D1426743

S C Y T H I A

Urals

St

Rhône
Alps
Rhône
Pyrenees
Ebro
Adriatic Sea
Tiber
Rome
ITALY
MACEDON
Black Sea
Caucasus Mts.
Caspian Sea
Ox
GREECE
Aegean Sea
Athens
CARTHAGINIAN
Sparta
Antioch
SELEUCID
Ecbatana
PARTHIA
Carthage
Mediterranean Sea
Seleucia-on-Tigris
Tigris
EMPIRE
Alexandria
Babylon
Euphrates
Susa
Persepolis
Zagros Mts.
PTOLEMAIC
EMPIRE
EGYPT
Oxyrynchus

SOUTHERN
ARABIA

Arabia

Mediterranean to China *c.* 300 BCE

p e s

Altai Mts.

3

XIONGNU
TRIBE

DONGHU
TRIBE

Tien Shan

Tarim Basin

CTRIA

YUEZHI
TRIBE

Yellow

Kunlun Shan

Wei

Yellow
Sea

Hindu Kush

Indus

EASTERN ZHOU
DYNASTY

Himalayas

East China
Sea

MAURYAN EMPIRE

Ganges

Pataliputra

Yanzi

Erannoboas

8

a

11

12

INDIAN OCEAN

0   250   500   750   1000 miles

EX LIBRIS

ANCIENT WORLDS

An Epic History of East & West

MICHAEL SCOTT

HUTCHINSON
LONDON

1 3 5 7 9 10 8 6 4 2

Hutchinson
20 Vauxhall Bridge Road
London SW1V 2SA

Hutchinson is part of the Penguin Random House group of companies
whose addresses can be found at global.penguinrandomhouse.com.

Copyright © Michael Scott, 2016

Michael Scott has asserted his right to be identified as the author of this Work in
accordance with the Copyright, Designs and Patents Act 1988.

First published by Hutchinson in 2016

www.randomhouse.co.uk

A CIP catalogue record for this book is available from the British Library.

ISBN 9780091958817

Typeset in 11.5/15 pt Garamond MT Std
Jouve (UK), Milton Keynes
Printed and bound by Clays Ltd, St Ives plc

For Alice and the bean

You may give them your love but not your thoughts.
For they have their own thoughts.
You may house their bodies but not their souls,
For their souls dwell in the house of tomorrow,
   which you cannot visit, not even in your dreams.

KHALIL GIBRAN, *The Prophet (On Children)*

Contents

Part III: Religious Change in a Connected World

Acknowledgements

A book such as this is impossible without the support and encouragement of others. From the inception of the idea my agent Patrick Walsh at Conville & Walsh has offered tremendous (and humorous) support; and my editors at Hutchinson, Sarah Rigby and Richard T. Kelly, alongside Jocasta Hamilton and the rest of the fantastic Hutchinson team, have been indefatigable in their encouragement, ideas, comments, suggestions and good humour. Thank you to you all for believing in me and in this book.

I am grateful also to Mandy Greenfield for her copy-editing, and to Jeff Edwards for drawing the maps.

To research such a vast expanse of history requires access to some of the great library institutions in the UK and abroad. I have been privileged to work in the British Library, London Library and Institute of Classical Studies Library in London; the University Library and Classics Faculty Library in Cambridge; the Sackler and Bodleian Libraries in Oxford; the University Library in Warwick; the British School at Athens library in Greece; as well as the Green Library at Stanford University in California. Thank you to all these institutions, and to their wonderful staff, for making the research such a joy.

But a book of this kind also requires the ongoing support and input of scholars from a vast array of specialist fields, who have kindly given their time and energy to open up their worlds of study for me and help develop my ideas in discussion, both in person and via email. It is without doubt one of the best aspects of this profession, and particularly this project, to have the opportunity to engage with such a broad range of fascinating and insightful people from across the world, and I have been deeply heartened by the enthusiasm with which they have responded in kind to this project. My thanks go to Prof. Robin Osborne; Prof. Paul Cartledge; Dr John Patterson (Cambridge); Prof. Giorgio Riello and the Global History and Culture Centre team (Warwick); Prof. Lee Dian Rainy (Memorial University of Newfoundland); Prof. Jeffery Lerner (Wake Forest University); Dr Christopher Baumer (Switzerland); Prof. Julia Shaw (UCL); Prof. James Hegarty (Cardiff); Prof. Simon Payaslian (Boston University); Dr Peter Frankopan (Oxford); and Prof. Ian Morris (Stanford). In particular, my sincerest thanks also go to Prof. Walter Scheidel at Stanford for hosting me during my visit and for his encouragement, insight and advice.

My rock during the writing of this book – and of many more years besides – has been my wonderful family, and especially the woman I am now lucky enough to call my wife, Alice. Her energy, loyalty and love give inspiration and resolve, comfort and enjoyment in equal measure. Alice and I are now expecting our first child. And so while this book is a history of ancient worlds for our present global times, I also hope that it will be of use to our child, growing up in a future which, while we cannot comprehend it, will without doubt be even more globally interconnected.

Note on Transliteration

Greek and Roman names and terms have been transcribed in English using their most common (mostly Romanised) forms, with key terms italicised for ease of reference. Chinese names and terms have been transcribed using the Hanyu Pinyin system (although popular alternatives are sometimes given in brackets), again with key terms and literary titles italicised. Names, terms and literary titles in all other languages (e.g. Armenian, Pali and Sanskrit) have been transcribed using their most well-recognised English counterparts, again with key terms and literary titles italicised.

List of Maps

List of Plate Illustrations

*T*he ants were as big as wild foxes and they bored tunnels into the earth, mole-like, excavating soil into towering piles on the surface. It was said to be dangerous for any human to look directly at these piles, for they were laced with gold – the best and brightest in the world, shining with lethal lustre under the burning sun. The local people, however, could not be dissuaded from desiring the gold for themselves.

Mounting wagons attached to their fastest horses, they would approach at midday – while the ants were busy digging deep below – and cart off as much earth-and-gold mix as they could. They had to move quickly and silently, though, lest they alert the ants, who would then swarm back to the surface to attack and pursue the thieves across the landscape. The locals would scatter chunks of flesh in the hope of distracting the ants from the chase, but not all of these wily insects were taken in. Some made directly for the humans and their wagons, and engaged in close combat to the death . . .[1]

*

Welcome to India – at least as it was described by a Greek called Megasthenes, on the cusp of the third century BCE.[2] Megasthenes paints a vivid picture of a world full of remarkable creatures, capable of extraordinary feats. The gold-digging, man-killing ants, he claimed, fought so hard against the human thieves because they understood the worth of gold and were willing to sacrifice their lives rather than part with it.[3] In other parts of India, as Megasthenes relates, one might encounter tigers twice the size of lions; monkeys larger than the largest dogs; winged scorpions, and flying serpents whose urine could blister and putrefy human skin; other serpents so huge they could swallow stags and bulls whole; and dogs with jaws strong enough to hold lions fast in their grip.[4] Towering over them all was the Indian elephant, larger than any elephant of Africa, whose counterpart in the sea was the whale, five times the Indian elephant's size.

Megasthenes' interests were not confined to beasts: his India was home to exotic humans, too. He records tales of tiny men, and men as tall as giants; some men with no noses, and other men without mouths who fed by inhalation, but could be killed by too harsh a smell; men whose feet – sporting eight toes on each – were turned backwards; men whose heads were canine, and who made conversation by barking.[5]

Megasthenes' text is not the fanciful concoction of a Greek slumbering in the far-flung afternoon sun of Athens or Sparta. In fact, it is the first ever eyewitness account by a Western observer of the plains of India surrounding the Ganges.[6] And while his narrative survives to us today only in fragments as repeated by later writers (who often, understandably, challenge the veracity of his account), he remains fundamental to our understanding of ancient India, offering us an in-depth analysis of how Indian society worked in comparison to his own.[7] Megasthenes, after all, was not some random traveller who stumbled into India by accident. He was the first official Greek ambassador to the royal court that ruled over the majority of northern India at this time, based in the city of Pataliputra (modern-day Patna). This was the court of the man whom Greeks called King Sandrocottus, better known in Indian history as Chandragupta Maurya, founder of one of India's great dynasties.

Megasthenes was appointed to his position by Seleucus Nicator ('the Victor'), former general of Alexander the Great, subsequent ruler of the Seleucid Empire that stretched from the coast of Asia Minor on the Mediterranean, deep into central Asia (via modern-day Afghanistan) and down over the Hindu Kush into north-western ancient India (today's Pakistan). From his privileged vantage point, Megasthenes presents us with a highly informed insight into how the physical magnificence of Chandragupta's palace compared to that of rulers in the West.

Pataliputra, he tells us, was situated at the meeting place of the great Ganges and Erannoboas Rivers and was laid out like a parallelogram, its wooden walls perforated by sixty-four gates and supporting 570 watchtowers. A deep ditch was dug all around, serving not only as a defence against attack, but also as a handy receptacle for all of the city's sewage (the stench of which must have assailed the eyes and nostrils of visitors, especially in the warmer months). But the splendour of the interior of the king's palace, Megasthenes claimed, far surpassed that of the great Persian palaces of Susa or Ecbatana in Asia Minor, hitherto considered by the Greeks to be the summit of luxurious extravagance. The royal parks abounded with tame peacocks and pheasants, shady groves and evergreen trees. Parrots followed the king, hovering above him in large numbers, and huge artificial lakes, brimming with fish, were exclusively for the pleasure of the king and his son.[8]

Megasthenes even records how King Chandragupta spent much of his day: judging legal cases while continually being massaged with wooden rollers to keep his blood flowing and his muscles loose. When not in session, he could be found sacrificing or hunting, which he did within his own parks (by shooting arrows from a platform) or out in the wild on the back of his favourite elephant. His every move, Megasthenes tells us, had repercussions for his people: when he washed his hair, a great festival was celebrated by the population of Pataliputra. For the king's person embodied the power of his royal city: it was the tradition for Indian rulers, Megasthenes explains, to take the name of the city as part of their royal title. Chandragupta was Pataliputra, just as Pataliputra was Chandragupta.[9]

Megasthenes describes the local populace as generally tall and of proud bearing, attributes that he credited to the abundant and fertile local soil. He relates, to his own amazement, how everyone seemed to be free and that no one was a slave – a state of society unheard of in the West. Law and order, he argued, were very simply maintained: no one could write, so everything was recited from memory, and anyone shown to be guilty of providing false witness had their hands and feet cut off. Anyone who maimed another person was punished in kind and their hands cut off, too. If anyone took the eye or hand of an artisan, they were put to death. The result – to Megasthenes' astonishment – was a society in which, unlike his own, almost no theft took place.[10]

Naturally curious as to how this very different world had come to pass, Megasthenes refers to Indian legends that link the birth of their society to his own Greek gods of the Mediterranean. Dionysus, he tells us, once invaded India with an army and, having settled there, taught the Indians how to make wine, build cities and establish law and justice.[11] Fifteen generations later, according to the same legends, the Greek hero Heracles was born among Indians and founded Pataliputra.[12] It appeared, then, that India and Greece, far from being disparate worlds, had been explicitly interwoven from the earliest times, sharing gods, traditions and practices in kind.

Of Megasthenes the man, we know little.[13] He was not, however, a pioneering figure. The first books on other parts of India had been written back in the sixth century BCE, for the Persian kings who had ruled what was now Seleucid territory and who, indeed, named the people living in the region of the Indus River as 'Indians' (a name the Greeks then applied to people from all over India).[14] The Greeks themselves had been talking about India since the fifth century BCE, the age of the 'father of history', Herodotus (who had also heard tell of the gold-digging ants). By the following century Greek physicians were aware of, and using, Indian remedies for the treatment of eye and tooth disease, even bad breath.[15]

Before Megasthenes' time, however, no one had realised the true extent of Indian territory, or of the wider world in which they lived. When in the *330s–320s* BCE Alexander the Great conquered all in his path, from Greece to the shores of the Indus, he and his comrades expected to find the end of the world, and instead were left to wonder at how much further the earth might stretch.[16] It is testament to an extraordinary expansion of horizons that, thirty years later, Megasthenes was a Greek envoy to the Indian dynasty that ruled the greater part of this vast expanse.

The court of Pataliputra, moreover, was well accustomed to entertaining ambassadors.[17] Megasthenes tells us that an entire department of Chandragupta's government was dedicated to looking after foreigners resident in India: to seeing that no wrong was done to them, dealing harshly with anyone who took unfair advantage of them, tending to them when they were sick and ensuring they were properly buried when they died.[18]

India was not the only place where the boundaries of the world were being pushed back at this time.[19] Megasthenes' contemporaries were sent to investigate other societies at the margins of the known world, and their reports, too, survive for us today in fragments. A man called Patrocles went sailing round the Caspian Sea; another, Demodamas, explored central Asia.[20] We know that after Megasthenes' retirement, his successor as Seleucid ambassador to Chandragupta's court was Deimachus, who wrote his own reports on what he observed.

The flow of information was not solely in the direction of the curious West. Two centuries after Megasthenes, a Greek king called Menander, who ruled a kingdom in the area of ancient north India (whose power extended perhaps as far as the royal capital of Pataliputra), became the principal character in a written dialogue with an Indian Buddhist monk called Nagasena.[21] This question-and-answer session between king and monk became an important Buddhist text in the following centuries (some even claim it as one of the finest works of Indian prose), and it spread far beyond India. In fact the text is known to us today through its inclusion in the Burmese and Chinese canons of Buddhist literature.[22] One Greek king's questions in northern India were, it seems, read very widely indeed.

The Ancient 'World' – or 'Worlds'?

Megasthenes' story poses a question for anyone interested in history, and particularly ancient history. When do we ever hear about such *interconnected* history, in schools, at university or in the public domain? Where are the courses, curricula, syllabi and books that cover these kinds of interactions between cultures in the ancient – or even more modern – periods? So much of what we study about the past is defined by strict disciplinary, temporal, geographical or thematic boundaries, which means that knowledge about our past is uncovered, written about and taught in clearly demarcated silos, seemingly detached from one another, and into which the interconnected worlds witnessed and explored by the likes of Megasthenes, Deimachus, Patrocles and Demodamas simply do not fit.[23]

We have accepted this delineated and divided picture of history to such an extent we have even convinced ourselves that, in studying one piece of the past, we are really studying it all. In my field of Greek and Roman studies, books are often published with titles ending '. . . *in the Ancient World*'.[24] Yet on closer inspection what is really meant by that title is the Greco-Roman world of the Mediterranean basin, where Greeks and Romans lived like frogs around a pond. 'The ancient world' has become an accepted shorthand for a very narrow zone of human interaction, centred around a single sea: our self-imposed boundaries have lured us into mistaking a part for the whole.

Of course, some scholars of the Greco-Roman worlds have attempted to look further afield – with limited success.[25] Despite, for example, Braudel's breakthrough writings on the connectivity of the Mediterranean basin, few have followed him in seeking to tie the Mediterranean as a 'unit' into a wider global perspective.[26] Those who have tried – and so challenged the distinctive 'Europeanness' of Greek and Roman ancestry – have, on occasion, met with stiff and vocal resistance.[27] Instead, comparative and connective studies of ancient cultures (particularly between Greece, Rome and China) have taken place in particular thematic silos, such as on the issues of trade and travel,[28] on the comparison of empires and systems of state power,[29] in attitudes to war and peace[30] and (by far the most energetically) in the field of literary, philosophical, legal, musical and scientific endeavour and discovery.[31]

Such a narrow focus must look bizarre to any onlooker, when we can point to the testimonies of men such as Megasthenes who engaged with a larger world that they perceived as fundamentally linked (in this case, by shared gods and heroes) to their own. That Chandragupta's court had a special department to handle foreign visitors surely ought to make us painfully aware that our highly delineated approach to history simply does not represent the reality of our past.

Those who study the Greeks and Romans are not, of course, the only culprits. We know lots about ancient civilisations in China, central Asia, India and elsewhere, all fervently studied in schools and universities and discussed in ever-growing volumes of scholarship. But in all these arenas scholars have concentrated overwhelmingly on their given civilisation, as if each were its own ancient world.[32] Across university departments, across countries, whole tribes of historians study and write about their worlds without feeling the need to raise their eyeline to the wider context of the different human civilisations living and breathing at the same time around the globe, even when the connections sit glaringly before us.[33] We are, in the twenty-first century, a global community.[34] And yet, at the same time, ironically, we seem to prefer to write and read about our history as if it happened in unconnected, compartmentalised chunks.[35] But what if we undertook to tell a bigger story – not of a monolithic 'Ancient World', but of many and diverse ancient worlds?

Writing Ancient Worlds

For me, the clinching argument as to why we should think about ancient worlds rather than any individual ancient world is twofold. First, the story of Megasthenes is only one strand in a connected web of entanglement and interaction that bonded ancient humanity together. As recent narratives of trade across the ancient world have shown us, by the first century CE Chinese silk was being worn by the aristocrats (both women and men) of Rome and Carthage. Roman merchants were sailing as far as southern Arabia and Tamil India, and it was claimed that fifty million sesterces annually were passing from Roman coffers into India, in exchange for precious spices, incense and other luxury goods. Rome, too, was exporting: worked glass, silver and gold, as well as precious stones, the worths of which were well known to the Chinese Han emperor (as were the delights of Indian spices).[36] And with the movement of these goods, and the people who transported them, travelled a cornucopia of ideas, knowledge and beliefs that would change the very fibre of ancient cultures from the Mediterranean to China and beyond.

But even more importantly, as we stand in the eddies of a new era of globalisation in the twenty-first century, with China keen to build a new Silk Road to connect East and West through trade, it is crucial that we realise we have been here before. As goods were travelling from the Mediterranean to China and vice versa at the beginning of the first millennium CE, ancient Mediterranean historians, such as Diodorus Siculus (the first author to quote the works of Megasthenes on India), Strabo and others, sought to write a new kind of 'universal history' that could encompass the entirety of their known world.[37] As such, studying our ancient past not only opens up for us a world of entanglement and global connectivity, but offers us, amid the tempestuous waters of our own global age, an exemplar of how humankind has reacted to and thought about the interconnectedness of humanity previously – so helping to contextualise the dangers and opportunities that we now face.[38]

This book seeks to remind us of an era of emerging world consciousness in our ancient past, which in many ways mirrors the position we find ourselves in today. Its focus is not on the objects that were transported, but on the developing relationships within and between human communities, as well as those between human and divine worlds, from the sixth century BCE to the beginning of the fifth century CE.

Within that span, my focus is upon three specific 'moments'. Part I concerns the sixth century BCE and focuses on man's relationship to man, as negotiated through politics; Part II concerns the third and second centuries BCE, examining the relationships forged between ancient communities through warfare; and Part III concerns the fourth century CE, investigating the developing relationship of man and god(s), as played out through adoption, adaption and innovation in religious belief. Each part takes as its point of departure a date and event crucial to these developing relationships, and made famous in the conventional annals of Western ancient history that remain so dominated by study of the Greeks and Romans: for Part I, it is 508 BCE, and the invention of democracy in Athens; for Part II, 218 BCE, when Hannibal the Carthaginian crossed the Alps with his elephants to invade Italy; and for Part III, 312 CE, when the Roman emperor

Constantine fought the Battle of Milvian Bridge, paving the way for his takeover of the entire Roman Empire and, in turn, for Christianity's ascent towards becoming the official religion of the Roman world.

I have chosen to examine these particular moments in time not merely because important things happened then in the Mediterranean, but because what makes these moments so remarkable is that similar developments in human relationships were also occurring at these times in cultures stretching from the Mediterranean through to China. Moreover, these three moments – and the relationship developments they represent – also signify stages in the developing connectivity of an ancient globalised world. From separated parts of the world seemingly turning to consider similar issues at similar times in the sixth century BCE, we will see how, increasingly, individuals had to make decisions based on ever-wider spheres of interaction (in the third to second centuries BCE), and how the emerging links between 'worlds' had in turn a profound effect upon the ability of ideas to spread, and on the ways in which man's relationships with this world and the next developed in the fourth century CE. And through it all, we will also see how this developing globalisation – and the debates in man's relationships that it sparked, enabled and influenced – in turn changed the way ancient societies thought about the achievements, institutions and beliefs created in their own past.

In Part I we will investigate how democracy came about in Athens as a revolutionary form of government, at the same time as a republican constitution was born in Rome; and at the same time as Confucius, in China, was at the height of his influence, developing his own political philosophy about how society should be run, how man should interact with his fellow man, and trying to convince those in charge to follow his ideas. Confucius was not aware of contemporary developments in the Mediterranean, but Rome and Athens were strongly connected. (As we will see, politically speaking, Rome even briefly studied at the feet of Athens.) In each arena, the desire for political change seems to have been motivated by a similar set of circumstances, but a very different kind of political settlement was established, subject to the particular cultural landscape and current events. These settlements, however, proved momentous.

In Part II we 'sing of warfare', great maker and unmaker of worlds. While the Carthaginian Hannibal crossed the Alps with elephants to challenge Rome for supremacy of the Mediterranean, rulers in Asia Minor were struggling to maintain the integrity of their empires from attacks on all sides; new kingdoms were being born by the sword in central Asia; and in China the First Emperor (a man who would be buried with a bodyguard of terracotta warriors) strove to unify the Chinese people by force into one world against the nomadic communities to the north and west. Rome's republican constitution was facing its greatest test, while in China the ideas of Confucius were at risk of being effaced from human memory. The glory days of the democracy of Athens, meanwhile, had become merely that: a memory. This was an era in which the fate of the ancient world lay in the hands of a small group of young male warriors and rulers, whose lives would be dedicated to reshaping the boundaries of their realms and the relationships between the communities they strove to control. But their decisions were increasingly shaped by events further afield, as the ancient world from the Mediterranean to China became steadily more interconnected – until, in the 140s BCE, its history was soldered together once and for all.

In Part III we see religious change and innovation sweep across that now-connected ancient world, as man rethought his relationship to the divine. As Christianity began to be accepted in the Roman Mediterranean and some outposts in Asia, Hindu worship was being fundamentally reorientated under India's ruling Gupta dynasty, while Buddhism was spreading to, and attaining the status of an official religion in, China. In some cases these were new faiths that had reached communities along a flourishing web of connective tissues linking the ancient world. Others had developed over long periods within their respective realms. Yet all of them had to operate and evolve under the auspices of individual rulers, kings or emperors governing from the Mediterranean to China. And by the efforts of these leaders to stabilise, unify and expand their realms within this now-connected world, these religions – including their practitioners and hierarchies, and the art and architecture they inspired – would be refashioned as if in the fires of a crucible and given new positions within their respective societies, always in intriguing relationships to power.

In the spirit of Megasthenes, I hope this book can help to open our eyes to ancient worlds: how they functioned, developed and interacted, and how they helped to shape our world today.[39] It is a story of beauty, diversity and glory – also, it should be said, one of violence, ambition and avarice – but I believe the telling of it can only deepen our appreciation, from the perspective of today's globalised world, of how much we have always owed to interaction with one another.

PART I

POLITICS IN AN AXIAL AGE

TIMELINE

776 BCE: The First Olympic Games

771 BCE: Start of the Eastern Zhou dynasty (and the 'Spring and Autumn Annals' period) in China

753 BCE: The Founding of Rome

594 BCE: Solon is appointed archon of Athens and proposes popular reforms; a system of land taxation introduced in the state of Lu, China

575 BCE: Servius Tullius becomes King of Rome

560 BCE: Peisistratus seizes the Acropolis, makes himself tyrant of Athens, but is deposed.

556 BCE: Peisistratus becomes tyrant for second time, with help of Megacles

551 BCE: Confucius is born in Lu State, north-east China.

546 BCE: Peisistratus re-establishes himself as tyrant of Athens for third time.

534 BCE: Lucius Tarquinius Superbus becomes King of Rome

520 BCE: Cleomenes I becomes King of Sparta

517 BCE: Political crisis in Lu: Duke Ding and Confucius exiled from the state of Lu and go to the state of Qi

514 BCE: Hipparchus, co-tyrant of Athens, is killed by Harmodius and Aristogeiton

510 BCE: Hippias, co-tyrant of Athens, is expelled by a popular revolt supported by Cleomenes

510–09 BCE: The 'Rape of Lucretia' leads to the ousting of Tarquinius and the birth of Rome's republic

509 BCE: Battle of the Arsian Forest for future of Rome

509 BCE: Duke Ding and Confucius return to the state of Lu

508 BCE: Etruscan king Lars Porsenna tries and fails to take Rome; Horatius Cocles defends Rome

508–7 BCE: Would-be tyrant Isagoras is expelled from Athens and democratic reforms are instituted under Cleisthenes

501 BCE: Confucius receives his first government appointment under Duke Ding

497–5 BCE: Confucius and his disciples quit Lu after Duke Ding receives 80 beautiful girls from powerful Lu families. Confucius starts his second period of exile

496 BCE: Battle of Lake Regillus – Roman consul Aulus Postumius repels Tarquinius

494–3 BCE: Two 'Tribunes of the Plebs' are elected for the first time in Rome

490 BCE: The Battle of Marathon: Darius I, King of Persia, defeated by the Athenians

487 BCE: Athenian archonship becomes elective by lot

487–5 BCE: Confucius returns to the state of Lu

486 BCE: Xerxes I succeeds Darius I as Great King of Persia.

481 BCE: End of the 'Spring and Autumn Annals' period in China

480 BCE: Battle of Thermopylae, costly victory for Xerxes over Spartans

480 BCE: Battle of Salamis, Greek naval fleet defeats the armada of Xerxes

479 BCE: Battle of Plataea, Persian forces conclusively defeated by Greeks

479 BCE: Death of Confucius

475 BCE: Beginning of the 'Warring States Period' in China

454 BCE: A Roman delegation visits Athens to study its democratic functions. The treasury of the Delian League is moved from Delos to Athens

451 BCE: The First Decemviri come to power in Rome to judge

	findings of Roman delegation to Athens and to review the constitution
450 BCE:	A Second Decemviri chosen to continue deliberations, who then refuse to give up power
449 BCE:	Romans revolt against the Decemviri; Enacting of the Twelve Tables
447 BCE:	The Athenians start to build the Parthenon

INTRODUCTION

═══════

In 1981 the polymathic American writer Gore Vidal published a novel called *Creation*, in which he mischievously mixed up recorded ancient history with some clever inventions of his own. The novel follows an imagined Persian named Cyrus, reared in the court of the (very real) King Darius I, whose war against Athens would lead to the Battle of Marathon in 490 BCE. On account of his talent for languages, Cyrus is saved from the battlefield and sent by Darius as Persian ambassador to India (an assignment of the sort later entrusted to Megasthenes as Seleucid ambassador to the court of Chandragupta Maurya). By the time Cyrus returns to Persia, his old schoolfriend Xerxes, son of Darius, has assumed the throne and is poised to embark on his own invasion of Greece, which will culminate in the battles of Salamis and Plataea. Again, though, Cyrus is sent out in the opposite direction, this time as Xerxes' ambassador to China. Come the completion of that diplomatic mission, Cyrus is serving Xerxes' successor, after a peace settlement between Persia and Greece, and he is despatched to fulfil one last ambassadorial role – in Athens.

During his extensive travels Cyrus is fascinated less by the humdrum business of ambassadorial duties than by the stunning range of political and religious ideas that he encounters across the expanse of the ancient world. And here Vidal cunningly tinkers with, and elides the timeline of, history so that his fictional Cyrus does what no individual in the ancient world could truly have done: namely, meet and spend time with some of the foremost thinkers of the fifth century BCE – Zoroaster in Persia, Confucius in China, the Buddha in India, Socrates in Athens. Through this privileged position Cyrus is able to bear personal witness to a revolutionary epoch in the history of human thought.

This epoch has been a great and obvious boon to the cause of global history – notably so ever since 1949 when the German historian Karl Jaspers published his hugely influential *Vom Ursprung und Ziel der Geschichte* (*The Origin and Goal of History*). Therein Jaspers outlined his concept of an 'Axial Age' in the ancient world from the Mediterranean to China, dating from 800 to 200 BCE – a time when, across cultures and civilisations not necessarily themselves connected, there was an overlapping rejection of old wisdom and a search for new understandings and explanations across philosophy, science, religion and politics. For Jaspers, this was a beacon age in the landscape of human history, noteworthy for similar circumstances across Greece, China, India, central Asia and what we today know as the Middle East.[1] Two of the key religious innovations of this era – Zoroastrianism and Buddhism – we will meet in Parts II and III of this book. But this Part focuses on the revolutions in political ideas and societal governance that broke out, not in Darius's Persia, but in Athens, Rome and the state of Lu in China at the end of the sixth century BCE. In these crucial centres across the ancient world, as part of this Axial Age of thinking, the way in which man related to man was being rethought, and in some cases reborn in the furnace of revolution.

In Athens, an angry mob of Athenians gathered in a three-day riot against those in charge of the city, their grievances roused by the way Athens was being run and the people were being treated. All were convinced of the need for change; not one could have imagined they were on the cusp of inventing a new form of politics, one that defines our Western world today. In fact the individual who was to prove the crucial agent of change in this story – a wealthy sexagenarian aristocrat named Cleisthenes – was not even in Athens during the citywide riot. But in the heady days that followed, a vague proposal that Cleisthenes had made some time previously for the extension of power and influence to local communities and people was taken up and tried out. It was the world's first step towards democracy.[2]

In Rome, another angry mob of citizens — disgusted by the vile behaviour of their royal family, which had driven a much-admired aristocratic woman to suicide — had shut the gates of their city to their king. Led by aristocratic nobles, the Roman citizenry struggled to develop a new system of republican political governance, even while the king sent wave after wave of troops against the city walls in an attempt to take back his realm. The system that emerged from this struggle would steer a middle path between the injustices of kingship and the notion (seen as unpopular and impractical) of direct 'people power'. In time it would guide Rome to become the undisputed power of the Mediterranean.

Meanwhile, for the small state of Lu in what is today's eastern China, it was a time when state was pitted against state. Lu's duke was an ineffectual ruler, and its principal families exercised overwhelming and corrupt power. A man already in his early fifties took up his first official appointment within the state bureaucracy. His goal was a new form of governance and order, motivated by humaneness and justice, to be embodied in the figure of a wise and righteous ruler. His was a lonely fight — there were no avid crowds of citizens to back him up, just a few dogged supporters — and he would not live to realise his dream. But his ideas and teachings never died. He would be remembered across all China as 'the illustrious and perfect sage' and his influence begat a system of governance and a wider world-view that we still recognise today: one that bears his name, which was Confucius.

One cannot overestimate the impact that these three parallel births of new ways of envisaging man's relationship to man, in three very different societies, have had on our human story. In China, Confucius remains a towering figure who has for centuries defined much of the country's attitude towards education, philosophy, law, justice and governance.[3] We need look no further than Washington DC's Capitol Hill, home to the United States Congress, or to modern Italy where the office of 'praetor' only became obsolete in 1999, to see the lasting influence of the geography and politics of republican Rome.[4] And when in 1993 the 2,500th anniversary of democracy was marked to much hurrah across the democratised world, the debt to ancient Athens and the durability of *demokratia* ('rule of the people') was abundantly clear, for all that debates persist over how well the largely representative democracies of our time compare to the direct (if exclusive) participation of Athenians in their assembly (*ekklesia*).

The civilisations we study were not all fully aware of one another. The earliest accounts we have of the foundation of the Roman Republic make reference to the overthrow of tyranny in Athens, and Rome even sent envoys to Greece to examine its new constitution and draw lessons. Confucius, though, knew nothing of such struggles, drawing solely upon his own society's history for examples and inspirations to progress.

What drove change in all three worlds at this time was a nagging sense of injustice felt towards governance that was overwhelmingly autocratic, and a search for a better, even ideal society, against a background of conflict and civil unrest. In Greece and Rome these political revolutions were community-led and began without any kind of roadmap. In China, by contrast, Confucius sought to change the way the state was governed, with a very precise plan in his mind. Indeed he is arguably the first person in Chinese history to make absolutely clear what were his principles and ideas, despite the fact that Confucius always presented himself as a 'transmitter' of old ideas, rather than as an innovator of new ones.[5]

But whatever rhyming motivations were present in Rome, Athens and the state of Lu, what emerged – thanks to the particular traditions of each society and the specific nature of its contemporary problems – were three fundamentally different systems of government, based on different social contracts and different conceptions of man's relationship to man, ranging from power in the hands of one venerable ruler (China), through a 'middling solution' in Rome that balanced the powers of different parts of society, to direct mass people-power in Athens.

From our vantage point today, the survival of all three of these systems of government seems natural. Yet in unpicking their stories we will see that each was, in its infancy, extraordinarily fragile, its endurance by no means assured, extinction a risk at every turn. Not one of them – not even the pre-formulated ideas of Confucius – was born in its finished form: perfection required decades, if not centuries.

Crucially, too, the stories of their development have often come to us only in later ancient sources, sometimes conflicting and influenced by the purview of those later times. We cannot forget that to study history is also to scrutinise historiography and to observe how societies prefer to tell stories about themselves – stories that, ultimately, we are still reformulating today.

The end of the sixth century BCE is without doubt a fascinating moment in the history of not just one ancient society, but a much wider ancient world. It is a turning point in the development of human civilisation and in the conception of how we can, and should, relate to one another and act as a community. Even more importantly, the debates that took place then not only still guide us, but echo with surprising vitality in our modern world today. 'The past', in Faulkner's famous words, 'is never dead. It's not even past.'[6] How best to govern human society, to establish man's relationship to man, is a question we will never stop asking.

CHAPTER I

Athenian Democracy and the Desire for People-Power

5o8 BCE: the sun rose on the third day of the siege, and on the Acropolis – that ancient hulk of limestone protruding from the high ground at the heart of Athens, casting its shadow across great swathes of the community below. For centuries this towering rock had been both a beacon and a haven for those who lived by it. First conceived as a palace of kings, it was now crowned by a temple and a teeming forest of statuary dedicated to the all-powerful gods. It was this sacred, impregnable heart of their own city to which the people of Athens – united and resolute, according to Herodotus – now laid siege.[1] For up above them, in hiding on the citadel, were the Spartan king Cleomenes and a small Spartan army. Sparta was nestled deep in the Peloponnese, more than 200 kilometres from Athens. It's likely some of the Spartan soldiers were now asking themselves what they were doing so far from home. But Cleomenes had tied their fortunes to the political goals of a man now holed up beside them in the Acropolis – the Athenian aristocrat Isagoras, the city's chief magistrate (known as the *eponymous archon*). And, it was whispered, Cleomenes and Isagoras shared something else: Isagoras's wife, whom Isagoras was said to have 'loaned' to Cleomenes as part of their alliance.[2]

Isagoras and the Spartans had orchestrated the expulsion from Athens of some 700 families who were unsympathetic to Isagoras's leadership, along with his chief political rival. They had even tried to abolish the supreme governing council in Athens – the *boule* – in favour of placing political power in the hands of Isagoras's own supporters. But so badly had this sat with the mass of Athenian people that Isagoras and his Spartan supporters, vastly outnumbered and fearing for their lives, had headed for the high ground of the Acropolis. The people of Athens had united in a spontaneous revolt that would shake the city to its foundations and change the course of history.[3]

Herodotus read these events as the fuse to the fire of political revolution in Athens that would eventually lead to the creation of a new political system: democracy. Yet Athens' journey to this moment had begun more than a century before, and the system of democracy created after 508 BCE would undergo a long evolution even afterwards. Crucial to the story of democracy's emergence are the actions and intentions of key individuals, actions that ought to make us wonder if the end result was something anyone ever intended. In such matters the ancient sources do not always agree, even with themselves, and are susceptible to influence by the political outlook of their own times.

The Acropolis, in fact, had been the scene of a relatively recent siege two years before, in 510 BCE; and on that occasion Cleomenes and his troops had fought alongside Athenians. The object of their ire, hiding amongst the towering temples and gleaming statues, had been Hippias, brutal tyrant ruler of Athens who had held onto power by increasingly violent means since the death of his father Peisistratus seventeen years earlier. That siege could have proved an unbreakable stalemate, had it not been for a curious twist. An attempt to smuggle Hippias's sons out of Athens to safety was thwarted, and the sons fell instead into the hands of the Spartan army. The Spartans and their Athenian supporters now had leverage, and they bartered Hippias's surrender in return for the lives of his offspring. Within five days Hippias had abandoned the Acropolis and fled Athens, eventually to end up in the court of the mighty Persian king Darius I, who commanded his vast empire across the sea in Asia Minor. Athens, however, had not seen the last of Hippias and his urge to hold power over the city.[4]

Still, Hippias's departure at the time left a political vacuum in Athens, which had been almost exclusively under the control of a single family since Peisistratus first took the reins in 560 BCE. Now, as Athenians basked in the relief of release from tyranny, they faced the problem of what should fill its place.[5] The Spartans under Cleomenes – involved in Athenian politics at the behest of the sacred oracle at Delphi, which had passed on the command of the gods that Sparta insert itself in the Athenian struggle – had little interest in controlling Athens directly, but they did have a preferred candidate in Isagoras.

Isagoras's main rival was another aristocrat – Cleisthenes, scion of the powerful high-born Alcmaeonid family, which had been infamous in Athens for more than a century. He was also the grandson (on his mother's side) of a tyrant – after whom he had been named – from the nearby *polis*, or city-state, of Sicyon. Newly sixty at the time of Hippias's expulsion, Cleisthenes was arguably an unlikely candidate for the historic role of democracy's vanguard revolutionary.

In those two years between sieges of the Acropolis the fight over the direction of Athens' future raged like an inferno. Isagoras gained the advantage, though, when he was appointed from amongst an elite body of aristocrats to the position of chief magistrate for the year from mid-508 to mid-507 BCE. As *eponymous archon*, Isagoras had the power to legislate on how the city should be run. The only avenue left to Cleisthenes was to propose his ideas within Athens' more representative (but less powerful) public assembly, and to seek support for his cause among the mass of male citizen Athenians who came from a wider range of social classes. The open-air environment of the public assembly was a hard one in which to make headway for a relatively elderly Athenian. First he had to make himself heard and understood above an often-vocal crowd; then he had the grander challenge of convincing his fellow Athenians of the need for a radical shake-up of the city's political structures, at a time when many would have felt there was already quite enough change in the air. And yet, according to Herodotus, something remarkable happened. Though the *demos* (the mass of the people) had been 'formerly despised' by the leading men in Athens, Cleisthenes 'added the *demos* to his faction'.[6]

What this means has been hotly debated by historians, not least because the Greek word Herodotus employs to describe 'adding to one's faction' is *proshetairizetai*.[7] At the root of this word is *hetaireia*, denoting a small band of intimate comrades, nothing less than an aristocratic peer group. Thus we might see the birth of democracy having been attended by a familiar kind of Athenian aristocratic political manoeuvring: not a revolution but, rather, business as usual.

If revolution was not intended in those heady days of 508–7 BCE, what Cleisthenes seems to have proposed to get the people to join his faction was, for sure, dramatically new. His proposal is thought to have consisted of two main elements. First, Cleisthenes suggested that the smallest civic units – the *demes* (roughly equivalent to modern-day boroughs) – should form the basis for all civic engagement, rights and responsibilities. Second, much more controversially, those *demes* were to be grouped into a new series of ten tribes, replacing Athens' four traditional tribal groupings, which would form the basis of the way in which Athenians contributed their time, energy and ideas to the state.[8] What made these new tribes so revolutionary was that their composition was engineered so as to explicitly break up the aristocratic power-blocs inherent in the old tribal structure, giving each tribe an equal say and equal power in the running of the state. Even more radically, the choice of who from among these tribes was to be entrusted with helping to run the state (in most of, but not all, the roles) was to be made not by election, but by random lot, so ensuring everyone stood a fair chance.

Cleisthenes' ideas must have captured the Athenian imagination, for when the battle with his aristocratic rival Isagoras came to a head, it was he who had sheer numbers on his side and a legitimate claim to be the aristocratic leader of the people. Still, one must remember there was never any official motion in the name of 'democracy' put down for consideration by the organs of Athenian government. This was an idea carried on the wind, repeated, discussed, debated in private homes, in the fields, around the public fountains in the city's market place, at the theatre and in the gymnasium. A desire to empower the local community was not, however, the only thing on people's minds that drove them to give their backing to Cleisthenes' plan.

Despite Sparta's help in ridding them of a tyrant, the Athenians resented continued Spartan intrusion in their lives, distrusted Sparta's former ties to Isagoras and feared what the Spartans might do next. They were painfully aware of Athens' military shortcomings compared to Sparta, and even to nearer neighbours. In terms of the great bulk of Spartan and Spartan-allied military might that could be marshalled to march upon Athens, 700 soldiers was merely the tip of the iceberg.

Cleisthenes' ideas for civic reform, however, went so far as to make the *demes* the basis for both military and political organisation of the city. As such, they offered the possibility of a more effective fighting force of self-defence. No wonder those words on the wind caught the imagination and won the support of the people of Athens. They offered a solution to a multitude of problems: a chance to rid Athens of Spartan presence, a chance to reorganise their military capabilities, and a chance to give themselves greater say in the political process. In the fields, homes and streets of Athens, the word on people's lips was 'Cleisthenes'.

The strength of this popular support stung Isagoras into recalling Cleomenes and his Spartan troops in order to bolster his own position. Cleomenes had been willing to relieve Athens of a tyrant, but he had no enthusiasm for the project of Cleisthenes: he preferred the Athenian political system just as it was – in the hands of a group of aristocrats, and as a natural military ally for Sparta. Cleomenes now ordered the Athenians to expel Cleisthenes and his supporters from the city. When the people refused to stir, Cleomenes returned with his crack Spartan troops to enforce the operation – only to find himself, and those troops, with Isagoras up on the Acropolis, besieged in short order by the sheer pressing mass of the Athenian people.

Cleisthenes the Reformer?

What did Cleisthenes really want? Power and influence in Athens, without doubt, especially at the expense of his aristocratic rivals. But as to his subtler or more complex motives, Herodotus and Aristotle took different views. For Aristotle, Cleisthenes was an idealist, keen to reform Athenian politics for the sake of the people.[9] To Herodotus, Cleisthenes was simply emulating his maternal grandfather, the tyrant of Sicyon, by rejecting the current tribal divisions of the city – because, like the elder Cleisthenes, he had a pronounced loathing for the Greeks of Ionia, across the Aegean Sea in Asia Minor, whose older tribal groups Athens was said to have originally copied.[10]

Whatever his true motives, Cleisthenes was not himself among the Athenians besieging the Acropolis in 508 BCE. He was in exile at that time, along with hundreds of families who supported him. It is certain, though, that he had informers who brought him snatches of news from Athens post-haste. The site of the Acropolis had special resonance, because of actions taken in that place by Cleisthenes' ancestors more than a century before – actions that Isagoras and the Spartans had chosen to rake up as the pretext for his exile, rather than his proposed political reforms or his opposition to Isagoras. Instead, Cleisthenes stood accused of carrying a family curse.

At some point in the 630s BCE a man called Cylon – formerly a winner of the foot-race at the Olympic Games – had attempted a coup in Athens, having misread advice from the oracle at Delphi. As Herodotus puts it, Cylon, 'preening himself with thoughts of becoming a tyrant', attempted to seize the Acropolis as the public marker of Athenian power.[11] But such support as Cylon had for his cause crumbled, and he and his close friends sought refuge at the altar of the patron deity of Athens, Athena – a sacred site from which no one could be removed, lest such an action violate the sanctity of the goddess's home. Cylon and his men were promised by the magistrates of Athens that they would not be harmed if they surrendered and stood trial; but, having agreed to leave of their own accord, they were immediately killed. The man later found guilty of their murder was Megacles, a rival Athenian Alcmaeonid aristocrat, and great-grandfather of Cleisthenes.

Cylon's ambitions were not uncommon in the Greece of his day, for Greek society had been in flux for some time. Its established model of a few rich land-owning aristocrats controlling a large, disconnected population of poor land workers had been destabilised by a tenfold population increase as well as newly emergent paths to wealth, particularly the more efficient exploitation of mineral resources and trade, as well as a healthy economic growth rate.[12] As more people got richer, they too wanted a say in how their society was run. Greeks in communities across the mainland, the Aegean islands and as far south as Crete struggled with how to conceptualise what kind of political society was most appropriate to these new economic and social realities. Some Greek cities near Athens, such as Corinth and Sicyon, were taken over by tyrants – strongmen who managed to seize power and hold on to it (and even, in some cases, pass it on to their descendants over several generations). Others, like the community of Dreros on Crete, or Chios in the Aegean, seem to have made tentative moves towards establishing a new social and political deal, with rights and responsibilities for the whole community. In Dreros, a legal and constitutional code – the earliest so far found anywhere in Greece – was carved onto stone for all to see, outlining how the community was responsible for maintaining law and order (rather than individuals exacting their own justice), and seeking to even out the rights of the different socio-economic groups.

To whatever degree disparate Greek communities were aware of this tumult – most so, probably, in those cities increasingly connected by trade – anyone looking at Athens during the seventh century BCE would have perceived both a society doing very well for itself and, at the same time, a society in the grip of ever-worsening conflict and violence. Cylon's example had shown that no one man was strong enough to gain a firm grip on power in Athens. Instead there was constant friction between those who coveted such power. Proof that late-seventh-century BCE Athens was a violent place is provided by the earliest piece of legislation that survives to us from there: laws written by the legislator Draco, whereby almost all criminal offences were held to be punishable by death (hence the survival in English of the term 'draconian' to denote severe punishment).[13]

Megacles' penalty for the killing of Cylon, however, was *miasma* or 'pollution' – a curse that would sit for evermore on him and his descendants. The family was exiled from Athens, knowing that should they ever be permitted to return, the penalty could still be exercised again if Athens saw fit. It was on these grounds that Cleisthenes was expelled by Isagoras and his Spartan supporters.

Solon the Law-Giver?

It seems that in 594 BCE Cleisthenes' ancestors were recalled from their first exile. Athens' chief magistrate that year was a man called Solon, remembered by history as a legendary law-giver, wise adviser, sage and poet. The fragments of Solon's poetry that survive today represent our best contemporary literary evidence of conditions in Athens at the beginning of the sixth century, and of what Solon sought to do about them.

Solon was an aristocrat who had already served the city well as a military general and adviser during a conflict between Athens and the Greek city of Megara, over the ownership of the island of Salamis. He had had experience in trade and business outside the usual run of agricultural land-ownership. As such, he realised that Athens would now not only have to deal with its own internal civic strife, but would have to do so while battling for its prestige and possessions against other greedy and expanding Greek communities. He identified a desperate need for a system of government in Athens that would enable the city to face its external difficulties as a united entity. To that end, the selfish pursuit of individual goals had to be eliminated: what Athens needed, Solon argued, was fairness, freedom and good leadership. His appointment as chief magistrate came with extraordinary powers to improve the city's working.

As Solon described his own reforms in his poetry:

To the *demos* [the people] I have given such honour as is sufficient, neither taking away nor granting any more. For those who had power and were great in riches, I equally cared that they should suffer nothing wrong. Thus I stood, holding my strong shield over both, and I did not allow either side to prevail against justice.[14]

And, more dramatically still:

I did this by harnessing force and justice together with power, and I carried through my promises. I wrote statutes alike for those of high and low social status, fitting straight justice to each. If someone other than I had taken power, some ill-intentioned and greedy man, he would not have been able to control the people. For had I been willing to do what pleased the opposing party then, or what the others had planned for them, this city would have lost many men. That is why I made a stout defence all round, turning like a wolf among many hounds.[15]

Not for nothing has Solon been hailed as the original proponent of the 'third way' or 'middling solution',[16] which makes it worth our looking closely at how he put principles into practice.

Judging from the laws Solon drafted to solve its problems, Athens was riddled with factional politics that spilled over into murder on the streets. Land was in the hands of a tiny minority of aristocrats who fought one another for influence in every way possible: disputing boundaries, challenging inheritances, insisting on magnificent funerals to outdo one another, and pestering the law courts for increased penalties for their enemies' offences. At the same time, many poor Athenians were caught up in debt bondage: they owed so much to their land-owning aristocratic employers that they had to use their own bodies as guarantees for loans, and were often sold into slavery as a result.

The most dramatic of Solon's plans involved the cancelling of all debts overnight, and the elimination of the possibility of one Athenian citizen being enslaved to another. This was accompanied by a series of readjusted political rights for each of the social and economic classes of Athenian society. Crucially, Solon's reform package, known *in toto* as the 'shaking off of the burdens', sought to redistribute rights and responsibilities, but not equally. His was a system of moderate conservatism, in which each stratum of the community received what Solon thought it deserved, rather than equal standing with one another: thus it was a 'middling solution', what he called *eunomia* – 'good order' – and good enough, he hoped, to unite Athens in contentment and readiness to face its rivals as one.

Doubtless, those around Solon – especially those who had most to lose by his reforms – were angered. We might imagine him holding forth at an aristocratic *symposium* (drinking party), while some of his listeners, lying on couches with their drinking cups in hand, were less than impressed. But Solon was no naïve poet. As noted above, he saw himself as a wolf among hounds – hounds that might bite him hard, if so riled. According to some sources, he was also sufficiently skilled in dispensing the favours of political office as to let slip his plans for debt cancellation to certain friends, who promptly bought land with large mortgages – debts that were soon declared void, leaving those men as rich and unencumbered land-owners.

Solon left Athens not long after his reforms were enacted and his laws written up on wooden tablets for display in the *agora* – the large open market space at the base of the Acropolis, a daily meeting and trading point for most Athenians. Athens was stuck with its new deal. Did it work? Without doubt, the poor classes of Athenians felt the most immediate benefits from debt cancellation and the end of debt bondage. But ultimately Solon's reforms failed to create the more united front that Athens needed to function effectively. Within a decade of his departure, political infighting in Athens had risen again to such heights that in some cases there was no agreement on who should hold such crucial civic offices as chief magistrate; and in other cases, some of those elected to these positions refused to surrender their power at the end of their one-year tenure. Solon's dying days were overshadowed by the appearance of one man who sought to copy the example of other communities across Greece, by subjecting Athens to his sole rule by force: Peisistratus.

The Rule of Tyranny

This, though, was no easy task. Athenians were sharply divided in their allegiances to rival aristocratic families and their respective flag-bearers. These families did not resemble political parties in any modern sense: they had no ideological line or manifesto. Rather, they were factions engaged in seeking maximum political influence for themselves at the expense of others. Herodotus labels this period a time of '*stasis*' – of 'internal civic strife' – between the Athenian people of 'the plain', the people of 'the shore' and the people of 'the hill'.[17] The people of 'the shore' were led by Cleisthenes' father, now back from exile and once again at the forefront of Athenian politics. The people of 'the hill' (although we have no certain idea where, or whom, this grouping refers to) were led by Peisistratus.

Again, our ancient historians paint very different pictures of the *dramatis personae*. To Aristotle, Peisistratus was a man whose time in power benefited Athens; whereas for Herodotus, he was a heavy-handed thug and trickster. Herodotus relates how Peisistratus's first grab at power revolved around trying to seize the Acropolis, just as Cylon had attempted before. Keen to avoid Cylon's downfall, however, Peisistratus took with him a personal bodyguard of club-wielding thugs – a private army whose services he had tricked the Athenian assembly into granting him, by showing off an (actually self-inflicted) injury and slyly claiming that his life was in danger from nefarious enemies.[18] Now this private army took control of the Acropolis and intimidated the vital organs of Athenian government, and Peisistratus declared himself tyrant.

Tyranny in ancient Greece did not necessarily mean that the people suffered. Aristotle and Herodotus agree that Peisistratus eventually made the reforms of Solon actually work within Athenian society. Even Herodotus, who sees Peisistratus as little more than a bully, reports that he organised the affairs of state well, after taking control. Peisistratus's victory, however, was to be short-lived. As swiftly as he had gained the autonomy he craved, he was forcibly expelled by the combined power of his aristocratic rivals, who were unwilling to allow him sole rule. This alliance against Peisistratus would itself quickly dissolve into feuds over who or what would take his place. In an act of volte-face that seized the initiative, Cleisthenes' father Megacles invited Peisistratus to return, even offering his daughter's hand in marriage to cement a new grand family alliance. Peisistratus agreed.

Possibly just as tricky a customer as Peisistratus, Megacles then set about devising a scheme to convince the people – unwilling as they were to welcome home a tyrant – of the need for Peisistratus's return. His entrance back into society would have to be extraordinary. So it came to pass that standing beside Peisistratus in his chariot as he entered the city was the goddess Athena – or so it appeared to the citizens crowding the streets to marvel at such a sign of divine favour. 'According to some accounts', Aristotle notes, the tall and beautiful goddess was in fact 'a Thracian flower-girl from Collytus named Phye', dressed up in suitable splendour.[19]

The charade worked, the marriage went ahead and the alliance of families ruled Athens – until it became known that Peisistratus was having conjugal relations with his new wife 'not in the customary way'.[20] Though the meaning is unclear, it has been argued that this refers to anal sex: Peisistratus, while agreeable to a marriage of convenience, would not deign to father a child with a woman from a rival family. In response to this outrageous misuse of his daughter, Megacles broke off both the marriage and the alliance, and Peisistratus was again forced out of Athens. Some time later, however, Peisistratus – together with his own sons from a previous relationship, and with support from a number of Greek cities – returned once more to take Athens by force, and this time with a proper army. He faced the Athenians in battle near Marathon, finally took control of the city and held on to it for almost two decades until his death, whereupon he was succeeded by his sons, Hippias and Hipparchus.

As torrid as the origins of this tyranny may sound in summary, it's worth saying again that, in the view of Aristotle, this period was a golden age, in which Athens enjoyed great economic growth. The Peisistratids oversaw the opening of Athens' silver mines, so generating a new and lucrative revenue stream for the city. They oversaw the building of a magnificent limestone temple to Athena on the Acropolis. Within the *agora* they provided community necessities such as a new well and communal altars of the gods. And, crucially, it was under the rule of the Peisistratids that great civic occasions such as the City Dionysia festival, in honour of Dionysus, seem to have begun. This celebration brought the Athenians together in ecstatic worship of the god of wine and theatre, alongside the watching of tragedies composed and performed in his honour at the god's sanctuary at the base of the Acropolis.[21] That said, Aristotle was of the view that the Peisistratids sponsored such endeavours not so much for the noble aim of beautifying and ornamenting the city as with a mind to keeping the mass of the people occupied and leaving them no time to rebel – a stratagem used by rulers throughout history.[22]

Born in violence, the Peisistratid tyranny was dealt a mortal blow by brutal means. The succeeding sons, Hippias and Hipparchus, ruled Athens together until a murder plot was hatched by two men named Harmodius and Aristogeiton and carried out during the grand Panathenaia festival of 514 BCE. The Panathenaia celebrated Athena and her status as patron deity of the city and involved the whole citizen population, who gathered at the city gates before marching to the Acropolis to deliver a new ceremonial robe in which to cloak the sacred statue of the goddess.

Lurking among the celebrants of 514 BCE, however, were the would-be assassins Harmodius and Aristogeiton. They concealed swords in their ceremonial myrtle branches, waiting until they could get close enough to strike, whereupon they succeeded in stabbing Hipparchus to death. Harmodius, though, was immediately set upon and killed by guards, and Aristogeiton was taken into custody, so permitting Hippias to restore order. Aristogeiton died under torture devised by the understandably paranoid Hippias, who would cling on to power for four more years.

This epochal moment – 'the killing of the tyrant' – would be commemorated in Athenian art by a famous and heroic statue of Harmodius and Aristogeiton that stood in a conspicuous dedicated position in the *agora*. The statue that survives today through copies depicts the two heroes standing naked, young Harmodius bearing a sword ready to strike, the older bearded Aristogeiton with an arm outstretched as if protecting his young companion. This piece became such a symbol of Athens' civic identity that the Persians, when sacking the city in 480–79 BCE, took the statue back with them to Persepolis as supreme evidence of their desecration of Athens. It is said that when Alexander the Great conquered Persia more than a century later, he took pains to liberate the statue and return it to Athens.

Why did this pair wish to kill the tyrants? Again, the sources disagree. It seems clear that they were acting in accordance with a popular mood. After all, the Athenian state guaranteed free food for Harmodius's and Aristogeiton's descendants in honour of their achievements, and for years a popular drinking song celebrated the killing as having been prompted by a desire for equality: 'I'll carry my sword in a myrtle branch, like Harmodius and Aristogeiton, when they together killed the tyrant and brought equality before the law to Athens!'[23]

The great historian Thucydides, however – writing later on in the fifth century BCE – claims that the murder, whatever its consequence, was intended purely to settle a grudge. Hipparchus, having been spurned in love by Harmodius – who was already in a relationship with Aristogeiton – had gone on to slander Harmodius's sister, for which Harmodius and Aristogeiton together decided that Hipparchus (plus his brother) should pay the ultimate penalty.[24] As such, we must decide for ourselves which motive seems more plausible: the desire for liberty or the pursuit of vendetta.

Cleisthenes' family had been in exile since around 546 BCE. For some part of that period – during the 520s and 510s – they had resided at Delphi, nestled in the Parnassian mountains in central Greece, its venerated sanctuary of Apollo precariously terraced into the mountainside, with a small community of a thousand or so local Delphians gathered around it. By this time the oracle at Delphi was renowned across the Mediterranean and beyond. On consulting days – one day a month, for nine months of the year – queues would form to shuffle through the sanctuary, and individuals and community ambassadors stepped forward to put their questions to the oracular priestess in order to know the will of the gods.

However, Delphi in this period was in ruins. The temple of Apollo at the heart of the sanctuary, having burnt down mid-century, was a building site; and the process of fundraising and rebuilding was slow, painful and ongoing. While Cleisthenes sat in exile, the din of stone-cutting, sawing and chiselling must have filled his ears, along with the cries of the workmen as they hoisted heavy blocks of solid stone into place, and the trundle of cart wheels as more material was hauled up from the port 600 metres below. But Cleisthenes and his family were not mere passive observers of this construction work: Herodotus tells us that they bid for and won the contract to complete the temple's rebuilding, and set about the project with a flourish, deciding on their own initiative – and out of their own pockets – to complete the eastern face of the temple (that overlooking the altar where sacrifices to Apollo were placed) in luxurious marble.[25]

Such largesse was keenly noted, not least by the oracular priestess herself. Every time the Spartans came to consult at Delphi during this period, they were told that, before they did anything else, they ought to free the Athenians from the surviving tyrant Hippias. Who answered the call in 510 BCE but the Spartan king Cleomenes?

Creating a New World

As the third day of the Acropolis siege dawned in 508 BCE, the people of Athens who had risen up in united affront against Isagoras and his Spartan associates must have sensed this was another hinge-moment in more than a century of vying and grasping for power in Athens. But on this occasion an agreement was reached without bloodshed. The siege was lifted by a truce, allowing the Spartans to leave Athens, along with the disgraced Isagoras. The Spartans may well have wished to avoid combat, considering their small numbers too paltry to reply to a mass Athenian uprising. Isagoras probably wanted to live to fight another day. But if the Athenians left Isagoras and the Spartans alone, they did take out their anger on many of Isagoras's Athenian supporters, who were killed for being on the wrong side of public opinion.

As the dust settled and the dead were buried, Cleisthenes and his expelled family supporters were recalled. The people of Athens remained concerned that Sparta might return with a much larger army – concerned enough, Herodotus tells us, to consider an alliance with Persia for their protection.[26] Still, it was in this context of perceived danger that Cleisthenes' reform package, first espoused in the heady atmosphere between the two sieges of the Acropolis, was put into place. Instead of Solon's middling *eunomia* that gave everyone the amount of power they deserved, Cleisthenes' reforms offered the radical potential for direct and full 'people-power'.

As we have seen, their stress was on small local communities – the *demes* – as the building blocks for wider networks of community organisation and political and military representation. In each *deme* people gathered in local assemblies to debate, admit new members and reach decisions on how to run their own communities. At the same time, crucially, Cleisthenes' wider network of ten new tribes sought specifically to break the ties of loyalty to particular geographical areas and their dominant aristocratic families, by bringing local groups from widely separated areas together to fight in the army and participate in politics.

Groups of *demes* from the northern countryside of Attica were thus united with *demes* from the city of Athens and from the south-eastern coast of Attica – whether in battle or when participating and voting in the main Athenian assembly in Athens (which now had a new meeting place on the Pnyx hill, dedicated for evermore as the home of Athens' public assembly). Crucially, each of these new tribes contributed an equal number of people to Athens' permanent governing council, and every one of those people was picked by lot. Some parts of the old system remained: alongside the new board of ten military generals, chosen (one by each tribe) to lead the city's army, stood (until *c.*490 BCE) an overarching 'war *archon*', who was traditionally an aristocrat. Equally, not all offices in the city were open to all: for some decades yet, the position of chief magistrate (as once occupied by Solon) was restricted to certain classes of citizen.

Nevertheless, the effects of these reforms were remarkable. By 506 BCE Athens won in battle against its nearby rivals, Boeotia and Chalcis, a victory that Herodotus attributed to the new political system:

> While they were under the rule of despots, the Athenians were no better in war than any of their neighbours, yet once they got rid of despots they were far and away the best of all. This, then, shows that while they were oppressed they were cowards, as men working for their master, but when they were free, each was eager to do the best for himself.[27]

Throughout this period of civic strife, even after Cleisthenes' reforms began to take effect, the word 'democracy' was not used – it had not even been invented. Solon spoke of *dysnomia* ('bad order') versus *eunomia* ('good order'). In the lead-up to the sieges of 510 and 508 BCE we hear of *isonomia* ('equal order'). We have to wait until after the Persian invasions of 490 and 480 BCE before the idea of *demokratia* – the power of the people – is first conceptualised and mentioned.[28] The politics of Athens had yet a way to go to evolve into the democratic system of the era of the Parthenon and the Athenian Empire. But by the 460s BCE – half a century after the popular riot that began Athens' march towards its famed democracy – a new baby boy in Athens was named Demokrates, in honour of the system that was now the birthright of him and every other future adult male Athenian citizen.

Writing Ancient History

It is amazing just how much we can know about the events of 2,500 years ago thanks to the texts of such ancient writers as Herodotus and Aristotle, which have been copied and recopied through the centuries and augmented by more recent discoveries of ancient papyrus copies in the desert sands of Egypt. But the stories told of the intrigues of Athenian politics in the sixth century BCE continue to pose a number of problems for historians. What kind of stories do they tell, and to what end? Just how reliable are they? How can we be sure that what we *think* we know actually happened? Much is at stake in our answers.

Aside from the fragments of Solon's poetry in later texts, we do not have a single line attributable to an Athenian writer that can be securely dated between 594 and 480 BCE. Herodotus wrote in the 420s, nearly a century after Cleisthenes' reforms. The text *Constitution of the Athenians* (often attributed to Aristotle, but really of uncertain authorship, and only retrieved in 1879 from a rubbish dump in the ancient city of Oxyrhynchus in Egypt) dates to the 320s BCE, as do Aristotle's other major works that mention Athens' political system. A number of other local historians from the fifth and fourth centuries BCE are preserved for us in fragments and seem also to have been used as source material by the Greek historian, philosopher and essayist Plutarch, who wrote a biography of the life of Solon as part of a wider literary endeavour to write about worthy lives – but Plutarch's endeavour dates from the early second century CE.

All of the texts on which we rely, to understand this critical period, were written at a distance from events, with inevitable question marks over their factual accuracy. We must also consider the degree to which we shape our past to reflect our present: the stories told in the ancient sources, the selection and emphasis of the authors, tell us about how they and their society chose to remember their past. (As the ancient historian Robin Osborne has put it, 'history is not something that has happened, but something which ones makes for oneself'.[29])

There are clear instances where we may detect the degree to which the historical record has been edited and shaped. For instance, thanks to the chance survival of an inscribed list of those who held the position of chief magistrate in Athens during this period, we know that in the year 525–4 BCE the *archon* was Cleisthenes. This was in the midst of the tyrant rule of his arch-enemy Peisistratus – a time when, according to the surviving historical texts, Cleisthenes and his family were said to be exiled from Athens. What does this tell us? First, that the nature of 'tyrannical' rule in Athens must have been much more 'light touch' than the term implies today. Peisistratus can hardly have ruled by an iron first but, rather, through a more informal network of shifting alliances, using persuasion as well as force and, ultimately, depending on a groundswell of civic support. Second, what that inscription underlines is the extent to which the principal actors in these stories, and/or those later recording them, were themselves keen to change the historical narrative to suit present circumstances. It was simply more appropriate for Cleisthenes – in his later guise as champion of the new Athenian democratic system after 508 BCE – to be removed from any involvement with (or contamination by) what had gone before.

It is a truism that history is written by victors. More often, though, we contemporary readers of ancient sources have to deal with opinions of different writers that are essentially contradictory, especially when it comes to the analysis of the character of particular epochs, the motivations of particular individuals, and the estimation of their importance to political change. Was Peisistratus's reign a golden age, as Aristotle argued, or a period of trickery and guile in Athens, as Herodotus thought? Aristotle, we know, was more of a fan of a balanced constitution in which the 'middling' people (rather than the 'mass') held power; so perhaps it is no surprise that he favoured Peisistratus (as he did Solon). But Herodotus was only too keen to stress the tyranny of Peisistratus by erasing Cleisthenes from the list of *archons*.

Sources differ, too, over why the 'tyrant-killers' Harmodius and Aristogeiton did their deed during the Panathenaia festival: in pursuit of civic liberty, or for revenge within the sorry context of a bitter love triangle? And what motivated Cleisthenes to introduce his ideas for reform: a desire to improve the lot of the people or his hatred of the Ionian Greeks?

We remember and celebrate a new system of governance that introduced freedom and democracy, so prevalent in our world today. But were these outcomes anything the principal actors actively sought or envisaged, or were they an unexpected by-product of actions motivated by other concerns? In short, was the invention of democracy intentional or accidental?

Our frame is also shifted by the different opinions of ancient historians over whom – or what – was the crucial impetus behind the change. From Herodotus until the fourth century BCE, ancient sources focus on Cleisthenes' crucial role, whereas Solon is neglected – unmentioned, even, by Thucydides, who wrote at the end of the fifth century BCE. Thereafter, though, Cleisthenes recedes, to be replaced by an emphasis on the key role of Solon in setting Athens on its course. When, therefore, should we say that democracy's journey began? Who was its midwife? Can we bestow on Solon such a mantle, when in his own poetry he specifically disavowed full people-power and expressed his desire only to give each section of the population as much power as they 'deserved'? Unless some new evidence is excavated from the earth in Greece or from a rubbish tip in Egypt, we may never be able to answer these questions properly. And, even then, such new finds are likely to provide only a fresh opinion, rather than definitive proof.

Aristotle was personal tutor to Alexander the Great in an age when powerful individuals were once again taking over the Greek world at the end of the fourth century BCE. Should we be surprised that Aristotle is more favourable to the tyrant Peisistratus than Herodotus, who wrote as Athens' democracy was fighting for its life in the civil war that consumed Greece at the end of the previous century? It is, perhaps, little wonder that a portrait of Solon as a wise and just ruler dispensing power where it was due became more important in history from the fourth century BCE onwards, within a world that craved the emergence of another benign autocrat. Such an account of Solon surely attracted the interest of Plutarch, who sought to write the biographies of wise and courageous but autocratic individuals as exempla for the individual and powerful rulers of his world in the early second century CE.

For me, the fragility and uncertainty inherent in the story of democracy's creation is rather inspiring. What all the sources tell us – once we see through to their contradictions, cover-ups and reframings – is that the conception and development of democracy were never free from doubt, or from the influence of personal motivations, and were constantly recast by its principal actors and commentators, and then again by successive generations.

Neither the principal actors nor the wider public in ancient Athens could know what they would eventually create, and the course of this new political system could have taken a different turn at any number of points, thus to be remembered and celebrated in any number of different ways. Such an understanding should make us more aware of the chance-like nature of human civilisation, and of the need not to assume the inevitable survival of any aspect of our society but, rather, to fight actively for what we wish to remain part of our world.

That awareness must stay in our minds when we turn to consider the sources pertaining to our second political revolution occurring at the end of the sixth century BCE. Tradition has it that in 510–509 BCE – just as Athens was expelling a tyrant and poised to witness the enactment of Cleisthenes' plan – the Roman Republic was born in Italy. How does the ancient record treat the origins of this new form of political governance?

Writing the Story of the Origins of the Republic

The earliest literary sources we have for the formation of the Roman Republic come not in Latin, but in Greek, and were written some 300 years after the event, and little survives to us today of these original works. The first was by a Roman senator, Quintus Fabius Pictor, at the end of the third century BCE; the second by a Greek called Polybius, in the second half of the second century BCE. This was a period – as we shall see – in which the political and military power of the Greek world had faded and that of Rome was rapidly expanding. Quintus Fabius Pictor was an important figure in that expansion. Yet he was also a huge admirer of Greek history and historians. Thus, while he was a Roman witness to the expansion of Roman power over Greece (and other parts of the Mediterranean), Fabius wrote his history in Greek, in conscious emulation of Herodotus and Thucydides.[30]

Polybius, on the other hand, was held as a hostage in Rome in the 160s BCE and became close with the well-known and respected family of Scipio. He wrote not only a history of this turbulent period, but also an assessment of what had made Rome into such a dominant force – a process he attributed to Rome's military organisation and the strength of Rome's republican constitution.[31] Indeed, while he was a Greek, Polybius was inherently scathing of Athens' (now waning) democratic political system: he called its temporary ascendance 'a work of chance and circumstance' and lambasted 'the inconsistency of her nature'.[32] As is so often the case, the political circumstances of the era in which Polybius was writing fundamentally affected his assessment.

These historians, in trying to construct Rome's earliest history, were working on the basis of myth, rumour and conflicting accounts, even in respect of matters as basic as when exactly Rome was founded and when the republic began. Their way of identifying these crucial dates involved working backwards in time from a date they felt sure of. And in the forefront of these men's minds – not surprisingly, given that one was Greek and the other was writing in Greek – seems to have been Athens' own dramatic history of crisis and change in the period 510–508 BCE. The foundation of the republic was a moment in which the people of Rome had expelled a tyrant king. The people of Athens had expelled a tyrant in 510–9 BCE. For ancient Greek (or Greek-speaking Roman) historians, this was a pleasing coincidence.[33]

Working back from that date, historians of the time added up the estimated lengths of each king's reign, so as to come up with a date for the foundation of Rome itself (by Romulus and Remus) at some point between 813 and 729 BCE. Fabius thought it should be dated to 747 BCE, although the date was eventually 'established' as 753 BCE by the writer Marcus Terentius Varro in the first century BCE (putting Rome's foundation at around the time of the 'starting date' for Greece's own history with the first Olympic Games in 776 BCE). Roman history itself, then, was dated through the cultural and political similarities between Greece and Rome, as desired by historians writing at a time when Rome was emerging as the superpower of the Mediterranean.

From the second century BCE the early history of Rome – its kings and particularly the foundation of the republic – was thus viewed through Greek-tinted glasses, especially by Greek-speaking and Greek-facing historians.[34] And in the writings of Polybius we see the first

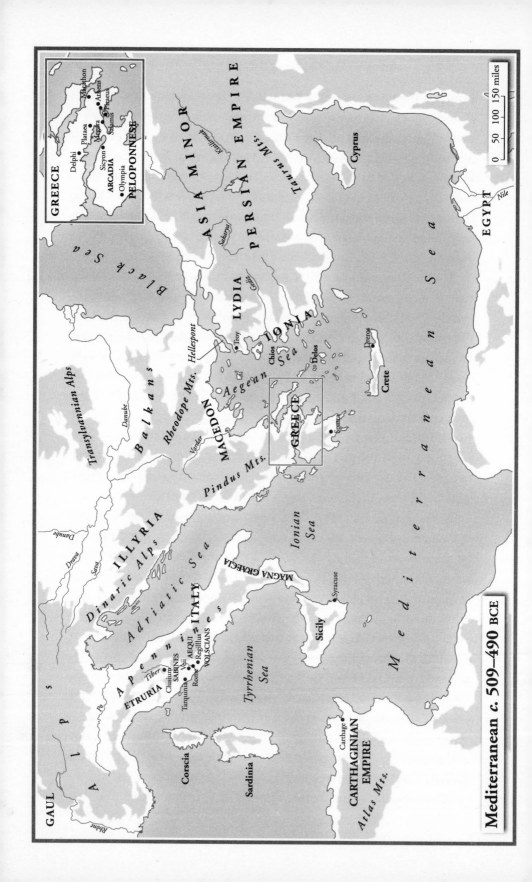

Mediterranean c. 509–490 BCE

GAUL

A l p s

Rhône

Po

Transylvannian Alps

Danube

Drava

Sava

Danube

Balkans

Rhodope Mts.

Black Sea

Dinaric Alps

ILLYRIA

Adriatic Sea

Apennines

ETRURIA

Clusium
Tarquinia
Veii
Rome
Regillus
SABINES
AEQUI
VOLSCIANS
Tiber
ITALY

Corscia

Sardinia

Tyrrhenian Sea

Sicily

Syracuse

MAGNA GRAECIA

Ionian Sea

Pindus Mts.

MACEDON

Vardar

GREECE

Sparta

Aegean Sea

IONIA

Chios
Delos

Crete

Dreros

Troy

Hellespont

Rheodope Mts.

Sardis

LYDIA

Gediz

ASIA MINOR

Kızılırmak

Sakarya

PERSIAN EMPIRE

Taurus Mts.

Cyprus

EGYPT

Nile

Mediterranean Sea

Carthage

CARTHAGINIAN EMPIRE

Atlas Mts.

0   50   100   150 miles

GREECE

Delphi

Plataea
Marathon
Megara   Athens
Sicyon   Salamis   Piraeus
ARCADIA
Olympia
PELOPONNESE

in-depth attempt to compare the political constitutions of Rome and Greece, in which Athens' democracy is disparaged, whereas Rome's is praised and compared to the political constitution of the Greek city of Sparta.[35] Even centuries later, fresh linkages or comparisons were being sought. Kings of Rome were said to have been descended from aristocrats from Corinth in Greece, or tutored by Greek intellectuals.[36] Rome itself was claimed to have been founded either by Romulus and Remus, as a Greek colony sent out from Arcadia in the Peloponnese, or perhaps even by the offspring of the Greek hero Odysseus and the witch Circe.[37]

Within Roman society, historical texts were not the only avenue for telling stories about the past. From around the beginning of the second century BCE epic poems and plays also performed this function. In the nascent Roman theatre, *fabulae praetextae* (historical plays) were performed at annual public celebrations in Rome, and they not only reshaped but also created historical traditions about the foundations of the city, its kings and the origins of the republic. One example is *Brutus* by Lucius Accius, from the late second century BCE/early first century BCE. Its plot concerns the expulsion of the last king of Rome and the role played by Brutus in setting up the republic. Accius's patron belonged to the family of Brutus's descendants, so the author's sympathies may be guessed easily enough.[38]

In the first century BCE, and particularly during the final crisis of the republic mid-century, a multitude of historians became concertedly interested in writing about the early history of Rome. Here we have the work of Diodorus Siculus ('of Sicily'), the first person to quote the works of Megasthenes and his description of India (as well as a large number of other earlier historians) as part of his vast forty-tome endeavour offering a geographical and temporal overview of world myth and history down to his own times, including – and ending with – the story of Rome.[39] Towards the end of the first century BCE we also have a history written by Dionysius of Halicarnassus, who covered Rome from its origins (which he, too, thought were Greek) through to the third century BCE.[40] And roughly contemporary, composed under the rulership of the new Emperor Augustus, the massive work of Livy in 142 books, *Ab Urbe Condita* ('From the Founding of the City'), began to appear.

The ancient literary sources that speak to the foundation of the

Roman Republic are thus a maze, all produced long after the events described and always heavily influenced by the intellectual milieu and political realities of the author's time atop whatever were his literary goals. The result is a murky mix of myth, legend and propaganda, its deficiencies clear to and acknowledged by authors such as Livy, who, in the introduction to *Ab Urbe Condita*, bemoans the lack of official records from the period – often said to have been destroyed when the Gauls invaded Rome in 390 BCE – and explains how he has had to resort to private and often contradictory accounts kept by or passed down within the great families of Rome. And all of this led to Rome's origins – and its conversion from a monarchy to a republic – being a matter of constant debate and discussion, retelling and reformulation amongst historians, orators, politicians and playwrights, all of which fed into the ongoing larger discussion about what it meant to be Roman, and what Rome stood for in the wider world.

We have other clues to help us date the foundations of the republic. In 304 BCE the Romans supposedly discovered 204 nails hammered into the wall of the magnificent civic temple of Jupiter Optimus Maximus on the Capitoline Hill. Since tradition decreed that one nail be fixed for each passing year, the Romans deduced that the temple had been dedicated in 509–8 BCE – that is, right in the heart of our assumed moment of significant change. More recent archaeological investigation has confirmed that we can tie the substantial development of Rome's temples on the Capitoline Hill to the last part of the sixth century BCE.[41] As a result, some scholars have expressed pleasant surprise as to how accurate ancient dating of the foundation of the republic seems to have been.

In any event, the link between the narrative of Roman and Greek (Athenian) political upheavals runs deeper than simply an overlapping date. Implicit in the narratives of Rome's transition from monarchy to republic are ideas, triggers and catalyst-like individuals that we can immediately recognise from the political intrigues of Athenian politics in the centuries leading up to the development of democracy. Nor should these links particularly surprise us. These were two cultures heavily engaged with one another: there was huge cultural and economic contact between Greece and Rome during the sixth and into the fifth centuries BCE. The techniques of tile-making, for example, were said to have been brought to Rome from Corinth, and local imitations of Corinthian vases seem to have been dedicated as sacred objects on the Capitol in Rome around 600 BCE. Large amounts of Athenian pottery have been found deposited in Rome from the sixth century BCE, part of a very healthy export market that Athens had with Italy. And in the period immediately after the creation of the republic, enormous numbers of Athenian red-figure drinking cups (*kylikes*) seem to have been imported, used and thrown away in Rome.

Yet more crucially, Rome continued to take lessons from Athens even after the foundation of their new body politic. In the turbulent first half-century of the republic, as the people and leaders of Rome struggled to find a balance between the rights of the masses and the power of the minority, Roman law-givers would travel to Athens to investigate the Athenian legal framework and constitution – particularly the reforms of Solon, whom the Romans considered to have faced a dilemma similar to their own – and bring back ideas to implement at home. This connection would continue through to the period of Greece's absorption into the Roman Empire in the later second and early first centuries BCE. Nevertheless, the outcome of this process was a fundamentally different political system from Athenian democracy, one that attempted to balance representation of the people with the ongoing majority power of an elite. The tension between these forces was present throughout the crucible years when the republic was born, and they were indelibly part of the structure that emerged from the fire.

CHAPTER 2

Rome, the Republic and the Perfection of Government

The bet, Livy tells us, was sealed over drinks. King Lucius Tarquinius Superbus ('the Proud') was away fighting. His sons, in the company of their cousin, Lucius Tarquinius Collatinus, had enjoyed a full evening of feasting when, 'heated by wine', they fell to wondering what their wives were up to at home. They laid bets and returned to their respective residences to find out who was right. The king's sons discovered their wives enjoying themselves at parties. But Collatinus's wife Lucretia was securely at home, spinning cloth with her maids, just as Collatinus had wagered.

One of the king's sons, Sextus Tarquinius, took Lucretia's beauty and virtue as a kind of provocation. Some nights later, while a guest at his cousin's house, he stole into Lucretia's room by night and demanded at knife-point that she submit to him sexually. When this failed to persuade her, he threatened to murder her along with a male slave and arrange their naked bodies so as to support a story that he had disturbed them both in an act of adultery and carried out a summary execution. Lucretia faced disgrace whichever way she turned. 'With this menace,' Livy wrote, 'Sextus Tarquinius triumphed over her virtue' and raped her.[1]

Afterwards Lucretia called together her father, husband and the men of the family, asked them to swear vengeance on Sextus, then took her own life. Livy – writing centuries later, under the first Roman emperor, Augustus – recounts the oath these men took:

> By this guiltless blood before the kingly injustice I swear – you and the gods as my witnesses – I make myself the one who will prosecute, by what force I am able, Lucius Tarquinius Superbus along with his wicked wife and the whole house of his freeborn children by sword, by fire, by any means hence, so that neither they nor any one else be suffered to rule Rome.[2]

We should not be surprised that Livy offers such detail on the circumstances surrounding the creation and evolution of the republic. In writing for a new era of Rome's history and for a new sole ruler, Livy's tale offered both a series of implicitly flattering contrasts (Augustus was nothing like the tyrannical kings) and a set of carefully balanced lessons about what good rule and heroic individual dedication to the cause of Rome ought to look like. Livy had much material from which to choose: Rome's revolution required a more careful social and political balancing act than that in Athens, and it took far longer to achieve.[3] Equally, as Polybius later made clear, the city was beset by almost continual warfare, which played a crucial role in forging the particular nature of its constitution. As a result, when Roman ambassadors went to Athens to do their research on Athenian governance in the mid-fifth century BCE, they found a society that, though it had begun its revolution at the same time as that of Rome, already looked very different indeed from their own.

Lucretia's body was carried into the centre of Rome and laid out in the Forum, the beating heart of the city. The man who spoke her eulogy was Lucius Junius Brutus (later the titular hero of Accius's play). Plutarch tells us he was the king's nephew. But, for Brutus, such a close family tie to power had carried a sting in the tail. He was the son of Tarquinius's sister and a man called Marcus, one of the richest men in Rome, who had died soon after Brutus was born. Tarquinius responded to this family tragedy by ordering the murder of Brutus's elder brother and by seizing Marcus's estate and wealth. Brutus himself had only escaped being murdered by the king, as a child, on account of his apparently artless (thus unthreatening) nature, for which he had earnt the nickname 'Brutus' ('simple'), and would be educated alongside the monarch's own sons.

Plutarch, though, argues that Brutus's 'simplicity' was really a cunning ploy to ensure his own survival. When he was sent among the royal children to the oracle at Delphi, one of the boys arrogantly asked the god which of them would rule Rome after Tarquinius. The oracle was said to have replied, 'Whoever is the first to kiss his mother.' While the royal sons rushed back to Rome to find their mother, Brutus fell down and kissed the ground, 'mother earth'. On the strength of having such wits about him, Brutus was, in Plutarch's estimation, always bound for glory. He duly rose through the ranks as a trusted servant of the king, becoming his second-in-command. But given the grounds that he had to bear Tarquinius ill will, it is little wonder that Brutus saw in Lucretia's suicide a cause for rebellion.

With Tarquinius out of the city, as Lucretia's lifeless body was laid out in the Forum, Brutus stepped forth to deliver the eulogy. If the main square of the city (with all its daily business of buying and selling) strikes us as a strange setting for funeral rites, we should remember that it was routine for elite funerals, by the time Livy was writing, to include an oration in the Forum. Not least because the Forum was no mere market place but, rather, the real heart of Rome, the original meeting point between the city's rival communities, the place where the idea of Rome itself had been forged. Surrounding the people that day as they pressed forward to see Lucretia's body and hear Brutus's oration were reminders of and memorials to the foundation of Rome, its protector gods, its political lineage, and the engineering prowess that had turned the marshy ground of the Forum into a paved arena for spectacle.

As the people stood to hear the story of Lucretia's self-sacrifice, and of the royal sons' atrocious behaviour – from the mouth of a man who had seen and suffered the brutality of the king at first hand – they were surely reminded of everything Rome had set out to be, and of the greatness it had achieved, in contrast to the wretched manners of its current ruling family. Brutus's words boiled the blood of the Roman people, inciting revolution in the place where Rome itself had been conceived. And Brutus's authority as second-in-command after the king further swung the allegiance of Rome's army to his cause.

When Tarquinius Superbus returned from campaign, he found not only his sons in exile, but the gates of Rome barred and his own army turned against him. As Tacitus expressed it snappily, come the late first century/early second century CE, in the very first sentence of his history: 'Kings held the city of Rome from the beginning. Brutus established freedom (*libertas*).'[4] (It was this picture of Brutus's role in overthrowing the king and establishing freedom that was said to have convinced his descendant, Marcus Junius Brutus, to join the famous plot of 44 BCE to assassinate the dictator Julius Caesar on the Ides of March.)

Kings Bad and Good

The date, probably, was 510–9 BCE. Tarquinius Superbus had been king for twenty-five years. His reputation in later histories has, understandably, been sullied, the better to justify his unceremonious ousting from power. In particular he is seen to disrespect the organs of Rome's government under his control, working people to death during the building of the city's mighty sewer system, while constantly fearful of revolt. (Livy relates that he was accompanied everywhere by bodyguards.[5])

The story of his original ascent to power speaks yet more ill of him. Son of a previous king, but not in a position of direct succession, he had married a daughter of the current king, Servius Tullius, then conspired with his ambitious sister-in-law Tullia Minor to murder both her husband and his wife, after which the plotters would marry each other. Having won over a number of aristocrats to this plan, Tarquinius marched to the council chamber in the Forum with an armed squad of militia and sat on the king's chair, proclaiming himself King Tarquin. When the aged king came to confront him, Tarquinius picked him up and dumped him into the street. Struggling home, dazed and confused, Servius was set upon and murdered, perhaps at the instigation of Tarquinius and his own daughter, Tullia. Worse, Tullia even ran over Servius's lifeless body in her chariot, spattering her clothes with his blood, in a street that was known ever after as *vicus sceleratus*, the 'street of crime'.[6] Thus began the reign of Tarquinius Superbus, 'the Proud'.

The infamy of all this is worsened by the positive reputation enjoyed in later histories by Servius Tullius. His was a rags-to-riches story: born to a slave in the royal household (or, in a different version, conceived from a phallus emerging from a fire), he eventually married the daughter of the king. His accession, however, was not a simple matter of inheritance. In contrast to Tarquinius, who had literally seized the throne for himself, Servius Tullius was elected to it; but not, as had traditionally been the practice for previous monarchs, by a vote of the people of Rome. Servius Tullius was, according to Livy, Rome's first king to be appointed solely by the Senate, Rome's aristocratic council. And yet despite his lack of people-power credentials, many of the ancient sources characterise his rule as one that introduced significant political and military change, as well as economic, artistic and architectural expansion, all of which hugely benefited Rome. Indeed, scholars today argue that his reign has been used by the ancient historians as something of a 'catch-all' for the origins of systems of government much admired in their own day. In comparison to Tarquinius Superbus, Servius Tullius was, for the ancient historians, a hero.[7]

Most notably he is said to have undertaken a census of all inhabitants of Rome and their property, on the basis of which he divided the people into classes that regulated their service in the army and the way in which they engaged in the politics of the city. First came the *equites*, the city's wealthiest citizens, who often acted as the army's cavalry (alongside small special groups for engineers and musicians); then classes graded from one to five, according to different degrees of wealth; followed by a class of the poorest citizens, often known as the *proletarii* (which literally means 'capable only of producing children for the state', but from which we take the term 'proletariat'). The classes were each divided into *centuriae* or 'centuries'. These groupings had both political and military functions, as the mini-communities in which these people voted and fought.

The gathering of these classes in a political assembly was called the *comitia centuriata*. Each century had one vote, irrespective of the number of people it contained. The *equites* had eighteen centuries (thus eighteen votes); the engineers and musicians had two each; 'Class 1' had eighty centuries; the second to fourth classes had twenty centuries each; the fifth class had thirty centuries; and the *proletarii* had a mere one – so imbuing the system with a heavy bias towards the richer classes, who always voted first. Indeed, in any vote, once a majority was reached – which could be achieved just by the numbers of the *equites* and 'Class 1', if they were all in agreement – the count was discontinued, which meant that the poorest class rarely got to vote at all. As Livy put it: 'Gradations were introduced so that no one should seem to be excluded from the right to vote, but all the power should remain with the leading men in the state.'[8]

This system reflected realities that were military as much as political or social. The *equites* were cavalry, upon whose shoulders, spears and fearless horses rested the primary responsibility for victory in battle and thus the defence of Rome. It was, to an extent, natural that they had a greater say in the state's decisions. Servius Tullius's system of suffrage (with some changes to the number of centuries in Class 1) lay at the basis of the Roman constitution throughout its history, and it was this body that 'elected' the republic's top officials and passed laws, as well as declaring war and peace. Notices would be posted days before elections were to be held. In the immediate run-up there would be conventions in which candidates made speeches, opinions from magistrates on new laws or foreign policy would be heard, and then the entire citizen body would break up into its centuries. Before any voting could take place, the gods had to be consulted to ensure that the day was auspicious for making decisions. A priest examined the entrails of an animal to decide if the vote should proceed. If he said no, everyone went home. But if the entrails appeared propitious, the vote began.

Such a mass of people required a massive space, so the votes of the *comitia centuriata* took place on a large open field, the Campus Martius, just outside Rome's city walls. Each century, when it came to their turn to vote, filed slowly through a system of lanes and barriers into a fenced-off area. Every citizen had a vote – they cast a pebble into baskets to signify yes or no. The counts were overseen by officials, who also had responsibility for counting the ballots and declaring the outcome: whichever way the majority voted, so went the vote of that century. The lower classes had to hang around the Campus Martius for hours, watching the laborious process, discussing amongst themselves which way they should vote, observing how the upper classes had voted, and waiting to see whether they would even get a chance to vote themselves. If every century had to vote before an overall majority was reached, the procedure could last longer than a day.

This system of suffrage introduced by Servius Tullius more than half a century before Rome's revolution of 510–9 BCE was now at the heart of a new kind of government, in the aftermath of the expulsion of Tarquinius Superbus. The novel dispensation was known in Latin as *res publica romana* – the 'public thing of the Roman people', from which was born the term 'the republic' and our descriptor of a particular kind of political constitution: republicanism.[9] According to Livy, using the *comitia centuriata*, the people of Rome elected two 'consuls' (joint leaders) to replace the position of the king as holder of *imperium* – the power to raise and command the people and armies of Rome.[10]

Baptised in Fire

The first two consuls, elected in 509 BCE, were Brutus and Collatinus: the man who had incited the people to exile Tarquinius, and the man whose wife had killed herself in shame, in response to the demands of Tarquinius's son. The term 'consul' may well have derived from the word for 'co-ploughers' in the field: two sets of hands on the tiller of state, each keeping a check on the other.[11] Alongside them was a *rex sacrorum* – a priest whose job it was to perform the religious functions formerly undertaken by the king, and who could never be a member of the Senate or hold political office. And advising the consuls, as they had done for Rome's kings, was the hugely influential and unelected aristocratic Senate, consisting of around 300 members who served for life.

Within its first year the new republic was put to the most exacting of tests. Livy claims that Brutus's first act as consul was to gather the people of Rome together to swear an oath never again to be ruled by a king, so that they would not be swayed by whatever grandiose promises and bribes a king might make, in an attempt to reclaim his throne.[12] Brutus is also said to have argued in public that since his co-consul,

Collatinus, was part of the Tarquin family (he was the ousted king's cousin once removed), then he should be exiled rather than hold office. Though Brutus himself was the nephew of Tarquinius Superbus, Collatinus did not fight the accusation and agreed to step down as consul, being replaced by Publius Valerius 'Poplicola' (the 'people's friend').

Tarquinius Superbus, having been barred from Rome, did not take his exile lightly. He had fled to the nearby community of his ancestors, the Etruscans, who at this time were more powerful (and controlled more land) than Rome or the alliance of Latin cities (known as Latium) to which Rome belonged. Indeed, Rome was effectively sandwiched between the powerful Etruscans to the north and the strong and successful cities of Magna Graecia ('Greater Greece') to the south. Rome had in many ways benefited from this position, as a natural portal for trade going north–south and east–west. But it also suffered by proximity to such powerful neighbours. One of Etruria's strongest cities, Veii, was a day's march from Rome. And while other Latin and Osco-Umbrian cities had opted for similar political reforms to Rome (particularly the replacement of a king with elected magistrates/consuls), the Etruscans still resolutely believed in a monarchy. Now an Etruscan-descended king, Tarquinius, sought their help in order to regain his throne.[13]

Heading an army recruited from the Etruscan stronghold cities of Tarqunii and Veii, Tarquinius Superbus advanced on Rome. His agents had already been at work in the city, trying to reverse popular opinion and undermine the oath Brutus had made the people swear. These agents even managed to convince the sons of Brutus (Titus and Tiberius) to turn against their father. Brutus was forced, then, to choose between the sons he loved and the stability and survival of Rome and its new republic, which he had helped to found – not to mention his own personal survival. He chose the republic and himself, and so had to endure the sight of his own children being executed for treason. After such a horror, on top of so many other grievances, Brutus's hatred of Tarquinius could hardly have burnt higher. More than merely denying Tarquinius the throne in Rome, Brutus wanted his adversary to suffer just as he, Brutus, had been made to suffer. When in 509 BCE Tarquinius launched his attack on Rome at the Arsian Forest outside the city, his son Arruns, leading Tarquinius's cavalry, spotted Brutus's corresponding position at the head of the Roman forces and charged at him. Brutus now welcomed the chance to kill Tarquinius's son, his own cousin.

In the heat of battle, amid the thunder of cavalry hooves, Arruns is said to have cried out:

> Over there is the man who drove us into exile from our native land. Look! He is himself decked out with our trappings, as he comes proudly on! O gods, avengers of kings, be with us![14]

Brutus and Arruns charged at one another, with such ferocity that their spear-points drove clean through each other's shields and into flesh. Mutually impaled, they tumbled from their respective mounts and lay sprawled among the carnage, their spears rising like masts from each other's bodies, twitching in the air with every breath of wind. The battle raged on, with the thunder of hooves and the thump of fresh casualties falling to the ground around the fallen leaders. Neither side, however, seemed able to dominate. Eventually, as night fell, the vying forces withdrew. Livy relates a legend that in the night air a voice from the forest – thought to be that of Silvanus, a god of the woods – had pervaded the battlefield, professing victory to the Romans, but only by the smallest of margins: the Etruscans, it was whispered on the winds, had lost one man more than the Romans.[15] The republic had been saved – for now.

And so Rome's first pair of consuls were both out of office within a year: one had stepped down of his own accord, the other had perished on the battlefield defending the fledgling republic. Brutus's place was taken by the father of Lucretia, who died soon afterwards, to be replaced by one Marcus Horatius. The surviving consul, Publius Valerius 'Poplicola', had celebrated Rome's victory at the Arsian Forest with a triumphal homecoming and procession, in which he had ridden in a chariot to the Capitol, the central and sacred hill of Rome, before pronouncing a stirring eulogy over Brutus's body. He now sought to calm fears that he had ambitions to overturn the republic himself and become king. The people pointed to Poplicola's house, increasingly bejewelled with rich ornaments and decoration, and its similarity to the former abode of Tarquinius, now demolished. In response, Popli-cola, 'the people's friend', had his own house levelled in the dead of night and spent the rest of his consulship homeless and begging a bed at night from friends. This extraordinary act of self-denial proved a huge success at the polls: Poplicola was elected consul four times between 509 and 504 BCE.

Thwarting the ambitions of Tarquinius Superbus, though, was far from Rome's only military challenge. The final years of the sixth century and the early years of the fifth saw Italy subject to great desta-bilisation. The Etruscans, despite their power, were increasingly threatened by invading hordes of Gauls from the north. At the same time, mountainous tribes in central Italy, such as the Sabines, Volscians and Aequi, started to push out into the fertile plains occupied by Rome and its Latin neighbours.

Rome had a long history with the Sabines. According to myth, Rome's founder Romulus had invited the Sabines to share in a Roman festival, at which the Roman men had stolen the Sabine women and married them forcibly so as to increase Rome's population. This out-rage, known as the Rape of the Sabine Women (from the Latin *rapere*, 'to seize'), had led to war, until a peaceable settlement was worked out, such that a Sabine king had even ruled in Rome after Romulus. Now, centur-ies later, Romans and Sabines were at war again.

As consul, Poplicola appeared well placed to deal with the situation – one of his ancestors had supposedly helped to reconcile the Romans and Sabines in Romulus's day. Initial military victories against the Sab-ines allowed Poplicola to strike another legendary deal: he persuaded one Sabine leader – Attus Clausus from the city of Regillus – to move to Rome with his family and his dependants, all 5,000 of them. Rome once again benefited by the increase in manpower. But there were many Sabines (not to mention other mountain tribes) who could not be neu-tralised in the same way, and who continued to threaten not just Rome's territory, but the very survival of Rome itself. Poplicola died fighting the Sabines in 503 BCE and was buried on the spot where the house he had purposefully torn down once stood.

While the Sabines menaced Rome, the persistent Tarquinius Superb-us persuaded another Etruscan king, Lars Porsenna of Clusium, to bring his even greater forces to bear down on Rome in 508 BCE. Polybius, writing more than 300 years later, is the first ancient source to recount how the Etruscan king came to the very gates of the city, but other ancient sources give contradictory accounts of what followed. Tacitus and Pliny claim that Porsenna managed to capture Rome, forcing her to yield territory, hostages and power to the Etruscans for some years, before Rome finally managed to throw off the Etruscan yoke and re-establish the republic for good.[16] But others, including Polybius, speak of a heroic and successful defence of the city and republic, in which both the Roman army and individual Romans played a part.

Among the Roman commanders standing in Porsenna's way was Publius Horatius Cocles 'the Cyclops', nephew of the consul Marcus Horatius and known as 'the Cyclops' on account of having lost an eye in combat. This deficiency did not stop Cocles from heroically defending the wooden bridge over the Tiber that led to the Sublician gate near the centre of Rome, until the rest of the Roman army could retreat inside the city walls and the bridge itself was destroyed. Wounded, Cocles leapt into the Tiber, fully armoured, and attempted to swim across, but he drowned.[17] Livy doubts this account, but then both he and Dionysius of Halicarnassus relate a yet more heroic version, whereby Cocles used the bodies of the slain as shields and threw every weapon he could find at the Etruscans, whirling around like a man intent on suicide and taking others with him, until finally, wounded all over, he jumped into the Tiber and emerged on the other side, there to be carried in triumphal procession through Rome and subsequently showered with honours.[18]

Both Polybius and Livy record that Lars Porsenna was set back but not defeated by Cocles' antics. He was, however, struck by these Roman displays of courage. Following Cocles' valorous saving of Rome, Gaius Mucius Scaevola (as his full title would soon become), a Roman aristocrat, was captured in Porsenna's camp as he attempted to assassinate the Etruscan king. When hauled before Porsenna, Mucius is said by Livy to have told him:

> I am your enemy, and as an enemy I would have slain you; I can die as resolutely as I could kill: both to do and to endure valiantly is the Roman way. Nor am I the only one to carry this resolution against

you: behind me is a long line of men who are seeking the same honour. Gird yourself therefore, if you think it worth your while, for a struggle in which you must fight for your life from hour to hour with an armed foe always at your door. Such is the war we, the Roman youths, declare on you. Fear no serried ranks, no battle; it will be between yourself alone and a single enemy at a time.[19]

In riposte, Porsenna ordered Mucius to be roasted alive until he revealed the full details of Rome's plot – at which threat Mucius, of his own volition, stuck his right hand into an open fire to show his scorn for the pain Porsenna threatened to inflict. Beside himself with wonder at the act, Porsenna let Mucius go, saying:

> I would invoke success upon your valour, were that valour exerted for my country; since that may not be, I release you from the penalties of war and dismiss you scathless and uninjured.[20]

Mucius returned to Rome, there to earn the nickname 'Scaevola' – meaning 'left-handed' – along with much honour, for his fearless courage and devotion to the Roman cause. Porsenna, weighing up his allegiance to Tarquinius against his respect for Roman courage and his wariness at what it might take to conquer such a people, agreed to conclude a peace treaty with Rome.

Still, Tarquinius's efforts to regain the throne did not cease. Around 496 BCE (the exact date is disputed) an alliance of Latin towns, traditionally allies of Rome, went to war against the city under the command of a now-aged Tarquinius and his last surviving son, Titus. The two sides met at Lake Regillus in the territory of Tusculum to the southeast of Rome. Commanding the Roman forces was a man called Aulus Postumius, who had been appointed dictator in Rome. This post had come into being not long after the creation of the republic, in recognition of the fact that in times of great trouble – of which the early republic seemed to be having its fair share – it was critical to have a clear chain of command and no delay in the decision-making process. Having two consuls – dual helmsmen of state – aided by the Senate was all well and good, but if the very survival of Rome seemed in jeopardy (so the argument went), then the state needed to be able to appoint a single head with emergency powers to pursue particular ends, after which he would step down.

It is said that when the rival forces engaged at Lake Regillus the zeal of the Roman army was sharpened by their awareness that they faced the last king of Rome and his final surviving descendant: here, then, was their chance to wipe out that line and close once and for all that chapter in their history. Postumius was in Rome's front ranks, encouraging his men. Tarquinius Superbus was correspondingly conspicuous, and tried to ride straight at Postumius so as to strike him dead, only to be deflected and forced to retreat. Despite this setback, the battle began to favour Tarquinius and his allies. Postumius – seeing that even Roman soldiers zealous to kill the king were turning back – ordered his own personal bodyguard to kill any Roman who retreated. According to Livy, this order forced the Roman army to re-engage with renewed vigour, but still it wasn't enough. In desperation, Postumius begged his aristocratic cavalry to dismount and fight on foot alongside the exhausted Roman soldiers. The resultant sight of all troops sharing the risk, shoulder-to-shoulder, is said to have re-fired Roman hearts and begun the rout of Tarquinius and his men. Pledging rewards for those who were first into the Latin camp, Postumius led the final and successful charge.

Building a Working Republic

Such triumphs made Rome the largest, wealthiest and most powerful community in Latium in the early fifth century BCE. As a result, the public and particularly the religious heart of the city was much adorned during the first thirty years of the republic. There was a spate of temple-building in Rome between 509 and 480, with edifices erected in honour of Jupiter, Juno and Minerva, Saturn (also used as the city's treasury), Ceres, Liber and Libera, Mercury and the Dioscuri – the twin brothers Castor and Pollux. This last temple, vowed by Postumius following the victory at Lake Regillus and completed by his son, was especially vast, with a footprint of 32 x 50 metres. Roman temples, unlike Greek ones, were often raised up on a large podium with a grand, sweeping staircase at the front. The staircase and podium at the front of the Castor and Pollux temple in the Forum was so prominent – approximately 7 metres high – that it was used as a speakers' platform from which to address the crowd, and the temple itself was, on occasion, used as the meeting place for the Senate.

Such a frenzy of major civic infrastructure projects in the immediate aftermath of the establishment of the republic would not be repeated during the rest of the century, since Rome's battles were far from over. Throughout the fifth century BCE Rome had constantly to prove its worth in the face of attacks from neighbouring communities such as the Sabines, the Aequi and Volscians, as well as the Etruscans – each group seeking to maintain and expand its own areas of influence. Rome was at war in almost every year of this period. In 390 BCE the city was even sacked by Gauls from the north. Rome's eventual mastery of Italy – not to mention the rest of the Mediterranean – came on the back of a long, hard-fought struggle in which outcomes often hung precariously in the balance.

Through it all, the nascent republic also had to respond to the internal difficulties and demands that perpetual war brings. Shortly after the initial victories against Tarquinius Superbus, the soldiers of Rome returned home to find themselves financially destitute. While kings had been exchanged for elected consuls, little else had changed in the Roman political system since the time of Servius Tullius. Debt bondage – outlawed in Athens by Solon a century before – was still practised. Food shortages were rife and Rome's economic vitality was hampered by a limited ability to trade, owing to the ever-present menace posed by its hostile neighbours (there was a notable decline in Greek-imported pottery in Rome during this period); while an expanding population meant more mouths to feed and growing tensions over land distribution. Rome, for all its early successes, was thus fast becoming a perilous place.

The situation came to a head when Rome's foot-soldiers – the lower of its social classes – marched out of the city in protest at debt bondage and encamped on a nearby hill. As the Roman historian Sallust later put it with gusto:

> The Senate abused the Plebs [the lower social classes] as if they
> were slaves, and threatened their lives and bodies as if the senators
> were kings ... The plebs, pressed by this savagery and by debt
> while at the same time they endured tribute payments and service
> in constant wars, occupied the Mons Sacer and the Aventine in
> arms ...[21]

Given that Rome was at war and in desperate need of its army, the
Senate hastily despatched one of their own, Menenius Agrippa, himself
a victorious general, to barter a solution. It is said by Livy that Menenius argued that the Roman *res publica* was like a body in which the belly
and limbs could not survive without one another: the belly needed the
limbs to bring it food, but it nourished the limbs in turn. If the
limbs stopped feeding the belly, in short order they, too, would become
weak. The *res publica* had to stick together.[22]

The result of this hillside agreement was not so much the eradication of poverty and debt within Roman society, but the insertion into
the new republican system of government representatives who would
look out for the interests of the lower classes. Up to this point all magistrates in Rome were selected from amongst the members of its
unelected aristocratic Senate. But around 494–3 BCE the first two
magistrates representing the lower orders were elected, with power of
veto over any action proposed by the government that they considered
contrary to the interests of the people they represented. These magistrates were sacrosanct – meaning that it was a heavy crime to harm
them in any way – and were responsible for convening special assemblies solely for the plebeians, which met in an open-air space by the
Forum called the Comitium, where a bronze statue of the heroic Cocles
kept watch over proceedings.

These new magistrates were known as 'Tribunes of the Plebs'. Such
a sense of people-power was enshrined in their offices that the term
'Tribunes', endures in modern democracies and in newspaper journal-
ism. But in ancient Rome the election of the Tribunes of the Plebs
pointed to an uneasy dichotomy – the so-called 'Conflict of the Orders' –
in Roman republican society between the Plebs and the Patricians. The

Patricians were those from specific aristocratic clans (in Latin, *gentes*), while the Plebs were defined as – well, everyone else. They represented the two opposing sides in an ongoing social and political struggle to alter the balance of power within the republic, one that would persist for most of its existence, with relations not infrequently tense.

For example, some sources argue that Gaius Marcius Coriolanus (later the subject of Shakespeare's tragedy) was descended from one of the early Roman kings, and failed to win an election to consulship mainly because he was distrusted by the Plebs. Subsequently, during a time of famine, Gaius Marcius argued that grain shipments from Sicily ought to be withheld from the Plebs until they relinquished their right to have tribunes. The rest of the Senate refused to support their fellow aristocrat and he was put on trial by the tribunes and exiled from Rome.

The relationship did enjoy more harmonious moments: other aristocrats enjoyed plebeian support and were re-elected to the consulship on numerous occasions. Moreover, groupings within the Roman citizen body were divided into many more shades than simply Plebeian and Patrician. Since many aristocratic and rich households in Rome were not necessarily part of one of the special clans that made up the Patricians, the Plebeians contained their own 'elite' – and it was these men who were at the forefront of the battle for more political power. In contrast, the massive numbers of real urban and rural poor in Rome and the surrounding area – those of the bottom social class – were, while technically Plebeians, rarely more than bystanders to the conflict.

Increased social and political tensions between Plebeians and Patricians flared up again in the 460s BCE. The Tribunes of the Plebs blocked all legislation for five years, while demanding that the powers of the new consuls be more clearly defined. The patrician consuls enjoyed an exceptionally broad range of powers: they were, for example, the ultimate arbiters and interpreters of all laws. Attempts in 457 BCE to mollify the tribunes by increasing their numbers from two to ten were a failure, and legislation was resisted for a further three years. Finally, in 454 BCE, the tribunes proposed that the entire legal framework of the state be reviewed, codified and published. In looking for alternatives and comparisons, a committee of three men chosen to undertake the review turned to Greece and to Athens. They even visited the city to study how the reforms of Solon had grown into the working direct democracy that was now thriving in the city.

Athens had not been the only city to experiment with principles of equality and community law and order in the seventh and sixth centuries BCE. In fact, there were cities with different shades of democratic process much closer to Rome at the time, amongst the Greek colonies in Sicily, where the city of Syracuse, for example, seems to have operated a system of political ostracism that was very similar to that of democratic Athens. But what drew Rome to Athens – apart from its trading links and a Roman love for Athenian drinking vessels – was above all the fact that, by 454 BCE, Athens was by far the most successful example of a democratic city in the Mediterranean. Its democracy had resisted the seemingly unstoppable power of the Persians and was now at the head of a flourishing Aegean empire.

Seeking Answers Across the Sea

What did the Roman delegates arriving in Athens find greeting them when they stepped onto land in the port of Piraeus? They would have seen a bustling business centre, with ships docking from all over the Mediterranean. In amongst the trading vessels in the different natural harbours of the Piraeus promontory, the Roman visitors would no doubt have been treated to the sight of Athens' formidable navy. This armada of *triremes* (their front noses hardened with bronze, to ram and destroy enemy ships) was the strong arm of the burgeoning Athenian Empire. The formidable fleet had been funded by the silver mines under Athens' control, which were first exploited by the tyrant Peisistratus and further developed by the fledgling democracy. Crucial in that development process had been the Persian invasions of Greece in 490 and 480–79 BCE.

Soon after democracy had been established, Athens had sent a small number of ships to assist a rebellion against Persian rule by Greek cities situated along the west coast of Asia Minor. The rebellion was put down, but the Persian king, Darius, had decided that Athens needed to be taught a lesson and that Greece – an outcrop of land on the margins of his mighty Persian Empire – should be brought under his dominion. In planning his campaign, Darius was aided by Hippias, exiled tyrant of Athens; and in 490 BCE Persian forces landed some 42 kilometres from Athens at the bay of Marathon.

The battle that followed was a stunning victory for Athens in which, according to the later sources, it incurred only 192 casualties, all of whom were buried together in a single honorary mound that still stands proud today. The remains of the Persian army took to their ships and eventually retreated back to Asia Minor. Darius died unsatisfied, and his son Xerxes took the throne, intent on realising his father's goal. In 480 BCE Xerxes returned with a massive land army and fleet to terrorise Greece and destroy Athens. Many Greek cities decided to acquiesce; even the Delphic oracle originally told an Athenian delegation that resistance was futile. In the charged atmosphere of Athens' democratic public assembly, on the Pnyx hill opposite the Acropolis, the people of Athens debated what to do. At the heart of the debate was the Delphic oracle's second piece of advice: to trust in 'their wooden walls'. What did that mean? For some, it invoked the old wooden palisade that ran around the Acropolis: perhaps the gods would protect them if they took refuge once more in the sacred impregnable fortress at the heart of their city. But for others, the oracle was clearly referring to the wooden walls of their ships. The debate raged, but finally the ships won the day. The Athenians abandoned their city, with women, children and old men retreating to the island of Salamis off the Athenian coast, and every able-bodied man took to his oar.

The Athenians were forced to watch their city burn as the Persians flooded through its streets. Xerxes set up his throne on the hills overlooking the bay of Salamis, intent on savouring every moment of the triumph he expected to be delivered by his Persian navy, which vastly outnumbered that of the Athenians. What happened next has become legend: one of the deadliest battles in naval history, decided by a brilliant strategic coup.

Once the Persians were drawn into the narrow straits between Salamis and the mainland, their superior numbers counted for naught. The Athenians knew those shallow waters well. Their ships had been at sea for only a short time, were not waterlogged, and so moved and turned faster. The result was a resounding victory for Athens, with much of the Persian fleet grounded or sunk and as many as 40,000 Persian sailors drowned. Xerxes, having seen this catastrophe from on high, retreated from his vantage point and left Greece thereafter, abandoning his land army to be defeated by a coalition of Greek cities the following year.

The victory at Salamis gave Athens the impetus to put itself forward as the natural candidate to lead the alliance of Greek cities and states. That alliance, while wishing to exact revenge on Persia where it could, was essentially defensive in nature, and Athens' fleet was vital to it, for its *triremes* spread out across the Aegean. But in the years between Salamis and the arrival of the Roman ambassadors, Athens' role was transformed. In 454 BCE itself, Athens chose to move the communal treasury of the alliance from its neutral position on the mid-Aegean island of Delos to Athens – seen by many as the moment when Athenians claimed the Aegean as their empire.

The Roman ambassadors, as they moved towards the city centre, would have travelled along a newly fortified corridor that joined the city and the port, encased by high protective 'long walls', which ensured that Athens had access to its powerful navy, plus the benefit of a constant supply of food and goods as these arrived into port. As the noises of carts, animals, creaking containers and people reverberated round this corridor, the ambassadors would have made their way to a city increasingly resplendent with imperial spoils. At its heart, imperturbably, was the Acropolis. Its temples had been burnt by the Persians, and the Athenians had sworn not to rebuild them until they had gained revenge, so the charred marble and limestone remains marred the skyline as a bitter reminder of what, for Athenians, was unfinished business. (Within five years Athens would sign a peace treaty with the Persians and call it a victory, then begin work on building the Parthenon, funded by the taxes extracted from its empire.)

Once in the environs of the *agora*, in which was situated the council chamber of the democracy and the chief magistrate's office, where copies of all Athenian laws were published – laws they were so keen to consider – the Roman delegation would have known they were in the midst of a city on the brink of a golden age. Coming from a city continually beset by war – able to survive but not decisively defeat its many enemies, governed by a political system of the same vintage as Athens and yet lacking any comparable cohesion internally or power beyond its borders – these Roman visitors must surely have beheld the bustling heart of Athenian democracy and empire and felt a profound jealousy.

Athens' democratic system had been steel-reinforced by its response to the Persian invasions. When Darius invaded at Marathon, the democracy was in its infancy, but the victory won by the hoplite (foot-soldier) ranks of Athenian citizens had bolstered confidence in the new dispensation, which had determined the organisation of the city's military units. Far more important, though, was the triumph of Salamis – a battle won not by aristocrats astride expensive horses, or even by well-to-do citizens who could afford their own hoplite armour, but by the sheer strength of the men who took to the oars to row the *triremes*. Amid the sweat and stench of the rowing galleys, the lowest classes of Athenian citizens had strained every sinew in order to save their city. It is no accident that in the years after Salamis the word *demokratia* came into use, and that the pace of Athenian political evolution picked up, such that by 454 BCE every citizen had the same rights to speak in the assembly and to serve on the governing council. Even the chief magistrates were decided by lot, rather than by election, from amongst the full complement of male citizens. It is thought that two-thirds of Athens' male citizen population – perhaps 50,000 people at the time – sat on the top council at least once in their lives.

War, of course, had been a constant feature of Rome's immediate environment: the city was at war every year, often to ensure its own survival in the turbulent century after the founding of the republic. In certain ways this pressure had pushed Rome in the same direction as it had Athens. The ceaseless threat of warfare had forced the Roman Senate to make swift concessions to the masses, such as creating the Tribunes of the Plebs, since they simply could not afford to lose such manpower.[23] But on the other hand it was also the spectre of war that encouraged the embedding of a political system in which the ability to defend the city carried with it an enhanced say in political affairs. Thus, though Rome had come to abhor kings, one man might nonetheless be granted dictatorial powers – if only temporarily – in order to protect the city. The men who assumed such authority generally exhibited no inclination to cling on to it, once their duty was done.

In 458 BCE Rome found itself at war simultaneously with the Sabines and the Aequi. One of Rome's consuls was besieged, and in panic the Senate and the remaining consul appointed a dictator, Lucius Quinctius Cincinnatus. This aristocrat, who had consistently opposed more legal rights for Plebeians, had lost everything when his son had been convicted of aggressive action against the Tribunes of the Plebs. He now ran a small farm outside the city, and he was at the plough when envoys came to inform him of his appointment as dictator. Cincinnatus donned his toga and, without delay, joined the fight for Rome's survival. Within fifteen days he had summoned every man of fighting age, subdued the Aequi in battle, resigned the dictatorship and returned to his plough without a single action to alter the political status quo – the very model of service to Rome.[24]

War, then, made heroes such as Cincinnatus, but also served to propagate a code of values through which the Roman elites more generally proved themselves in defence of their community, so earning the gratitude and respect of the mass of people.[25] Crucially, all the key battles for Rome's survival were fought on land. There was no equivalent of Salamis in the Roman imagination: no moment when the onus fell so heavily, or was borne so heroically, by the lower classes of society. As such, war made a case for the merits of a hierarchical social system in which the richer classes justified their political voice by sterling displays of courage in defending the state.

The Roman ambassadors to Athens were not interested in carrying a model of thriving direct democracy back with them to Rome. Indeed, they must have been astonished that the Athenians used random lot to decide who sat on their juries and supreme councils or served as chief magistrates. Some scholars (notably, Fergus Millar) have argued that Rome's republic – particularly in its later period in the second and first centuries BCE – can be called a democracy, especially since there was no property qualification for voting in Rome's elections.[26] But in reality – as we have seen, and as Polybius argued – Rome's constitution was much more about balancing the will and power of the different sections of society.

Everyone Has Their Place

The idea that Rome conceived of its society as being made up of different, discrete sections is crucial to understanding the contrast between republican Rome and democratic Athens. We saw earlier how the Roman *res publica* was described as being like a body in which the belly and limbs could not survive without one another. This kind of argument, which we will also see emerging in relation to ancient Indian society in Part III of this book, never appears in the political thinking of those looking at democratic Athens. While Rome thought in terms of different sections of society/the body performing different, discrete functions in order for the community to work, in Athens there was much more overlap between the roles played by members of the community. In Athens a citizen was a voter in the assembly, a potential council member of the *boule*, a hoplite in the ranks of the army and/or a rower in the navy, a potential candidate for the position of chief *archon*, and a member of the juries in the city's law courts. Each Athenian citizen performed a multitude of roles to ensure that the community could survive. As a result, no section of Athenian society could ever really be labelled as a part of the separate body with only one function to perform.

What did interest the visiting Romans were the 150-year-old reforms and law codes of Solon, inscribed by the chief magistrate's office in the *agora*. Solon's 'middling', balanced solutions for society, his principle of *eunomia* or 'good order', which appealed so much to Aristotle, also made a great deal of sense to Romans of 454 BCE. Solon's reforms would later be epitomised by the orator Cicero as *concordia ordinum*: a unity and concord of purpose amongst the orders of society, which Cicero went so far as to compare to music:

> Just as in the case of string instruments or flutes or singing, a certain harmony must be maintained out of distinct sounds . . . and this harmony, arising out of a blending of very dissimilar notes, is nonetheless made concordant and in agreement, so a *civitas* [political community] is made harmonious by the common agreement of the most dissimilar elements through a blending of the highest,

lowest and intermediate orders as if they were musical notes. What
the musicians call harmony in song is concord in the state, the
tightest and best bond of safety in a state, and it can in no way exist
without justice.[27]

In this moment of 454 BCE it is intriguing to imagine what the
state of Rome thought of the state of Athens, and vice versa. In the
half-century since their respective revolutions had begun, they had
faced comparable challenges, harboured similar aspirations and developed very different political systems. On the Roman side there had to
be that degree of jealousy: Athens was poised to take over the Aegean
and remake itself in shining resplendent marble. Rome, meanwhile,
was trapped in political stalemate, with no decisions having been
passed for years, and still suffering regular attacks from its neighbours
that threatened its very survival.

Athens' attitude towards Rome, I suspect, was one of perplexity. As
we have seen, Greek historians of the time were very much focused on
Cleisthenes as the heroic figure in their political story, to the extent that
Thucydides makes no reference to Solon whatsoever. So as the Athenians watched the Romans poring over Solon's law codes, perhaps their
reaction was to shake their heads and wonder why the Romans did not
raise their eyes and see the incredible vitality of the direct democracy
around them. Little did they know that in the following century many
among them would be calling for one wise and just ruler to take
control.

Certainly the Roman commissioners took their fact-gathering mission in Athens seriously. The review took three years, until in 451 BCE
the committee of three submitted their report to a ten-man patrician
commission (a *decemvirate*), who were given a year (during which all nor-
mal offices of the state were disbanded) to formulate a new legal code
by which the republic might function, and to which all parties might
agree.

The result was a set of ten laws or 'tables', as they were known.
Two further tables were added by another commission the following year – this one including some Plebeians. But this commission,
it seems, refused to step down at the end of its tenure, behaving

arrogantly, even tyrannically, such that the *decemviri* earnt the dread nickname of 'The Ten Tarquins'. Indeed, in an episode horribly reminiscent of the attempted rape of Lucretia that led to the demise of the monarchy, the *decemvirate* leader Appius Claudius even tried to rape a young girl, who was then killed by her own father so as to save her from disgrace. The Plebs of Rome once again rose up and marched out of the city to protest from the same hill they had occupied in 494 BCE.

The Ten Tarquins were eventually deposed and dealt with, in the following year, 449 BCE, under the consuls L. Valerius Potitus and M. Horatius Barbatus. But the outcome of this period was the earliest surviving legal document issued by the Roman Republic. Known collectively as the Twelve Tables, this codification sought to combat the abuse of individual power; recognised the sacrosanct nature of a range of magistrates; ensured that all Romans had the right of appeal to any decision by a magistrate; and gave legal power to the decisions of the Plebs in their own assemblies; while also containing a wide variety of rulings on everything from what to do with dead bodies, to who could marry whom. Yet while this new code was intended to calm tensions between the different social and political groups within the republic, it also helped to cement even more firm distinctions between who was 'plebeian' and who was 'patrician': a Patrician, for instance, was not allowed to marry a Plebeian.

For Polybius, the development of the Twelve Tables represented a crucial turning point in Rome's history, perhaps even more meaningful than the overthrow of the monarchy half a century before.[28] Why? Because they gave Rome what Polybius thought was the very model of political government: a mixed constitution with aspects of monarchy (the consuls), aristocracy (the Senate) and democracy (the *comitia centuriata* and the *concilium plebis*), plus defined rights and responsibilities for each group within the system as laid out in law.[29] While Herodotus would argue that democracy had made Athens militarily dominant because everyone now fought for themselves and their way of life, Polybius contended that Rome's mix of elements worked, not only because it harnessed the skills and expertise (and financial power) of the different parts of Roman society and ensured they worked efficiently within a hierarchical structure, but also, crucially, because no one social class could claim the system for themselves or deny it to another.

What made Rome unique – and uniquely powerful in the centuries after 449 BCE – was its complicated system of checks and balances that kept all levels of society believing they had more to gain from the system than from debunking it. For Polybius, Rome had achieved, finally, through the 'discipline of many struggles and troubles', *concordia ordinum*. By the time Polybius was writing, Rome had nothing more to be jealous about in regard to Athens, for it was poised to take over the Mediterranean world.[30]

Still, there was considerable modification to the laws of the republic in the 250 years between its law code and the writings of Polybius, arising from the continual struggle between Plebeians and Patricians over rights and access to top magistracies. In 445 BCE, for example, the ban on marriages between Plebs and Patricians was lifted. In 367 BCE the law was changed to allow a Plebeian to become a consul.[31] By 342 BCE it was stipulated that one consul had to be a Plebeian. Many scholars have argued that it was only after this point – as Rome's political system settled the conflict between its orders – that Rome could begin to make real conquests across Italy and the Mediterranean.[32] In 172 BCE, for the first time in Rome's history, both consuls were Plebeians – an advance that had been a long time coming perhaps, but with Rome now holding sway as the sole great power of the Mediterranean, its grand ambitions and the perfection of its political system appeared to have met in the most extraordinary union.

CHAPTER 3

China, Confucius and the Quest for the Just Ruler

Rumour had it that Duke Ding, ruler of the state of Lu, was a man very easily distracted; and at some point between 497 and 495 BCE a plot was hatched to distract him from the very serious business of running the state. The heads of some of the leading aristocratic families in his domain asked Duke Ding if they might present to him eighty of the loveliest women they knew, so that he could decide which of them was the most beautiful.[1] The women were duly brought before the duke, who – unable to take his eyes off this delectable parade – may have failed to notice the one onlooker who shook his head in obvious disgust.

This was the duke's adviser, Kong Fu-Zi ('Grand Master Kong'), originally born as Kong Qiu but better known in the West – thanks to the Latinised translation of his name bequeathed to us by Jesuit missionaries – as Confucius.[2] Taking his leave of the room, the beauties and the duke, Confucius is said to have sung a sarcastic song to his disciple: 'A woman's tongue can cost a man his post; A woman's words can cost a man his head; Then why not retire to spend my last years as I please?'[3]

Possibly Confucius had cause to feel himself unkindly overshadowed on more than one count. His physical appearance is not believed to have won him many admirers: some sources speak of him as a tall and striking individual, but more characterise him as ungainly and unattractive, with a noticeable bump on his forehead, large pendulous ears and prominent front teeth.[4] In his behaviour, too, he was said to be unappealingly fussy: not liking rice from the public market, for instance, and refusing to sit down to eat unless his mat was absolutely straight.[5] But whether for meaningful reasons or highly superficial ones, as the fifth century BCE began, Confucius was doomed to find himself a prophet without honour in his own land. His great renown and influence, though considerable in time, were fated to be posthumous.

Though as historians we know the ancient world was deeper and richer than the Mediterranean – and though a twentieth-century novelist such as Gore Vidal could imagine for us a Persian envoy's meetings with Confucius – nonetheless the emerging field of scholarly comparison between Greece, Rome and China has rarely focused on this moment around the end of the sixth century BCE and the beginning of the fifth.[6] In part this is because we believe Greece and Rome had no direct knowledge of China until after the fourth century BCE.[7] As such, we are in the murkier realm of comparative (rather than connective) history. Greece–China studies have been principally focused on comparing the intellectual history and development of these two communities through their ethics, philosophies and science rather than their politics.[8] Comparisons between Rome and China have focused almost exclusively on the period of the Roman and Chinese Han empires in the first centuries CE, by which time these two cultures had made several attempts to send diplomats to one another's capitals. Such studies have focused not on the political ideologies inherent in Roman and Chinese culture so much as on the mechanics, problems and opportunities of empire, economy and trade.[9]

In bringing Confucius's story into direct comparison with the revolutions in political thinking and governance in Rome and Athens, we offer a very different kind of story of political change. By studying China in the same timeframe as a democracy was developing in Athens, and a republic in Rome, we have the opportunity to observe a moment not of societal revolution, mob-rioting and popular political change; but one in which an individual, attended by a few devoted followers, attempted calmly to convince the society's rulers to adopt a new way of political thinking and governance, a new formation of man's relationship to man, as their own.

Moreover – unlike in Rome and Athens, where the political systems that came to pass were by no means shining goals from the outset but, rather, compromises forged over time as circumstances allowed – in China Confucius developed his own very deliberate ideas for the way governance should operate, in order to offer a complete package of political, juridical and moral guidance for his society's rulers. He was perhaps the first person in Chinese history to do so, and yet would always claim to be a transmitter of ideas from the past, rather than an innovator of new ones.

The socio-political situations to which Confucius was responding did have huge overlap with the circumstances that gave birth to political revolution in Athens and Rome. Confucius evolved his thinking in the midst of a highly turbulent time in Chinese history, even more terrifying in some ways than the wars that beset Rome and Athens. As L. Shihlien Hsü puts it:

> The age of Confucius was marked by political chaos, revolutionary movements, moral degeneration, the influence of corrupt demagogues in office ... the domination of anarchism, extreme individualism, political transcendentalism, military despotism, selfish imperialism and unethical mercantilism.[10]

The Records and Heroes of Ancient Chinese History

Just as in considering Athens and Rome, we face equivalent problems of source availability in knowing the details of Confucius's life, his ideas and the society in which he lived. A collection of sayings attributed to Confucius survives: this is *Lunyü*, 'Conversations' or *Analects*, first compiled by his disciples in the century after his death. The earliest extant biography of Confucius, however, was composed by Sima Qian and appeared at the end of the second century BCE, some 400 years after the apex of Confucius's career.[11] This biography was part of

China's first-ever grand narrative history that sought to cover the events of the previous 2,000 years.[12]

However, in happier contrast to our Greco-Roman studies, we are much better endowed with surviving contemporary Chinese texts, such as the *Chunqiu* or *Spring and Autumn Annals*. The *Annals*, later claimed to have been compiled by Confucius, describe events from the late eighth to early fifth centuries BCE, from the point of view of the small state of Lu, which covered around 52,000 square kilometres and was home to fewer than one million people, at a time when the population of the lands of the governing Zhou dynasty totalled approximately fifty million. The *Annals* draw a picture of endemic conflict and suffering and do so in memorably terse shorthand: an entry for 609 BCE reads simply, 'Winter. Tenth Month. The state of Lu assassinated its ruler, Shu Ch'i.' One for 594 BCE offers: 'Winter. Locusts arose.' The record for 520 BCE ends simply: 'The royal house was in chaos.' And in 479 BCE sad news is stated just as succinctly (and provides good evidence that Confucius was, at the very least, not alone in creating the *Annals*): 'Summer, a day in the fourth month, Confucius died in sixteenth year of Duke Ai.'[13]

Thankfully, alongside the *Annals* we also have the *Zuo Zhuan*, the 'Commentary of Zuo', traditionally attributed to a contemporary and disciple of Confucius and covering the period 722–468 BCE. This is one of three extensive commentaries that unpack the elliptical notes of the *Annals* and offer us many stories surrounding Confucius's life. Also increasingly available to historians of this period are the findings of archaeological investigations in some of the Zhou dynasty's major epicentres.[14] Nonetheless, we are again broaching a historical epoch in which undisputed facts are few and far between, and in which later writers, including those very close to the protagonists in this story, have had a close hand in the representation of this crucial clash between personal ideology and political rule.

Confucius's mission in the court of Duke Ding had been to try to school the duke in how to be a good and conscientious ruler, with the hope that the rewards of his positive example would cascade down through the population. (As Confucius is reported to say in the *Analects*: 'if there existed a true king, after a generation humanness would certainly prevail'.[15]) Confucius's efforts were ended by the eighty beautiful women who turned the duke's head from the dry business of governance. But this, of course, was no accident: Lu's most powerful families preferred the duke to be an ineffectual ruler who allowed them to do what they liked – at best, a biddable tool for their own ends. And so Confucius quit the state for voluntary exile, making his living by offering his advice and wisdom to rulers in other nearby states. The *Analects* record his discontent: 'When right prevails below heaven, courtesy, music, and punitive wars flow from the sons of Heaven. When wrong prevails below heaven, courtesy, music and punitive wars flow from the feudal princes.'[16]

Confucius's time at the heart of government, as far as we know from the surviving sources, had been brief, a mere five years. In 501 BCE, aged fifty, he had been appointed to his first major job of political-administrative importance. As the chief magistrate of Zhong Du the inner part of the capital of the state of Lu, he was positioned within the select group of the *Ai* – the elders, the governing elite. Sources disagree over how high he then rose: some claim he became Minister of Public Works, or of Justice. Seemingly it was Duke Ding himself who sought out Confucius and gave him his first position within the ranks of the *Ai*.

It might appear that, at fifty, Confucius was somewhat long in the tooth to be commencing a career in high-level government; but he was younger than Cleisthenes was at the time of Athens' democratic revolution. Indeed, Confucius would later contend that his whole life's long experience had readied him for the moment, that his youthful decades had been devoted to the getting of wisdom. '[A]t 50,' he writes in the *Analects*, 'I understood the laws of Heaven.'[17]

Duke Ding's hold on power, however, was weak. The duke was poor, and his ancestors had, for several generations, been little more than ceremonial heads of state. Real power in Lu was divided between three influential families: the Meng-sun, Shu-sun and Chi-sun, whose occupancy of nearly every government office was considered to be a near-hereditary prerogative. In 517 BCE Duke Ding's elder brother had attempted to curtail the power of the families, only for him and the young Ding to be forced into exile. Joining them was Confucius, driven to follow by his deep-seated belief in the importance of supporting the appointed ruler and in his disgust for the usurpation of power.

However, in 509 BCE the duke's elder brother died in mysterious circumstances and Ding was allowed to return, along with Confucius, though neither was granted any real political influence. Soon after their return, the head of the Chi-sun household, who had run Lu in the duke's absence, also died, leaving a political vacuum and a black farce of political power-broking, during which time even a steward of the Chi-sun managed to make himself, effectively, dictator in Lu. The steward eventually fled in fear for his life, and Duke Ding was able to assert control. He invited Confucius into senior government, from where Confucius was recognised as an official adviser of the duke, until that day when eighty fair women hove into view.

The importance of the individual ruler within Chinese culture – and of that ruler's perceived character – is clear from the very way in which Chinese history is delineated and discussed. It is traditionally broken down into dynasties, always founded by an able and virtuous ruler, whose successors – so the historiographical narrative goes – rarely manage to live up to the founder's standards. Eventually a successor becomes so incapable of ruling that he and his family are replaced by a new, strong and virtuous ruler, who founds a new dynasty – and so on.

The first such dynasty to come into historical focus is that of the Xia from 2200 to 1750 BCE, based along the Yellow River near Luoyang, in the modern-day province of Honan in central-eastern China. The Xia were replaced by the Shang dynasty (1766–1122 BCE), followed by the Zhou (1122–256 BCE), then – eventually, after a hiatus – by the Qin 221–206 BC, then by the Han, who ruled through to 220 CE, expanded their empire to cover most of the territory governed by China today, and are increasingly studied in comparison to the Roman Empire.

The Book of Documents or *Shujing,* one of the earliest surviving Chinese historical sources (which some later sources claim Confucius had a hand in creating), is a compilation of rhetorical prose writings organised into dynastic eras of ancient history and used as an essential tool with which to formulate political philosophy from the time of Confucius onwards. According to the *Shujing,* the fall of the Shang dynasty came about expressly as a result of the shortcomings of its last leader, not least because his cruelty drove his own troops to mutiny. While we have seen something of this narrative of degeneration in the moral conduct of Greek and Roman rulers (Hippias, say, or Tarquinius Superbus) who seemed to engineer their own downfalls, the Book of Documents explains that in China the loss of power was thought to be caused by the loss of the mandate to rule, itself the gift of Heaven.[18] The dynamic founders of the Zhou dynasty that supplanted the Shang were King Wen and his brother King Wu, and it is said that Wu had simply called out, 'I come to bring peace, not to wage war on the people', to which the 'sound of the people knocking their heads on the ground in submission was like the toppling of a mountain'.[19]

Kings Wen and Wu have been credited with innumerable acts of philosophical and martial greatness: Wen is said to have established the coding for the Book of Changes, another of the classics texts of ancient Chinese history, which operated as a divination manual. Wu, who finally vanquished the last king of Shang in the Battle of Muye, is said to have given weapons to 170,000 slaves to fight alongside him, and to have faced many Shang soldiers, who immediately pointed their spears downwards as a sign that they did not wish to fight against him. (It is said that the last king of Shang responded to his defeat by covering himself in gold and jewels and burning himself to death inside his royal residence.)

The Zhous who succeeded Wen and Wu are said to have further burnished the reputation of the dynasty. Wu's son Zheng was still in infancy when he took the throne, but his uncle, the Duke of Zhou, who acted as regent, made no move to usurp power, instead facing down a number of Shang rebellions. These tales of heroic Zhou virtue formed a critical set of principles for later leaders in Chinese history to uphold. The ruler received his mandate from Heaven and was answerable to Heaven for his actions. As such, his first concern had to be for the welfare of his people, and should he fail to live up to expectations, then Heaven – having first indicated its displeasure by portents – would withdraw its mandate and confer it upon someone else.

The importance of divine backing for rule is similarly emphasised in the early history of Roman kings. There was no undisputed line of succession from father to son – instead, each candidate nominated by the city's elites had to be ritually 'seized' and subjected to the trial of inauguration, during which the gods were asked to show their acceptance of the choice by the sending of a favourable sign. (The word 'inauguration' has at its heart *augur*, the Latin term for a priest who interpreted divine signs.) Once acknowledged, the king thus ruled with religious authority. And even after the last king had been exiled, the notion of divine support for public power endured through the consular exercise of *imperium* – the right to control and direct Rome's people and armies – and in the elected position of the *rex sacrorum*, for whom favourable portents had to be shown.

Divine support also underpinned the power of the Zhou dynasty. As in Greece or Rome, in China there was an endless litany of gods responsible for all sorts of particular aspects of life. Yet crucial to the holding of political and military authority was one: Heaven. 'Heaven', according to Chinese thought, was itself a deity, which had its own will, could be pleased or angered by human action, gave or took away its mandate to rule and had to be placated by sacrifice.

Confucius was a huge admirer of Wen and Wu and of the Duke of Zhou, on account of their virtuous moral code. He believed they had created a golden age by behaving in an honourable, wise and just fashion, in turn forging *dao*, 'the Way' – a means of running a state such that good order and harmony would prevail among men.

In a telling example of how central the Zhou dynasty was to Chinese narratives of good governance and society, it is also in the Book of Documents created during this period that we see the first recorded use of the way in which China has ever since referred to itself: *zhongguo*. This translates as 'central/middle state/nation', and is the primary term used in Chinese sources to refer to China right up to the present day. (It appears in the official name for the People's Republic of China.[20]) *Zhongguo* can mean a particular emperor's capital; or the grouping of states in the Yellow River basin at the heart of the Zhou dynasty; or all Chinese territory and civilisation; or, more widely, the whole of the Chinese world. And in the centuries to come, during the Qin and Han dynasties of the third and second centuries BCE, another term came to equivalence with *zhongguo: tianxia*, which means 'all under Heaven'. Just as rulers were said to have received their mandate from Heaven, so what they ruled was 'all under Heaven'. The prize of good governance, in Chinese thought, was not just a central role in the world, but the rule of everything there was to rule.

Decline, and Hopes for Renewal

By Confucius's time, however, the Zhou dynasty had begun to mirror the traditional pattern of slow moral, political and military decline borne out in previous epochs. It was said that in 524 BCE, when Confucius was in his twenties, divine portents of disaffection with the moral standard of leadership under the Zhou had been vividly apparent – including typhoons and fires ravaging unchecked across four different states – and yet these omens were ignored.

The long span of the Zhou dynasty is divided by historians into two separate periods, that of the Western Zhou (1122–771 BCE) and the Eastern Zhou (771 onwards). Under the force of its early charismatic kings during the era of the Western Zhou, the area controlled by the dynasty expanded massively. But as a consequence of this expansion, the king had to appoint semi-independent rulers to keep control of different areas – not unlike the provincial governors (*satraps*) of the Persian Empire that stretched from the western coast of Asia Minor into central Asia at this time, or the governors appointed to different areas of the Roman Empire centuries later. But as the centuries went by in China, the king's authority declined as a result of this delegation of powers, with each ruler and his territory assuming the character of an independent state, leaving the dynasty as a whole to become what has been described as little more than a 'mad hatter's tea party'.[21]

In 771 BCE the Zhou were also confronted with a foreign invasion by the Quanrong tribe, based in the north-western region of today's China, who overran much of the fertile Wei valley in central China, fed by the Wei River, the largest tributary of the Yellow River. As a result of the invasion and the loss of such productive lands the Zhou were forced to move their capital east to the area of Luoyang: hence the beginning of the Eastern Zhou age, itself split into two major eras: the 'Spring and Autumn' periods' (771–481 BCE) and the 'Warring States' (475–221 BCE). These titles are based on the names of key texts that survive from each period: the *Spring and Autumn Annals* (*Chunqiu*) and the *Strategies of the Warring States* (*Zhan Guo Ce*), a commentary on actions and events compiled later, around the second century BCE. The era of the Eastern Zhou saw even greater turmoil and upset than the Western Zhou period. Scholars estimate that between 656 and 221 BCE there were 256 wars.[22] In the entire duration of the 'Spring and Autumn' era – just under 300 years – there were said to have been just thirty-eight years of peace. And in just 134 years of the 'Warring States' period, the ancient Chinese historian Sima Qian, writing in the second century BCE, estimated that 1.5 million people were killed.

This bellicose climate arose because, quite apart from the threats posed by nomadic peoples and expansionist tribes bordering the land of the Zhou, approximately 170 individual states were fighting internally with one another for territory and power, one of which was the state of Lu under Duke Ding. The capital city of the Zhou in Luoyang was said to have fallen into disrepair by the end of the sixth century: a place of cracked stones and broken bells, supplanted in importance by a myriad of smaller state capitals, all vying for pre-eminence.

By 481 BCE (around the time of Confucius's death) there were roughly ten warring states still in existence.[23] One of these, Qi, is thought during the period of the Eastern Zhou to have destroyed and consumed thirty-five others; another to have eliminated fifty-one states. Others simply moved their territory around like a population of locusts: the state of Xu moved five times in seventy years, covering more than 1,000 kilometres in the process.

As such, Confucius's world was constantly on the edge of imploding, as a population of roughly fifty million people made perpetual war on one another across hundreds of years. We have seen that warfare was a dynamic force in forging the conditions for political change in Athens and Rome. In Athens, war or the threat of same not only pushed its citizens towards mass riot in 508 BCE, but also crucially, at Salamis in 480 BCE, bolstered the fledgling democracy through a demonstration of the importance of the masses in defence of their city. In Rome, by contrast, the constant pressure of war enforced a continued willingness – despite the overthrow of the monarchy – to place authority with those who could afford to protect the city by the purchase of armour, chariots and horses.

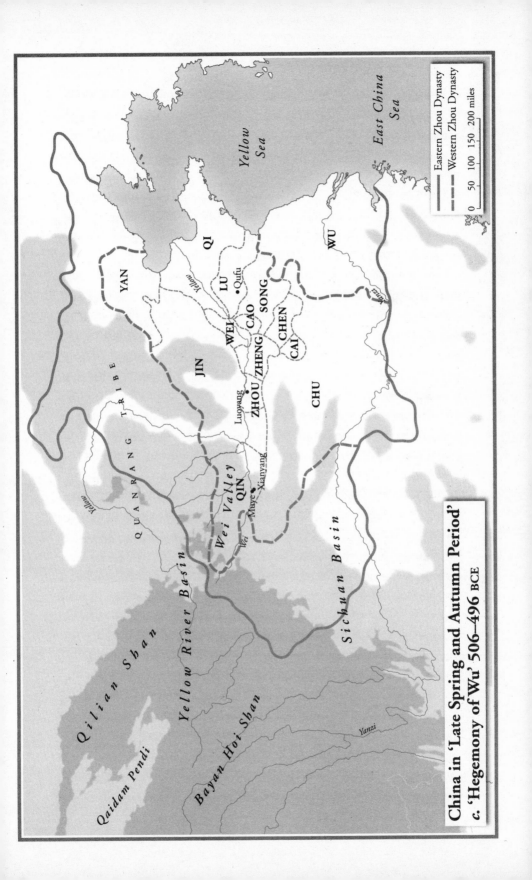

Qilian Shan

Qaidam Pendi

Bayan Hoi Shan

Yanzi

Yellow

QUANRANG TRIBE

Yellow River Basin

Wei Valley

QIN

Wei

Muye

Xianyang

Luoyang

ZHOU

ZHENG

Sichuan Basin

JIN

WEI

CAO

SONG

CHEN

CAI

CHU

Yellow

LU

Qufu

QI

YAN

Yellow Sea

WU

East China Sea

Yangzi

Eastern Zhou Dynasty
Western Zhou Dynasty

0 50 100 150 200 miles

**China in 'Late Spring and Autumn Period'
c. 'Hegemony of Wu' 506–496** BCE

Unlike the Greeks, the Zhou did not face an external enemy of the might and magnitude of the Persians. But the internal conflict faced by the states of the Zhou dynasty was on a scale that would have been unimaginable in either Athens or Rome, in point of the sheer numbers of combatants, the geographical extent of the conflict and its duration.[24] As a result, the military, economic and political reaction to the large-scale civil war amongst the states – while it had elements of both Athens' and Rome's reactions – created a very particular new balance of forces.

On the one hand, the need to fight endless wars against ever-growing opponents (as victorious states engulfed their defeated enemies) ensured a radical change in the make-up of the armed forces of the different states. The composition of armies transformed from a reliance on chariots provided by the aristocratic families, towards depending on the sheer brute force of large peasant armies, with some states fielding forces of up to 600,000 men.[25] As such – albeit for different reasons than in Athens (where the poor were important because they could row the warships) – the lower classes became crucial to a state's survival in the Zhou dynasty.

On the other hand, the ongoing need for each state to defend itself on land ensured that, just as in Rome, authority continued to be placed in the hands of the elites. What was different about the Zhou dynasty, however, was that the aristocratic rulers could not hope by themselves to organise such mass mobilisations as were needed to create huge armies, or provide the produce or finances necessary to feed and supply them. As such, political leadership of the Zhou states passed from a central leader surrounded by a small band of hereditary advisers towards larger, more centralised administration units who could perform the Herculean feats required to create and support armies that could, in turn, guarantee the survival of the state.

The outcome was a true government bureaucracy, staffed by a new junior aristocracy who earnt their positions through learning and skill. An entire social and political class, the *Shi* ('Gentlemen/Scholar-Bureaucrats'), developed within this meritocratic environment, and Confucius and his family were members of that class. Such a development would have been unthinkable in Athens, where every citizen was supposed to take an equal part in running the democracy. In Rome, too, no central administration emerged: rather, over time, the *cursus honorum* – a ladder of career opportunity – developed, such that any ambitious Roman would attempt to climb it, and which, in turn, made room at the top for what were termed *homines novi*: new men of state who were not from an aristocratic background, the most famous of whom was Cicero.

These military-administrative changes in the Zhou dynasty were accompanied by (and, no doubt, helped to encourage) a series of wider economic changes: substantial increases in trade alongside individual agricultural productivity, and a shift away from a model of communal agriculture practice (in which the majority of poor had worked on farms owned by the few), towards the development of the idea of private land ownership and a free market in goods, fuelled in turn by the introduction of coinage.[26] In 594 BCE – the same year that Solon introduced his reforms in Athens, among them the abolition of debt bondage – a not entirely different system of land taxation was introduced in the state of Lu, which required peasants to pay taxes on their own incomes rather than provide labour service to the state.[27]

By the end of the sixth century BCE, as Confucius entered high government office, the state of Lu and the other surviving states around it enjoyed a peculiarly dynamic but simultaneously stable society. Peasants and farmers were now deemed to be of more importance to their state since they formed the backbone of the army, and had more opportunities to improve their own position in life, thanks to the changes in agricultural practice and increases in commerce – leaving them more well off, it has been argued, than peasants in nineteenth-century China.[28] The state capitals were lively places, filled with aristocrats enjoying hunting and archery; scholars poring over enormous books made up of slabs of wood held together with thongs of leather, like venetian blinds; artisans and merchants making and plying their wares; and the streets bustling with carriages, feasts and festivals. The aesthetic hallmarks of the time were fine silken clothing, carefully wrought bronze and delicate pottery.

The rule of the elites had not been questioned in the same way as it had in Athens and Rome. Rather, it had been strengthened by the development of successful administrative bureaucracies, which made states fit for war and gave greater numbers of people a vested interest in government. So while no one state could count on its survival in an age of civil war when the map was redrawn on a regular basis – and while any state ruler (such as Duke Ding) could be ineffectual and controlled by surrounding elites – the system of government itself had, in many ways, never been more inclusive, stable and secure.[29]

Shaping a Sage

Confucius's family was of that new *Shi* class of 'Gentlemen/Scholar Bureaucrats' groomed to serve in the state administration. His father, Kong He (said to have been enormously tall and very ugly), was an officer in the service of the powerful Meng family, and he was already seventy years old and blessed with nine daughters by the time Confucius was born. But a male heir was what Kong He had desired most dearly. The mother, from a poor and little-known family, so later sources claim, was between sixteen and twenty when she and Kong He conceived the child. The baby was given, along with his 'personal' name of Kong Qiu, the 'courtesy' name of Kong Zhongni ('the Younger brother of Mud Mountain'), after a nearby peak onto which his mother had climbed in order to pray for safe delivery of a boy, and because his head at birth was said to resemble the peak itself.[30] Kong He, though, died not long after Confucius was born. His mother, it is said, was not allowed to attend the funeral because of her inferior social class, and she soon moved with the young Confucius to the state capital, Qufu. There, with the help of the Meng family – as befitting his father's rank and service – Confucius received a good education.

Aged nineteen, he married a woman of whom history records nothing; and at twenty he lost his mother, who had staunchly refused to abandon him after his father's untimely (if not unexpected) death. One of the central tenets of Confucius's teachings was filial piety: the need to obey one's parents, care for them in old age and give them a proper funeral with full mourning. Confucius sought out his father's grave and buried his mother in the next plot, before mourning her death formally for three years. (As the *Analects* later put it: 'our master's way is simple: loyalty and consideration'.[31])

Over the next thirty years Confucius acted as a clerk in the state granaries; then as official supervisor of the pasture lands belonging to the state; and eventually he rose to become a 'leader of the knights', a high position within the *Shi* class, which – given the *Shi*'s preoccupation with administration – was almost certainly one in which he wielded pen rather than sword. Through it all, Confucius's watchword was continual meditative self-improvement: 'to learn, and not to think over [what one has learnt] is useless: to think without learning is dangerous'.[32]

And yet Confucius, for all his cultivation, had reached the limit of what a person of his background could be expected or allowed to achieve. In his attempts to have an impact on the highest authorities in the land, he was continually thwarted by the older aristocratic families who still held sway in Lu and beyond. This cap on his ambitions was also due, it was said, to his blunt, critical manner, which was better suited to teaching than to politics. He chastised one of his own disciples for collecting an unjust tax on behalf of the powerful Chi family, Confucius's stern view being that principles should come first.[33] Indeed, it was to teaching that Confucius now turned, so gradually building his reputation as a wise man. But in the *Analects* he professes to set no great store by fame: 'I am not worried that nobody knows me. I seek to become fit to be known.'[34]

In time, rulers of several states did come to know of Confucius and were interested in hearing from him. His reputation developed as that of a man steeped in knowledge of ceremony, genealogy, manners and ritual; one who could reinterpret the learning of former times and apply it to the problems of the present. He was known, too, to like archery, fishing and charioteering, and to play a version of the lute (being of the view that musical harmony could encourage a broader kind of consonance among men and communities). This, then, was a man with a rounded philosophy; and state rulers, ever conscious that they should maintain the mandate of Heaven, were ready to listen to a famously wise man – if not necessarily to heed him.

When Confucius first went into exile in 517 BCE alongside the young Duke Ding, they resorted to the neighbouring state of Qi. Its ruler, Duke Jing, beset as he was by problems of government, asked Confucius what 'kingcraft' properly consisted of. Confucius's reply was strikingly simple and conservative: 'When a king is king and the minister is minister, when the father is father and the son is son' – that is to say, when no one tries to usurp a position that is not rightfully theirs.[35] But such responses did not earn Confucius ongoing favour: Duke Jing soon tired of the teacher and dispensed with his counsel. Confucius's stress on continual learning and self-improvement, lest virtues degenerate into evils, set a high personal bar for rulers to clear, and possibly made him a rather wearying sort of adviser to have around.[36]

It is a shame that his advice against the usurpation of power was not heard within the state of Lu, where the three main powerful families vied with one another to act as if they were the Duke of Lu. Or, rather, perhaps it is a shame that Confucius did not wish to give his advice to these usurpers. We know, for example, that he turned down at least one offer of employment from the steward of the house of Chi, who managed to make himself dictator in Lu for a short while before the successful return of Duke Ding. Why did Confucius so steadfastly throw in his lot with the young Duke Ding? Probably it was for the simple reason that he was the rightful ruler of the state of Lu and, as such, deserving of Confucius's advice. After all, the state of Lu had a noble ancestry: its founder and first ruler was no less a man than the Duke of Zhou – the upstanding moral regent whom Confucius much admired, and who had been fundamental in helping to formulate *dao* ('the Way'), by which one could govern a country so as to produce the greatest well-being and happiness of the people.

We can only guess at the advice Confucius gave Duke Ding from our understanding of his ideas more generally. In the *Analects* Confucius is reported as saying that a just ruler must take care to achieve three things: sufficient food for his people, enough troops for their protection and, above all, the people's trust. If any of these had to be sacrificed, first should go the troops and then the food, because, without trust, 'a people cannot stand'.[37] Polybius, Greek-born historian of the Roman Republic, had a very different view of what united the body politic, namely that it was crucial that the mass of the people held the right to confer honour and inflict punishment, because these 'were the only bonds by which kingdoms and states . . . are held together'.[38]

One cannot overstate the stress placed by Confucius's system of thought upon how the individual could affect his own life, those of others and indeed the course of history, through the application of strenuous self-cultivation and improvement. The system was founded upon key concepts, the first being *Ren* ('love, benevolence, kindness'). This word, used forty times in the *Analects*, denotes a standard for the way in which man behaves to fellow man.[39] It applies to the way a ruler acts towards his people, and to the way members of an individual family act towards one another, as well as to the way the community as a whole works together to cultivate a community spirit sufficient to triumph over individual greed. It is a character trait that can only be achieved through strenuous moral effort.

Alongside *Ren* came ideas of *Zhong* ('loyalty') and *Shu* ('consideration'). In one of the most famous lines from the *Analects*, Confucius was asked which word best sums up the duty of man. His reply was *Shu*: 'do not do unto others what you would rather not have done to you'[40] – the 'golden rule' of reciprocity, of which near enough every ethical system or religion that one could name has put forward its own version.

Confucius required the conduct of all men to be unimpeachable, but particularly that of the ruler, since 'if a ruler is set on good, his people do good. The king's mind is the wind, and the grass is the minds of the people. Where the wind blows, so the grass bends.'[41] A good ruler in turn was created by adherence to three critical concepts. The first was *Te* – 'virtue/moral force'; the second was *Yi* – 'righteousness'; and the third was *Li* – 'adherence to all habitual, customary and socially accepted rites'.[42] Without righteousness, courage was pointless: 'a gentleman with courage but without righteousness will cause disturbances; a common man who possesses courage but not righteousness will become a thief'.[43] Indeed, everything should be refused in life – including life itself – if it was not compatible with righteousness.

Li, like many other Confucian virtues, was a lifelong endeavour. By perfecting and observing the rites and traditions of society through long periods of book-learning, education and self-cultivation, and by ensuring the rites were observed and practised with real emotion and belief rather than simply performing them for their own sake, a ruler would retain the mandate of Heaven. More widely, Confucius believed that the pursuit of *Li* would ensure a civilising and controlling influence on the excesses of the nobility, and provide wider improvements for the whole community.

The original meaning of the word *Li* is 'sacrifice' – as in religious sacrifice, part of the rituals and rites that the word later came to denote. Such connections stress the overlap between religion and behaviour within the Confucian system. Indeed, in China, the system of teaching associated with Confucius has never been known as Confucianism, but, rather, as *Ru Jiao*, 'Doctrine of the Literati'. The *Ru*, however, also links back to the scholar officials who were direct successors of religious experts trained to perform ceremonies in the Shang dynasty.

Yet it would be a mistake to understand Confucius's ideas as a religious system or belief – or indeed to see Confucius as a religious man in his own right. His ideas operated within a religious world in which the power of Heaven – and the mandate it offered to a ruler – was strong and important, but his ideas are ultimately concerned with behaviour in the human world. As such, they can best be described as an ethical-political system for good government and wider socio-political harmony.

Ancient Global Approaches to Politics

How do Confucius's teachings and political outlook compare to what was prevalent in contemporaneous Athens and Rome? First, one must confront a figure who was not active in the centre of events but was, rather, an ungainly, unattractive, intractable, awkward gadfly type of man, who spent his time studying, advising when he was asked, and only coming into the management of state affairs late in life. Confucius was not interested in change for change's sake, or for his own advancement. Instead, he was concerned that the rulers of his day could meet the heavy demands of the violent and uncertain world in which they lived with a moral code and a sense of justice and reason that compared favourably with the founders of the Zhou dynasty.

Confucius, unlike the Romans who sent ambassadors to study the political constitution of Athens, had no comparative light by which to steer. Instead, his focus was resolutely on re-creating the golden age of the past, on following the example of earlier periods of Chinese history to locate and pass on the best answers by which to steer the state's future. History, then, was a mirror by which Confucius sought to help rulers see their faults. He was, as he himself argued, a transmitter of the best ideas from the past, not an innovator of new ones.

To that extent, Confucius resembles the Athenians of the late sixth century BCE, who also had an inherent suspicion of 'the new' and preferred innovation to be draped in the trappings of a return to the past, or at least explicitly sanctioned by the gods.[44] He is far removed, however, from the radical democratic thinking that erupted in Athens. Equally, though his ideas chime with Rome's preference for the reins of power to remain resolutely in the hands of the aristocrats, Confucius would have seen little sense in the system of elections and regular 'office-holding' that defined republican Rome in the absence of its kings. Polybius argued that the strength of the Roman system came from its checks and balances that gave each section of society some power, but not too much, and ensured that everyone felt they had more to gain from being in the system than working against it. And while Confucius too was much invested in the idea of balance in society – in his case between the cosmic forces of Heaven and Earth – in contrast, his system did not seek to barter for people's loyalties; rather, to ensure all arrived at a wise and honourable understanding of the respective stations they occupied.

And yet we would be wrong, I think, to see nothing 'democratic' in Confucian teachings – for one thing, because his system applied equally to all people, not just rulers. To Confucius, the people were an intelligent and critical check on erroneous tendencies in government.[45] For another, because Confucius believed a ruler's mandate was predicated on his doing good by his people, and that failure in this duty constituted grounds for his disposal, whether by Heaven or by human hand. (Indeed, it is these 'democratic' elements of Confucianism that are today being heavily underlined, in order to make Confucianism attractive in the twenty-first century.[46])

Overwhelmingly, however, Confucius's focus was on the internal struggle for self-improvement by an individual. Paramount to his system was that the ruler behaved in the proper manner, for all else flowed from him and his character. Such thinking was a natural consequence of the social and political hierarchies of China: powerful individuals had always ruled, even if, in Confucius's day, the power of the Zhou dynasty was diffused amongst its constituent states, each with their own rulers, who each in turn had to deal with the powerful presence of a number of rich families trying to usurp control from them. But a comparable situation had, of course, pertained in both Athens and Rome, and more widely in Greece and Italy, before their revolutions. Rome had turned on and expelled its king. Athens had turned on and expelled a tyrant. In both cases the individual character of a ruler had been a critical factor. The Roman king Servius Tullius was heralded as a good man who created much that the republic sought to maintain, whereas Tarquinius Superbus (the 'Proud') appeared to embody everything a bad ruler could be. Similarly in Athens the expelled tyrant Hippias was thought to have thoroughly earnt his reputation for intolerable cruelty.

That Confucian stress on the disseminable virtues of one wise ruler never had a comparable hearing within the evolving Athenian democratic system, though – because there were no individuals in whose hands power was so concentrated. Athens depended on everyone: roughly two-thirds of its population could expect to hold high office at least once in their lives. And even its more prominent figures were hailed for military ability and courage far more than for any bookish desire for self-improvement. The people of Athens got their education in how to be democratic citizens through a complex communal process acted out within civic and religious events, rituals and festivities. The 'bad citizen' was one who fundamentally opted out of this routine of public engagement, to whom was applied the scornful epithet *idiotes* ('private person'). If we seek an Athenian analogue to Confucius, the man who springs to mind is perhaps Socrates: also something of a gadfly, also not greatly blessed in the looks department, but clearly a man of high ideals and strong exhortations – so much so that he suffered a fate worse than Confucius's neglect, being condemned to death by Athens, at least in part because people wearied of his constant criticisms.

We must wait until the heyday of Athenian democracy is done – at the end of the fourth century BCE, as power in Greece again shifts back towards autocrats and monarchs such as Philip of Macedon and Alexander the Great – to witness a revived focus on the importance and character of the individual. Philosophers such as Plato and Aristotle were interested in the ideal characteristics of individuals, particularly those of a putative 'just ruler', and were not above getting their hands dirty in the business of politics. (Plato made several journeys to Syracuse in Sicily in a sadly ill-fated attempt to train one particular set of rulers to be better kings.) The political-philosophical writer Isocrates even wrote open letters to Philip of Macedon hoping, praying, exhorting that he be the just ruler Greece so desperately needed.[47]

Equally in Rome, while many of Confucius's virtues in a ruler overlap with those that were praised within Roman society – *Ren*, for example, feels strikingly similar to *humanitas*; *Te* and *Yi* to *dignitas* and *auctoritas* – the principal characters of the republic are in no way expected to spend their lives in constant and austere self-improvement. In the early republic, key figures such as Poplicola were distrusted by the people because they seemed bent on the assumption of too much power. It was the outward gesture of burning his house and appearing to be humble that made Poplicola for ever 'the people's friend' – not any reputation for austere and diligent private study. Even the near-mythical figures who humbly set aside the plough to serve Rome as temporary dictators were honoured for their ability to resist the exercise of power – not for dispensing it in a just and moral fashion.

It is not until the last heady decades of the republic – when critics such as the senator Cato bemoaned the lack of morality inherent in the key figures of the time – that we start to see a re-emergence of the importance of individual morality, justice, learning and righteousness. This persists into the period of empire, when once again an individual emperor was in charge of a political system far more comparable to Confucius's China, and we find Roman and Greek writers debating the importance of individual character and the pitfalls when a ruler displays obvious deficiencies in same (to speak only, for instance, of Nero).

The reality is that Confucius struggled to have his message heard, even within China. Indeed, during the difficult and dangerous 'Spring and Autumn' period of the state of Lu it is easy to see why a solution demanding so much strenuous effort from individuals within the court – especially when espoused by a blunt individual possessed of little obvious charm or persuasiveness – fell on deaf ears.

After Confucius's attempt to school Duke Ding was foiled by the cynical device of the eighty desirable women, he set forth with some disciples in a convoy of carriages across the war-torn lands of the Eastern Zhou for his second period of exile – initially to the court of Duke Ling in the state of Wei, but his teachings also failed to gain any real traction there. In the decade that followed, Confucius travelled through many other states within the Zhou kingdom – the Qu, Cheng, Wu, Pu, Cai and Cao – offering his services as a teacher at every stop.[48] His self-imposed second exile was of the same duration as that of Solon from Athens roughly a century before. Solon, whose poetry extolled a kind of moral balance and desire for justice that Confucius might have endorsed, could in the end claim far greater reward for his thought within his own lifetime than Confucius ever could. Even in his absence from Athens, Solon received a hearing in influential circles. He pops up in historical narratives around the Mediterranean in Egypt and Cyprus, and even supposedly advised King Croesus of Lydia that wealth did not amount to happiness. But Solon, too, was given cause to reflect that a wise man's advice is heeded only on rare occasions, and imperfectly even then.

Confucius's bitterness at his lack of success and his inability to keep staunchly to his own teachings is recorded in the *Analects*, when he responds to a charge that he consorted with rulers unworthy to receive his wisdom:

'Master, I have heard you say that when a man does evil, a Gentleman should stand aloof . . . How could you join Bi Xi?'

'Yes, I said so,' replied the Master. 'But is not a thing called hard that cannot be ground thin? White, if left will it not turn to black? Am I a gourd – can I hang without eating?'[49]

At the age of sixty-nine – after ten unsuccessful years attempting to convert rulers across the Eastern Zhou to his teachings – Confucius arrived back in Lu with that same small following who had joined him in exile. His return had been orchestrated by one of his advocates who had remained in the state and who had managed to win the favour of the newly appointed ruler, Duke Ai. Confucius's return, however, would not be marked by his appointment to an important position within government. Instead he was grudgingly accepted back into court, where his ideas continued to be disparaged, and in short order he had to face up to the deaths of two of his favourite disciples and that of his own son. These must have been bitter reminders of the always fragile and now receding influence that he had managed to exert upon the world.

In his final years, he worked as a private teacher, becoming the first person in Chinese history to set up a school of this sort, one that taught his system of learning and behaviour and which, crucially, was open to all. 'From the man who paid in dried meat upwards', Confucius is recorded as saying in his *Analects*, 'I have withheld teaching from no one.'[50] He died in 479 BCE, just as the Athenians were securing the defeat of the Persian invasion and the success of their democratic experiment. Confucius's few remaining disciples built huts near his grave and mourned him for three years. But perhaps the best summation of his life is that recorded in the *Analects*, attributed to a gatekeeper who, on being told that someone had been sent on Confucius's behalf, replied: 'Confucius? The man who knows it's no good, but keeps on trying anyway?'[51]

Rivals in the Field of Ideas

Some readers, surveying what Confucius made of his life in the years that he was allotted, might wonder why we remember him at all – this man who was shunned by the powerful figures of the time, regularly driven into exile, and who ended his days teaching, in return, amongst other payments, for dried meat. The question becomes even more problematic when we realise that Confucius was not alone in his mission to offer wisdom to rulers and their governments. The upheavals of this fraught period created a market in ideas for how to improve society, and many thinkers offered different solutions to the same problems. While Confucius was teaching his system of *dao* ('the Way'), a very different concept of the Way was being formulated – one that emphasised 'action through non-action', spontaneity and simplicity, and the linking of one's desires with the natural rhythm of the world. The principal text that embodies this approach, known more broadly as Daoism, is *Daodejing* (*The Way and the Power*).[52] And the text's author – according to later sources – was a man called Laozi.

Most scholars acknowledge today that Laozi never really existed.[53] His name, which simply means 'old or venerable teacher', has been attached to the *Daodejing* as its sole author, when in reality the work is the result of numerable authors over a period of time. And with the invention of an individual author for the principal work at the heart of Daoism, so too developed stories of competition between Laozi and his 'contemporary' Confucius. Their relationship, according to later sources, was characterised by intense rivalry because of their conflicting ideas about how society should be run, which can be summed up as Confucianism insisting that mankind could affect *dao,* the Way, of the world, and Daoism insisting that humans can only follow the Way. In some classic Daoist texts Confucius is thus depicted as a student of Daoism sitting at Laozi's feet; or alternatively as a deceiver who bends the ears of rulers with rubbish about moral duty.[54] That competition between their different ideas was to persist long after these two men – one real, one fictional – had died.

Laozi (once he had been invented) was not even Confucius's only antagonist in the field of ideas. Also overlapping with his lifetime was a figure known as Mozi, who argued that ritual and music, by which Confucius set great store, were a waste of time, and instead emphasised austerity, self-restraint and simplicity. Shouting to be heard also were the 'Strategists', who argued that success was all that mattered; and the 'Logicians', who used argument rather than past precedent and historical example to decide things.[55] Within a century, as the 'Spring and Autumn' period gave way to that of the 'Warring States' and yet more intense conflict (en route to the emergence of a single ruling dynasty),

China was living through an era known as the 'One Hundred Schools of Thought', among which the teachings of Confucius were but just one contender.[56]

But if the memory of Confucius's teachings was at first preserved by just the few disciples who survived him, Confucianism would find new interpreters and champions. In the fourth century BCE, as Plato and Aristotle began to pontificate on the notion of the just ruler, so in China did a vocal disciple of Confucius emerge, known in the West as Mencius.

Mencius gathered his own disciples around him, and was principally responsible for collecting the extant sayings of Confucius into the text we now call the *Analects*, so establishing the tradition of Confucius as a man worth listening to. 'Ever since man came into this world,' Mencius proclaimed, 'there has never been anyone greater than Confucius.'[57] But while preserving Confucius's teachings, Mencius was also a producer of his own, who sought to elaborate on what Confucius had offered. Mencius's writings pushed Confucianism from a largely passive force (waiting to be asked to advise, slinking off into exile when no longer wanted) towards its having an active social role in educating the people (fitting, perhaps, to Confucius's late-life efforts as a school teacher for anyone and everyone).

Mencius also advocated a role for the people in decision-making. Confucius had never offered examples of when popular opinions should be taken into account, but Mencius argued that 'the people are the most valuable part of a country; the spirits of the land and of the grain are second; the ruler is the least' – a contention that brought Confucianism nearer to Polybius's view of what made the Roman Republic work, in so far as distribution of honour and punishment were in the hands of the people.[58]

Mencius's brand of Confucianism faced its most authoritative challenge from another school of thought known as Legalism, developed in embryonic form by a man called Shang Yang, and eventually formulated as a fully functioning governing philosophy by a man called Han Fei in the third century BCE.[59] Born in the state of Wei, Shang left to eventually become an adviser to the rulers of Qin, a small and fairly backward state in the extreme west of the Zhou dynasty. The ideas he took with him, subsequently developed in Qin by Shang and later by Han Fei, were at the heart of what would eventually be formulated as the Legalist approach to power.

Legalism sought to give all necessary power to the state, to ensure its ability to defend itself and its people. It contended that, in so doing, the interests of the state should trumpet ethical and moral issues. As part of that system, Legalists argued that there needed to be a comprehensive law code and a set of punishments for offences against the law. Rather than relying on an idealisation of the past, or on the actions of a just and sage ruler to enthuse his people to follow his example, as did Confucians, Legalists sought to regulate the way in which everyone lived their lives under the law.

As different rulers of surviving Zhou-dynasty states fought one another for survival in the ever more violent cycle of destruction that was the 'Warring States' period, they did so with different philosophies of government and rule being poured into their ears by these travelling proponents. Like a petri dish in which curious new things are grown with surprising speed, the states of Zhou-dynasty China embraced the 'One Hundred Schools of Thought' as part of their desperate attempts to resist destruction and emerge victorious. The Legalism of Shang Yang and Han Fei would prove indispensable to the one state that came to rule them all. And this endorsement of Legalism, at first, posed a major threat to the endurance of Confucianism. However, it was over time to provide a springboard by which Confucius's ideas would surmount their detractors and obtain the highest position of influence.

Coda

Since Karl Jaspers first argued for his famous concept of an 'Axial Age', some scholars have doubted the degree of unity that can be perceived across different ancient civilisations in this period of enlightened change. Most recently, Ian Morris has argued that the only real observable 'unity' is, in fact, the *diversity* of thought in both East and West.[1] That said, Morris is also keen to stress that, clearly, something extraordinary *did* happen around the time of the mid-first millennium BCE; and it cut across the boundaries of different ancient societies. He argues that in previous millennia 'tipping points' were often reached when disruptions created by the expansion of civilisations brought about, in turn, their collapse. What was extraordinary about the period under our study here is that those exact kinds of disruptions did *not* lead to societal collapses. In other words, this was a turning point in history because, as Morris puts it, 'history did not turn'.[2] Instead, societies mutated and evolved, staying one step ahead of the chaos they had generated.

They did so in part through the fundamental reassessments of man's relationship to man that we have examined in the preceding chapters. The political revolutions and philosophies created in this period were, without doubt, essential to the successes of ancient societies in responding to and keeping ahead of the problems they begat. In Athens, Rome and the state of Lu, war coupled with a number of internal societal triggers led to the state, spearheaded by particular individuals, seeking political alternatives that better balanced the needs and demands of the populus and better protected the community from external threat. In all cases the results were fragile new political ideologies, subject to revision, which we know about mostly through later sources. In some cases these sources sought to link the stories of revolution together; and, in all cases, they adapted and represented the story of conception, birth and development so as to reflect the given society's current political concerns and priorities. This is, of course, the nature of history; but given that these political ideals have survived to our own time, with much still at stake upon them, we ought to be keenly aware of the uncertainty and fragility inherent in these systems that we now so often take for granted.

One of my favourite stories from antiquity that makes much of the quirks of fortune can be found in Herodotus: the so-called 'Persian Debate'.[3] Following an attempted revolt, leading Persians (including the future king, Darius) meet up to decide on what the future political system of the state should be. One (Darius) speaks for monarchy, another for oligarchy, while a third – in a manner that Herodotus's late-fifth-century BCE Greek audience will have recognised as utterly anachronistic – advocates democracy. They eventually agree that monarchy is best, but cannot agree on whom should be king, so they agree to leave it in the lap of fate and the gods: the owner of the first horse to neigh after sunrise will claim the throne. So Darius and his attendant cook up a cunning plan: the attendant rubs his hand over the genitals of Darius's horse's favourite mare and, at just after sunrise, proffers the appealing hand to the horse – which neighs in delight, so winning the day for Darius. Herodotus's Greek audience doubtless relished the thought that the leadership of Persia hung upon such skulduggery. But for us, the 'Persian Debate' offers a much bigger lesson, which arguably neither Herodotus nor his audience wanted to hear or heed: namely, that similar tricks and turns and quirks of fate may play a determining role in any and all societies.

Today we tend to associate revolutionary zeal with youth, by which light Cleisthenes and Confucius may strike us as somewhat senescent figures. Lucius Junius Brutus, who stiffened the resolve of Romans to shut out their king, at least was in his mid-thirties. But Confucius alone among the key figures in our story knew what it was that he sought to achieve. In Rome and Athens, on the whole, they merely knew what they wanted to avoid. But it was in Rome and Athens where reforming ideas became realities with immediate success. Confucius died without having exerted meaningful influence on more than a handful of souls.

We have seen three quests for political change, driven by broadly similar problems and circumstances, leading to three very different propositions for political governance: direct democracy, 'mixed' republican government, and Confucius's concept of the hard-working, constantly self-improving, just and wise ruler governing all. The differences between these systems are clear, and they arose among societies facing disparate challenges, given to different proclivities. But their similarities are perhaps more fascinating – in particular, the way in which Confucius, the Romans and eventually the Athenians (after the fourth century BCE) all agreed on the need for, and importance of, a Solon-like individual who apportioned responsibility, not necessarily equally but as was merited, around whose neck the garland (and the burden) of governance could safely be hung.

At the same time the articulation (and adoption, in the case of Athens and Rome) of these political systems has been linked, both by ancient and modern historians, with changing fortunes for these cities on the wider stage. Herodotus saw Athens' military victories against other Greeks (and subsequently the Persians) from the end of the sixth century as expressly connected with its adoption of democracy, as citizens now fought for a system in which they all had an equal say. Josh Ober has recently argued that the open economic markets and exchanges of knowledge fostered by Athenian constitutional change from Solon onwards – alongside its ability to harness the skills and abilities of foreigners resident in the city – enabled Athens to move ahead of its contemporaries in Greece during the sixth century, driving continuous innovation and learning and, thus, economic growth.[4]

All three societies would, before the end of the first millennium BCE, see power vested in the hands of one ruler. In the case of Athens, this happened in a little over two centuries after the emergence of democracy, as Athens and Greece itself were overwhelmed by the might of Philip of Macedon, Alexander the Great and the subsequent

Hellenistic monarchies. In the case of Rome, what Polybius saw as the exemplary form of its mixed republic won it control of the Mediterranean (and Greece) by the start of the second century BCE. But that balanced constitution would topple, leading to civil war and the institution of an emperor. In the case of the Zhou dynasty there always was a ruler, but, at the same time as Rome's republic mastered the Mediterranean, one among the warring states – Qin, where Shang Yang had seeded his Legalist ideas – managed to establish its rule over all the rest, so initiating a new dynasty and a new age in Chinese history, with a new supreme emperor at its head.

It is time to move our story on, into this era of the third and second centuries BCE, when human communities renegotiated their relationships through warfare, conducted by a fresh generation of young military commanders, and redrew the ancient world map. But just as in this Part the redrawing of man's relationship to man had an impact on the community's relationship to others (as, for example, between Rome and Athens) and on the relationship between humans and the divine (for example, the reliance on divine approval for political change in Rome, Athens and China), so this next era of community renegotiation explored in Part II is also critical to our understanding of the continuing development of the political constitutions that we have seen blossoming in Athens, and especially in Rome and in China.

As Rome rose to dominance across the Mediterranean, Polybius took stock of how its political constitution had helped it achieve such power. In China – which saw the ascent over all of a single state, one that followed Legalist ideas – the survival of Confucianism hung in the balance. And while the heavy footsteps of countless soldiers and raiders echoed across the ancient world, and the political debates continued to rumble on, this was also a crucial moment of growing connections within the Mediterranean: between Asia Minor and central Asia, and between central Asia, India and China. From this era of war, not only would rulers have to take increasing account of the plots and plans of others spread over an increasingly wide geographical area; but a landmark meeting of East and West would be achieved in the depths of central Asia and, with it, a permanent connection would be made across vast ancient terrain.

PART II

WAR AND A WORLD IN CHANGE

TIMELINE

═══════════

323 BCE: Death of Alexander the Great in Babylon

c.300 BCE: Megasthenes working as Seleucid ambassador to Chandragupta Maurya at Pataliputra

281 BCE: Pyrrhus of Ephesus invades Italy

280 BCE: Ai Khanoum founded by Seleucid king Antiochus I

268 BCE: Ashoka becomes emperor of the Maurya dynasty in India

264 BCE: First Punic War begins between Rome and Carthage

256 BCE: The army of Qin state captures the city of Chengzhou, China, ending the Zhou dynasty

250 BCE: Former satrap Diodotus rebels against Antiochus I, creating the Greco-Bactrian kingdom in central Asia

247 BCE: Hannibal born

241 BCE: Roman naval victory off the Aegates Islands ends the First Punic War

232 BCE: Ashoka dies; the Mauryan Empire starts to decline

229 BCE: Death of Hamilcar Barca, Carthaginian general and father of Hannibal

223 BCE: Antiochus III comes to Seleucid throne

221 BCE: Philip V formally assumes the throne of Macedon

221 BCE: Qin Shi Huangdi defeats China's other warring states, claims Mandate of Heaven

221 BCE: Diodotus II is overthrown by Euthydemos to rule in Bactria

218 BCE: Construction of parts of a Great Wall to defend China initiated by Qin Shi Huangdi

218 BCE: Second Punic War begins. Hannibal leads his army over the Pyrenees and Alps

217 BCE: Hannibal defeats Roman forces under Caius Flaminius at Lake Trasimene

217 BCE: Ptolemy IV of Egypt wins victory over Seleucid King Antiochus III at Raphia

216 BCE: Hannibal crushes Roman forces at Cannae

215 BCE: Philip V seeks an alliance with Hannibal

213 BCE: The 'Burning of the Books' in China

212 BCE: Antiochus III heads east to Bactria

210 BCE: Death of Qin Shi Huangdi, buried with army of 8,000 terracotta warriors.

208 BCE: Antiochus III wins Battle of the Arius River against Euthydemos of Bactria

206 BCE: Antiochus III recognises the Greco-Bactrian kingdom and Euthydemid dynasty

206 BCE: China's Qin empire collapses, civil war begins

205 BCE: Roman general Scipio Africanus invades Africa to defeat Carthage

203 BCE: Antiochus III signs a treaty with Philip V to divide Egypt

202 BCE: Battle of Zama, Scipio Africanus defeats Hannibal, ending the Second Punic War

202 BCE: Liu-Bang defeats Xiang Yu, founds the Han Dynasty, becomes 'High-Emperor' Gaodi

200 BCE: Gaodi makes peace with Maodun, leader of the Xiongnu

200 BCE: Demetrius I becomes king of Bactria

197 BCE: Roman victory over Philip V at Cynoscephalae; Hannibal flees Carthage for Tyre

196 BCE: Flaminius enjoys triumph in Rome; Antiochus III crosses Hellespont

196 BCE: Gaodi issues edict sympathetic to Confucianism

195 BCE: The death of Gaodi. His empress Gaohou wields power.

192 BCE: Rome sends troops to Greece to fight with Philip V against Antiochus III and Hannibal

190 BCE: Antiochus III decisively defeated by Rome back in Asia Minor at Magnesia

187 BCE: Death of Antiochus III

185 BCE: Mauryan dynasty in India formally dissolved

183-2 BCE: The deaths of Scipio Africanus and Hannibal

176 BCE: Yuehzi migrate west following defeat by Xiongnu

145 BCE: Ai Khanoum taken over by Sacas

141 BCE: Emperor Wu comes to throne in China and initiates era of expansion

126 BCE: Ambassador Zhang Qian reports back to Emperor Wu following ten year excursion to the West

INTRODUCTION

The view was one that many among them had thought they would never see. Perched high in the Alps, with snow swarming around the steep peaks and bitter winds bellowing through the narrow passes, Hannibal – commander of the Carthaginian army – turned to address his men. He gestured to the panorama that now confronted them: the horizon which, for days, had been obscured by sheer, oppressive rock-faces, ice and blizzards, but which now opened up to reveal not merely an escape, but a paradise.

Beneath the rocky Alps the green fertile plains of the Po valley of northern Italy stretched out before these fighting men. The Alps had afflicted them with frostbite and had left thousands of their comrades dead, their bodies quickly encased in ice and covered in snow, lost beneath the eerie beauty of the deadly shifting sea of white that thickened with each passing day. But now within sight was relief from those bitter elements, and the promise of plentiful food and open grazing for their animals.

All that was needed, Hannibal urged, was one final push through the high summit pass to the welcoming pastures below. And beyond that restful Elysium, their general reminded them, was the enemy they had come so far to destroy: Rome. The inhabitants of the flat plains ahead, the Gauls, had only recently been conquered by the Romans and they – Hannibal insisted – would welcome the Carthaginian army with open arms. And so, fuelled by their desire to escape the torments of their frozen world, to enter that promised land of respite below and to attain their ultimate goal of confronting the might of Rome, Hannibal's men prepared themselves for their final descent. It was to be the worst part of their entire journey.

*

Hannibal's heroic march with his army across the Alps in mid- to late November 218 BCE has captured the imagination of generations, making it one of the most famous military endeavours in history. It inspired generals such as Wellington and Napoleon – the latter made a comparable journey centuries later – as well as artists from Goya and Poussin to J. M. W. Turner. It stands as an example of human courage and tenacity in the face of awesome adversity. And what makes the achievement even more impressive is Hannibal's relative youth: barely thirty years old when he succeeded in this undertaking, younger even than Brutus when he took the momentous decision to oppose the King of Rome and champion revolution in the very city against which Hannibal now marched.

Hannibal's Alpine crossing was the start of a military campaign and a sequence of events that would, ultimately, decide who was master of the Mediterranean. Yet, exceptional as he undoubtedly was, Hannibal ought to be seen within the wider ancient world of this time, as a distinguished representative of a select band whose actions would alter the balance of global power and recast the balance and nature of the relationships between communities across the globe. This is a moment in human history (from the end of the third century BCE to the middle of the second) when a handful of rulers and military commanders, from the Mediterranean, across Asia and all the way to China – many of them notably young – marched, sailed, fought, schemed, ruled and died in their quest to redraw the maps of their dominions, carve out new territories and secure themselves against extinction.

What makes this period all the more important to the idea of a global ancient history is the fact that the actions of each of these leaders not only affected their own fortunes but, increasingly, impacted on the considerations, decisions and achievements of each other's. Heralded by the sound of war trumpets and the march of fighting men, these

1. Solon of Athens: aristocrat, poet, law-giver – and father of democracy? As chief magistrate in 594 BCE he proposed political reforms designed to promote good order (*eunomia*) throughout society by satisfying both the *demos* [the people] and the rich and the powerful, since each would receive what Solon thought they deserved – though not equal standing.

2. The heroic statue of Harmodius and Aristogeiton, which stood in the Athenian agora, commemorating the mortal blow this duo struck to the Peisistratid tyranny of Athens in 514 BCE. Their joint assassination attempt, which killed one of Athens' two tyrants, was celebrated in song and captured a popular mood. Yet Thucydides would later claim that the killing was really an act of revenge occasioned by a bitter love triangle.

3. A study in Roman courage: the lone defence of the Sublician bridge against the Etruscans by Publius Horatius Cocles, as imagined by the French painter Charles Le Brun *c.* 1642–3. The hovering figure laying a laurel on Horatius is a personification of Rome. Basking in the foreground is a river god embodying the Tiber itself.

4. This silk painting (probably Song dynasty, 960–1279 CE) depicts Confucius *c.* 500 BCE lecturing students on the subject of filial piety. The obligation to obey and care for one's parents throughout life was one of the central tenets of Confucius's teachings, and he had practised what he preached.

5. What did Hannibal of Carthage look like? No reliable likeness survives, though we are sure he was not as fair-skinned as European painters pictured him. This, by the German Johann Rasso Januarius Zick (1730–97), depicts the boy Hannibal as he accepts his father Hamilcar's urging and swears an oath of eternal enmity against Rome (signified by the shield that bears the legend SPQR, Senatus Populusque Romanus.) Legend has it that in later life Hannibal told of the oath to Seleucid king Antiochus III as the two men plotted to take on Rome together.

6. Hannibal's march across the Alps in 218 BCE, made in order to challenge
Rome for supremacy of the Mediterranean, is among the most famous military
endeavours in history. We can't be sure over which of the six or so known passes
through the Alps Hannibal led his army, with its train of elephants, horses and
pack animals. We do know that treacherous weather and topography made a huge
problem for the army, oblivion beckoning at the first misplaced footstep. This
famous engraving imagined such a scene for an *Illustrated History of the World for
the English People*, published in the 1880s.

7. Antiochus III, barely twenty when he assumed the Seleucid throne in 222–1 BCE following the murder of his elder brother. His challenge was to unify a vast realm under his sole rule. His fate was to live a life at war, moving east to west and back again in defence of his empire's boundaries. His efforts in the east earned him the title of 'The Great'. Pressing west into Asia Minor, he became the enemy of Rome. But following a rout by Roman forces at Thermopylae in 191 BCE, Antiochus quickly lost everything he had struggled to achieve.

8. Philip V assumed the throne of Macedon in 221 BCE aged only sixteen, but in his forty-two-year reign he witnessed the growing interconnectedness of the Mediterranean. Facing complex networks of alliance within Greece, he tried to create similar arrangements in his own favour, only to wind up as the focus of alliances directed against him. In 215 BCE he made a deal with Hannibal and began ten years of war with Rome. Later he allied with Antiochus III against Egyptian king Ptolemy V, but was decisively defeated by the Romans at Cynoscephalae in 197 BCE, so ending his days as a loyal servant to Rome.

leaders forged an increasingly interconnected world, such that a mere eighty years after Hannibal crossed the Alps, the historical sources of the Mediterranean and those of China converged for the first time – from which point the ancient world took on the character of a chessboard in which every individual move had implications for the whole.

As they listened to their commander, Hannibal's troops had had plenty of time to consider the stakes of their Mediterranean-based conflict, and to reflect on what they had already endured to reach this point. They had encamped near the summit for two days, waiting for stragglers and for the slower-moving parts of the army's enormous snaking train. Over the previous nine days they had marched into the mountains, climbing slowly into arctic conditions that now surrounded them on every side. It was said that they were the first to cross the Alps with an army since the Greek hero Heracles (he whose legend as the Indian-born founder of Pataliputra was extolled by Megasthenes, Greek ambassador to India). Heracles, it was said, was also the first to force a route through the Alps wide enough for men and baggage trains, slaughtering the local tribes who stood in his way.[1] But as Hannibal and his troops had progressed further into the belly of the mountains, the passes had narrowed, leaving them vulnerable to attack from the surviving descendants of those tribes Heracles had once attacked.

Hannibal's forces had been subject to depletion since setting out from their Carthaginian bases in southern Spain in the early summer of 218 BCE. At that outset his army had boasted 90,000 infantry, 12,000 cavalry and some thirty-seven elephants.[2] Having left some of his troops to fight in Roman-controlled north Spain, dismissed others and lost even more to desertion, Hannibal crossed the Pyrenees with a far leaner army, on whom the mountains exacted a further toll. By the time they had made it through and on towards ancient Gaul and the western banks of the Rhone River that carves through modern-day France, Hannibal had just 50,000 in his infantry and 9,000 cavalry men, though his contingent of elephants was intact.[3]

As they reached the foothills of the Alps, Hannibal sensed fear and trepidation spreading among his men, and he chided their hesitation. Were they not troops of mighty Carthage that had conquered Spain?

Had they not crossed the Pyrenees? Were they not the men who had just cowed a force of Gauls while traversing the mighty Rhone, taking not only men, but also elephants across its violent waters? Would the Alps be any different? Had the envoys from the friendly tribes waiting for them on the other side come to Hannibal on wings, rather than using the very same paths they would now use? And, with such a prize in mind as Rome itself, would any hardship be too great to endure?[4]

It was early November when the army began to climb.

*

Not a single Carthaginian source survives to tell us of Hannibal's legendary adventures en route to Italy, or of the campaigns that would follow.[5] Two contemporary Greek accounts, since lost, were dismissed by the ancient writer Polybius as 'the kind of common gossip one hears in the barber's shop'.[6] Conversely, Polybius would claim that he had personally surveyed the landscape and followed Hannibal's route to ensure his account was as accurate as possible.[7]

Polybius, one of the first surviving ancient sources to tell us of Rome's revolution and conversion to a republic, was an astute observer of politics and war in history, and particularly of 'how, and under what political system, the Romans in less than 53 years succeeded in subjecting almost the whole inhabited world to their sole power – an achievement unique in history'.[8] He attributed Rome's mastery, on top of its enviable location and resources, to its mixed and balanced constitution, forged through almost three centuries of external conflict and internal tension between the Patricians and the Plebs.[9] And Polybius interrupts his historical narrative of Hannibal's campaigns against Rome specifically to ponder Rome's political constitution, as he argues that 'it was at its best and nearest to perfection at the time of the Hannibalic war'.[10]

Quintus Fabius Pictor, the first Roman to write about the origins of the republic (albeit in Greek), was himself a soldier in the conflict against Hannibal. Livy, writing his history of Rome about two centuries after Hannibal's attack, focused closely on the supreme test Hannibal posed to Rome, as did a number of later historians writing about Rome's military history, such as Appian.

Despite these important sources, however, we are still not entirely sure over which of the six or so known passes through the Alps Hannibal led his company. We do know that during the first day of the ascent his extended convoy was threatened by an ambush by a local Gallic tribe, the Allobrogians, and that with great cunning they managed to fend off that threat. But if Hannibal and his men thought they would now be left alone to continue their journey, they were wrong. The tempting target of the heavily loaded baggage train was too much for the Allobrogians.

As the Carthaginians marched further into the mountains over the next seven days, they continued to suffer onslaughts along their flanks: each time horses reared, bucked and fled in terror as confusion spread through the ranks. Local warriors sent rocks bounding down the gorge walls, leaving trails of death and uproar in their wake. Animals and men were trampled, skewered and sliced to pieces. On open ground, control would have been quickly re-established, but Hannibal's army was marching through narrow, uneven passes, with little room for manoeuvre and, even worse, a precipitous drop on one side for much of the time. With every incursion, more bewildered animals were pushed off the path, skidding to their deaths down the grey mountainside, taking with them much-needed supplies. Hannibal was losing not only animals, but the means to sustain his army on the march ahead. He had no choice but to go on the offensive, ordering his men to kill, in confused hand-to-hand combat.

Finally, on day nine, his surviving men saw the green pastures of the Po valley, and they camped, rested and re-formed in preparation for the descent. It was little more than six months since they had set out from southern Spain and, despite Hannibal's inspiring words about taking on powerful Rome, the survival of his entire army was now in jeopardy. Their supplies were so low that one of his subordinates even suggested they resort to cannibalism.[11] Meanwhile, the snow was falling more heavily each day. It was only a matter of time before it became so deep that the paths out of the Alps would be cut off and they would all starve or freeze to death.

By day twelve Hannibal could let them rest no longer. The army pushed onwards. The enemy now was not tribal fighters, but treacherous weather and topography. Snow fell so thickly that it was impossible for the troops to see where the path ended and faded away into a precipice. One misplaced footstep or stumble, and oblivion beckoned. A day into the descent, Hannibal and his army arrived at a spot where the majority of the path had been destroyed, carried away in a landslide. There was no way they could edge the elephants or baggage animals along the remaining splinters of pathway. Casting around for another route, Hannibal saw that a new snowstorm made any change in direction impossible: the densely packed ice from the previous winter lay under the fresh fall, with the result that the men slipped on the unseen ice, and animals, heavy with their packs, broke through it with their feet, only to be trapped on account of the weight of their burden.

The only way was forward, and for that to be possible, Hannibal's men would have to remake the very landscape of the Alps. The soldiers were set to work building up the path along the cliffside, gouging out space from the rock-face, and packing the area where the track had fallen away with anything they could find to make it stable enough again to pass over.[12] It was back-breaking, perilous work but, within a single day, the army had created a pathway wide enough for the horses and pack animals to cross. Hannibal led them forward and down out of the mountains, into the pastures immediately below the snow level. The animals were left to feed, while Hannibal returned with his crack troops to the ravine, to help his men make the path wide enough and strong enough for the elephants. These poor beasts – unable to graze in such conditions, and with little left in the army provisions that could alleviate their enormous hunger – were stuck on that freezing narrow ledge for three days, the army working tirelessly around them.[13] Finally the elephants were able to cross and move down into the plains below (the region of modern-day Turin) along with the exhausted troops, who 'looked more like beasts than men in outer appearance and general condition'.[14]

Hannibal had led his train on an arc around the Mediterranean coast to make it to Italy. Yet, as he entered the Po valley – the start of the effort to reach the gates of Rome itself – he had already lost 70,000 men from his infantry, half his cavalry and, almost certainly, a number of elephants. Those soldiers and animals that survived were malnourished, bruised and battered, exhausted, terrified and despondent.[15] And their war, in truth, had only just begun.

But as Hannibal moved to challenge Rome for mastery of the central and western Mediterranean, there was equivalent activity in the eastern Mediterranean, across Asia and in China – where other young leaders, too, were making momentous decisions that would serve to draw our ancient worlds into closer orbit and recast the relationships between them.

As I noted in my Introduction to this book, the world of Megasthenes, Greek ambassador to India, was one in which the eastern Mediterranean, Asia and India had been connected by the conquests of Alexander the Great. In the aftermath of Alexander's death, the lands he had conquered had divided into competing power-bases that came to be heavily involved with one another and, eventually, with affairs in the western Mediterranean.

In Greece itself, around the time Hannibal was preparing for his march from Spain to Italy, King Philip V assumed the throne of Macedon, aged merely sixteen. Philip sought to expand his own influence within Greece and to link up with Hannibal in order to inflict even more damage on Rome (though, as events transpired, he would have to revert to a more defensive strategy against redoubtable Roman opponents). In other words, he wished to create and manipulate connections across the Mediterranean, only to find an interconnected alliance ranged against him.

Then there were the Seleucids, who ruled a vast domain stretching from the eastern shores of the Mediterranean deep into central Asia and the northern parts of India. (It was the first Seleucid monarch who sent Megasthenes to India.) As Hannibal marched across the Alps, the new Seleucid king was Antiochus III, a fresh-faced man-boy in his early twenties. His task was to unify, connect and stabilise a sprawling realm under his single rule. His fate was to spend his life at war, moving across his territory from east to west and back again, defending its boundaries from incursions at each side. To the west Antiochus, like his Seleucid predecessors, had to deal with the advance of Rome, plus the irritant that was Egypt. To the east, in central Asia, he was challenged by new players, particularly the state of Bactria (occupying much of today's Afghanistan), rich in gold and ruled by successive ambitious warrior kings. And to the south, Antiochus still had to reckon with the fading and splintering remnants of the once-splendid and powerful Indian court, kingdom and army founded by Chandragupta Maurya, especially since Bactrian rulers regarded Chandragupta's once-proud kingdom as potential rich pickings.

In China the Qin state, having embraced the developing philosophy of Legalism (not Confucianism) as its governing mantra, moved from its shadowy spot on the western edges of Chinese territory to conquer every other warring state by 221 BCE. At the head of this new dominion was Qin Shi Huangdi, who had come to power twenty years before at the age of fourteen, and who now became the First Emperor of Qin. Like Antiochus and the Seleucids, like Rome as its influence expanded across the Mediterranean, Qin Shi Huangdi set himself to rule a vast empire of fifty million people with iron discipline. His monuments would be legendary but in his grand mission he was to fail, so passing the mantle and the challenge to a new dynasty – the Han.

Concerned by the threat of invasion from the nomadic tribes that surrounded China to the north and west, Qin Shi Huangdi ordered the erection of defensive structures that were linked up to form a 'Great Wall', which the Han would further extend. Battling the nomadic tribes was a lifelong obsession for these emperors, for whom stability on their borders was a key tenet of their attempts to unify their realms. The thrust of their policy alternated between invasion, blockade, accommodation and bribery. Invasion and blockade led to the flight of certain tribes to the west. But the outcome of accommodation and bribery was also to create a powerful nomadic Xiongnu empire on China's borders, which drove yet more numbers west. And so began a great migratory ripple that would eventually crash into the complex, interconnected world of central Asia, where Bactrian, Parthian, Seleucid, Indian and Indo-Greek rulers sought to carve out for themselves new and improved dominions.

As Hannibal struggled across the Alps in 218 BCE, opening a new phase in Carthage's fight with Rome for supremacy in the Mediterranean, he doubtless understood the gravity of what he was attempting.

As he rallied his troops to look down onto the Po valley and prepare for the battles ahead, the challenge of the future must have seemed vast and daunting. And yet he could not have imagined more than a fraction of it, at best. Hannibal and his generation were to exercise power and fight, for glory and for survival, in an increasingly wide world – one in which the systems of governance whose births we charted in Part I struggled to survive at times, but at others were decisive in the redrawing of the global map and of the relationships between its constituent communities.

By the 140s and 130s BCE Rome was master of the Mediterranean, having destroyed Carthage and razed Corinth in Greece to the ground, while the Han ruler, Wudi, was poised to begin his own expansion of China westwards. Waves of nomadic tribes fell upon and took over Bactria – the first event to be recorded in both Western and Eastern historical sources. It would not be long before those connections grew into unbreakable networks, stretching from Rome to the capital of the Chinese Empire in Luoyang. The ancient world would never be the same again.

CHAPTER 4

A New Generation Arises

From his boyhood Hannibal was steeped in warfare, schooled in its conduct by his father Hamilcar, who, as legend would have it, also bred in young Hannibal a burning antagonism towards Rome.

Hamilcar died in Spain in 229 BCE, commanding Carthaginian forces that had spread out to take control of much of the southern half of that country. Hannibal had been in Spain for half his life – he was only nine years old when Hamilcar took him and his brother Hasdrubal there from Carthage on the North African coast (in modern-day Tunisia). His mother remained in Carthage and it is uncertain whether Hannibal ever saw her again. Instead he was reared at Hamilcar's side, educated, we think, in Greek language and literature by a Spartan teacher.[1]

We know that Hamilcar died in a battle with an Iberian tribe at which Hannibal and Hasdrubal were both present. According to the first-century BCE historian Diodorus Siculus, Hamilcar, finding himself and his forces almost surrounded, took a different route from that of his sons in order to throw their enemies off-track. Galloping heroically until he was overtaken by his pursuers, he turned his horse into a nearby river, wading deep into the middle in full armour, where he drowned under the weight of his horse, his diversionary tactic having bought the time for Hannibal and Hasdrubal to escape.[2] Hannibal was eighteen, on the verge of adulthood, now without the father who had guided him, long without a mother, and within a foreign territory that, while mostly under the Carthaginian thumb, was not without its dangers. What he bore within him, however, was a cause.

It is famously said that when Hannibal, towards the end of his life, came to meet Antiochus III, master of the Seleucid Empire to the east, he told of how his father, before taking him from their homeland to Spain, had made him swear an oath never to show goodwill to the Romans: an oath, some sources even say, of eternal enmity.[3] Another Roman source claims that Hamilcar said joyfully of his two children, 'I am rearing these lion cubs for the destruction of Rome!'[4] History – as ever – is written by the victors, but in this case the victors chose to portray an enemy whose eventual defeat brought them honour: a man who had dedicated his life to opposing them and who, as every Roman source admits, came very close to being their conqueror.

While Hannibal mourned his father in 229 BCE, in Greece Philip V, a boy of eight, was being groomed for the throne of Macedon, guided by one of his father's cousins who acted as regent. The foreign-policy objectives of Macedon were to expand its influence south, to deal with unfriendly neighbours to the west (who were supported, perhaps, by Rome) and to resist invading tribes from the north.

In Asia the Seleucid ruler Seleucus II, father of the future Antiochus III, faced the threat of greater Roman intervention on the western borders of his world, while having to resign himself to the loss of territories to the east, where the hyperactive and expanding kingdom of Bactria had just gained a new and ambitious ruler: Diodotus II.

The flux was all the greater since in India the last great Mauryan king, Ashoka, had lately died, so beginning the break-up of the once-proud empire of Chandragupta Maurya, upon which neighbouring realms now feasted like vultures.

Meanwhile in China the state of Qin had just won one of its greatest military victories against a rival state, in its march towards total domination of the Chinese world, led by the future Qin Shi Huangdi.

By 229 BCE, then, the ancient world from the Mediterranean to China was in serious flux: because of fraught and resisted Roman expansion in the west; instability, intense rivalry and dynastic struggle in the centre; and seemingly unstoppable Qin expansion in the east. Here we can see a historical crux-point: the mindsets of a new group of young rulers and commanders were taking shape; likewise the military and political landscapes they confronted and took charge of. Within ten years, the reins of power had been handed over: Hannibal, in his mid-twenties, leading the war for Carthage; Philip V taking full command of Macedon, at just sixteen; Antiochus III, barely into his twenties, ruling the enormous Seleucid Empire; and Ptolemy IV, twenty-one, in control of Egypt. Young men taking great and fateful responsibilities upon their shoulders, they put down their stakes in the game and rolled the dice.

Resisting Rome in the West

Roman sources tell us that Hamilcar was descended from either the father or brother of Dido, the fabled first queen of Carthage. Since Dido's heart was broken by Aeneas, progenitor of Rome, such that she burnt herself alive to escape her grief, it's easy to see why the family's descendants might have borne a grudge.[5] But Hamilcar had his own reasons to be wary of Rome.

By 237 BCE, the year he and his sons quit Carthage for Spain, Rome and Carthage already had a grisly history. The First Punic War between these two Mediterranean powers had ended only four years earlier, with Carthage the defeated party. Its fleet had been destroyed in a sea battle off the coast of Sicily and it was now being forced to remove its troops from Sicily and the surrounding small islands; to hand over all its Roman prisoners; and to pay the huge sum of 3,200 talents of silver in instalments to Rome over the next twenty years. The Carthaginian treasury was left so destitute that it could not afford to pay the professional soldiers it had hired to fight Rome on its behalf.

Polybius argues that Carthage's reliance on mercenary troops was always a fatal weakness, in contrast to Rome's use of citizen forces and allies.[6] Consequently Carthage did not pay adequate attention to the state of its armed forces, who never entered battle believing that the survival of their homeland was at stake.[7] Perhaps yet more crucially, when things went wrong a mercenary army could turn vicious. And so, in 240 BCE, 20,000 unpaid mercenaries turned on Carthage seeking retribution, besieging the city and inciting the local North African tribes to join them in open rebellion. The war that followed was labelled by some ancient commentators as the most impious of all time: the mercenaries castrated their pay-masters and the Carthaginian people cut off the mercenaries hands, broke their arms and legs and cast them into a pit to die. Hamilcar – leading the remaining loyal Carthaginian army – besieged and starved to death thousands of rebels in a narrow canyon know as 'The Saw', murdering those who surrendered.

But if Carthage won a reprieve, Rome was not done with its demands, and in 238 BCE it made known its intention to have the island of Sardinia, traditionally a Carthaginian possession. Carthage would not only have to surrender and evacuate its forces, but also pay an additional 1,200 talents to Rome in fines, at the peril of renewed war if it refused. The notion of another conflict with Rome was untenable. The First Punic War – beginning in 264 BCE, after Rome had initially been invited to protect Sicilian cities that were threatened by the expansion of Carthaginian power – had become about much more than drawing a line between the zones of influence of Carthage and Rome. It had become a struggle for dominance over the central Mediterranean. In the early stages of the war Carthage had seemed sure to prevail. Previously Rome had fought all of its expansionary wars on land, while Carthage had long been a seafaring power with a great navy to control the sea lanes around the Mediterranean coast. Rome had sought to compete, building a navy from scratch by copying the style of the Carthaginian warships and adding a *corvus* (a bridge that could hook onto enemy ships and enable soldiers to engage in hand-to-hand combat on deck).

But Carthage had also built up its land forces in Sicily, including the transporting by ship of military elephants from Africa. The Roman army was terrified of these huge beasts, since they knew not how to fight them. It was only in 250 BCE that they developed the successful tactic of hurling javelins at the elephants until they were so deranged by pain that they rampaged uncontrollably. Fuelled by this growing intelligence over the enemy, Rome also began to threaten Carthaginian supremacy at sea, first laying siege to its strongholds on Sicily, then defeating its navy off the island's coast.

Hamilcar commanded Carthage's Sicilian forces after 249 BCE, in the final stages of the war. Leading a force predominantly composed of mercenaries, his tactic was to win enough small skirmishes to keep the war in Sicily at stalemate, but he knew he could not push for outright victory, not least because he was lacking the full support of Carthage itself.

From what we can gather, Carthage's political system was not unlike that of republican Rome. Two 'kings' were elected annually from amongst the wealthiest families (a decision Livy and Polybius thought comparable to Rome's consular system) and they ruled in conjunction with an assembly of aristocrats (not unlike the Roman Senate), alongside an administrative bureaucracy, a panel of judges and a more popular assembly, which supposedly held a final vote if the kings and aristocratic council could not agree. To Polybius's mind it was this casting vote of the people that gave them an overweening power, unlike the balance of monarchical, oligarchic and popular elements in Rome; and he thought it a key factor in Carthage's eventual besting at Roman hands.[8]

Polybius further argued that the Carthaginian system was infected by greed at a level unknown in Rome: open bribery was rife, and nothing that resulted in profit could be considered disgraceful.[9] Powerful aristocratic families (including Hamilcar's) were keen on popular support, but also had the means to buy it, the better to sway the organs of state towards their preferred decision. Unlike in the fierce aristocratic rivalry and struggle for popular support that beset Greece in the sixth century in the run-up to its democratic revolution, there was no need for the recruitment of a beautiful woman dressed up as a goddess to hoodwink the people in Carthage.

Hamilcar's family was, however, not alone in seeking to convince Carthage of a particular plan of action. In foreign policy the state apparently had two main rival camps of opinion: one led by Hamilcar, who advocated confrontation with Rome; the other by Hanno 'the Great', who sought to ignore Rome and concentrate on building Carthage's power in Africa. This rivalry was the reason Hamilcar never got the support he needed to win his fight against Rome in Sicily: Hanno won the argument to confine Carthaginian efforts and manpower to

African soil. When Rome crushed Carthage's fleet off Sicily, they did so because Carthage's attention and forces were largely committed elsewhere.

Hamilcar was thus doubly embittered, come the end of the First Punic War: by the Romans and their expansionist desires, and by his own people for not fully taking his side. As Carthage began the push-back against its unpaid mercenaries in 240 BCE, the battle between Hamilcar and Hanno continued to rage in the state's council chamber, its assemblies and in the streets. The stakes were high: in Carthaginian tradition a military general seen to have failed faced execution. Hanno, in this confrontation at least, would prove victorious. But Hamilcar, thanks to his pitiless prosecution of the war against the mercenaries, managed to escape with his life and political status just about intact. Unsurprisingly, though, he did not dally in Carthage, heading for Spain with his sons in tow.

For Hamilcar, Spain was a new beginning: a territory to which none of the big Mediterranean powers had yet fully laid claim, but with which Carthage had strong trading connections. Carthage could take control, so rebuilding its treasury and compensating itself for its loss of Sicily and Sardinia to the Romans. And now was the time to strike, since Rome, too, was alive to the opportunity of expansion into Spain and was starting to extend its reach down from the Pyrenees. Hamilcar knew very well that success would bolster his reputation and influence within the Carthaginian aristocratic council and among the people. It was a goal he would pursue ceaselessly until his death.

*

Hamilcar's Carthage was by no means the sole antagonist of mighty expansionist Rome in those years before 229 BCE. The kingdom of Macedon in northern Greece had been the epicentre of Alexander the Great's empire, extending all the way through Asia to India. Macedon was, and always had been, very different from the city-states of southern and central Greece: while Athens was busy with democratic revolution, Macedon remained resolutely a monarchy, engaged in trading luxuries with other ruling families near and far, and building massive, lavishly appointed funerary monuments for its dead kings.

After the splintering of Alexander's empire, Macedon remained – just about – the pre-eminent kingdom in Greece, ensuring its dominance through a delicate and difficult balance of military and diplomatic pressure with the different alliances of Greek states to the south; with competing kingdoms to the west such as Epirus; and with wild tribes to the north, such as the Dardanians; as well as with the few independent cities in Greece, including Sparta and Athens.

What had become of Athens' proud democracy by this time? Alexander had treated Athens with respect on account of its heritage – which is to say that he had stopped short of burning it to the ground, the fate he reserved for other cities that rebelled against him – and, indeed, he permitted its democracy to continue to function. Alexander had supported democracies in other cities that he liberated as part of his conquest of Asia – for instance, in Ephesus, on the island of Chios and in Erythrae.[10] But following Alexander's death, Athens had fallen under the sway of powerful Macedonian governors who tampered with its system, introducing a bar of property ownership for those who sought to qualify for citizenship, even adding two new tribes to its celebrated democracy, expediently named after the governor and his father. In 287 BCE the Athenians had had enough: the sources report a new democratic revolution, though it is very unclear to what extent Athens got back full control of its affairs or returned to anything like the direct radical democracy of its heyday.[11]

Indeed, if one were seeking an example of democracy in action in the third century BCE, one would look everywhere other than Athens. Scholars of this period have pointed to functioning democracies on Cos, and at Miletus, Iasus and Calymna on the Asia Minor coast. The Seleucid king, Antiochus I, who was known to be keen to get rid of democratic constitutions where he could, had remarked that the city of Lysimacheia on the north-eastern Aegean coast was a democracy as of the 270s–260s BCE.[12] But what must have really galled proud Athenians was a blossoming democracy much closer to home – the Achaean League of central and southern Greece, of which Polybius writes, 'no political system can be found anywhere in the world which favours more the principles of equality, freedom of speech and true democracy'.[13]

The Macedonian King Demetrius II died in 229 BCE (the same year as Hamilcar) while fighting the wild tribes to Macedon's north. His heir, eight-year-old Philip, was too young to succeed and so one of Demetrius's cousins, Antigonus, stepped in as regent and guardian to Philip. The state faced a variety of threats on all sides, but Antigonus succeeded in pushing the northern tribes back across the Macedonian frontier, then turned his attention to uprisings in central and southern Greece, where anti-Macedonian sentiment was boiling. But while he was thus engaged, a new war broke out on the western and northern fringes of Greece – with Rome.

Rome had been largely uninterested in Greece, mainly because from 264 BCE onwards it was fighting for survival against Carthage. But with the conclusion of that war, and Rome's growing interest in Sardinia and northern Spain, the Senate's attention was now also turning to the east, and in particular to a semi-barbarian tribe who occupied the north-western edge of Greece and the land as it tips round the top of the Adriatic Sea towards Italy – the Illyrians, led by Queen Teuta.

Teuta had lately ordered the murder of a Roman envoy who had been so arrogant as to question the way in which the Illyrians governed themselves, and to intimate that Rome might teach them a lesson. The murder of a diplomat – however undiplomatic he may have been – was, inevitably, grounds for a Roman campaign. In 229 BCE the Romans marched into Illyria, supported by their now pre-eminent fleet in the Adriatic, ostensibly seeking to punish Queen Teuta. But the key issue at stake was Illyrian piracy in the Adriatic, then wreaking havoc in the trading sea lanes, not only for Rome but for its allied cities on the east coast of Italy. Consequently Rome moved to establish a permanent presence on Greece's north-west coast by annexing a strip of coastal land about 120 miles long and 20–40 miles wide, along with many of the outlying islands, including Corcyra (modern-day Corfu).

This was the first time that Rome had established control over Greek mainland soil (as opposed to taking over Greek colony cities in Sicily and southern Italy); and the newly annexed territory was, at one point, separated from Macedon by just a single valley. Despite this sudden proximity, though, it doesn't seem that Antigonus and the young Philip regarded Rome's presence as an immediate threat. Antigonus in particular was too busy dealing with a mutiny in the Macedonian army, his soldiers exhausted by the conflicts that had seen them fighting continuously for more than a decade. Nor was any respite forthcoming: the Illyrians, stymied by the Romans in their pursuit of riches through piracy, gave vent to their frustrations by attacking Macedon, an assault Antigonus would spend the rest of his life trying to fend off. Arguably, however, Antigonus and young Philip should have given more thought to Rome's aspirations. (For one thing, some historians have argued that Rome was actually the inciting force behind the Illyrian attacks on Macedon.[14])

The ambitions of Rome did not stop in Greece. In 229 BCE an official communiqué was making its way slowly across the Mediterranean – its author the Roman Senate, its destination Asia, its intended recipient Seleucus II, King of the Seleucid Empire.[15] The letter presented Rome's formal request that Seleucus respect the autonomy of the city of Ilion, on the western coast of Asia Minor, abutting the Aegean. Ilion had a famous history, for it was once known as Troy, taken by the Greeks more than a millennium before in the wake of ten long years of war made immortal in history by Homer's *Iliad*. More vitally for Roman interests, Ilion's inhabitants were the ancestors of the Roman people, since it was a fugitive Trojan, Aeneas, whose descendants founded Rome. Troy mattered deeply to the Romans.

But the message sent to Seleucus II was more deeply indicative both of Rome's growing interest in Asia and of its sense of its own power. The Romans had defeated Carthage; taken Sardinia and Sicily; were establishing beachheads in Greece and advancing into northern Spain; were even sending athletes to compete in the Olympic Games; and now they were fully emboldened to make demands of the King of the Seleucids.

*

In truth, the Roman Senate could hardly have picked a less opportune moment to petition Seleucus II, who wanted no new problems in the midst of an already troubled time for his vast, unwieldy empire – one that stretched for thousands of miles from the western coast of Asia Minor on its Mediterranean side; down into the Middle East; and all the way east into central Asia. As such, Seleucus was better placed than anyone to understand the reality – and feel the burden – of the entangled nature of the wider ancient world.

Within this sprawling territory lay a patchwork of different cultures, tribes, languages and power systems, separated not only by vast distances, but also by difficult and treacherous terrain. The king could not be everywhere at once, and relied – as had Alexander and the Persian rulers before him – on a network of *satraps* (governors) who ruled in his name. Though the Seleucid ruler remained more powerful than the Zhou ruler in China in the era of Confucius – who also, given the vast territories and numbers of his people, had to rely on individual 'mini-rulers' to keep control of individual states – just as in China, the Seleucid system created problems, as cities and tribes rose up in rebellion and declared independence; as *satrap* governors dreamt of more power and defied their king; or even as rivals from within the imperial family sought to challenge the sovereign power.

Seleucus had seen all of these problems in the decade before 229 BCE. Seven years previously, a newly independent kingdom had been declared in Asia Minor on Seleucid territory, centred on the city of Pergamon near the western coast of Asia Minor, and newly ruled by (the self-styled) King Attalus. Seleucus, however, could do little about this encroachment, not least because his power had already been significantly weakened by a challenge much closer to home. In 239 BCE his younger brother, Antiochus Hierax – 'the Hawk' – had proclaimed himself king, leading a revolt in conjunction with a number of powerful allies from the northern limits of the Seleucid borders. To make matters worse, in the three years between Antiochus Hierax's defection and the emergence of Attalus's kingdom, Seleucus had also had to face down open rebellion in one of his empire's richest and most powerful cities, Babylon. Seleucus had managed to contain and force Babylon back into the fold, but when he faced Antiochus Hierax in battle in 235 BCE, he was humbled and forced to strike off a larger chunk of northern Asia Minor from his lands, leaving it to his brother and his supporters.

Seleucus was no stranger to family feuding. In fact, the open war with his brother was only the final chapter in a wider dynastic

power-play over his own claim to the throne. Seleucus's father, Antiochus II, had fathered children by two different mothers. One – Laodice,
from Asia Minor – was the mother of Seleucus and Antiochus Hierax.
The other, Berenice, was Egyptian, daughter of the King of Egypt,
Ptolemy II. Egypt had long been a sizeable thorn in the side of the
Seleucid Empire. In fact, the Ptolemies – another dynasty and kingdom born of the splintering of Alexander the Great's empire – had
over the previous century already fought two wars with the Seleucids
in dispute over the boundaries of their respective territories, particularly in the area of modern-day Israel and Palestine that was then
known as Coele-Syria. The most recent conflict with Egypt had not
gone well for the Seleucids, and it was then that Antiochus II had
been forced to divorce Laodice and marry Berenice, as part of the
peace deal.

When Antiochus II died, the question, of course, was who should
succeed: the eldest son of Laodice, or the child of Berenice, daughter of
Ptolemy? When Berenice called on her father to help ensure his grandson's accession, Laodice promptly had Berenice and her son killed,
making Seleucus king. The Egyptian ruler was – understandably –
incensed by the murder of his daughter and grandchild; and so began
the third war between Egypt and the Seleucids in 246 BCE, just as
Seleucus II came to the throne. It would last until 241 BCE, the same
year that Carthage lost its war with Rome. But the peace that was eventually agreed would yet again reveal the precarious nature of Seleucus's
position, as he was forced to concede new territories in Coele-Syria and
even the port of the great city of Antioch on the western coast of Asia
Minor.

The ongoing tussles with Egypt underlined the other major problem facing such eminences as the Zhou dynasty and the Seleucids: the
endless porous boundaries of their kingdoms, impossible to guard and
maintain at every juncture. In 229 BCE, as Seleucus II – vulnerable
king of a still-mighty but significantly crumbling empire – read the
official request from Rome seeking autonomy for Ilion/Troy on his
western border, he was also having to confront yet greater upheaval
and instability to his east.

Instability in the Centre

The kingdom of Bactria – roughly 3,000 kilometres east of Babylon, its heartland where northern Afghanistan is found today – lay at the very fringes of Seleucid control. It was one of a number of provinces at the junction between Hellenised Asia to the west, the vast steppes and plains of nomadic central Asia to the east, and India to the south. Bactria was, as a result, at the very limits of Greek influence as forged by Alexander the Great a century before. Its frontier looked out over very different worlds; a melting pot of contrasting cultural traditions from all directions. As the historian Arnold Toynbee once put it, Bactria was a roundabout 'where routes converge from all quarters of the compass and from which routes radiate out to all quarters of the compass again'.[16]

Bactria – not to speak of the surrounding provinces of Sogdiana, Parthia, Margiana, Aria and Drangiana, some of which were under Bactrian influence while others were independent in their own right – was accustomed to lying at the outer edge of empires. The Assyrians, we think, and then more certainly the Persians had tried to bring these areas within their realms, with a good deal of success.[17] When Alexander the Great marched through Persian territory in the 330s and 320s BCE, he had found the Bactrians willing allies against Persia, albeit less willing to accept Alexander as their ruler. Alexander eventually managed to exert control using both the stick and the carrot. He married a woman from nearby Sogdiana; settled fellow Greeks throughout the region; and founded/renamed about a dozen new cities (after himself), which fed upon the lively trade and commerce that passed naturally through the area, including the city of Kandahar in modern-day Afghanistan. Moreover, he brutally quashed both internal revolts and invasion attempts by nomadic tribes to the east and north. And yet by the time of Alexander's death in 323 BCE, Bactria was still in turmoil, its governance fought over frenetically by various Greek mercenaries, who briefly styled themselves kings, before being murdered by their rivals.

Attempts to subdue Bactria, made by Alexander's generals in the immediate aftermath of his death, bore little fruit. But when the dust finally settled and the fragmented kingdoms of Alexander's former empire had assumed a more or less consistent shape, King Seleucus I of the Seleucid Empire set out to establish a firm hold over Bactria. By 305 BCE he was victorious, not least thanks to naked imitation of the actions of Alexander the Great: marriage between Seleucus and a Sogdianan woman; a period of extensive Greek colonisation of the area, backed up with light-touch governance; huge investment in building more cities; and the ever-present threat of force, where it was thought necessary. Seleucus I now commanded an empire of 1.5 million square miles, containing roughly thirty million people – not incomparable in size and population to that of the Zhou dynasty in China.

Seleucus I and his son, Antiochus I, paid close attention to their newly won territories and to the surrounding provinces, especially as they were – just as Alexander had been – consistently at risk from incursions by nomadic tribes from even further east. In 293–2 BCE, when nomadic raids destroyed an entire city, Seleucus recognised that a stronger physical presence was required, and put his son in charge of the eastern half of his empire. Antiochus I set up command in Bactria and spent more than a decade defending the eastern frontier. This was a golden time for the region. Gifted with fertile land that was ideal for horse-breeding, benefiting from the increasing trade flowing through the region from east and west as well as from India in the south, and buoyed even further by the introduction of a fixed silver coinage based on the standard used in Athens, Bactria boomed.

One of the new settlements, at Ai Khanoum (in modern-day northeastern Afghanistan), was a central location for the minting of this new coinage. The city's architecture bears witness to how deeply Greek culture was infused into the multitude of traditions around this hub – a Greek gymnasium built with oriental motifs; oriental-style temples with Greek columns and capitals; a theatre for 6,000 people; a palace complex and substantial one-storey housing in local mud-brick and whitewash paint, all secured within strong fortification walls.[18] And in Ai Khanoum was erected one of the greatest pieces of evidence for the international flavour of Bactria during this period: a monument dedicated to the founder of the city, a Greek named Kineas, and inscribed with sayings copied in around 275 BCE by one Clearchus, who made a

10,000-kilometre round trip from Ai Khanoum to Delphi in central Greece. Clearchus returned to inscribe the philosophical maxims of the world-famed oracle on the city monument: 'in childhood, be well behaved, in youth have self control, in middle age behave justly, in old age be of wise counsel, in death be without sorrow'.[19] (As a discursus on the Ages of Man, it compares to Confucius's schema as recorded in the *Analects*: 'at 15 I was bent on study; at 30 I could stand; at 40, doubts ceased; at 50, I understood the laws of Heaven; at 60 my ears obeyed me; at 70 I could do as my heart lusted and never swerve from right'.[20])

Bactria's golden age couldn't last. In 281 BCE Seleucus I was assassinated, forcing Antiochus I to leave Bactria and head west to secure his throne. He, his son Antiochus II and his grandson, Seleucus II, were, as we have seen, wholly consumed with war in the west. They had little time for Bactria, although they depended on it for regular supplies of men and fast horses. The result, almost inevitably, was revolution, driven by local resentment of the way in which Bactria and its environs were being sucked dry for their far-away 'ruler' and, in turn, how the absences of men, horses and a strong ruler left the otherwise blossoming Bactria more susceptible to nomadic raids from the east. Either during the reign of Antiochus II or during the dynastic conflict that embroiled Seleucus II, the provinces of Bactria and nearby Parthia took matters into their own hands.

The local governor of Bactria, Diodotus, drove the region to independence and turned himself into King Diodotus I. Much the same happened in Parthia under its governor – then king – Andragoras. By 245 BCE Diodotus was the official ruler of the independent kingdom of Greco-Bactria, also encompassing the surrounding provinces of Sogdiana, Margiana and Aria, and by 239 he had, like Parthia, officially broken all ties with the Seleucid Empire. Seleucus II had to accept the loss of two major provinces on the eastern borders of his realm, the third major province he had lost (the first, to the Attalids, being Pergamon in the west) in just ten years.

But Seleucus II was not the only one forced to watch this new efflorescence of independence in central Asia. A tribe called the Parni, based just south of the Caspian Sea, were also weighing the potential for a power-grab, not least because the newly proclaimed King of Parthia,

Andragoras, was now struggling to maintain his authority and borders. The Parni, under their leader Arsaces, swept in to take charge, killing Andragoras in the process. In Bactria, meanwhile, as Diodotus I died and Diodotus II ascended to the throne, there was much to celebrate – not only the undisputed ascension of the son of the self-declared king, making the 'Diodoti' a true ruling dynasty; but also a treaty made with the new King Arsaces of Parthia, so that both parties would respect each other's borders. And what Diodotus now looked to was the opportunity for further expansion south – towards India.

*

The Mauryan dynasty had swept to power across India at the time of Alexander's death a century earlier in the late 320s BCE, led by a relatively youthful emperor in Chandragupta Maurya. According to Plutarch, while still in his teens Chandragupta had met Alexander:

> Androcottus [Chandragupta], when he was a stripling, saw Alexander himself, and we are told that he often said in later times that Alexander narrowly missed making himself master of the country, since its king was hated and despised on account of his baseness and low birth.[21]

Chandragupta was, and remains, a legendary figure in Indian history, not least for the manner in which he assumed power by the final overthrow of the unpopular Nanda dynasty, storming their capital at Pataliputra. The Nanda had ruled northern India for almost a hundred years, having fought Alexander (and nearly lost, so Plutarch tells us). In the wake of Alexander's death, Chandragupta expanded his empire still further by stealing back territory in north-west India that Alexander had acquired earlier in the decade.

By the time Seleucus I's wars brought him to India c.305 BCE, Chandragupta's hold on Alexander's former territory was so strong that Seleucus could do no more than make a treaty with him, acknowledging Mauryan control over the north-west lands as well as those of the Hindu Kush mountains, the region around Kabul and Kandahar and stretching west into the Gedrosian desert. In return Seleucus received 500 Indian elephants trained for use in battle, which he soon put to good use back in the west. (Some ancient sources say Megasthenes was involved in the negotiation, his performance earning him the appointment as Seleucus's ambassador to Chandagupta's court at Pataliputra.[22])

So began a rich period of cultural and financial interchange between the Seleucid Empire and India. Greeks were certainly curious to know more of India, while India in turn absorbed a number of Greek traditions, including figurative art, coinage, language, and possibly even theatre. Chandragupta's son, Bindusara, is said to have expressed significant interest in Hellenic culture, once officially requesting from Seleucus I sweet Greek wine, Greek figs and a Greek sophist – an intellectual from whom to learn about their culture. (Reportedly Seleucus sent the wine and figs, but declared that 'in Greece, law forbids a sophist to be sold'.)

The Mauryan court, however, hardly needed Greek accoutrements to impress: its opulence surpassed the wildest dreams of any Greek. Only the luxury-loving Persians, according to Megasthenes, could even imagine the riches on display, but could not hope to compete.

Splendour came at a price. Chandragupta was said to be so paranoid about potential assassination that he changed bedrooms frequently to confuse any potential plotters. In later Buddhist legends, Chandragupta chose to renounce his throne willingly in favour of Bindusara, who was then succeeded by Ashoka in 270 BCE. This succession, however, according to several of the later ancient sources, seems to have been violently contested: following a protracted dispute between rival claimants to the throne, it is said that Ashoka assured his own succession by killing almost all of his ninety-nine brothers.[23]

But a counter-story survives today by way of the enormous contemporary rock-cut inscriptions littered across Ashoka's former empire, proclaiming his laws, edicts and achievements (also relating that his brothers were unscathed and held important positions in his court). The inscriptions – discovered on the frontiers with the Seleucid Empire to the west, and deep into Afghanistan at important settlements like Kandahar – were cut onto cave walls and giant free-standing rocks, but also onto enormous 40–50-foot stone monoliths erected across his realm. These pillars, weighing nearly fifty-one tonnes each, were often topped with a series of sculptured animals: four lions, for example, sitting back-to-back, guarding the column and surveying the land around them. The Ashoka inscriptions (of which about twenty survive today) are the first deciphered examples of writing in Indian history, and they reveal not only a complex society, but one in command of a vast territory and integrated with a variety of surrounding communities. These permanent memorials to Ashoka's acts were written in Greek (testifying to the ongoing influence and use of Greek in the region), Irano-Aramaic and Prakrit, so ensuring that they were intelligible to as wide a range of people as possible, both within his empire and outside it. In the texts Ashoka demonstrates familiarity with most of the ruling dynasties of the eastern Mediterranean. As such, they are an incredible testament to the connected nature of this part of the ancient world.

For all that the literary sources have to say of Ashoka's ruthlessness and cruelty, they also report a remarkable change in his character and outlook. The Sanskrit text *Ashokavadana* relates how Ashoka eventually converted to Buddhism – a religion that had flowered as another outpouring of the Axial Age in the sixth and fifth centuries BCE, as a consequence of the life and teachings of the Buddha in India. The embrace of Buddhism seemed to encourage Ashoka to devote his kingship to public welfare rather than territorial expansion (and to spread the message of Buddhism further afield, as we shall see[24]). At home Ashoka supposedly became selfless to the detriment of his rule, giving away nearly everything he owned in order to inspire the people to share in his vision. Central to that vision was the concept of *dharma* – a crucial tenet of Hindu and Buddhist worship, though its precise meaning has not only varied between religions, but also over time and even within individual faiths. At the root of *dharma* is the idea of order, either at an individual level (e.g. 'the right way of living') or at a cosmic level ('cosmic order'). Whatever its particularities of meaning, however, the essential idea is that its presence, and its preservation, are essential for the continuation of a balanced society and world. How to achieve it? As Ashoka put it in one of his rock edicts: 'the noble deeds of *dhamma* [*dharma* in the Pali script] and the practice of *dhamma* consist of having kindness, generosity, truthfulness, purity, gentleness and goodness increase among the people'.[25]

Despite surface similarities, this was a very different philosophy of governance from that of Confucius, who advised rulers to seek continual self-improvement, govern by example and so earn the mandate of Heaven – rather than surrender one's worldly goods in the hope of making people nicer to one another. Economist and Nobel Laureate Amartya Sen has argued that Buddhism as a belief system, and Ashoka's adoption of its principles in governance, are actually examples of democratic ideology which suggest to us that democracy's origins, usually located in late sixth century BCE Athens, were not exclusively Western.[26] But there is reason to doubt that Ashoka, or other Buddhists of his time, would have identified themselves with the radical democrats of ancient Athens. Ashoka's experiment, moreover, was certainly not so successful. Despite warnings from his ministers and his son, Ashoka continued the great giveaway until he was left, according to the *Ashokavadana*, with just half a piece of fruit and long lamentations on his new-found impotency.

Ashoka died in 234 BCE – in the same decade that Diodotus and Arsaces took Bactria and Parthia to full independence – and it is telling that we are unsure who replaced him. Just as the Seleucid Empire was withering on all sides, so, too, the once-great Mauryan Empire had attained its zenith and begun to collapse – not least, in some scholars' view, because of Ashoka's decision to convert to Buddhism and try to improve the lot of his people rather than defend his kingdom. Some argue that different successors broke the empire apart to rule as independent kingdoms; others say that a sole ruler managed to hang on for a little longer. But without doubt the territories of north-west India – so long a mixture of Greeks and natives, once belonging to Alexander and then to the Mauryans – now began to form small independent political communities. More importantly, as Diodotus II took the Bactrian throne in 229 BCE, he saw his opportunity for Bactrian expansion in the Mauryan territories north of the Hindu Kush mountains. The remains of the Mauryan Empire were ripe for conquest. As one Indian scholar has commented, 'India needed men of the caliber of Porus and Chandragupta to ensure her protection, but she got [in Ashoka] a dreamer.'[27]

Making an Empire in the East

It is 246 BCE. Hannibal is a newborn in Carthage. Diodotus I is establishing an independent state, with himself as king, in Bactria. And 8,000 kilometres east of Rome a fourteen-year-old boy called Zhao Zheng has inherited control in the state of Qin, its capital at Xianyang, based in the Wei river basin in what is now the city of Xi'an in the Shaanxi province of central China.

For the first six years of Zheng's rule day-to-day power rested with his prime minister, but once Zheng turned twenty (in 240 BCE) he assumed the reins. He was to be unbelievably successful: by 221 BCE he had taken Qin from the status of one among many warring states and made it the sole and victorious survivor, uniting under the Qin banner much of what is now central China for the first time in its history and establishing himself as Qin Shi Huangdi: the First Emperor of the country of Qin.

Zhao Zheng's success was partly down to geography. The Qin heartland – the Wei valley – was on the western edge of the Eastern Zhou dynasty in the 'Warring States' period. Its secluded distance from the epicentre of events meant that it was not such a natural target for aggression (rather as Rome's location on the western margins of Mediterranean events allowed it room to develop[28]). The state of Qin was also protected from the other states to a large degree by the mighty Yellow River and a number of mountain ranges. The Wei, moreover, was an extremely fertile and productive area, ensuring that the Qin were well supplied and self-reliant. (Again, Rome was similarly blessed with an abundance of natural resources on its doorstep.)

Nevertheless, the state's preferred guiding principles of governance also had a significant impact. Despite its protected position, Qin had not fared well during the first hundred years or more of the so-called 'Warring States' period (475–221 BCE). A change was wrought in 361 BCE when the then-ruler retained as his adviser Shang Yang, proponent of the embryonic philosophy of Legalism that was officially adopted by the state in 359 BCE, its credo being 'Wise men make laws, stupid men are constrained by them.'

Legalism, the reader may recall, was a system in almost direct opposition to the teachings of Confucius, insisting that central government establish and uphold strong laws and carry out harsh punishments, to ensure the absolute authority of its rule, the productivity of the state and its survival against enemies. In his lifetime Confucius's ideas had failed to persuade a single devoted ruler; his imitator Mencius at least adapted Confucian teachings to make them more facile. Shang Yang, though, converted a state to this way of thinking, with manifold results.

Over the next century the state of Qin's fortunes was dramatically transformed, with order and tranquillity becoming the status quo. It also expanded its dominion to the south, overcoming the neighbouring states of Shu and Ba. With this increased territory, the Qin state instituted a series of massive irrigation projects to further improve the fertility of its terrain and, with a bigger population, it built up a powerful army. Such achievements were not without casualties. Shang Yang himself finally fell foul of his enemies at the Qin court who resented his influence. For his supposed 'crimes' – fighting as a 'rebel' against them (and the state) – he suffered the appalling punishment that his own system of government demanded: his body was torn apart by chariots galloping in opposing directions.

When the young Zhao Zheng took full control of the Qin state in 240 BCE he and his advisers capitalised on their existing advantages (geography, philosophy of government, a centralised streamlined bureaucracy) and pressed for further expansion. During this period the other major figure in the development of Legalism as a coherent philosophy of government – Han Fei – also arrived in the state of Qin, hoping to wield similar power to that of his Legalist predecessor, Shang Yang. While his work on further formulating Legalist ideas was welcomed and devoured by Zhao Zheng, Han Fei himself was not to reap the benefits. So terrified was Zhao Zheng's prime minister that Han Fei would supplant him in his position of authority that – despite being an old fellow student of Han Fei – he convinced the emperor to have him imprisoned and killed.

The surrounding warring states fell to Qin in quick succession: the Han in 230 BCE, the Zhao in 228, Wei in 225, Yan in 222 and finally Qi in 221 BCE. In the *Wuzi*, a classic work on military strategy attributed to Wu Qi, admiration for Qin's martial prowess is made plain: 'Qin's nature is strong. Its terrain is difficult. Its government severe. Its rewards and punishments are reliable. Its people do not yield: they are all belligerent.'[29] During this enormous conquest, Qin Shi Huangdi survived at least three assassination attempts (by dagger, lead-weighted lute and solid-metal wrecking ball). He was said to have had hundreds of tunnels created underneath and between his palaces, so that he could move unseen by would-be assassins (or evil spirits).

From his new fastness the First Emperor then began to look to the vast nomadic lands of central Asia, to the west and to the north. Yet neither Qin Shi Huangdi nor his ruling peers thousands of miles to the west could possibly have envisaged the impact that conflict with these tribes over the next half-century would have – not only upon China, but also on the Greek kingdoms at the eastern edge of the Seleucid Empire in Bactria and Parthia, as a migratory wave was unleashed.

*

Looking at the globe as it stood in 229 BCE, we can see the ancient world in extraordinary flux. Rome's expansion had been manfully resisted, but ultimately unchecked in the west; while instability was created in the centre; and Qin's rise to power continued in the east.

Carthage, having lost its first war with Rome, was building a new power-base in Spain under Hannibal's father Hamilcar, in order to strengthen its position in the Mediterranean. Rome, steered by its republican system, had extended its influence into Spain in the west and into Greece to the east, and was looking to project its power even further east into the Seleucid Empire. The Seleucids, under Seleucus II, were losing battles at their borders in the east and the west; break-away new dynasties like Bactria and Parthia were being formed under opportunistic dynasts such as Diodotus I and Arsaces; and rulers like Diodotus were looking to profit from the disintegration of old empires to the south in India, thanks to the potentially ruinous good intentions of King Ashoka. And in China the state of Qin, under Zhao Zheng, was poised to subjugate all states under its rule.

Many strong currents were in play, and in hindsight it may be tempting to read Rome's rise, in particular, as obvious and unstoppable. Yet in the 220s BCE, despite Rome's obvious successes, this scenario was far from assured.

Upon the death of Hamilcar, leadership of the Carthaginian forces passed to the elder son, Hasdrubal – his brother Hannibal was simply too young. Hasdrubal preferred diplomacy to war and over the next eight years by skilful negotiation he extended the reach of Carthage further north into central Spain, right up to the River Tagus (which ambles across Spain and Portugal from east to west and empties out into the Atlantic Ocean near Lisbon). Hasdrubal's masterstroke was to seal a diplomatic deal with the Romans, determining their respective spheres of control within Spain. Since Roman influence seeped southwards from the Pyrenees, and Carthaginian control northwards, the dividing line agreed on by Hasdrubal and the Roman command was the Ebro River, Spain's second-largest after the Tagus, running almost parallel with the Pyrenees from its source in the mountains in northern Spain, and gushing out into the Mediterranean on the central-eastern Spanish coast. Carthage thus had free rein over the vast majority of Spain, including a number of mainly Roman settlements south of the Ebro that Hasdrubal otherwise agreed to leave alone.

Despite having emerged victorious from the First Punic War, Rome was possibly content to settle with Hasdrubal like so: it considered Spain the least of its worries while it contended with an invasion of Gauls from central Europe into northern Italy. In the time that Rome had invested in building influence in Spain, established a bridgehead in Greece, demanded independence for Troy in Asia and sailed the Mediterranean to take advantage of its supremacy at sea, as wrenched from Carthage, the Gauls had meanwhile laid waste to the countryside of northern Italy and stirred up rebellion amongst the resident Gallic tribes in this region, over whom Rome just about exerted dominion.[30] In every military campaign season over the next five years Rome was forced to send an army into northern Italy to subdue its northern residents and eject the invaders.

In the east the beleaguered Seleucus II had felt the burden of empire profoundly as he trekked from one end of his demesne to the other and back, attempting to counter every threat. Finally his resistance gave out: around 225 he suffered the ultimate humiliation for a monarch, dying not in combat, but by having fallen from his horse. His eldest son, Seleucus III, succeeded him. In 223 BCE Seleucus's younger brother Antiochus waved his elder sibling off, as he sought to regain some of their father's lost territory by taking on the newly proclaimed King Attalus of Pergamon. Seleucus, though, was promptly murdered by his own army en route, probably because they were reluctant to fight for such an inexperienced general against such a battle-hardened veteran as Attalus. And so, at no older than twenty, Antiochus became king of a hugely turbulent Seleucid Empire.

In Macedon, 221 BCE saw the time finally come for Philip, aged about sixteen, to step out from behind his regent uncle and become King Philip V. In Egypt in that same year Ptolemy IV came to the throne, probably in his early twenties and faced with the prospect of continuing to wrangle with the Seleucid Empire for control of Coele-Syria. Meanwhile in Spain Hasdrubal's diplomatic skills could not save him from assassination at the hand of the slave of a Celtic king whom he had killed in battle. Hannibal, now twenty-six, was elected general by popular vote of the Carthaginian troops in Spain, a decision later ratified by the Senate in Carthage.

In a fast-changing world the mantle of rule had passed to a new generation of young rulers. Within three years Hannibal tore up the treaty Hasdrubal had bartered with Rome, swapping diplomacy for war and laying siege to the Roman town of Saguntum south of the Ebro River. From there he began his march across the Pyrenees. His family name, lest we forget, was Barca, meaning 'lightning flash'. And as one Roman commentator would later evoke it, Hannibal 'burst his way through the midst of the Alps and swooped down upon Italy from those snows of fabulous heights like a missile hurled from the sky'.[31]

CHAPTER 5

Making Connections

In spring of 215 BCE the fleet of Rome spied a Macedonian ship making its way from Italy to Greece across the Adriatic Sea. The Romans sent light fast craft to intercept it. Initially the Macedonian vessel tried to outrun its pursuers, but the slender frames of the Roman ships moved with ease over the surf, gaining on their prey. Recognising the futility of their position, the Macedonians turned and surrendered. On board was Xenophanes, an Athenian ambassador for Philip V of Macedon, and three envoys whom – by their dress, accents and manner – the Romans took for Carthaginians.

Asked to explain himself, Xenophanes claimed he had been making his way to Rome with an offer from Philip of an alliance, only to be cut off by Hannibal's Carthaginian forces, who by now had spread out from the Alps down into Italy and were seemingly unstoppable. But the Romans were made suspicious, particularly by the Carthaginian company that Xenophanes was keeping. They proceeded to interrogate the slaves and attendants on the boat, and what they uncovered was a document that struck fear into the heart of the Roman commander. Immediately he ordered that the document (and the ambassadors) be conveyed to Rome in the fleet's fastest ships – with each of the captured men in a separate boat, so that they were unable to communicate and falsify their story any further.[1]

The document was the draft of a treaty alliance, not between Philip V of Macedon and the Romans, but between Philip and Hannibal. Its terms were simple: Philip would invade the east coast of Italy with approximately 200 ships, ravage the coast and make war on the Romans, helping Hannibal in his quest to humble Rome (and, in the process, forestalling any further Roman incursions into Greece). With Rome defeated, Hannibal would control all of Italy and its possessions. In return, Hannibal would then sail with his men to Greece to fight with Philip against his own Greek enemies, helping once again to re-establish the undisputed power and supremacy of Macedon.

Carthage and Macedon, situated on different continents over 1,500 kilometres apart, were nonetheless united in their desire to check the single power that menaced them both, and ready to help each other to improve their respective spheres of influence. Moreover, in proposing to link their worlds like so, Philip and Hannibal were asserting themselves as leaders. As the fates of their predecessors had shown them all too clearly, these young men, if they were to survive, had to command the respect of their troops, the loyalty of their people and – yet more difficult – of their allies, not to speak of the admiration (however grudging) and circumspection of their enemies.

In the eastern Mediterranean the young Ptolemy, newly ascended to the throne of Egypt, would soon exert himself similarly – locking horns with the inexperienced young Seleucid emperor Antiochus III, who was forced in turn to demonstrate his own worth while he wrestled with the inheritance of the vast and vulnerable territories bequeathed him by his father. The challenge of being a single ruler across a vast expanse was one Antiochus shared with the First Emperor of Qin, similarly taxed to unify his new world after centuries of endemic conflict, to protect its boundaries against a gathering collection of nomadic enemies, and to ensure his nascent dynasty's survival.

The only way, it must have seemed, to survive and prosper on this ever-expanding chessboard of the ancient world was to think in terms of coordinated strategies of attack and defence.

Making Alliances in the Mediterranean

It is easy to understand why Philip believed alliance with the prowess of Hannibal was worth the price of taking the fight to Rome. His father and uncle had been plagued by tribal invasions to the north and west of Macedon, which had only lately (and barely) abated. But Macedon also had enemies to the south. When Philip assumed the throne in 221 BCE, his official title was not only King of Macedon, but also General of the Hellenistic Symmachy. In other words, he was the head of a league of Greeks who all had something to fear from the growing power of a rival Greek collective – the Aetolian League, which occupied much of central Greece.

In 220 BCE Philip – as head of his Hellenistic league – declared war on the Aetolians. It would be a messy conflict: each time the military campaign season began, Philip marched his troops down into central and southern Greece (as Sparta in the southern Greek Peloponnese had decided to side with the Aetolians), only to hear rumours of a possible invasion of Macedon and return home, or else spend most of his time dealing with dissatisfied, mutinous members of his own league.

Philip's troubles were not helped by the reappearance of the Romans in Greece. One of the terms Rome imposed on the Illyrians (having established their bridgehead of land on the west Greek coast) was that no Illyrian ship could sail south beyond an agreed point, without Roman say-so. But in 220 BCE two Illyrian commanders took it upon themselves to lead ninety ships into the Adriatic to glut themselves with piracy, the traditional livelihood of Illyrian warriors. In the summer of 219 BCE Roman troops marched back into northern Greece to punish the Illyrians for their transgressions. Philip held off his own attacks further south, to watch what the Romans would do next – and with good reason. Rome's full attention was now on Illyria and Greece. Normally each of Rome's consuls was assigned a different area of military operations to oversee during their year in office, depending on where Rome's governing bodies felt needed the most attention. It was an unmistakable statement of intent that, in 219 BCE, both consuls were sent to Greece to oversee operations.

Philip probably felt very much alone as the clouds of war gathered over Greece. However, Rome's focus – and Philip's too – was abruptly and decisively switched from the east to the west in 218 BCE, as reports came in that Hannibal had marched over the Alps and into Italy. Some have argued that it was from this moment that the idea of an alliance with Hannibal entered Philip's mind, and it was certainly espoused by some of his confidants, including the recently scolded Illyrian prince Demetrius, one of those responsible for the piracy that had brought Rome crashing into Greece, but now a trusted adviser and military commander of Philip's.

Philip and Demetrius did not simply sit and wait for further news of Hannibal's movements. They established a relay system of messengers to bring them the latest news from the Italian front with all due despatch. In the summer of 217 BCE Philip sat at Nemea, 600 kilometres south of Macedon, helping to celebrate the Nemean Games in honour of Zeus. As the athletes limbered up and the pressing crowd cheered in anticipation, a messenger arrived directly from the Macedon capital, with news that Hannibal had secured his greatest triumph yet – full-blown victory over the gathered Roman army in central Italy.

Philip's interest in athletic competition melted away, as did his entire military agenda. Within months he had settled the war between Greek leagues by way of a peace treaty, and he did so principally by stressing the importance of greater Greek unity at a time when attentions might usefully be turned elsewhere. Polybius tells us that one of the dignitaries at the signing of the accord offered this observation: 'If you desire a field of action, turn to the west and keep your eyes on the war with Italy, so that, wisely biding your time, you may some day at the proper moment compete for the sovereignty of the world.'[2] Philip certainly understood the advice and what was at stake, but was in no mood to heed the suggestion that he bide his time. Spurred on by his piratical confidant Demetrius, he spent the winter of 217–16 BCE building a fleet for a new operation.

While Rome was preoccupied with Hannibal, Philip's aim was to land 5,000 men on the Roman protectorate zone along the Illyrian coast, at the same time as sending ground troops in from the Macedon side to occupy the area – in other words, a simultaneous

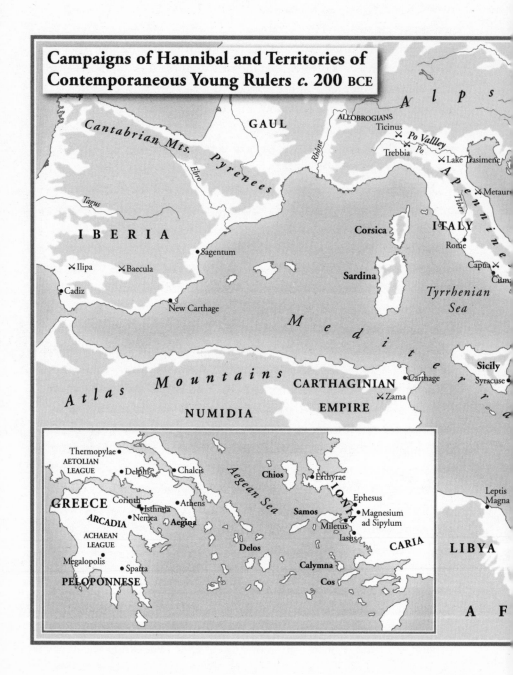

Campaigns of Hannibal and Territories of Contemporaneous Young Rulers *c.* 200 BCE

Cantabrian Mts.

GAUL

ALLOBROGIANS

Pyrenees

Ticinus ✕

Po Valley

Rhône

Ebro

Trebbia

Po ✕ Lake Trasimene

Tagus

✕ Metaurus

Tiber

Corsica

ITALY

I B E R I A

Rome

✕ Ilipa   ✕ Baecula

Sagentum

Capua ✕

✕ Cum.

Cadiz

Sardina

Tyrrhenian Sea

New Carthage

M e d i t

Sicily

A t l a s   *M o u n t a i n s*   CARTHAGINIAN   ✕ Carthage   Syracuse

✕ Zama   EMPIRE

e r r a

NUMIDIA

Thermopylae ●

AETOLIAN LEAGUE

● Delphi

● Chalcis

Chios   ● Erythrae

Aegean Sea

Ephesus ●

Leptis Magna

GREECE   Corinth

● Isthmia   ● Athens

Samos   ● Magnesium ad Sipylum

ARCADIA   ● Nemea   Aegina

Miletus ●

Iasus ●

CARIA

LIBYA

ACHAEAN LEAGUE

Megalopolis ●

● Sparta

Delos ●

Calymna

PELOPONNESE

Cos

A   F

Carpathians

Danube

Drava

Sava

Transylvannian Alps

Danube

Black Sea

inaric Alps

ILLYRIA

riatic Sea

DARDANIA

Balkans

Rhodope Mts.

THRACE

MACEDON

Pindus Mts.

EPIRUS

ASIA MINOR

Pella

Lysimacheia

The Chersonesus

Troy

SELEUCID EMPIRE

annae

Tarentum

Crotona

Corcyra

Cape Colona

Cynoscephale

Taurus Mts.

Ionian
Sea

Cyprus

Crete

Tyre

Panium

ean

Sea

Gaza

Raphia

Alexandria

PTOLEMAIC EMPIRE

Siwa Oasis

Nile

RICA

EGYPT

0   100   200   300 miles

pincer movement. This would not only expand Macedonian control, but also provide a secure base from which to launch any future operations into Italy.[3]

If that was the grand design, Philip's first sortie must have severely dampened his spirits. Another Illyrian prince, in league with Rome, made a desperate appeal to the Romans for help to fend off Philip's fleet. Rome despatched a meagre ten boats, and yet Philip, hearing that the Romans were on their way, panicked, expecting the appearance of the entire Roman fleet. He retreated immediately, his ships scattering as they desperately tried to find safe harbour – all fearing the appearance of Roman masts on the horizon. Instead, Philip's weak-kneed withdrawal would be grounds for jibes at his expense for years to come.

Negotiations for an alliance with Hannibal were already opened and, despite Rome's seizure of the envoys in the spring of 215 BCE, this treaty was signed by the summer. Polybius records the official text of the document, which had undergone significant changes since its spring draft: Philip was no longer promising to invade Italy alone, but only to help Hannibal. There was a mutual agreement to support one another if either was invaded, and if Hannibal made peace with the Romans, then part of the deal was that Rome would not turn its military machine upon Philip.[4] Expectations of what Philip might accomplish militarily had been pragmatically scaled back; equally, by 215 BCE Hannibal's conquest of Italy was beginning to look less assured.

*

For all his deathless accomplishments, Hannibal remains an enigma to us. Unlike Alexander the Great, whose profile is commemorated in surviving statues, busts and coins, no official portrait of Hannibal exists. He left no written record, save for a single inscribed monument in southern Italy. The sources that chart his life are all Roman or Greek, and written with the benefit of hindsight. To some, Hannibal is a fearsome and strategically brilliant enemy, who managed to command an army composed of a patchwork of nations, to perform incredibly difficult feats of endurance and bravery; a man who tested Rome to its very limits, and even displayed an impressively dry wit. To others, he is a cunning shape-shifting devil, devoid of principles or any sense of justice, remorseless in pursuit of victory. For others still, he 'had a thirst for human blood which inflamed him at the core of his being'.[5] Nonetheless, all admire his ability to survive constant hardship, deprivation and uncertainty. Like a rock structure that only gets harder when compressed by tectonic forces, so too, it was generally agreed, Hannibal was at his most formidable when under extreme pressure.[6]

And he was pressurised from the outset, though not always by the enemy on the battlefield before him. When Hannibal ripped up his brother-in-law's diplomatic treaty with Rome by laying siege to Saguntum, the Romans – wishing to keep their focus on Illyria and Greece where both consuls had been sent – sought a diplomatic solution by going behind Hannibal's back.[7] Hannibal's fate in Spain still depended on the vagaries of political infighting back home in Carthage, a place packed with the same enemies who had so hampered Hamilcar's campaigns in previous decades. The Roman historian Quintus Fabius Pictor even went so far as to claim that Hannibal had kick-started his march towards Italy in 218 BCE principally because he was worried that his enemies in Carthage would soon persuade the Senate to remove him from command.[8] Thus Rome's appeal to Carthage directly to rein in their renegade young general, sending its most senior ambassador to Carthage's supreme aristocratic council, had a high chance of success. But in the tense atmosphere of this meeting, pride and brinkmanship seem to have got the better of both sides. The Roman ambassador brandished his toga and – according to Polybius – told the Carthaginians that in its folds it held both war and peace. The Carthaginians asked him to let fall from his toga whatever the Romans wanted, to which the ambassador said he let fall war. The Carthaginian high command replied simply, 'We accept.'[9]

Hannibal had prepared for a war on multiple fronts. Before attacking Saguntum he had sent 20,000 men to Africa from Spain, in case Rome attempted a revenge attack on Carthage. A similar number of men, drawn from the various North African tribes under Carthage's command, were then directed back to Spain. With the largest army in the Mediterranean behind him, Hannibal now engaged in an act of pure theatre, making a 750-mile round trip to the city of Cadiz on the western Spanish coast to pay homage at the sanctuary of Heracles-Melqart, a Greco-Carthaginian deity identified with the same Heracles that Megasthenes had said was born in India. In doing so, Hannibal was copying the historical example of great leaders to the east (taught to him in boyhood, we assume, by his Greek tutor): not only the Athenians heading to the oracle at Delphi before the Persian invasions, but, even more meaningfully, Alexander the Great's journey to the sanctuary of Zeus Ammon at Siwa in the Egyptian desert before he set out on his campaign to conquer the world a century before.[10]

And yet, still, Hannibal's prospects were not as promising as they might have seemed. He had been unable to sail from Spain to Italy in the first place because of the superior Roman fleet that prowled the Mediterranean Sea and could bear a Roman army to Carthage or Spain with great despatch. On arrival in Italy, despite telling his men that the Gallic tribes in the north would flock to his banner, Hannibal could not fully put his trust in those tribes: they would side with whoever looked to be victorious. And soon enough he was directly confronted by Rome's highly adept legions, which he had to counter with a depleted, exhausted army, some frostbitten elephants and a straining supply chain stretched over some of the most inhospitable territory in Europe.

He retained, at least, the element of surprise. Rome, hearing that Hannibal had crossed the Alps in fifteen days in mid-November 218 BCE, went into panicked freefall, not least because their army was initially in the wrong place. Roman troops (under the command of the consul Publius Cornelius Scipio) had sailed from Italy earlier in the year to confront Hannibal in Spain – only to find, while en route, that he was already in Gaul. The Scipios were a well-known aristocratic family in Rome who had served the republic with distinction. (In time the family's patronage of Polybius would result in their highly favourable presentation within his famous history.) Now Scipio returned as quickly as he could to Italy, to make ready for the Carthaginian arrival in the Po valley. Hearing of Hannibal's descent from the mountains, Scipio marched to oppose his advance at the River Ticinus (just south of modern-day Milan).

Hannibal was known for his stirring speeches, but now he tried a different tactic. He took two Gaulish prisoners, who had attempted to oppose his plans for passage through the Alps, and forced them to fight one another to the death in front of his men, with the promise that the winner could go home free. Hannibal was demonstrating to his troops the nature of the fight they were about to engage in: death or victory were the only options, nothing in between. 'For either you must conquer, or die, or fall alive into the hands of your foes,' Hannibal cried out, 'and what awaits those who are vanquished and consent to flee or preserve their lives by any other means is to have every evil and every misfortune for their lot.'[11]

In the battle that followed, it was said that the two sides were so eager for the fight that Rome's javelin-throwers, who normally let loose storms of javelins on the enemy as their troops marched towards them, hadn't the time to throw a single volley before the two sides were enmeshed with one another. Scipio, as keen as his men, in so far as he wished to prove himself worthy of the consulship and his military command, was wounded, his life being saved by his seventeen-year-old son who led a heroic charge to rescue him from the battlefield. This boy, also called Publius Cornelius Scipio, was in due course to be Hannibal's nemesis.

Hannibal's victory at the Battle of Ticinus not only struck terror into Roman hearts, but also caused local Gauls to flock in their thousands to his banner, however little he trusted them. It is said that during the winter of 218 BCE Hannibal was so fearful of assassination by Gauls pretending to defect to him that he took to wearing a variety of wigs to disguise his identity.[12]

The elder Publius Cornelius Scipio, meanwhile, retreated a little further south to the River Trebbia. An honourable man, in defeat he now handed over command of the Roman army to his co-consul, who might have better luck. But with it he offered wise advice. Scipio saw how Hannibal, despite his success, was precariously balanced: the Romans had already begun to attack his over-extended supply line by sending troops to Spain to open up a new front in Hannibal's heartland. If the Romans held off from engaging him, then in Scipio's view Hannibal would soon have to order his men to pillage for food from amongst their new Gaulish allies, who would turn on the Carthaginians – thereby leaving Rome to simply mop up the remains. Such was Scipio's theory, but Polybius records that his co-consul, Tiberius Sempronius Longus, desired an outright victory and the glory that came with it.

On 21 December 218 BCE the two sides met at Trebbia with roughly equal forces. Hannibal's troops prepared by eating a hearty meal and rubbing themselves all over in olive oil, to keep out the biting cold. As the confrontation began, Hannibal displayed his trademark cunning: he stung the Romans with enough lightning attacks on their encampment to lure their glory-hunting consul Tiberius and his whole army to cross the ice-cold and chest-high swollen river towards his encamped position – and this before they had even breakfasted. Thus the Romans – hungry, frozen, exhausted and numb from the water – lined up in battle formation in heavy snow, to face not only Hannibal's rested, breakfasted and oiled troops, but also his elephants, now fully acclimatised to the cold after their Alpine crossing. In the battle that ensued, Hannibal's elephants caused enough disorientation and panic in the frozen opposition ranks for his cavalry and crack infantry to destroy a large portion of the Roman army.[13] But the younger Scipio, who survived the reversal, no doubt took note both of Hannibal's strategy and of his superior's blunders.

Hannibal's tactics had once again won out, but that winter took its toll. Many more of his men died, weakened by the mountainous crossing and now, once again, by the cold and wet. His horses contracted mange, and all but one of his elephants succumbed to disease. In early spring 217 BCE, as Hannibal rode his sole surviving elephant – known as 'Surus', or 'the Syrian' – through the Italian peninsula, the beast's broken tusk seemed a sign of the fundamental weakness of Hannibal's position. Luck seemed to have deserted him, too: amid the filthy conditions of the marshlands through which his army moved, he contracted ophthalmia and lost the sight in one eye.

Yet still Rome did not heed the older Scipio's advice to wait for Hannibal to exhaust himself. The new consuls for 217 BCE were equally keen to succeed where others had failed, and to write their names in the history of the republic. This was – ultimately – one of the chinks in Rome's armour. Polybius argued that the Roman system was set up to create men who were ready to endure anything in order to gain a reputation for valour.[14] That may have been true, but it also meant they were overly willing to risk anything. In addition, the limit on the term of this top position in the republican system of Roman government – while intended to ensure that no one individual could achieve tyrannical or monarchical power in Rome again – also meant that office-holders had only a short window in which to demonstrate valour, which inclined the incumbents to hasty actions rather than patient tactical responses, often to the republic's disadvantage. Such impetuosity amongst the Roman high command certainly helped Hannibal's campaign.

On 21 June 217 BCE consul Caius Flaminius chased after Hannibal's army, fearing it was making a push for Rome. Without any forward scouting parties, Flaminius's men marched straight into a landscape that Livy later labelled as 'born for an ambush'.[15] At Lake Trasimene (in modern-day Umbria in central Italy) the entire column entered a narrow space between the hills and the shoreline. In the mist coming off the lake, the Romans could hardly see Hannibal's troops bearing down on them, let alone their own ranks and standards. Within three hours, in a world of mistaken shadows and muffled cries, 15,000 Romans were butchered, many of them while standing up to their necks in the water of the lake, pleading for mercy.[16] When the sun finally burnt off the early-morning fog, it became clear that Flaminius himself – a consul of Rome – had been killed in the battle by a Gaulish spear.

This was the report carried 1,300 kilometres to Philip V of Macedon as he observed the Nemean Games – news that encouraged Philip to abandon his own war in Greece and seek an alliance with Hannibal, who surely seemed poised to conquer the mighty Romans. Philip may well have heard that the Senate of Rome remained in session from dawn until sunset for several days – unprecedented in Roman history – desperately debating its response to the calamity at Lake Trasimene. He may also have heard that Hannibal's troops were now staggering under the weight of the plunder they had taken, as they marched unopposed eastwards towards the Adriatic coast and southwards down through Italy towards its heel.

As early negotiations commenced in 216, Philip would certainly have heard tell of Hannibal's next – and greatest – victory over the Romans, at Cannae in south-eastern Italy. On 2 August 216 BCE Rome put into the field 80,000 infantry troops, the largest force in the history of Rome – half of whom had been drafted into the military that year and were untested in battle. Facing them were Hannibal's forces, buoyed up by their previous victories and many now clad in the pillaged garments of the Roman legionaries they had struck down at Trebbia and Trasimene. Hannibal, dressed just like his soldiers, was conspicuous only up close on account of his one sightless, expressionless eye. On that day Rome outnumbered Carthage by two-to-one; and yet Cannae became the worst defeat ever sustained by the armies of Rome in their history. Indeed they suffered, it has been argued, more casualties in a single day than any other Western army before or since.[17]

The reason was twofold. First, Hannibal, it is said, picked the day for the battle based on his knowledge of the alternating command of the Roman consuls on location with the army, in order that he might face the more ambitious – and thus rash – consul-commander. Second, against this unthinking eagerness for battle, Hannibal deployed his uncanny ability to place his troops in the position most appropriate to their particular fighting skill and, at the same time, keep sufficient control of them all so as to engage the Romans with a battle line that changed shape, even as it advanced to encircle and crush the enemy, like a spider incarcerating a fly in its web. Once more the young Scipio, in the Roman ranks that day, had to watch as more than half of his comrades-in-arms were killed, including another of Rome's consul generals, Lucius Aemilius Paullus, and more than half of its military high command: one proconsul, two quaestors, twenty-nine military tribunes, eighty senators and a number of ex-consuls, praetors and aediles. Injured Roman soldiers were said to have buried their heads in the mud to choke themselves to death, so ashamed were they at their fate.[18] Hannibal allowed burial only for Rome's consul, Paullus: the rest were left to rot in the summer heat where they had fallen.

The last words of Paullus, as he sat in pools of his own blood, were for his fellow leaders: 'Go tell the Senators to fortify the city of Rome and garrison it strongly before the victorious enemy draws near!'[19]

Hannibal was advised by his own lieutenants that he could dine on the Capitol in Rome within five days of victory at Cannae, if he pressed his advantage. In Rome the desperation was palpable, the rumours rife: many times the cry went up that Hannibal was at the gates of the city. After hearing the pleas of its dying consul, Rome despatched Quintus Fabius Pictor (later the noted historian) to Delphi to seek the advice of the oracle. But back at home, more desperate and gruesome measures were taken in the hope of capturing the goodwill of the gods: a Gallic man and woman and a Greek man and woman were buried alive, in dual sacrifice.

Polybius specifically sites his discussion of Rome's political constitution at the moment when it suffered its greatest defeat at Cannae. For it was in Rome's response that Polybius located the peculiar unbending will and character of the Roman system and its people, which would ultimately ensure its success. For all the panic that swept the city, Polybius argues that the system did its work – the threat of extinction forcing the republic's constituent parts (consuls, Senate and assemblies) to work seamlessly together.[20] Moreover, Rome's political and military system, founded on legendary tales of heroic defence, and sustained by the promise of high honours for such courage, ensured that its will to survive only hardened in the face of defeat.[21] Hannibal is said to have offered to ransom the Roman soldiers he took prisoner after Cannae. The Roman Senate, despite the pitiful position in which Rome found itself, refused. This, for Polybius, was the ultimate example of the granite will that Rome's system had created, and which would, ultimately, guide it to mastery of the Mediterranean.[22]

The Second Punic War, then, was far from settled. Hannibal was handicapped by his inability to rely on the long-term support of the Gauls who now made up the majority of his army. He was also undermined by Carthage's political system, which, despite his victories, could still be swayed at any moment by Hanno the Great, Hamilcar's old rival. Hannibal was evidently anxious to keep Carthaginian goodwill: in the aftermath of Cannae, while offering to sell his Roman prisoners back to Rome, he ordered the bodies of the dead Roman high command to be stripped of all their gold rings, which he then sent back to Carthage to be poured out before the Senate: a gleaming spectacle representing gory conquest. It worked: the Carthaginian Senate immediately voted to send Hannibal extra men and elephants (though most died of plague soon after their arrival in Sicily).

In truth, Hannibal may have been unwilling to risk an assault on Rome itself. He had, after all, turned away from attacking the capital after Lake Trasimene, detouring instead to southern Italy, after which his troops had to deal with the continual harrying of Romans, like flies bothering a wildebeest.[23] After Rome's refusal to buy back its prisoners taken at Cannae, Hannibal sent ambassadors to discuss peace terms, which the Romans, in what was later termed an act of stoic courage, also refused. Hannibal may simply have wanted to force them to the negotiating table in order to redress the balance of power in the Mediterranean – to curb their ambition and reassert Carthaginian influence. But he was facing an enemy even more dogged and determined under pressure than he was, able to fight on in the face of crushing losses for some time to come.

And now the seeming perpetuity of Hannibal's campaign in Italy started to drain his army's powers. In order to continue their campaign they needed new lands upon which to feast, just as much as they required crushing, ego-boosting victories against the Romans. After Cannae, Hannibal's men – even Hannibal himself – spent the winter engaging in 'Campanian-style luxury, wine-bibbing, whoring and all manner of dissipation'.[24] When they were forced back into their ranks in 215 BCE, Hannibal suffered his first real defeat in Italy when he was unable to take the town of Cumae, a failure Livy would attribute to the dissipation that preceded it. Defeat dented morale and prompted defections to Rome.

To make matters worse, the elder Scipio's policy of initiating war in Spain had begun to pay dividends: Hannibal had to divert some of his attentions and manpower back to these lands, where Roman victories further encouraged some Spanish towns and local kings to switch their allegiance to the republic. And while Hannibal had secured an ally in Philip of Macedon, against whom the Romans also now had to wage war, his other attempts at joining forces had not proved successful. He had begun negotiations with Hieronymous, the fifteen-year-old ruler of Syracuse in Sicily, only to see Hieronymous murdered by an anti-Carthaginian faction; followed by a Roman naval blockade of Syracuse that lasted two years, through which the city was only able to last out thanks to the genius of one of its residents, Archimedes – known to posterity as the man who leapt from his bath crying 'Eureka!', having determined how to measure the density of an object. In the teeth of the Roman siege, Archimedes devised all manner of defensive machines to help his city, including 'the claw' – a massive mechanical arm that could be dropped down onto ships to haul them out of the water – and the 'ray' – a system of fires and mirrors that created a laser-like beam of light capable of setting Roman ships on fire.

Such was the context of Philip's and Hannibal's watered-down alliance in the summer of 215. For the rest of the decade Rome and Hannibal were locked in a war of attrition, with both sides claiming victories and suffering defeats on two fronts: in Italy and in Spain. But this war had broader implications for other rulers around the Mediterranean. And for rulers further afield, such as Antiochus III, it bought them breathing space for their own business, free of expansive Roman ambitions. Closer to the centre of the Mediterranean, the Second Punic War had cost the young ruler of Syracuse in Sicily his life and led to a damaging blockade of his town. But arguably no one was buffeted more by this conflict than Philip V of Macedon. Panicking a second time at the arrival of the Roman navy off the Illyrian coast, he was so terrified that he burnt all his ships and retreated overland back into Macedon.

Philip's woes were not simply due to his own failed sallies against the Romans. Rome had been doing some allying of its own, to connect up the Mediterranean world and ensure that Philip's focus was not on them alone. To keep Philip busy and out of their hair, they had encouraged his enemies: the Aetolian League in Greece, and even King Attalus of Pergamon across the Aegean Sea, the man who had taken his kingdom to independence from the Seleucid Empire and who was now keen to expand his own influence. The result – so Livy and Polybius tell us – was a Philip increasingly humiliated, so irascible and uncontrolled as to be unrecognisable to his fellow Greeks. In July 209 BCE he was at the height of his woes: Attalus arrived with his forces on the island of Aegina off the coast of Athens; the Romans were stationed in central-western Greece, poised to trap Philip's army in a pincer movement; and a Carthaginian relief fleet had failed to reach Macedon.

Philip was at the sharp end of a connected Mediterranean turned against him and bearing down on him. While attending the Nemean Games he lost himself in wine and stumbled drunkenly around the sanctuary, amongst the crowds of Greeks gathering to celebrate in honour of Zeus, pretending to be an ordinary citizen dressed in pauper's clothes without his crown, but acting like an emperor. He demanded and took everything he desired, insisting on having sex with any woman who took his fancy – be she a prostitute, married, unmarried or widowed – and berating any man whose wife or mother would not succumb.[25] Forced to take to the battlefield against the Romans in the midst of his revels, Philip was thrown so hard against a tree that his helmet split in two, after which he returned to his debauchery.

It was at around this time that the Romans made a momentous decision. In 210 BCE they elected a new commander in Spain who, at the age of twenty-five, was chosen without previously having held the traditional senior public offices – an achievement unprecedented in the annals of Roman history. The man so elevated was the younger Publius Cornelius Scipio, whose exploits in battle had scarcely left time for him to complete the traditional *cursus honorum* of Roman politics. But he had seen at close quarters Hannibal's tactics, and had noted the terrible consequences of underestimating the Carthaginian general in battle or seeking an improvidently quick victory in the name of personal valour. Scipio now burnt with the same energy and determination as Hannibal: they would be well-matched opponents in the final reckoning between Carthage and Rome.

Unifying Worlds under a Single Leader in Asia and China

As Hannibal and Rome sat in stalemate and Philip succumbed to alcoholic gloom, 8,000 kilometres to the east Qin Shi Huangdi revelled in his accomplishments. Since defeating the last opposing warring state and opening a new era by the unification of China under his rule, he had ruthlessly pursued his goal of knitting together even more tightly the states now governed by the Qin, and had achieved a success of which Rome could still only dream.

Qin Shi Huangdi had ordered the melting down of all weapons held in conquered territories and the demolition of rival capital cities; and he had organised the population into groups for mutual surveillance, ensuring that everyone kept each other in check. At the same time he had physically drawn together the vast expanse of Qin territory with a new system of roads covering 4,250 miles – all radiating out from the triumphant Qin capital at Xianyang – and had introduced a policy of empire-wide standardisation in everything from weights to currency and language. It is estimated that in the years after 221 BCE one-tenth of the population of China was working as forced labour for the state.

Behind it all stood the unbending philosophy of Legalism – law and order underwritten by heavy punishment to ensure the authority of the state. In an example of the obliteration of diversity used to vilify the First Emperor by the later Han dynasty (and thus of dubious actuality), the emperor was said in 213 BCE to have banned anyone other than academics from owning philosophical texts of all other branches of political and social thought that had been spawned during the era of the 'One Hundred Schools of Thought'. All books surrendered were burnt. 'Anyone who uses antiquity to criticise the present', the decree supposedly ran, 'shall be executed along with his family.' And 470 scholars who disapproved of the emperor's methods were said to have been killed, some reputedly buried alive.[26] Among the texts being burnt were those of Confucius and his disciples. As such, the very survival of the Confucian system was later claimed to have hung in the balance, dependent on how thoroughly the emperor's agents prosecuted their campaign of confiscation and incineration.

The emperor now imposed a body of imperial statutes to guide local officials in every kind of law-and-order issue, and it regularly handed out punishments such as death, castration and hard labour. But his reconfiguration went beyond simple laws. In the first great history of China – the *Shiji*, written in the late second century BCE – its author,

Sima Qian, recounts how the emperor summed up his own efforts in his official publications:

> The First Emperor has created a new beginning, he has put in order the laws, standards, and principles ... All under Heaven [*tianxia*] is unified in heart and yielding in will. Implements have a single measure, and graphs are written in the same way ... He has rectified and given order to the different customs ...[27]

In other words, the emperor had declared previous conceptions of the mandate of Heaven to be outmoded: now the ruler, sage and mandate of Heaven were one and the same, and there was no need for a wise man such as Confucius to advise the ruler in this new world, since the ruler embodied everything the world needed. In spite of his proclaimed godliness, though, the emperor persisted in well-founded fears for his life: he was attacked at least once by bandits within his own borders, and was said to prefer, as a precaution, to rule from the shadows.

Rather like Hannibal, the First Emperor is a hard character to unravel – not least since many later historical sources purposefully portray him as an evil and arrogant man, an unworthy ruler in comparison to later dynasties. It was said, for example, that he was born illegitimately to a concubine, and that he later commandeered the first-person pronoun (the equivalent of 'I') for his exclusive use. What is without doubt, however, is that he was a tough and ambitious ruler, intent not only on consolidating and maximising his huge territorial gains, but also on defending them without compromise from the nomadic tribes to the north and north-west.

What better way to do so than by defining the boundaries of the Qin Empire with a wall? Building walls at borders had long been a favoured Chinese tactic. In 450 BCE the north-eastern state of Qi had built a barricade along its border with the nomadic groups to the north. From 300 BCE the business of defending the northern boundary of the warring states had been taken even more seriously, with the creation of a bank of earth that rose along the edges of the kingdoms of Qin, Wei and Yen. Soon after 221 BCE Qin Shi Huangdi sent one of his most trusted generals and hundreds of thousands of workers along the 'Straight Road' (now radiating out from Xianyang for 600 miles towards Inner Mongolia), their mission to build a wall of more than 500 miles along the limits of the new Qin Empire.

Connecting to older fortifications built by smaller states, the Qin now had a defensive line of around 3,000 miles stretching from Liaodung on the coast (near modern-day Korea) westwards to the northern bend of the Yellow River and on to Lintao, closing off the northern and north-western border of the empire from attack. The high walls of pounded earth stopped the swift, stinging attacks of nomadic horsemen, gave a greater sense of unity and community to the new Qin Empire, and heightened the perceptions of the First Emperor of Qin as a man who could achieve the impossible. It was a feat the impact of which still defines China today – most of the Great Wall of China that is still visible to us dates from the fourteenth to seventeenth centuries, built during the later Ming dynasty, but it is constructed along roughly the same route as that established by the First Qin Emperor.

The great wall came at a huge cost, and not merely financial. It consumed innumerable lives in its construction, but the dead bodies of exhausted workers were simply compacted into the stone and earth as cement. In one heart-breaking story that has become one of China's great folk tales, the wife of a worker at the wall came to search for his body after he died, only to find that it had been employed in the wall as cement. Her weeping, it was said, moved the wall so that part of it collapsed, exposing hundreds of bodies, from which she was able to retract her husband's. Having buried him with honour, she drowned herself.

The work of unification and reinforcement under his rule did not, however, mean that Qin Shi Huangdi set aside his plans for expansion. Facing the Qin – on the other side of the wall – were three main nomadic tribes, identified in Chinese sources as the Yuezhi, the Xiongnu and Donghu. The construction of the wall had perturbed these groups, encouraging them to adapt their loose nomadic lifestyle towards a more organised militancy. Now, as the Qin armies poured into the nomadic pasturelands of what is today Inner Mongolia, they displaced the Xiongnu further northwards, causing more consternation within the wider region. The Xiongnu, though, were the weakest of the three tribes – treated with contempt by the Donghu and forced to send a regular hostage to the court of the Yuezhi, a tribe about 400,000 strong.

Around 215 BCE the Xiongnu ruler, Touman, decided to send his son, Maodun, as hostage, after which he promptly attacked the Yuezhi. The second-century BCE historian Sima Qian tells us that Maodun correctly recognised this as a ploy by his father to have him killed by the Yuezhi, since he favoured his other son to succeed him as ruler. Touman's plans were thwarted when Maodun managed a daring escape back to his home tribe on a fast horse. Recognising his son's bravery, Touman gave Maodun command of a cavalry of 10,000.

With these troops under him, Maodun set about creating an elite force. Like the soldiers of Qin Shi Huangdi, they were trained to absolute obedience – to shoot their arrows wherever Maodun directed them with one of his own. In their ultimate test (and Maodun's great act of revenge against his father), Maodun first shot at his favourite horse: the horse was killed in a hail of arrows. Next he shot at his favourite wife: the wife was riddled with arrowheads. Then he shot at his father's favourite horse: no hesitation, the horse was speared 10,000 times. Finally, Maodun took aim at his father – and the last sight the old man saw was a flock of pointed arrowheads falling upon him with lethal speed, blotting out the sky as he was enveloped.

Maodun took full command of the Xiongnu around 209 BCE, executing his stepmother, younger brother and anyone else who would not bend the knee. Over the next seven years he transformed the reputation of his tribe, leading an increasingly militant and highly trained Xiongnu army to victory over their neighbouring Donghu, and even against the Yuezhi. The result was the beginning of the great forced migration of the Yuezhi westwards, out of the path of the Xiongnu, across the vast steppes of central Asia. Within sixty years the Yuezhi would be displaced in their entirety, forced to travel more than 2,500 kilometres west, washing up in the kingdom of Bactria in central Asia, with predictably transformative consequences.

Having set his immediate rivals on the run, the fearsome Maodun had turned his attention back to the Qin Empire. What he saw was a kingdom in the midst of a difficult and painful rebirth. On 10 September 210 BCE – in the same year the young Scipio was elevated to command of Rome's armies against Hannibal in Carthage – Qin Shi Huangdi had died while touring his lands. His death, it was said, was due to his ingestion of mercury tablets, ironically prescribed to him by alchemists as he searched for the fabled elixir of life to secure the title of 'The Immortal', on which he had insisted throughout his reign.

Qin Shi Huangdi did at least attain a version of immortality, after his burial-tomb complex was discovered in 1974 by local farmers sinking a new well. Work on this mausoleum began soon after he became the ruler of Qin, and was no doubt vastly expanded once he had declared himself First Emperor. Sima Qian tells us that 700,000 workmen were brought to labour over the lower slopes of Mount Li not far from the Qin capital, chosen by the emperor for its rich seams of jade and elegant landscape. The tomb mound of the emperor – sealed even to this day – is a pyramid shape located deep down in an excavated area about a football pitch in size. Surrounding the emperor is a microcosm of the city from which he ruled: a necropolis providing everything he might need in the afterlife. Reputedly a hundred underground rivers were created from mercury, and the ceiling of the necropolis was decorated with heavenly bodies, looking down on rammed-earth walls and giant gateways protecting offices, halls and stables.

And lined up in rank to guard the emperor were roughly 8,000 soldiers – or, rather, life-size sculptures in terracotta, each individually designed to reflect their different statuses and specialities, and originally painted in an array of colours.[28] In addition to this vast infantry sat ready 130 chariots, 150 cavalry horses and a bevy of officials, acrobats and musicians, alongside a vast cache of armour and weaponry waiting to be deployed. Today the terracotta warriors look on in eternal vigilance, just as they did when they were buried out of sight more than 2,200 years ago. Thrown in amongst the silent watchmen at the time, however – so the ancient sources say – were a number of live subjects: not just the childless wives of the emperor, but also the craftsmen who had created the tomb and its warriors, so that they might never let slip the secrets of the emperor's resting place – the cruellest imaginable repayment for all their fastidious labours.

The First Emperor of Qin got the burial honours he sought, but despite the work that had gone into his young empire, it was swiftly torn apart after his demise. The initial problem was one of distance. The emperor died at a location that was fully two months by road from his capital – sufficient time, following the announcement of his death, for potential rebellions to take root and even for challenges to the Qin capital, before the emperor's close circle of officials could return. His entourage tried to cover up his death for as long as they could, employing piles of rotting fish to mask the growing stench of the decaying corpse on the long journey home.

A second and more pressing problem was who should succeed Qin Shi Huangdi. He had more than one son, and each was supported for the throne by several of his most trusted officials. Over the following months one of the emperor's eunuchs, Zhao Gao, and his prime minister, Li Si, forced General Meng Tian – who had been responsible for overseeing the Qin Great Wall and combating the nomadic tribes in the north – to commit suicide, along with members of his family and one of the emperor's sons, whom Meng had supported to become emperor. Li Si and Zhao Gao subsequently installed the emperor's younger son (aged twenty-one) on the throne, but the collaborators were soon at odds. Zhao Gao executed Li Si and stepped in to rule, dominating the young emperor.

The biggest problem, however, was not this particular wrestling for power within the Qin court, but, more broadly, powerful individuals from across the Qin Empire using the window of disarray to fragment this lately unified world and restore the former authority of their respective states. And in amongst those jostling to reassert regional loyalties were men who simply saw an opportunity to improve their lot in life, with some unlikely alliances forming as a result. Zhao Gao and his puppet emperor soon found themselves opposed by a duke – Xiang Yu – and a low-born Qin official called Liu Bang. Liu, having failed to lead a group of forced labourers to work on the terracotta-warrior tomb, had deserted the emperor's service and, in the aftermath of Qin Shi Huangdi's death, joined forces with Xiang Yu. Soon enough Xiang Yu and Liu Bang were competing with one another to be the first to take the capital, Xianyang.

Zhao Gao's response was to kill the newly enthroned emperor and install another. But the second candidate, wise enough to suspect Gao might reprise the trick, had Gao himself murdered and then, keen to save his own skin, willingly handed over the capital to the first rebel to arrive with sufficient forces – which was Liu Bang. By 207 BCE, just three years after the death of the First Emperor of Qin, the Qin Empire was dead with him. So, too, were the safety and security that the Qin Empire had provided with its strong and stout borders: the Xiongnu had, unsurprisingly, been watching the collapse of the Qin with intense interest and now seized the day to recapture much of the land they had lost between 221 and 210 BCE, spilling over the rammed-earth walls, left unmanned and uncared for because all attention was on the dynastic succession unfolding in Xianyang.[29]

More was to unfold. Liu Bang could not hold on to the capital for long: he was forced to yield it to Xiang Yu, who promptly killed the retired Qin emperor, divided up the empire into nineteen kingdoms, with himself as overlord, and settled the Kingdom of Han on Liu Bang as his consolation prize. Liu Bang was unwilling to settle for such spoils and by 202 BCE he had pursued and defeated Xiang Yu. So began the second unifying dynasty in Chinese history: that of the Han, who would rule China, with only one brief interruption, for more than 400 years.

*

If Liu Bang – formerly a low-born official, deserter and renegade war leader – was looking for an exemplary sole ruler in his own time, then he could have done worse than to contemplate the first years of Antiochus III of the Seleucid Empire.

And yet Antiochus's reign had started out with so little to recommend it. Thrust into the kingship of the enormous, cumbersome and crumbling empire after the murder of his elder brother by his own troops, just months into his reign, Antiochus III had a long list of crises to deal with and very little experience to bring to the task. The first crisis was the question of who might rule after him if he died, or – as seemed more likely – was murdered. Barely twenty, Antiochus had understandably not yet turned his thoughts to children and heirs. But now, his court advisers preached, there was little else that mattered. Quickly he married his first cousin, the daughter of King Mithridates II of Pontus from up near the Black Sea, and in 220 BCE their first child was born – the first of eight, as it would come to pass.

With his heir apparent in place, Antiochus still had a menu of crises from which to pick. His empire – at least in name – stretched from the eastern Mediterranean coast to central Asia, and presented him with gathering clouds of war to his west and ongoing turmoil and dynastic upheaval to his east. On the west, in Egypt, another new young ruler, Ptolemy IV, was keen to prove his mettle and improve on recent gains made at Seleucid expense – Egypt having previously annexed not only the disputed territory of Coele-Syria along the Levant, but also land further north up to Antioch. But Antiochus was also taxed by a pressing rebellion in the east, one that had sparked in the vacuum of power made by the swift successive deaths of Seleucus II and Seleucus III, followed by Antiochus's relative neglect while he was preoccupied with securing his family line. This revolt in the east was led by the provincial governor of Persis, a man named Molon, who was quickly joined by his brother Alexander, *satrap* of nearby Media.

East or west? Where should Antiochus move first? He chose to divide his resources and act on two fronts: he set off to lead the campaign against Egypt while his generals were despatched east. However, a lack of preparation and training amongst the rank and file led to panic, and the generals refused to engage Molon and Alexander in battle. The brothers, recognising their opportunity, moved to expand their area of control south into Babylonia and Mesopotamia, the cultural and agricultural heartland of the Seleucid Empire.

Antiochus was faring little better in the west when he received the news of his generals' failure. Faced with the prospect of further losses on both fronts, he decided to halt his own campaign before it had really even begun: he would leave Egypt and concentrate all of his resources on defeating the pretenders to the east. The problem now, however, was money. Molon and Alexander had occupied some of the richest parts of the kingdom, denying Antiochus vital resources to pay his troops, who were now threatening mutiny. Thus the King of the Seleucid Empire was forced to borrow money from one of his advisers, in return for which he had to promise his creditor an ongoing official position of influence at the heart of government.

With his army just about secured, and lessons learnt about which of his generals he could trust, Antiochus finally began the march eastwards to face Molon and Alexander in Apollonia. There, with as much royal pomp as he could muster, he drew up his troops. And it seems that the left wing of Molon's army, faced with the sight of the Seleucid king and the forces at his disposal, simply lost their nerve and deserted en masse. Antiochus, seizing the initiative, was able to overcome the remaining combatants with relative ease. Showing incredible foresight, he treated these rebels leniently, allowing them back into his own ranks – since, after all, he had need of every able-bodied man. As for Molon, he had committed suicide at the end of the battle, but Antiochus, far from satisfied, had his corpse crucified.

With that much achieved, Antiochus may have been minded to turn his attentions back to Egypt. Almost immediately, however, he was beset by a second rebellion, and by his own cousin – a man called Achaeus, who had marched with Antiochus's brother, Seleucus III, on the fateful journey north to confront King Attalus of Pergamon, during which Seleucus had been murdered. But by all accounts Achaeus had not been involved in the murder, and thereafter acted honourably to avenge the new king's death. Antiochus in return had made Achaeus a governor of much of Asia Minor. Now, though, complex court politics had converted a loyal follower into a rebel. Surrounding Antiochus was a thunderstorm of claim and counterclaim from different factions as to who was loyal to him and who was not – not least because he had taken to killing anyone he felt was disloyal, or else too powerful.

Achaeus, considering himself falsely accused of treason, but all too aware of the fate Antiochus reserved for traitors, decided to strike first. Mustering his army, he attempted to march straight into Syria and take over the Seleucid court, but his troops refused to countenance attacking the sovereign and so Achaeus had to be content with promoting himself to King of Asia Minor.

Antiochus – boldly, in light of his many travails – decided to ignore Achaeus's escapades, gambling that a victory against Egypt would solidify his position sufficiently for smouldering rebellions to peter out of their own accord. With the resources of Babylonia and Mesopotamia once again at his disposal, he turned to take on the young Ptolemy IV of Egypt. In 219 BCE these two young men clashed over the land of Coele-Syria in what was the fourth Egyptian–Seleucid contest of this kind in history.

As Hannibal and his men began their long march more than 3,500 kilometres to the west, Antiochus was making slow but steady progress along the coast of the Levant, taking back cities held by the Egyptians ever since the failures of his father. Like the hands of a clock, these two leaders were advancing around opposite sides of a Mediterranean clock-face. By 218 BCE, as Hannibal crossed the Alps, important cities such as Antioch and Seleucia were back in Antiochus's hands, as well as the well-defended city of Tyre at the south-eastern corner of the Mediterranean Sea, the original homeland of the Carthaginians, famous for producing a unique and sought-after purple dye squeezed from the glands of thousands of murex sea snails that are native to the region. By early 217 BCE, as Hannibal was enjoying success on the battlefields of Italy, Antiochus was even commanding territory south of the River Jordan. Ptolemy IV, however, was not entirely defeated. He had spent the previous two years, while Antiochus painfully reconquered his lands, building and training a fresh army, which he now released into the field.

On 22 June 217 BCE, the forces of Antiochus III drew up against those of Ptolemy IV on the open dusty ground at Raphia (present-day Rafah in the Gaza Strip). This was to be a clash of epic proportions, not unlike that of Hannibal against the Romans at Cannae the following year. In the days running up to the confrontation, both sides had engaged in minor skirmishes. Antiochus had even sent a defector from Ptolemy's camp silently back in, under cover of night, in an effort to assassinate the Egyptian king. The assassin made it all the way into Ptolemy's official quarters – only to find that the king had taken the wise precaution of sleeping in another tent.

Unimpressed by Antiochus's tactics, Ptolemy now drew his troops up for battle. Though they were about the same age, Antiochus had aged beyond his years, having already, in the first six years of his reign, defeated several rebellions and captured many cities while traversing thousands of kilometres from west to east and back again. For Ptolemy, on the other hand, this was the first big military test of his rule. He had the better-trained and bigger army: Polybius estimates his numbers at 75,000, Antiochus's at 68,000. But this was also a battle of animal might: Antiochus had 102 large Indian elephants against Ptolemy's seventy-three African bush elephants (smaller, more aggressive, but less obliging). Antiochus's elephants were clad in armour and carried on their backs a wicker cageload of troops armed with javelins and spears. Goaded into action by a trained 'elephant corps', these lolloping pachyderms gradually picked up momentum, their movements becoming more regular, the terrifying thud of their huge weight as it hit the ground making a vibrating beat that struck fear into their opposition. As the elephants neared the enemy lines, their speed making them an unstoppable force, their huge size blotted out the sun as the noise of their approach filled the ears and obscured the strangled cries of those they trampled underfoot.

At Raphia it was not only Ptolemy's troops who were scared of Antiochus's elephants. Ptolemy's own African elephants – panicked by the strange smell and intimidating size of their Indian counterparts – were said to have turned and fled. In the titanic confrontation of troops that followed, Antiochus attempted a daring move beloved of Alexander the Great: heroically leading the charge himself. Yet by the time Antiochus could get back to assess the overall strategy and take command, Ptolemy's troops had already scattered Antiochus's army, most of whom had fled into the walled city of Raphia where Antiochus was, humiliatingly, forced to join them.

Ptolemy's victory was celebrated with a monument that survives today, first erected by Egyptian priests in 217 BCE. The text is crowned by an image of heroic Ptolemy on a rearing steed, watched by his queen, poised to throw a javelin into the enemy. The text proudly proclaims Ptolemy's achievements in Greek and in Egyptian demotic and hieroglyphs (the two forms of scripts the Egyptians used for document writing):

He conquered [Antiochus] in great and noble fashion. Those of his enemies who were able to come near him in the battle, he stretched out dead before him . . . He compelled Antiochus to fling away his

diadem and his royal hat. Antiochus fled with his escort . . . in pitiful and sorry fashion after his defeat. The most part of his troops
endured grievous distress . . . They suffered hunger and thirst. All
that he left behind was taken for spoil . . . Then the king took as
prey much people and all the elephants. He took possession of very
much gold and silver and other precious things, which were found
in the several places, which Antiochus had held, brought thither
under his dominion. He caused them all to be conveyed to Egypt.[30]

The reward for Ptolemy was the official religious sanction of the
Egyptian priesthood and his recognition as a true Pharaoh of Egypt.
This young ruler had achieved what all the young leaders across the
Mediterranean sought: the respect of their communities and the loyalty
of their people. Antiochus, on the other hand, is said by Polybius to have
blamed his failure on the cowardice of his troops, and later made a peace
settlement with Ptolemy for division of the disputed territories.[31]

A reverse, then, for Antiochus. However, he now made it his prior-
ity to deal with his rebellious cousin, Achaeus. For the next three years,
while Hannibal was rampaging through Italy and negotiating with
Philip, Antiochus relentlessly pursued Achaeus. Finally, come 214–13
BCE, he had him besieged in the city of Sardis, not far from modern-
day Izmir in Turkey. Achaeus was tricked into an escape attempt,
thinking he was to be carried to safety, only to find himself promptly
escorted to Antiochus. Having sacked and destroyed Sardis, murdering
every person found within it, Antiochus turned to his cousin. Perhaps
it was the pent-up fury of having had to chase him for so long; perhaps
he was frustrated by the victory denied to him by Ptolemy in Egypt; or
perhaps, like Qin Shi Huangdi, Antiochus was learning that violence
and discipline were indispensable tools in leading a patchwork empire.
Whatever his motives, Antiochus visited a terrible punishment upon
Achaeus: his genitals were cut off whilst he was still alive; he was
decapitated; and, in the ultimate insult, his head was sewn onto the
skin of a donkey. Compounding the disgrace, the butchered remains of
Achaeus's body were crucified.

Antiochus III, then, had certainly put down a marker of his authority. Despite his failure to secure an outright victory against Egypt, he

was now the secure, undisputed and unrivalled leader of his empire, facing no major rebellion, and with access to the full might of the resources of his kingdom.

It was time for him to attempt the most difficult of all his challenges: the re-establishment of Seleucid rule in the east, at the very borders of the Hellenic world. From 212 until 205–4 BCE Antiochus III thus absented himself from Mediterranean affairs. It was a gamble, but arguably a needful one. Rome had tweaked the Seleucid tail back in 229 BCE with its express concerns over the independence of Troy, but was now far too busy fending off Hannibal in Italy and Spain, and keeping Philip of Macedon occupied in Greece, to be of any concern to Antiochus. Indeed, by combining with Attalus of Pergamon to harass Philip, the Romans were even lightening Antiochus's load on his western frontier.

And so, naming his eight-year-old son as his co-king, Antiochus set off eastwards with something between 70,000 and 100,000 men, and enjoyed a stream of rapid victories over the kings of Armenia, Media and even stubborn Parthia. In 208 BCE Antiochus turned to the greatest prize of them all: Bactria. An independent kingdom since 245 BCE, Bactria now teemed with a thousand lucrative cities – a shining jewel in the midst of central Asia. However, it was no longer ruled by Diodotus II, son of the governor who had proclaimed himself king, but by a shadowy figure called Euthydemus. History cannot determine whether Euthydemus hailed from Magnesia in Thessaly or Asia Minor; whether he was a provincial governor or a frontier general before he came to power by *coup d'état*; or even when that coup took place (perhaps around 221 BCE in the wake of the revolt of Molon). But Euthydemus was certainly the antagonist when Antiochus drew up his forces at the River Arius, three days' march from the Bactrian capital of Bactra.

If Antiochus's lead-from-the-front style at Raphia had lost him the battle, here on the Arius it was essential to his victory. Euthydemus, though he enjoyed a reputation for battle-planning, did not appear at the head of his troops, while Antiochus – right in the midst of the action – gained the upper hand. His horse was killed by a spear, and as horse and rider came crashing to the rocky ground, several teeth were knocked from Antiochus's jaw. But Antiochus won the day, for all that his victorious grin must have been a bloody sight to behold.

Antiochus pushed onwards to Bactra and besieged the capital for the next two years, forcing Euthydemus to the negotiating table, though the Bactrian ruler still clung to two beliefs that he considered to be trump cards. The first was that, having seized the throne from a man who was descended from a traitor to Antiochus's father, he ought to be treated not as an enemy, but as an ally. The second was that if Antiochus was to return to the Mediterranean, he would have desperate need of a strong ally on his eastern frontier – just as in the golden era of the Seleucids in the early third century BCE, when Seleucus I governed the west and his son Antiochus I garrisoned the east against nomadic invasion. It was this second argument that carried weight with Antiochus, acutely aware as he was of how stretched his defences were.

And while neither Antiochus III nor Euthydemus could have known it at the time, nomadic incursions into Bactria would only worsen as the Sacas, who roamed the lands immediately abutting the furthest reaches of Hellenic influence, were themselves pressed west by the arrival of nomadic tribes fleeing from earlier Qin (and, shortly, Han) expansion.

Antiochus granted Euthydemus's argument, but had less regard for the man advancing it. In Euthydemus's son Demetrius, however, Antiochus was said to have recognised a future ally. He thereby granted Euthydemus the title of king, on the condition that Bactria supplied food, troops and elephants to Antiochus's army in return. Buoyed by success, Antiochus turned to the communities of Greeks and Indians living in the north-west of India at the foot of the Hindu Kush. There he met a local ruler, a man called Sophagesenus, who had carved out command in the region from the remnants of the Mauryan Empire, and agreed a treaty of friendship with him, for which Antiochus was supplied with more Indian elephants. Thus, as he returned west from seven years away, Antiochus held the largest-known army of elephants in the ancient world. More importantly, he returned having done something no recent Seleucid ruler had managed: to hold undisputed dominion over a vast world that spanned an area from the Mediterranean to central Asia. He had managed to stem the disintegration of his kingdom, unify it under his rule and make himself respected and feared.

By April 205 BCE Antiochus III was back in Babylon. He had survived against the odds, and while in many cases his victories were insubstantial in terms of lands acquired, their propaganda value was huge. In the fabled city where Alexander the Great had died, Antiochus declared himself 'the Great King', in imitation of Alexander and of the Persian kings who had ruled before him. And as Antiochus the Great looked out from Babylon once more towards the Mediterranean, he must have contemplated a new world of opportunity.

In Egypt, Ptolemy IV had suffered a precipitous decline after defeating Antiochus at Raphia. Having fallen into drunkenness, he died leaving a five-year-old successor in his place, surrounded by advisers and courtiers keen to assume the reins of power. In Greece, Rome could no longer persuade the Aetolians to fight a war on its behalf against Philip: the Aetolians had sued for peace and Philip had gladly taken the deal. In Italy, Hannibal, having endured a never-ending seesaw of success and failure against the armies of Rome, now perceived that his enemy had claimed for itself what Carthage had thought was its 'new empire' in Spain. His brother had died in battle and the support he received from Carthage continued to appear ambivalent. And so Hannibal took this moment to inscribe for posterity his journey and achievements on the walls of the temple of Juno Lacinia at Cape Colonna, in the toe of southern Italy. He must have sensed that his opportunity to humble Rome was drawing to a close.

In 205 BCE the chessboard of the ancient world was gazed on by a set of leaders with older, wiser, more war-weary eyes than had beheld it two decades before. Some had more hope for the future than others. Hannibal, now in his forties, had probably seen the writing on the wall, for his efforts to harass Rome to the negotiating table. The Roman general Scipio, who had faced Hannibal repeatedly in battle from the ranks since he was seventeen, was now thirty, invigorated by victories in Spain and ready to confront Hannibal head-on. Philip, in his thirties, was conceivably relieved to be no longer the target of concerted Mediterranean attack from east and west. Antiochus the Great, also in his thirties, was enjoying high fortunes on the crest of his unified realm that connected the Mediterranean to central Asia, and was ready to engage in the splintered warfare and politics of the Mediterranean; meanwhile his old adversary, Egypt – post-Ptolemy IV – looked to be in utter disarray.

In central Asia the cunning older Euthydemus and his young son Demetrius were bedding into their roles as rulers of Bactria and guardians of the Seleucid Empire against the nomads to the east. In China, Liu Bang, head of a new dynasty, ruled over a newly unified Han Empire. And champing at the bit on the north-western borders of this nascent world were the highly trained and lethal forces of the Xiongnu, led by the young, fearless and pitiless Maodun.

They had all, in their different ways, recast the relationships between their respective communities and, in so doing, tied the ancient world closer together, largely by violence. They had spread war simultaneously across multiple theatres, seeking to expand their respective influences and bolster their prospects by alliances. Some had even succeeded in creating huge, unified, stable communities under single rule. And the results of these moves – particularly the seemingly chaotic migrations that had been initiated in the east – would in turn come to connect these worlds even more tightly together. The final act of this crucial era was nigh.

CHAPTER 6

Empires in East and West

I t is said that the early life of Liu Bang was characterised by a disreputable fondness for idleness, drink and women. Following his ascension to power, however – as Gaodi of Han – he became a driven man. Little wonder that later histories tell of how a dragon seemed to hover above him at portentous moments in his childhood, or that his high forehead, nose and sharp whiskers even gave him a dragon-like appearance, as if he were pent up with elemental powers.

Over Gaodi's seven-year rule he faced two main tasks not much different from those put before predecessors such as Qin Shi Huangdi – or, indeed, far-flung rulers such as Antiochus the Great of the Seleucid Empire. How could such a vast expanse of populated territory be both effectively governed and defended at its boundaries? China had long meditated on these topics.

The debate over the ideal system of government was one Confucius and his disciples had wrestled with, albeit as one of the 'One Hundred Schools of Thought' vying for the preferment of those in power. Gaodi had first-hand experience of the delicate balance required to govern more than fifty million subjects: how one had to delegate just enough power to those whose support one required, but not so much power as to sharpen their rivalry and aspirations. He had, after all, exploited just such a situation to rise to his present eminence.

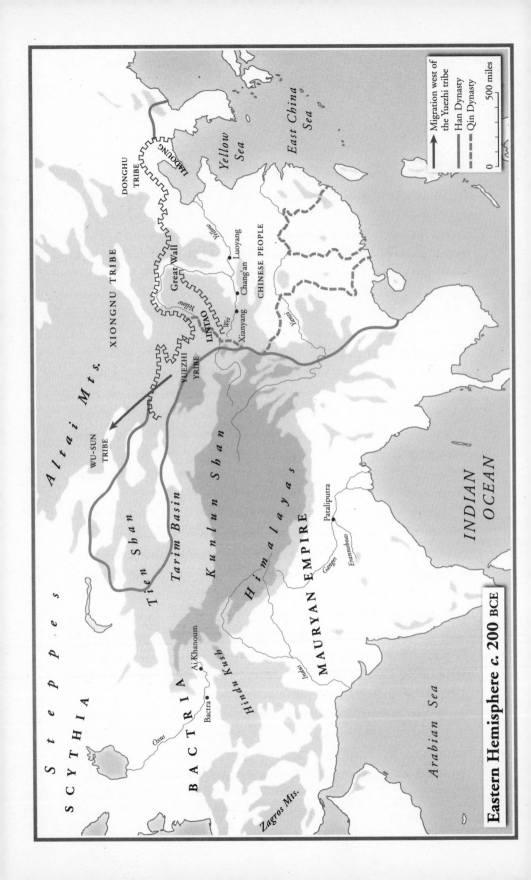

Migration west of
the Yuezhi tribe
Han Dynasty
Qin Dynasty

500 miles

0

Steppes

SCYTHIA

Altai Mts.

XIONGNU TRIBE

DONGHU
TRIBE

LIAODONG

Yellow
Sea

*East China
Sea*

Great Wall

Yellow

Luoyang

Chang'an

CHINESE PEOPLE

Xianyang

Wei

LINTAO

Yellow

Yangzi

YUEZHI
YRIBE

WU-SUN
TRIBE

Tien Shan

Tarim Basin

Kunlun Shan

H i m a l a y a s

MAURYAN EMPIRE

Pataliputra

Erannoboas

Ganges

Indus

*INDIAN
OCEAN*

Ai Khanoum

Hindu Kush

BACTRIA

Bactra

Oxus

Zagros Mts.

*Arabian
Sea*

The second problem had also been part of China's history since the very first defensive wall was constructed in the fifth century BCE. Now, though, it was more pressing than ever, because the nomadic tribes to the north and north-west were led by an equally charismatic, dragon-like character, a man called Maodun.

A comparable dual challenge would, over subsequent decades, come to preoccupy the Roman Republic, too. With Hannibal inscribing a mournful autobiography of his efforts on temple walls in southern Italy, and the young Scipio leading Roman troops, Rome was poised to launch a proactive counter-offensive against Carthage. It was about to push back once more against Philip V of Macedon, to become much more directly involved in Egypt; and, just as Antiochus sought to expand his dominion into the Mediterranean, it was inevitable that Rome would come to clash with the Seleucids as well.

A range of strategies would be tried by these powers to ensure compliance amongst those over whom they had control, and to define the borders of their power. The end result would be the creation of two mega-empires at either end of the ancient world, and instability amongst numerous competing groups in between.

Defending the Boundaries

As Liu Bang, now Gaodi, had been locked in his battle for power within China, Maodun, leader of the Xiongnu, had started to push back against the rival tribes all clustered along the north and north-west frontiers of the new Han dynasty. According to Sima Qian's grand Chinese history, which dedicated an entire section to the story of the Xiongnu, Maodun had a way of dealing with his rivals. The Donghu were said to have demanded of Maodun one of his father's best horses (one of those spared the killing spree that Maodun had ordered of his troops, in order to prove his authority against his own father). And Maodun is said to have given it freely. Then the Donghu demanded his favourite wife. To keep the peace – or perhaps to lure his opposition into a false sense of security – he gave her, too. Then they asked for land. This time Maodun refused, claiming that land – nothing else – was the basis of a nation. He launched a furious attack on the Donghu, killing its leader and turning his head into his own personal drinking goblet.

At the same time Maodun had spearheaded the overrunning of the Qin Empire's protective walls, occupying much of the fertile land in the Yellow River basin. By the time Gaodi had established himself at the head of the Han dynasty in 202 BCE, the Xiongnu were in complete control of this productive region, becoming, as a result, a much more organised, hierarchical and sedentary empire. Though the match was of David-and-Goliath proportions – the Xiongnu were at most a million people, versus the fifty-million-plus population of Han China – it was a battle in which, over the next thirty years, the Xiongnu were to have the upper hand.

In 201–200 BCE Gaodi set off, personally leading his Han army, with the aim of pushing the Xiongnu back out of the rich pastureland. For a man who had risen to power on the back of hard-won military victories, this campaign was an unanticipated disaster from the beginning. As they headed north in winter, roughly one-third of his men suffered frostbite in their fingers, rendering them useless on the battlefield. At the same time, the Xiongnu masked their inferior numbers by making traditional nomadic lightning attacks on horseback, then quickly retreating, having caused maximum damage and confusion. To this tactic Maodun added a twist: after such attacks, his men would feign retreat in just enough disarray to encourage contingents of the Han army to pursue them, straight into an ambush. One such ploy succeeded in luring the Han emperor himself into a charge, and he was quickly surrounded by Maodun's troops, cut off from his army. For seven days the emperor was besieged – the future of the nascent Han dynasty, and of China, was now in Maodun's hands.

But later Chinese sources suggest that Gaodi used a trick of equal guile to save himself. He appealed to Maodun's wife to lobby her husband for his release, advising her that if she did not oblige, then his last act would be to send Maodun a gift of a bevy of beautiful women who would claim his affections and leave his wife out in the cold. (Perhaps Gaodi knew the sorry tale of Confucius's failure to claim Duke Ding's attention, after eighty beauties had been paraded in front of him.)

The ruse appears to have worked: Gaodi was allowed to return home with his frostbitten tail between his legs. In 200 BCE he recognised Maodun's strength in a peace agreement with the Xiongnu, which treated them and their leader as equals with the Han dynasty and emperor. The peace was known as *heqin* – 'peace through kinship relations' – and was cemented by the Han sending a royal princess accompanied by substantial quantities of silk, textiles, food and wine.[1] For their part, the Xiongnu simply pledged to make no further invasions of the Han realm.

Having secured peace in his time, Gaodi could turn to the matter of how his realm should be governed. Legalism had been the mark of the Qin dynasty, whose ruler had set himself up as a new paradigm – ruler, sage, and power over 'all under Heaven'. But such a formula had, ultimately, failed to ensure the Qin's survival. In casting around for an alternative, Gaodi, at the end of his life, began the Han dynasty's journey towards the adoption of Confucianism as its guiding philosophy.

Confucianism had been narrowly saved from extinction in the (supposed) mass burning of the books initiated by Qin Shi Huangdi in 213 BCE. In 196 BCE Gaodi issued an edict reasserting the need for educated men to be recruited to the administration in order to run the government. It was the first step in a return to the promotion of the *Shi* class, from which Confucius himself had emerged; and a gesture to the renewed prioritisation of education, a key tenet of Confucian ideas. For all that progress had been gradual, Confucianism was now taking on the appearance of an old idea whose time had finally come.

A new phalanx of civil servants needed somewhere to live and work, and Gaodi was open to the idea of a new capital city. The old Qin capital of Xianyang was thus replaced by a new city, built a couple of kilometres away: Chang'an. Founded in 195 BC and populated initially by the forced relocation of about 150,000 people from other regions of the empire, Chang'an would become a city brimming with scholar bureaucrats, political and military advisers and, in time, foreign traders.

As Chang'an was founded, Gaodi passed away. In his dying days, as he banqueted in his home town, he is said to have extemporised a lyric called 'Song of the Great Wind' to sing for friends, which underlines his ongoing worry over how to defend his realm:

A great wind came forth,
the clouds rose on high;
Now that my might rules all within the seas,
I have returned to my old village;
Where will I find brave men
to guard the four corners of my land?[2]

He might have added to this baleful tune the question of whom he might appoint as a worthy successor. Officially Gaodi was replaced by his son, Hui, who assumed responsibility for completing the walls of the new Han capital at Chang'an. But in reality power was in the hands of Gaodi's wife, Gaohou. Indeed, Hui willingly handed over the reins to his mother, having seen the way in which she dealt with two of her enemies: a former concubine of her dead husband, and their child. The child she is said to have poisoned; the woman she first treated like a convict – ordering her head shaved, forcing her into hard labour. Eventually she decreed that the poor woman's limbs be severed, her eyes gouged out and her ears sliced off, after which she was dumped in a latrine. When Hui was brought to witness what his mother called a 'human pig', he is said to have fallen ill for a year. He told his mother he was incapable of such cruelty, then handed over power and devoted his life to sex and drink.

In 192 BCE Gaohou – also known as the Empress Dowager Lü – was forced to despatch another tearful princess bride to Maodun. The princess was understandably distressed by the fate that awaited her: the reports coming back spoke of a life far from the exquisite comforts, perfumes and silks of the Han court, instead describing domed lodgings with felt walls and a diet of horse-meat and fermented mare's milk. This was not for a lack of silk: the Han were sending it to the Xiongnu in large quantities, along with their princesses. But the Xiongnu seemed to prefer to sell this fine stuff on to the West: in this way – thanks to the excellent transportation skills of the nomads of central Asia, and to the trade networks of Bactria and the Seleucid Empire – silk eventually made its way to the Mediterranean, where it would become, in centuries to come, the most prized Roman import from the East.

The Empress Dowager Lü herself narrowly evaded the fate of betrothal to the Xiongnu leader. Maodun – understanding the power behind the Han throne, and seeing in Gaohou someone capable of extraordinary violence comparable to his own – appears to have written to propose a liaison between himself and the older empress. Her reply was diplomatic, thanking him for his attentions, but stressing her age and the poor state of her hair and teeth.

If Maodun was unsuccessful in obtaining the empress, he was unstoppable in his campaigns to increase the territory of the Xiongnu, this time at the expense of other nomadic tribes in the region. The Xiongnu's reach grew incessantly under Maodun, until his death in 174 BCE. Just two years before, according to the Chinese historian Sima Qian, Maodun reported to the Han emperor (by then free of the influence of the Empress Dowager Lü, who had died in 180) that:

All the people who live by drawing the bow are now united into one family and the entire region of the north is at peace. Thus I wish to lay down my weapons, rest my soldiers and turn my horses to pasture, and forget the recent affairs [of once again raiding the Han Empire] and restore the old pact, that the peoples of the border may have the peace that they enjoyed in former time, that the young men may grow to manhood, and the old live out their lives in security, and generation after generation, enjoy peace and comfort.[3]

It seemed perhaps, for one brief moment, that with the creation of a more stable Xiongnu Empire, the Han dynasty and the Xiongnu might live peacefully side by side. Yet Maodun's dream was short-lived. His son, Jizhu, regularly encroached into Han territory, and the emperor was forced not only to continue to send him a Han princess, alongside fine silks and other goods, to maintain the status quo; but also to establish heavy garrisons along the frontier of the Yellow River to prevent the Xiongnu from comprehensively breaking their side of the bargain.

In 162 BCE the Han emperor acknowledged the division of sovereignty and culture that separated the Xiongnu from the Han, making a case to the ruler of the Xiongnu that the people north of the Great Wall – where men wielded the bow and the arrow – were subjects of the Xiongnu, while the people south of it – who dwelled in houses and wore hats and girdles – were part of the Han dynasty. 'We', the emperor implored his Xiongnu counterpart, 'must be as parents to them all.'[4] But his entreaties fell on deaf ears.

One of the tribes that Maodun had brought under his control in the 170s was the Yuezhi, based to the west of the Xiongnu. As a result, large parts of this tribe, who had already begun to move westwards in response to earlier Xiongnu expansion, vacated their territory and headed further west in search of a new home. By the late 160s they had occupied the territory of another tribe, the Wu-sun. The son of Mao-dun, while spurning the overtures of the Han emperor, was still hungry for victories to emulate those of his father and provide much-needed booty that he could redistribute amongst his commanders in exchange for their loyalty; and so, in the late 160s BCE, he allied with the Wu-sun to attack the Yuezhi. He is said to have killed the Yuezhi king in battle, then to have followed his father's preference in having the king decapitated and his skull fashioned into a goblet.

In disarray, the Yuezhi fled yet further westwards, and even the Wu-sun, under no pretensions about what they could expect from their alliance with the Xiongnu, vacated their territory and headed south. The Yuezhi exodus would not stop until, in the 140s, it came crashing down on Bactria's doorstep, north of the River Oxus, at the very northern tip of Afghanistan – and this just as Rome asserted its mastery of the Mediterranean by finally razing to the ground the cities of Carthage and Corinth.

*

In 202 BCE, as Gaodi made himself sole and undisputed ruler of the Han in the east, Rome took a monumental step towards the creation of its own Mediterranean-wide empire. It did so by tackling head-on the enemy it had fought for the past sixteen years at the very boundaries of its own influence: on Carthage's home turf. The years since 210–9 BCE, when Hannibal had carved an account of his actions on the temple in southern Italy, had been bleak for the Carthaginian cause and especially for Hannibal. In 207 BCE his brother Hasdrubal, marching overland from Spain to bring reinforcements to Hannibal in Italy, had been engaged and defeated by two Roman armies, after which the Romans decapitated Hasdrubal and tossed the severed head into Hannibal's camp. The following year, Hannibal had not fought at all. In 205 BCE the last Carthaginian possession in Spain had fallen to Rome, which proceeded to make peace with Hannibal's ally, Philip V of Macedon. That same year Carthage had sent out one final fleet of thirty ships and 15,000 men to Italy to bolster Hannibal, but they had made land some 600 miles north of Hannibal's position and were simply out of his reach.

Though Rome still had an enemy on its home turf, Roman sources suggest that Hannibal had privately conceded to friends long ago that he saw no hope of capturing further territory in Italy.[5] Indeed, he was said to have recognised 'the destiny of Carthage', which seemingly no longer featured his longed-for dominion over Rome.[6] Amazingly, since this was a man whose name had for years struck dread into the heart of every Roman, it was now as if Hannibal 'was no longer in Italy'.[7]

In 204 BCE the highly driven Scipio took the fight to Carthage's back yard, landing with his men in Africa. He secured enough victories in the hinterlands to force the Carthaginian Senate to summon home Hannibal's other brother, Mago, along with his forces. But Mago died en route, and so the Carthaginians had no option but to recall Hannibal himself to defend the city. Yet, once again, Hannibal seems to have been grievously let down by his Carthaginian overlords, who failed to send sufficient ships to southern Italy for him to embark all of his troops. Hannibal faced a desperate choice from a menu of unappealing options: to wait for more ships, which might not even be forthcoming; to build ships himself, however long that took; or to leave a large number of men and horses behind and set sail without delay.

In the end the choice he made was a brutal one. Indeed he built more ships, but on the shores of Italy, as his carpenters and workmen rushed to construct seaworthy vessels, his soldiers built another set of structures – piles of rotting dead. These were the carcasses of some 3,000 elite horses that had faithfully carried their masters into battle; of innumerable pack animals that had ceaselessly carried the necessities and booty of Hannibal's campaigns; and of some 20,000 slaughtered soldiers, supposedly from rebel Italian communities who had turned to Hannibal, seeing in him a relief from Roman rule, but who had refused to leave their own home shores to continue that fight in Africa, thereby paying the ultimate price at the orders of their leader.[8] Perhaps by such slaughter Hannibal had learnt the lesson Polybius would later point out: Carthage relied on foreign troops to its disadvantage, whereas Rome relied on its citizens and closer Italian allies.

The Carthaginian Senate now panicked: Scipio was coming ever closer, and with no sight of ships on the horizon they sued for peace, blaming the entire war on Hannibal who, they told Scipio, had acted contrary to their wishes. As Livy commented, 'it is not the Roman people whom Hannibal defeated in battle so many times and put to flight who have conquered Hannibal, but the malice and envy of the Carthaginians'.[9] Some argue that hanging the noose around Hannibal's neck was but another example of the vicious politics of the Carthaginian high command. Others, more generously, contend that it was simply a stalling tactic to buy Hannibal more time to make it home to Carthage's defence. In any event, a provisional settlement was established in 203 BCE whereby Carthage would abandon Spain and Italy and all the islands between Spain and Africa; hand over the majority of its fleet; pay a large fine; and provide Rome with grain. This was to surrender everything that Hannibal and Hamilcar had striven to take for Carthage.

As the agreement was being finalised, Hannibal at last reached the shores of his homeland, landing 100 miles south-east of Carthage at Leptis Minor (in modern-day Libya). One can only imagine the strangeness of his return. He had left North Africa aged nine, and he was now in his early forties. His entire adult life had been spent expanding the power and influence of a place where he had spent so little time, and whose leaders had been inconstant in their support, to the point of effectively stabbing him in the back. Now, in spring 202 BCE, perhaps buoyed by news of Hannibal's return to North Africa, the Carthaginians in Carthage unexpectedly breached their peace agreement with Rome by attacking some enemy supply ships. Scipio responded by plundering towns around Carthage and leaving them to burn. In desperation, the Carthaginians sent messengers to Hannibal to urge an immediate attack on Scipio. Hannibal is said to have given them short shrift, telling them he would attack when he was ready. In early autumn 202 BCE he marched to Zama, a five-day journey from Carthage.

Scipio must have known that a battle between Hannibal and himself was inevitable, for he had prepared for it well. It was perhaps the battle for which he had been waiting all his life – one in which he no longer had to follow the orders of others, in the manner that he had witnessed slaughter at Ticinus, Trebbia and Cannae. Now Scipio was in charge and could face Hannibal head-on. At Zama, Scipio drew up 29,000 infantry and 6,000 cavalry. Amongst his men he could boast not merely Roman soldiers who had lost their fathers in Hannibal's devastating victory at Cannae, but even veterans of Cannae such as himself. These soldiers, shamed for their defeat, had been formed into two legions and sent to fight in Sicily immediately after Cannae, banned from returning to Italy until the war was over. Few had been willing to associate with them. But Scipio, who at that time had command of the province, had realised their potential and, as a survivor of Cannae himself, had earnt their trust and loyalty. Now, as battle-hardened veterans desperate for revenge, the legions of Cannae had come to Africa under Scipio to recover their reputations. It was of little matter that they had only limited experience of fighting in the hot, dusty climate, since Hannibal was no better versed, never having fought on his home continent.

What Hannibal did know was the strength of Scipio's forces. He had sent spies to reconnoitre, only for them to be captured; yet Scipio, rather than killing them, gave them a tour of his camp followed by a grant of provisions and an escort back to Hannibal. So intrigued was Hannibal by Scipio's actions, it is said, that he requested a meeting between them. Leaving behind their armies, accompanied by only a few horsemen and interpreters, Hannibal and Scipio faced one another. The man who had wounded Scipio's father, caused the annihilation of Rome's armies and threatened Rome itself stood talking to a man who, at the age of seventeen, had saved his father in battle against Hannibal, survived Hannibal's crushing victories, and now held both of their futures in his hand.

Hannibal blamed fickle Fortune, and advised Scipio not to tempt fate. Hadn't he, Hannibal, once almost been master of Italy, who now stood here defending his home city? He urged Scipio to consider revised peace terms, less onerous than the ones Carthage had already agreed to and then broken. Scipio replied by chiding him like a schoolmaster: how could Rome – after Carthage had violated an agreed peace – consider a new one with less burdensome terms? No, said Scipio. 'Either put yourself and your country at our mercy or fight and conquer us.'[10]

The next day, 19 October 202 BCE, Hannibal and Scipio joined in battle on the dusty open plain of Zama. Against Scipio's 35,000, Hannibal had 36,000 infantry, 4,000 cavalry and eighty elephants arranged in the front line. In his ranks, too, stood his hardened veteran soldiers, some of whom had been with him since the beginning of his march from Spain over the Alps and into Italy. Yet the majority of his soldiers had been quickly assembled from North African tribes still loyal to Carthage. And his elephants were mostly young and untrained, secured in equally swift order since his return to Africa. Their smell wafted over the battlefield, the ground shaking with their stamping and bellowing, but Scipio had a novel plan to counter them. In the troop formation opposite these enormous beasts, he created lanes such that when they charged – which they could only do in straight lines – his men simply opened up those lanes to let the elephants pass through. At the same time, Scipio's trumpeters strained their lungs to play as loudly as they could, so disorientating and deranging the animals that some turned back and crashed into Hannibal's own troops.

In the heat of the sun, the battle continued all day. The Carthaginian and Roman cavalries engaged, with the Carthaginians soon being chased from the battlefield, the Romans in hot pursuit on their horses. Meanwhile Hannibal and Scipio sent their infantries in wave upon wave of attacks. Neither side could get the better of the other. As the disgraced survivors of Cannae engaged in hand-to-hand combat with Hannibal's veteran troops from that same battle, bitterness, anger and frustration clouded the air, clamorously apparent in the savagery of the fighting, the cries of the wounded and dying, and the screams of jubilation from those who cut down their enemy. Polybius would argue that it was only a stroke of marvellously timed fortune that broke the bloody stalemate. In the fading light of the day the Roman cavalry, having charged off hours earlier into the hazy distance in pursuit of the Carthaginians, now returned to the battlefield just in time to help provide the necessary manpower to encircle the final line of Carthaginian infantry.[11] Many thousands of Carthaginians died, many thousands were taken prisoner and some managed to escape, including Hannibal, who fled on horseback and would ride 120 miles over two days at full gallop to evade his pursuers. It was the last land battle Hannibal ever fought, and the first he ever lost.

Early the following year (while Han ruler Gaodi was captured and held hostage by the Xiongnu leader, Maodun) Hannibal returned to Carthage to officially report to the Carthaginian Senate that he had lost the battle – and they the war. Carthage surrendered to Rome. As a symbol of their submission, Scipio led Carthage's fleet out into the bay and burnt the ships in full view of the city. As the flames licked the sky, Scipio's reputation in Rome was reaching similar heights. He was one of the first Roman generals in history to be given an official name that originated from the scene of his greatest and most crucial victory: 'Scipio Africanus'.

Zama was more than just another battle between Carthaginians and Romans – it was a contest for regional supremacy, and Rome's victory assured it undisputed masterdom over the western and central Mediterranean and surrounding coastlines. At the very borders of its influence, Rome had cemented its reputation and rule by seeing off its most determined enemy. Yet the eastern Mediterranean still eluded its grasp. Rome had agreed a peace with Philip V of Macedon in 205 BCE, despite having sent troops into Greece, because in the final analysis it could not afford to be fighting on two fronts with the invasion of North Africa looming. Now, for three principal reasons, the situation had changed.

First, and most obviously, Rome was free of the Carthaginian front and could turn nearly all of its attention east. It was, however, obliged to keep one eye on its back yard: Hannibal had been storming across Italy for most of the last decade, inciting particularly the rebellious Gallic tribes of northern Italy to join him. With Hannibal gone, there were many scores to settle and many wavering rebels to put back firmly under the yoke. In the first decade of the new century, 200–190 BCE, Rome would be dealing with Gallic uprisings in northern Italy almost continuously, just as it had been doing in the 220s, which back then had forced it to agree diplomatic and unfavourable terms for the division of Spain with Hasdrubal.

The second reason was that Philip had continued, even after his peace with Rome, to throw his weight around in Greece and the Aegean. In particular he had turned to piracy in order to raise funds, a policy not appreciated by many of the business- and trade-minded independent island states of the Aegean, such as Rhodes.[12] On the back of his haul from the shipping lanes, Philip had begun in spring 203 BCE to build himself a new fleet, having incinerated the last one in fear of the approaching Romans. The following year, as the Romans finally defeated Hannibal, Philip was busily attacking towns in the Black Sea and islands in the Cyclades, such as Samos; and defeating the Rhodian navy. By now he was taking on Attalus of Pergamon, one-time ally of Rome, and also the cities of Caria on the coast of Asia Minor. Though Philip was losing as much as he was winning, doubt lingered in Roman minds: for all his false starts and setbacks, might this Philip be another Hannibal? If they did not fight him in Greece, would they finally have to fight him in Italy?

The third reason for Rome to look east, however, was the one that weighed heaviest – the arrival back on Mediterranean shores of Antiochus III, now Antiochus the Great. The King of the Seleucid Empire was riding high on his successes in Parthia and Bactria. His ranks had been swelled with fighting elephants, thanks to his deals with the Bactrian king and Indian leaders. His opponents for the throne were either dead or in hiding. Having returned to the western coast of his empire, he had scores to settle, most obviously with Egypt. But here, again, Rome could not rest easy. Would Antiochus – in his thirties, with plenty of fight still in him and an empire bigger and stronger than anything else abutting the Mediterranean – really be content with his present sphere of influence? What was to stop the Seleucid Empire being Rome's next Carthage?

Mastery over the Mediterranean

Rome was not alone in its vigilance of Seleucid activity. Also watching closely were the squabbling ministers who had served Ptolemy IV, and now the boy-king Ptolemy V in Egypt. And so, too, was Philip V of Macedon.

Philip and Antiochus had always had something of a competitive relationship. In 223 Antiochus had come to the throne in his late teens, as had Philip in 221. They had grown through their twenties hearing reports of each other's struggles for dominance within their own realms. Now, in 203 BCE, they were both in their mid- to late thirties. The lately dubbed Antiochus 'the Great' had a secure empire and a replenished treasury to his name, while Philip was hampered by much the same predicaments with which he had begun in 221. Personal jealousies apart, Antiochus and his future ambitions were also now a real threat to Philip and his operations in the Black Sea and along the coast of Asia Minor. As a result, in 203 and 202 BCE, Philip, while causing havoc in the Aegean, simultaneously entered into negotiations for an alliance with Egypt that was designed to counter Antiochus, cemented by marriage between the infant Ptolemaic ruler and one of Philip's daughters.

Philip, however, was playing both sides. In 201 BCE an envoy from Rhodes reported to the Roman Senate not only Philip's warring behaviour in the Aegean, but also that Philip and Antiochus had agreed a pact to divide Egypt and its territories between them. Rome had to be concerned: about the threat posed to Italy by Philip; about Antiochus's potential enlargement of his empire into Egypt; and about how any future Philip–Egypt or Philip–Antiochus alliance might impact on Rome and its freshly won control of the central and western Mediterranean. This was a new kind of geopolitics, in which vast swathes of the Mediterranean and Asia were caught up in a complicated network of alliances, implications and consequences. Indeed, Polybius would explicitly blame Rome's decision to go back to war with Philip on the increasing 'symploke' – 'interconnectedness' – of the ancient world.[13]

While Roman strategists may have felt that another war was inevitable and necessary, most Romans felt otherwise. The consul for 200 BCE was Publius Sulpicius Galba, who had special responsibility for affairs in northern Greece. He called on the Roman assembly of the people to vote for war against Philip. But as the groups of citizens filed through the voting gates to drop their tokens in the baskets, something astonishing became apparent. By an overwhelming margin, it became clear that the assembly had ignored the advice of the Senate and the wishes of the consul: they had voted 'no' to further conflict, 'worn out' – Livy would say – 'by a war of long duration and great severity, weary of hardships and perils'.[14]

Publius, urged on by a Senate disgusted at what they perceived as a lack of backbone, called an informal meeting on the Campus Martius just outside Rome's walls – the site dedicated to the public, after it had been ripped from the possession of Rome's last king, the place where not only did Romans vote but where Rome trained its soldiers and its generals were received in triumph. There, the war-weary people of the city gathered. 'Not in five months, as when Hannibal came from Spain, but in five days after he sets sail from Corinth, Philip will arrive in Italy,' Publius cried out in warning. 'Compare him at least with Pyrrhus [an invading Greek commander of the early third century BCE] . . . When Pyrrhus attacked he shattered [Italy] with a blow and came a conqueror almost to the gates of Rome!'[15] Harangued by these fearful proclamations, the people consented to a re-vote in which, persuaded that offence would be the best form of defence, they voted for immediate war, with the proviso that no veteran of the African campaign against Hannibal should now be made to fight in Greece against his will.

The machinery of war cranked slowly into action. Roman ambassadors were sent to raise allies amongst the Greek leagues and island- and city-states, and unexpectedly came across Philip in Athens, whereupon they served him an ultimatum: stop causing trouble for the Greeks or face the wrath of Rome. Philip's response was to ignore them; Athens' response was to abolish the honours it had earlier voted to Philip V. Those honours had been to associate Philip with the roots of Athenian democratic governance as prioritised by Cleisthenes in the sixth century BCE: its tribes, into which all the citizens were divided, and which acted as the units in which the people of Athens had voted and gone to war. The glory days of Athenian democracy were long gone, but its cultural and historical legacy endured. To be part of Athens' social, political and cultural fabric remained a huge honour, and that much had been bestowed on Philip by associating him with an Athenian tribe, but was now withdrawn. The Athenians instead created a new tribe of citizens in the city, named after Attalus, King of Pergamon, one-time ally of Rome, and long a major thorn in Philip's side.[16]

Philip in turn continued his campaigning in northern Greece and into the Black Sea. The Roman people, angered by his disregard for Rome's authority, now had a full-measure resolve for war. A new ultimatum was issued, demanding that Philip either submit to tribunal for the damage he had done to Greece or else fight. Philip was bullish in his response and accepted the Roman challenge. In mid-September 200 BCE Rome landed 25,000 men on the west coast of Greece.

As head of the Hellenic league, Philip spent much of his time battling other leagues that held power-bases in central and southern Greece, as well as remaining independent city-states Sparta and Athens. Back in 217–15 BCE he had abandoned war with these groups in anticipation of turning all his energies to help Hannibal attack Rome, but had resumed his bullying tactics after being forced to make peace with Rome around 205 BCE. Now Rome was invading Greece to act as its protector from Philip. What ensued was a drama of alternating combat, diplomacy and backhanded double-dealing between Rome, Philip and the leagues and independent cities of Greece, which came to a head in 197 BCE.

On a foggy day in central Greece, the Roman army, while groping to locate Philip's troops, encountered him on the hills of Cynoscephale (literally, the 'Dog's Head') in Thessaly. Skirmishes between scouting parties steadily grew into an entanglement of both armies in and around the hills. With the Romans were Greek troops from Crete, as well as troops and elephants from their newly won territories in Numidia; but it was not the elephants that would prove decisive this time. Much more important was the Roman style of fighting. Roman soldiers were trained to fight as a single large unit, but also as individuals, while Philip's forces fought always and only as unified groups. On open plains the superiority of the coordinated fighting unit was hard to match, but on the difficult broken terrain of the hillsides of the Dog's Head, Rome's more flexible fighting style came into its own.

And so – whereas in China, Maodun's flexible, lightning fighting style had not only led to the capture of Gaodi, but the acknowledged equality of his David to the Han Goliath – in Greece the Roman Goliath now broadcast the superiority of its own flexible fighting style to the Mediterranean world. It was, remarkably, the first time a Macedonian army – indeed, an army from any part of Greece – had been bested by Romans in a straightforward battle on Greek soil. Philip, suitably chastened, now sued for peace.

The Romans, however, found themselves with a delicate balancing act on their hands: they now had to decide how to shore up their influence and establish stability in the region, without investing huge amounts of manpower that they simply could not afford. On the one hand, Philip's enemies in Greece wanted their revenge. Equally, Philip had challenged Roman authority, and any Roman weakness might further embolden him – and indeed the rest of Greece – to side with one of the other great players in the region, in particular Antiochus the Great.

On the other hand, Rome could not simply kill Philip or remove him from power, since they needed a strong man at the northern borders of the Mediterranean world, just as they needed a strong buffer on the southern Mediterranean coast (which was in large part why they had held off from destroying Carthage completely, despite calls to do so from some of the more bombastic senators). If a policy of leniency carried problems with it, so undoubtedly did the act of cutting off one's nose to spite one's face. Rome was in the same quandary of governance as faced by Antiochus over his Asian empire, one that had led him to do a deal to allow the truculent Euthydemus in Bactria to rule as a strong eastern protector of the Seleucid Empire. For Rome, though, the issue was yet more vexed because of the competing voices within Greece.

At the Isthmian Games of 197 BCE – amid the athletic competitions, feasting and burnt offerings to the gods – the victorious Roman army general, Titus Flaminius, delivered one of the most unexpected speeches recorded in antiquity. The Romans had come on the pretext of liberating Greece from Philip of Macedon. But no one expected them to keep their word, especially given their recent new position as master of the central and western Mediterranean. As Greeks from all over the Aegean piled in to the tiny sanctuary of Isthmia, near the Corinthian canal, whispers and rumours of what the Romans had decided ran rife among the people crammed in around the temples and statues.

There, Flaminius began to talk of freedom. He offered a declaration from the Senate of Rome that all Greek cities in Europe and Asia were to be free. Philip V of Macedon was now directly accountable to the Senate of Rome and would pay reparations for his crimes. The final words of the announcement were drowned out as deafening cheering broke out amongst the assembled masses, so much so that a herald was forced to move through the crowd to repeat the declaration for those who had not heard it, those who perhaps thought they had dreamt it and those who just wanted to hear it again. The cheers were so loud it was said that ravens fell dead from the sky, scared to death at the tumult.[17] No one paid any attention to the athletes that day, and Titus Flaminius was almost torn apart by the surging crowd of well-wishers who wanted to shake him by the hand and offer him their profuse thanks. On that heady day in 197 BCE no one seemed to appreciate a deep irony that would, in time, come to bite: Rome was now not only the guarantor but also the dictator of Greek freedom. By the late 190s Rome would depose the man who had been ruler of Sparta since 207 BCE, calling him a tyrant-oppressor of freedom rather than its king.

After their hugely popular intervention at the Isthmian Games, the Roman ambassadorial team held another meeting – this time with representatives of Antiochus the Great. Since the Seleucid king had returned to Babylon and re-entered Mediterranean geopolitics in 205 BCE, Rome had treated him with courtesy and cordiality. They had heard the warnings brought to them by Rhodian ambassadors to be on the lookout for Antiochus's expansionist plans. They had heard pleas from the Egyptian court for help. But whatever concerns they had harboured, Rome had until now had enough to contend with, thanks to Hannibal and Philip. It had watched Antiochus's moves from afar without major objection, even meeting him in 198 BCE to renew the usual pledges of friendship.

This was in spite of some extremely active territorial expansion on Antiochus's part. In 203 BCE he had moved to retake a number of cities in Asia Minor that had at one time or another fallen out of the folds of the Seleucid Empire. The following year, having signed an agreement with Philip to carve up Egypt, he began the fifth war between Egypt and the Seleucids over the disputed territory of Coele-Syria, still in Egyptian hands since Antiochus's failure to defeat Ptolemy IV at the Battle of Raphia back in 217 BCE. Most of the towns in this long-war-torn region now acquiesced to Antiochus without resistance, but one held out: the fortified city of Gaza, just 33 kilometres from the battlefield at Raphia, where Antiochus had suffered his one really humiliating defeat. The battle-hardened leader would not make the same mistake twice. This was the city that had held out against Alexander the Great for more than five months when he had besieged it as the final prize before his own invasion of Egypt. Now Antiochus the Great had come to do the same. Polybius singles out the people of the city of Gaza for their courage, steadfastness and ingenuity in resisting the might of Antiochus's army.[18] Yet by autumn 201 BCE, Gaza had fallen.

That December – as Carthage was stripped of its glory by Rome, as Philip was rattling the sabre in the Aegean, and it was leaked that he was making pacts with Antiochus about future divisions of the country between them – Egypt panicked. It was torn apart by revolution; its drunken ex-ruler was dead; and its new ruler's age was not even in double digits. Philip had betrayed Egypt in negotiating with Antiochus, and now Antiochus – having taken back all the disputed territories to which Egypt had held on for so long – was poised to enter Egypt itself. A delegation was despatched from Alexandria to Rome to ensure the Romans knew that the fate of Egypt hung in the balance. Rome's response was lukewarm, at best. As part of their mission to Greece they may have tasked one senior Roman official with the role of tutor to the infant Ptolemy V – not exactly the response the Egyptians were hoping for.[19]

Nevertheless, Egypt did manage to put up a defence with a successful counter-attack in 200 BCE, forcing Antiochus to reconquer some of the land he had swept through the previous year. As a result, in the same year that Rome poured its forces back into Greece, Antiochus was to be found taking to the field against the Egyptians at Panium at the foot of the Golan Heights. Alongside him was his eldest son, also called Antiochus. At twenty, the younger Antiochus proved himself a chip off the old block by leading the cavalry, who proved decisive in the battle, routing their Egyptian counterparts and subsequently turning on the Egyptian infantry in a pincer movement with troops led by the elder Antiochus the Great, who must have felt massively assured in his authority by the prowess of his son on the battlefield.

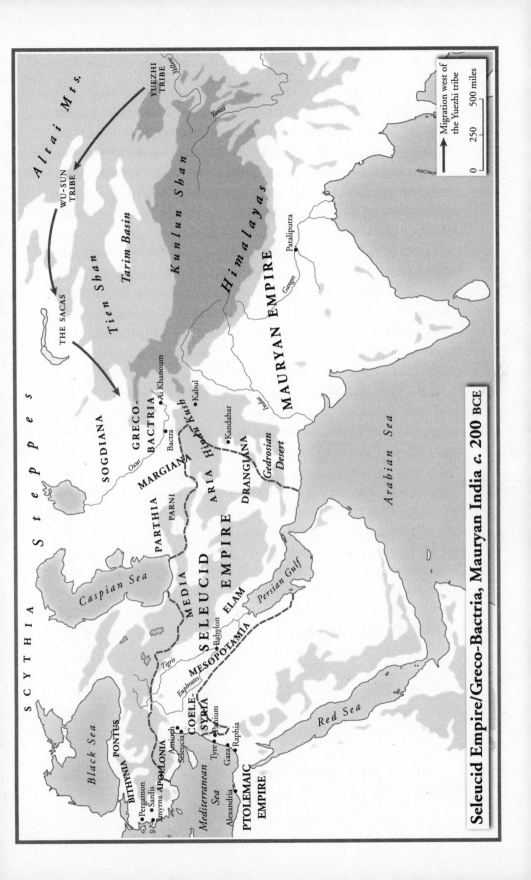

Seleucid Empire/Greco-Bactria, Mauryan India c. 200 BCE

Migration west of the Yuezhi tribe

0   250   500 miles

YUEZHI TRIBE

Yellow

Altai Mts.

Yanzi

WU-SUN TRIBE

Kunlun Shan

Tien Shan

Tarim Basin

Himalayas

MAURYAN EMPIRE

THE SACAS

Pataliputra

Ganges

SCYTHIA Steppes

SOGDIANA

GRECO-BACTRIA

Ai Khanoum

Hindu Kush

Kabul

Oxus

Bactra

Indus

MARGIANA

ARIA

Kandahar

DRANGIANA

Gedrosian Desert

PARTHIA

PARNI

Caspian Sea

Arabian Sea

MEDIA

SELEUCID EMPIRE

ELAM

Persian Gulf

Tigris

MESOPOTAMIA

Babylon

Euphrates

Black Sea

BITHYNIA

PONTUS

Pergamon

Sardis

Smyrna

APOLLONIA

Antioch

Seleucia

COELE-SYRIA

Tyre

Panium

Gaza

Raphia

Mediterranean Sea

Alexandria

PTOLEMAIC EMPIRE

Red Sea

Egypt lay open for conquest. And so, too – with Philip embroiled in war with Rome and all eyes trained on central Greece – did the northern coast of Asia Minor: that mix of independent Greek cities held or conquered by Philip (while he had terrorised and pirated his way around the Aegean) and small but wealthy kingdoms, including the Attalids at Pergamon, one of the breakaway states that had at one time been part of the Seleucid Empire, now allies of Rome and honoured by Athens.

In 199–8 BCE Antiochus turned north and advanced with his forces all the way up through Asia Minor until they reached the Hellespont, the narrow channel of water – in what today is north-western Turkey – that separates Europe from mainland Asia. At this symbolic barrier had once stood the massed armies of the Persian king Xerxes as he prepared to lead them into Greece for the ill-fated invasion of the early fifth century BCE. Now, a little under 300 years later, Antiochus, Great King of the Seleucid Empire, gathered his own troops on the brink of a momentous decision. Alexander the Great had established an empire that spanned Europe and Asia. Might Antiochus achieve something comparable in reverse?

Rome was not unaware of Antiochus's abrupt change of focus. Towns that he had attacked on his way north, such as Smyrna, had been advised to send a direct appeal to Rome. Some thought that Antiochus was coming to Philip's aid; others that he was looking to secure Seleucid domination over as much of Asia as possible, yet would not stray into Europe. Either way, the Roman Senate was alarmed, not least because their man on the ground in Greece had just offered a Roman guarantee of freedom not only to the cities of Greece itself, but also to the Greek cities on the coast of Asia Minor – cities now very much under the influence of Antiochus the Great.

With the cheers for Greek freedom doubtless still ringing in their ears, Flaminius and the Roman commissioners thus met Antiochus's representatives. The Roman message was clear: Antiochus was to free any city he had taken that had belonged to Philip or the Ptolemies; and not to sail over the Hellespont into Greece. The problem was that Antiochus was already in the process of crossing into Europe.

By 196 BCE he had landed in the Chersonesus – the modern-day Gallipoli peninsula, that finger of European land jutting down into the Aegean Sea, helping to form the narrow channel of the Hellespont before it widens into the Sea of Marmara. Antiochus had then moved with his men to Lysimacheia (destroyed the year before in the Roman war against Philip), where he quickly began restoring the city and gathering together its fragmented population to act as a base for his operations in Europe. (This was the same city that, ironically, one of his ancestors had pointed to, disdainfully, as one operating under a full direct democratic constitution.)

Upon finally meeting the Great King at Lysimacheia in October 196 BCE, the Roman ambassadors were initially cordial: in their informal meetings the conversation flowed easily. However, in their official audience, according to Polybius, the Roman delegation chose to be brusque, setting out Rome's demands, stating that those cities in Asia Minor that had belonged to Philip had been won in war by Rome, and asking, moreover, exactly what the Seleucid king was doing in Europe. 'For if it were not with the intention of attacking the Romans, there was no explanation left that any reasonable person could accept.' With these words, Polybius recounts, the Romans ceased speaking.[20]

In the tense silence that followed, the canny Antiochus replied with a delicate mixture of diplomatic sidestep, bluster and bluntness. The Romans should not concern themselves about Egypt, he argued, for he was about to sanction a marriage between the young Ptolemaic ruler and his daughter, creating an equitable alliance between the kingdoms. As for advancing into Europe and rebuilding Lysimacheia, he was not conquering new territories, but reclaiming those once won by his ancestors. And as for Roman demands to dictate affairs along the coast of Asia Minor: 'he did not understand by what right the Romans raised a controversy with him in regard to the cities in Asia. They were the last people in the world who had any claim to do so. They should refrain entirely from interfering in the affairs of Asia, seeing that he never in the least degree interposed in those of Italy.'[21] Any city that wanted to be free, Antiochus said, would have its autonomy from his grace, not that of Rome.

The conference broke up, with the Romans withdrawing to lick their wounds. Now apparent before them and Antiochus were the boundaries of their respective worlds – Greece and the western Mediterranean were the affair of Rome, while Asia, Egypt and a little bit of Europe were the business of Antiochus and his son-in-law-to-be, Ptolemy V. Would Rome and Antiochus learn to keep one another sweet, as Gaodi and Maodun had managed to keep the Han and Xiongnu dynasties rubbing along together? Or would one or the other, or both, decide that this map of the spheres of influence as drawn was simply not satisfactory?

Since Ptolemy was a mere thirteen, the wedding was delayed for two years, whereupon the boy married Antiochus's ten-year-old daughter, Cleopatra. While this child-marriage had been forced on a defeated Egypt, it seems they were allowed to choose the location, which they did with a nod to history: it was Raphia, the site of the Ptolemaic victory over Antiochus in battle more than twenty years previously. This was not the only wedding Antiochus had to attend in the period: he also married his son and co-king, Antiochus the Younger, to his daughter, Laodice. This was the first time a Seleucid had wed his own sibling, although it was a practice long established in the Egyptian court. Antiochus the Great is even said to have offered another of his daughters to King Eumenes II of Pergamon, to cement an alliance with that independent kingdom in Asia Minor, but the offer was refused. However, in between these wedding festivities, Antiochus had been made aware of the presence of a famed visitor to his kingdom: none other than Hannibal.

Scipio Africanus had burnt the Carthaginian fleet and imposed taxing peace terms on the city, but he had not demanded that the Carthaginians hand over Hannibal. Between 201 and 197 BCE Hannibal had been experiencing life in Carthage for the first time since he was nine, and he found it not to his liking. According to Livy, he spent the time working hard to introduce legal reforms and to regrow the city's finances after the debilitating effects of more than fifteen years of war and the price of peace with Rome. By contrast, his enemies in Carthage – most of whom were connected in some way to the family of Hamilcar's great adversary, Hanno the Great – spent concerted time writing to Rome with fabricated tales of how Hannibal was in league with their enemies.[22] Scipio Africanus – exhibiting the authority of a man who had parleyed with Hannibal and bested him in battle – defended his old adversary's reputation in the Senate. Still, the Romans in turn sent an embassy to Carthage to investigate the claims, part of its diplomatic endeavour to maintain control over the city without explicitly having to run it.

Without waiting for the outcome of this scrutiny, despairing of his home city, Hannibal escaped from Carthage with characteristic flair. Feigning to go out on a leisurely horse-ride, he rode instead through the night to his seaside estate, whence he travelled by ship to a small archipelago of islands off the Carthaginian coast. Recognised by some merchantmen, he invited them to dinner, got them drunk and, while they slept, fled in darkness, east along the coast of North Africa, coming at last to the city of Tyre, the ancestral home of the Carthaginian people. Here he was welcomed 'as a man distinguished with every kind of honour'.[23] In contrast, when Carthage found him missing, Hannibal was declared an enemy of the state and his house was burnt down.

From Tyre, Hannibal travelled north along the Mediterranean coast, deeper into the territory of the Seleucid Empire. At Antioch he met Antiochus the Younger and in 195 BCE, as plans for the wedding with Laodice were advancing, Hannibal moved to the resplendent city of Ephesus, where he met Antiochus the Great himself. Hannibal offered his services as an adviser to the king's dealings with Rome and – if Livy is to be believed – proposed a grandiose scheme by which he and Antiochus could take on Rome together.[24] It was to Antiochus that Hannibal told the story of the oath his father had made him swear just before he left Carthage as a boy: never to be a friend of Rome.[25] A new Mediterranean-wide partnership had been born.

While Antiochus and Hannibal were plotting in Asia, Rome had, it seems, shifted its focus once again away from Greece, back to the defence and control of its heartland territories in Italy – not least from the rebellious Gauls and Ligurians to the north in the Po valley and its surrounds. By 194 BCE not a single Roman soldier was stationed east of the Adriatic Sea: Rome had guaranteed Greek freedom, fired a warning shot across Antiochus's bows, kept a close eye on politics in Carthage, but physically contracted its military tentacles. Partly this was due, of course, to the need to deal with the threats in Italy. But it was also part of a wider design by which Carthage, having not been utterly destroyed, could act as a self-sustaining bulwark for Roman influence on the African coast, without Rome having to commit large numbers of its own troops. That said, Rome conceivably feared that it could not yet engage in a full-blown war in the eastern Mediterranean, and may have been reluctant to get its hands irremediably messy in the fragmented politics of Greece and Asia Minor. Perhaps, too, they hoped that Antiochus had heard their warning and that the dividing line between their worlds had been drawn for good.

At the same time Rome was counting the burgeoning profits of war, not only from the fines extracted from Carthage, but also from Philip V of Macedon. When Flaminius, so nearly crushed by gratitude at the Isthmian Games, celebrated his military triumph over Philip in Rome, his procession through the streets was accompanied by copious displays of Greek plunder: marble statues and weapons of all kinds, almost 50,000 pounds of unworked silver, silver shields, 114 gold crowns, almost 4,000 pounds of gold and almost 100,000 coins of different denominations. There was also Philip's own son, Demetrius, handed over as a hostage to guarantee peace in Greece. But that peace was shattered when Antiochus, perhaps at Hannibal's urging, invaded Thrace.[26]

In 194 BCE Antiochus marched around the top of the Aegean Sea, from his base in the Chersonesus into Thracian territory, so violating the boundary line drawn up in the disgruntled conference with Roman ambassadors at Lysimacheia. In response, Rome restated its position to Antiochus's representatives: leave Europe alone or face the prospect of war. The following year the Senate (in yet another example of Rome's careful approach to its authority in this part of the Mediterranean) sent a commission to Greece and Asia Minor to judge the mood of the commanding figures in the region. They interviewed King Eumenes II of Pergamon (who told them to declare war on Antiochus); they interviewed Hannibal (though we don't know what advice he gave); and they even met Antiochus, coming direct from the wedding of his daughter at Raphia and the declaration of his wife as a goddess. What no one could determine was Antiochus's ultimate goal. Was he prodding the sleeping dog of Rome, so as to see what the limits of its tolerance were? Or was he hell-bent on something grander – even Rome's outright destruction?

In the midst of this stand-off between the giant powers of the ancient Mediterranean, the small and fairly insignificant Aetolian League of central Greece saw an opportunity to win some advantage by inciting conflict. To Antiochus, the League whispered of how much Greece hated the yoke of Roman control and wished to be free (for all that its freedom was already, technically, guaranteed by Rome). In 192 BCE Rome panicked as rumours abounded that Antiochus, advised by Hannibal, was already in Aetolia, preparing to sail for Sicily. The Roman military officials, who had been sent to press Rome's advantage in Spain, were quickly redeployed across the Mediterranean to lead operations in Greece. Flaminius, still counting the gold coins from his last war on Greek soil, was re-despatched to keep the peace. Yet his efforts failed to stop the Aetolians making an official request for Antiochus 'to free Greece and arbitrate between themselves and Rome'.[27] Light-touch Roman diplomacy had failed, it seemed, to keep the Greeks in check.

Antiochus's response that autumn was to make a sacrifice at the city of Ilion – ancient Troy, still under Seleucid control, despite Rome's historical interest in and regard for its ancestral city. Before embarking for Greece with an army of 10,000 soldiers, 500 horses and six elephants, Antiochus wanted to ensure that his mission was following in the footsteps of the glorious military campaigns that had gone before. Historians have often wondered what was going through Antiochus's mind as he set sail for Greece. Had Hannibal been so instrumental in encouraging Antiochus into a clash with his old sworn enemies? Or did Antiochus really believe the Aetolian League when they told him that the Greeks would welcome him and rise up to evict the Romans and Roman influence (much as Hannibal had told his men that the Gauls and Gallic tribes in northern Italy would become the Carthaginians' firm supporters when they invaded Italy)? For sure, the Aetolians were incredibly keen to convince Antiochus that he would be seen as a liberator, going so far as to seize a town and then informing him that it had spontaneously revolted from the Romans, on hearing the news of his coming.

It is debatable whether Antiochus had a clear plan, or even a clear sense of what taking on Rome would constitute. He appears not to have been in any hurry to free the Greeks from their 'despot'. According to Polybius, he spent the winter in Greece, carousing in Chalcis and even marrying a young Greek woman, despite his advancing years and plentiful extant sons and daughters.[28] His spirits do not even appear to have been dampened by a conversation he had with Hannibal, reported later by the Roman author and grammarian Aulus Gellius. On showing Hannibal all his troops massed to enter Greece, Antiochus asked the distinguished general if these would be enough to combat the forces of the republic of Rome. Hannibal is said to have replied, 'I think this will be enough, quite enough, for the Romans, even though they are most greedy.'[29] Rome, having declared war on Antiochus in November 192 BCE, made preparations through the winter to show Antiochus what its greed amounted to.

The campaigning season of 191 BCE saw all the living potentates who had defined Mediterranean and western central Asian history over thirty years now pursuing their designs in Greece. What had begun as a series of conflicts on many fronts, spread out over a vast geographical distance, had contracted to one seething, tumultuous hotspot, set to detonate outwards. The Romans marched into Greece to eject Antiochus the Great – not only to re-establish Greek 'liberty' and reassert their authority over the region, but to put down the one remaining power that could challenge their authority over the Mediterranean itself. Antiochus marched into Greece perhaps believing himself a liberator at the beginning of his next great conquering foray into the western Mediterranean, possibly unsure of what he was getting into. Hannibal, as a military adviser, was at Antiochus's side, contemplating yet another clash with his old enemy. And Philip V of Macedon – one-time ally of Hannibal, then of Antiochus, and already defeated by the Romans – was in the middle of all of them. What Philip decided to do next would be crucial.

Hannibal advised Antiochus to regain Philip as an ally or else neutralise him as soon as possible. Unfortunately, Antiochus trampled over Philip's political sensitivities with all the grace of one of his elephants. He decided to support another Philip – Philip of the city of

Megalopolis, a pretender to the throne of Macedon and a sharp thorn in Philip V's side. Worse, Antiochus ordered Philip of Megalopolis to go to the battlefield at Cynoscephalae – the location of Philip V's defeat at the hands of the Romans in 197 BCE. The whitened and gnawed bones of his fallen warriors had lain on this hilly broken terrain for the past six years, unburied by Roman decree, weathered by the hot sun and the cold wind, feasted on by birds of prey and the beasts of central northern Greece. In what Antiochus hoped would be a grand gesture of the liberation he was ushering in, Philip of Megalopolis was sent to bury the skeletons. As his men set to the chilling task of interring these skulls and bones, Antiochus's intended gesture of unity for Greece seemingly so annoyed Philip of Macedon – probably because Philip saw in it Antiochus's intention to assume power and end Philip's own rule – as to send him running to the very people who had killed his men: the Romans. Perhaps it was a case of better the devil you know than the devil you don't. For the rest of his life Philip would remain in command of Macedon as a Roman ally, treated with honour and respect.

Having blundered thus, Antiochus drew up his men at Thermopylae. This narrow corridor, allowing passage from northern Greece to central and southern parts, had already played host to moments of enormous political and military importance in Mediterranean history. Thermopylae was where 300 Spartans had resisted the Persian invasion in 480 BCE; where invading Gauls had been routed in the third century BCE; and, now, where Antiochus, invading Greece to protect Greek liberty from the invading Romans, arranged his troops to face the Romans, who had come, they claimed, to assert their right also to assure the Greeks of freedom and to push Antiochus back to his own sphere of influence.

Antiochus knew his history: he sent men to guard the hidden mountain passes around the 'Hot Gates' (as Thermopylae's name literally translates) and prevent the sort of encircling manoeuvre that had undone the heroic Spartans almost 300 years before. But this time there was to be no heroic last stand by Antiochus and his men. Ancient sources claim that Antiochus fled back north with only 500 survivors, his army decimated, and soon afterwards left Greece for Ephesus with his Greek bride.[30] The final showdown for mastery of the Mediterranean had sounded not with a bang but a whimper. Its consequences, though, were impressive nonetheless. Rome was now the greatest power in the whole Mediterranean, and this easy victory over Antiochus the Great seems to have calmed any hesitation Rome might have had about facing up to Antiochus's empire, and even enflamed its desire to project influence further east – into Asia.

*

On 18 March 190 BCE, Lucius Cornelius Scipio crossed with Rome's army from southern Italy into northern Greece, so to begin the long march into Asia. By his side as his adviser and general was his brother, Publius Cornelius Scipio Africanus, hero of the Battle of Zama. Philip V of Macedon, who had received his son back from hostage in Rome in thanks for his support against Antiochus, now struck up a strong friendship with Scipio Africanus, one that both men furthered by correspondence throughout the rest of their lives. But Asia awaited, and by August the Aegean Sea was completely under the control of Rome and her allies, after Hannibal – now commanding Antiochus's navy – lost to the Rhodians, who had joined in the war on Rome's side.

Rome's forces moved into Seleucid territory as the campaigning season was coming to an end. Antiochus had entrenched his men to guard the route to Sardis and his naval base at Ephesus. At Magnesia ad Sipylum – a city about 65 kilometres north-east of modern-day Izmir, nestled at the foot of Mount Sipylus by the River Hermus – the forces of Rome and of Antiochus met in battle. It is thought that the armies were of similar size, although Antiochus's was composed of many more types of warriors, from the breadth of his vast and diverse empire. Both sides had elephants, and the Romans were now well accustomed both to utilising and combating these lumbering beasts. They sent spears flying towards the elephants' eyes, bewildering the animals with pain and confusion, causing them to turn and trample their own troops. Antiochus – a man who had spent his entire adult life on military campaign – once more took up a heroic position leading his cavalry wing, and smashed through the Roman lines and almost to their camp. Once again, however, just as in Raphia, he had forgotten his role as overall strategic commander. By the time he returned to the heart of the action, the Romans had broken his other wing and he could do little to prevent them overrunning his camp.

Livy records a fantastical sum of 53,000 dead in Antiochus's army, a mere 394 in Rome's.[31] Whatever the accuracy of these numbers, Rome's victory was absolute. Antiochus was forced to accept a peace treaty in which he abandoned his hard-won control over the coast of Asia and all of the lands west of the Taurus Mountains. Rome took possession of these former territories of Antiochus and dispensed with many (as 'gifts of Rome') to its allies – consummate diplomatic gestures to keep Greece and the eastern Mediterranean sweet.[32] In addition, Antiochus had to pay a huge fine. He was allowed to keep his throne and the remainder of his Asian empire – a now traditional Roman move, for how else could Rome seek to keep the eastern border of the Mediterranean well guarded? But the successful challenge to Antiochus's authority in the Mediterranean (as had happened to him and his ancestors so many times in the past) kick-started a chain reaction of rebellion across the vast plains of his hard-won kingdom.

Parthia – at the eastern end of the Seleucid Empire, only recently forced back into the fold – once again rebelled. In Bactria, Demetrius, son of the late Euthydemus (both of whom had exhibited renewed ambitions from the moment Antiochus headed back west in 202 BCE), now expanded the Bactrian realm as much as was possible, to the east and over the Hindu Kush into India.[33] New provincial governors, emboldened by Rome's successes, declared themselves kings of independent territories. Everything for which Antiochus had worked his whole life now crumbled. Three years later, aged fifty-three, he was killed in a street skirmish while looting the city of Elam to fund a campaign meant to re-establish his authority in the east.

Antiochus had learnt the hard way how a lifetime's effort to unify and solidify an empire under a single rule could be undone by a couple of poor outcomes on the battlefield. As appeared to be the fate of Seleucid rulers, he became hostage to an empire stretched so wide that it was almost impossible for any one person to keep it in check. In contrast, Rome to the west had not only done battle at its borders to the south and east – against both Carthage and Antiochus – in order to define the growing remit of its power and influence, but had worked hard and with guile to cement that influence and to balance its abilities and manpower with the size of the realm it sought to control, within a Mediterranean world in which everything and everyone was increasingly connected.

Far to the east of Antiochus, Gaodi, too, had defended and articulated the boundaries of his new Han Empire, had sought to mollify those at its borders, and had begun to focus on the development of a system of governance suited for such a vast realm and population. In expanding and developing their respective spheres of influence, Rome and the Han had created vast empires in both the west and east, separated in the middle by zones of increasing turmoil, dynastic overhaul and mass migration, which would, very soon, mesh to create a permanent connection between East and West.

Rome's final demand to Antiochus in the wake of the Battle of Magnesia was that he should hand over Hannibal to them. But the Romans were too late. Hannibal had already fled the royal court, in anticipation of just such a request. Three years later he would resurface as an adviser to King Prusias of Bithynia, ruler of a small kingdom on the shores of the Black Sea, whom Hannibal duly aided in campaigns against Eumenes II of Pergamon, a longtime ally of Rome. Hannibal had not renounced the pledge supposedly made to his father. Still, the reality of his position was, according to the Roman satirist Juvenal, a sad one: 'conquered, he fled into exile and there he sits, both might and marvellous, a suppliant at the king's vestibule, until such time as it should please the Bithynian tyrant to stir from his bed'.[34] In 182 BCE the Romans at last persuaded Prusias to relinquish Hannibal to them. Aged sixty-three, the mighty general had, at last, run out of options: he took poison in his own home rather than be captured. According to Livy, these were his final words: 'Let us now put an end to the great anxiety of the Romans, since they have thought it too tedious to wait for the death of a hated old man.'[35]

Coda

I n the same year that Hannibal died – 182 BCE – so, too, did his great antagonist Publius Cornelius Scipio Africanus. This was a man with a unique perspective on how the Mediterranean world had changed during his lifetime – in particular, how it had come to be dominated by Rome. Scipio had taken to the battlefield against Hannibal at Ticinus at the age of seventeen, as Rome fought for its life against the lightning Carthaginian invasion. He had seen his father defeated by Hannibal, and had witnessed at first hand the way in which subsequent Roman consuls underestimated Hannibal's abilities and tactics, first at Trebbia and then at Cannae, as Rome's survival continued to hang in the balance.

Scipio had risen up through the ranks at great speed, almost as demanded by the crisis in which Rome found itself. He had taken the fight to Carthage, defeated Hannibal in open battle and overseen the imposition of Roman influence in North Africa. Then he had advised his younger brother in the campaign to push Rome's influence east and take on Antiochus III. Through this extraordinary life, Scipio had seen the growth of resistance to Rome; its ongoing problems in defending its home terrain; its efforts, problems and preoccupations in expanding its influence across the Mediterranean; and the delicate balancing act that was required to keep control of such a world and ensure its boundaries were secure and stable. When Scipio first went to war, Rome was but one of the powers in the Mediterranean. By the time he died – and in no small thanks to his own leadership on and off the battlefield – the Mediterranean was Rome's world.

Scipio, though, had also seen how Rome's politics had both helped and hindered that progression. His family had had, and would continue to have, a long and illustrious role in Rome's republic. It was his adopted grandson, Scipio Africanus the Younger, with Polybius at his side, who would oversee the complete destruction of the city of Carthage in 146 BCE. Polybius argued then, as we have seen, that it was Rome's perfectly balanced and mixed government – never better than when under pressure – that had propelled it to dominance. That mix of oligarchic, democratic and monarchical power meant, for Polybius, that no one element rated itself to be in charge, unlike the democracy of ancient Athens, which, for Polybius, allowed 'the masses [to] make all decisions according to their random impulse' and which was 'like a ship without a commander'.[1] The result, for Athens, had been the eclipse of its democracy and power, leaving it with merely a symbolic cultural and historical value to rely on. Similarly, in Polybius's view, greed and too much 'people-power' at Carthage had brought about civic decay. In contrast, Rome's much more resilient system had triumphed.

And yet, as had become clear to Scipio when he saw consul after consul lunge for their moment of glory to try and defeat Hannibal, one of the faults in the Roman system was that while encouraging every man to seek a reputation for valour, its limited periods of high office prompted a short-termist view in decision-making. And what Scipio was also only too aware of was the potential for disagreement and disorder amongst the leading men of the city itself, just as Polybius had pointed out in Carthage. On their return from defeating Antiochus in Asia, both he and his younger brother were accused by jealous contemporaries of having taken bribes from the Seleucid king, and only escaped the charges by mobilising the goodwill of the people in their favour. Scipio is said to have retired from Rome as a bitter man in consequence, even refusing plans for his burial in the city, so as to deny Rome the honour of his bones. Perhaps he even guessed the truth: that it would be, in the centuries to come, this infighting for glory amongst the leading men of Rome that would bring the republic crashing down, only to be reborn as a system under one imperial ruler.

Four years after Hannibal and Scipio died, so too did Philip V of Macedon, who had known a mere eight years of peace throughout his forty-two-year reign. No one understood more than Philip the way in which the growing interconnectedness of the Mediterranean – the *symploke*, as Polybius would call it – had both helped and hindered the fortunes of individuals and communities. Philip had faced complicated networks of alliance within Greece, and attempted to create similar arrangements in his own favour: with Hannibal, with the Ptolemies in Egypt and with Antiochus. He had ended up perilously, however, as the focus of a number of alliances all directed against him, before finally being forced to choose sides as Rome pushed east. He died a loyal servant to Rome, a city that had managed successfully to ally and control large numbers of people to its cause.

Hannibal, Philip, Scipio – all young men who had led the charge during this era of change – were schooled in the fickle nature of fortune made even more unpredictable by the difficult and constantly changing world environment in which these leaders had to operate, as stressed upon Scipio by Hannibal in Livy's account of their face-to-face meeting before the Battle of Zama. But perhaps none of them understood fate's caprices so well as Antiochus III, who had died before them all in 187 BCE, having been saddled with the most sizeable problem: that of maintaining, unifying and stabilising under his rule a world that stretched from Europe into central Asia, and in which discord in one part could spread everywhere – a problem that Rome, as master of the Mediterranean, duly inherited. Antiochus's life had been spent criss-crossing East and West, ever mindful of the need to prove his worth to his own subjects and so maintain his rule, but also constantly watchful of what was happening outside his empire, and of the impact these events might have upon his world. His diligence in this regard earnt him his title of 'The Great'. But eventually his elongated empire came shoulder-to-shoulder with that of Rome. And it was at this juncture – crucially, in the decision not to respect his rival's boundaries, but to try to push beyond them – that Antiochus was made to taste the bitterness of fortune turning. Once defeated by Rome in the west, his whole empire was destabilised, like a run of dominoes, and he lost everything that he had struggled to achieve.

In central Asia the motto of leaders seems to have been 'Fortune favours the brave' – or, more accurately, the ruthless. Each of the micro-kingdoms in the region continued to grapple with one another for territory, and individual rulers were cut down by those even more desperate to rule. In Bactria the 'Diodoti' dynasty had lost out to the usurper Euthydemus by the time Antiochus III arrived. Euthydemus was in turn replaced by his son Demetrius, who – while Antiochus was being thoroughly beaten in the west – oversaw vast expansion of Bactrian influence east, deeper into central Asia, and south, into the former Mauryan territories. Yet soon enough the Bactrian throne was seized by another usurper, Eucratides, who in turn faced up to internal rebellion and invasion by the newly resurgent Parthia, pursued an expansion of Bactrian influence into India and was, according to one interpretation of the sources, killed by his own son. The son is said to have ridden his chariot through the rivulets of his father's blood and ordered the body to be left unburied, as food for the circling birds of prey.[2]

In the east, Qin Shi Huangdi had also acquired an acute appreciation of the difficulties of ruling a vast empire. In forging his united Qin dynasty, he ruthlessly pursued the moulding and interconnecting of the constituent parts of his world in a way that the Romans, and even Antiochus, could only dream of – but he endeavoured simultaneously to define its boundaries against the outside world. He did so not only by building roads and walls, but also by silencing the (often discordant) multiplicity of voices that had been such a feature of the 'Spring and Autumn' and 'Warring States' periods. In this way the 'One Hundred Schools of Thought' were harrowed down to just one: Legalism.

Qin Shi Huangdi's death, however, caused the collapse of that project into disarray, and the subsequent revival of other ways of thinking. The eventual emergence of Gaodi and the Han dynasty reignited the project of unity and solidarity under a single emperor ruling from a new capital city, but it also threw open the question of which philosophy of governance ought best to accompany it. In trying to expand his borders, Gaodi had suffered a degree of embarrassment, whereupon he was willing to accommodate the tribes around him, even to the extent of shipping off Han princesses and endless luxury goods to Maodun and his successors. In turn, Maodun and his Xiongnu were able to create their own empire, driving their own neighbouring nomadic tribes (chiefly, of course, the Yuezhi) off in migratory waves towards the west. And it was this great movement of human traffic towards the unstable 'roundabout' of central Asia that led to the first event ever to be recorded in the histories of both East and West.

Around 145 BCE the beautiful and ornate city of Ai Khanoum within the gilded kingdom of Bactria was invaded by neighbouring Scythian nomads known as Sacas.[3] A few years later a different nomadic tribe made incursions into Bactrian territory: the Yuezhi, who had been on the move since the nomadic territorial fighting on the borders of the Qin and Han empires back in the late third/early second centuries BCE.

In the west, Roman sources such as Strabo (writing in the first century BCE) and Justin (in the second/third centuries CE) speak of the overwhelming of Bactria by nomadic people who certainly answer the description we have of the Yuezhi at this time.[4] And we know of the mass movement of peoples from approximately the same time in the eastern sources, too, because in 139 BCE the new Han emperor, Wu, sent an ambassador, Zhang Qian, west to search for allies in a new assault that the Han emperor planned to unleash upon their old enemy, the Xiongnu. Zhang Qian took some time to report back: he did not return until 126 BCE, having journeyed thousands of kilometres, in which time he suffered capture and a ten-year imprisonment by the Xiongnu (even taking a Xiongnu wife during his incarceration). His report survives, however, thanks to the historian Sima Qian, who was composing China's first monumental history, *Shiji*, under Emperor Wu. Zhang Qian's communiqué must have made grim reading for the Han emperor: no nomadic tribes were willing to join him in his venture, not even the Yuezhi, with whom the ambassador had eventually caught up on the banks of the Oxus River. According to Zhang Qian, the Yuezhi were flush with gains lately made, having not only attacked Bactria, but brought it completely under their sway.[5]

Of even greater significance than this dovetailing of Eastern and Western histories is what came next. The ancient sources underline the wealth and tendencies to extravagance of the people of Bactria and the Indo-Greek kingdoms. Eucratides in Bactria, for example, created the largest and most valuable gold coin in the entirety of the Hellenistic world.[6] Zhang Qian's report also underlines how skilled were the people of this region in commerce, and how developed the networks of trade in this region already were: he was amazed to find bamboo and cloth made in the Chinese province of Sichuan for sale in Bactria.[7] At the same time, the nomadic tribes who had now come to hold power over Bactria were, by their wandering nature, also experienced transporters of goods. All manner of items had already been making their way haphazardly across this vast expanse, such as the silks given in tribute to the Xiongnu, which they traded onwards at a profit.[8]

So it was that by the end of the second century BCE, a meshing set of factors – a martial clash of cultures in central Asia and a subsequent expansion of Chinese power, a harsh physical environment that encouraged mobility and connectivity for the sake of survival, and the endeavours of human communities that appeared to have business and trade in their blood – had led to the emergence of a concrete and official commercial chain of interaction across Asia. Within decades this network connected China (from the massive 'nine markets' within the new Han capital at Chang'an) to Tyre (ancestral home of the Carthaginians on the eastern shores of the Mediterranean), and eventually to Rome. It would become known, in honour of the principal good that it carried, as the Silk Roads.[9] Zhang Qian himself made several further journeys this way, and elsewhere around Asia, before his death in 114 BCE, and was so well remembered for his role in charting its course that, it was said, mere mention of his name to anyone on the Silk Roads was a proof of good faith.

Around 100 BCE another Chinese mission was sent out by the Han emperor to meet the King of the Parthians, who despatched 20,000 horsemen to greet the imperial ambassadors, and sent envoys of his own to China in return. The Han emperor, according to Sima Qian, was delighted with these new contacts.[10] These developing silk routes would be crucial to world trade for most of the next 1,500 years, until Columbus discovered America and Vasco da Gama successfully navigated the southern tip of Africa, opening up new sea routes and markets for trade west and east. And alongside the goods that travelled along this new east–west corridor came ideas – not the least of which were concepts of the divine, which would have a fundamental influence on the relationship of man and god(s) across this now-connected ancient world in the centuries to come.

PART III

RELIGIOUS CHANGE IN A CONNECTED WORLD

TIMELINE

c. 563 BCE (or 480 BCE): Birth of the Buddha in India

150 BCE: King Menander (Milinda) converted to Buddhism by monk Nagasena

25 CE: Beginning of Eastern Han Dynasty

66 CE: Tiridates I of Armenia travels to Rome to be crowned by Roman Emperor Nero

68–75 CE: First Buddhist monastery ('White Horse Monastery') built at Luoyang

148 CE: Arrival of An Shigao in China as Buddhist monk and translator

220 CE: End of Eastern Han Dynasty and beginning of Three Kingdom Period in China

257 CE: Father of future Tiridates the Great murdered; Tiridates sent to Rome (and Gregory to Caesarea)

265 CE: Beginning of Western Jin Dynasty in China

284 CE: Beginning of reign of Roman Emperor Diocletian.

286 CE: First simultaneous translation of Buddhist text into Chinese completed by Dharmaraksa

300 CE: Ghatotkacha Gupta rules in India

303 CE: Diocletian initiates persecution of Christians in Roman Empire

303/314 CE: Conversion of Tiridates the Great to Christianity

304 CE: The Xiongnu break through into Northern China – beginning of Sixteen Kingdoms Period

306 CE: Constantine I declared Augustus by his troops.

310–11 CE: Chang'an and Luoyang destroyed

312 CE: Constantine defeats Maxentius at Milvian Bridge

313 CE: The Edict of Milan, enacted by Constantine and Licinus, decrees religious tolerance

314 CE: Constantine convenes Council of Arles

316 CE: Beginning of Eastern Jin dynasty in China based around capital at Nanjing

320 CE: Chandragupta I begins rule in northern India

324 CE: Constantine I defeats Licinius at Chrysopolis

324 CE: Meeting of Constantine, Tiridates, Gregory, and Pope Silvester

325 CE: Constantine I calls the Council of Nicaea; Gregory 'the Illuminator' dies

327 CE: Second Council of Nicaea

330 CE: Constantinople is founded on the site of old Byzantium as 'the new Rome;' Tiridates the Great dies

335 CE: Samudragupta becomes ruler of the Gupta Empire; Council of Tyre in Roman Empire

337 CE: Death of Constantine

350 CE: Huns begin to invade the Sassanid Empire

353 CE: First Armenian Council conducted by Catholicos Nerses

360 CE: Julian the Apostate is proclaimed emperor and attempts to revive paganism.

375 CE: Chandragupta II becomes ruler of the Gupta Empire.

376 CE: The Visigoths flee the Huns, entering the Eastern Roman Empire

380 CE: Edict issued by Emperor Theodosius on correct form of Christian belief and worship

381 CE: Emperor Xiaowu formally accepts and establishes Buddhism at his court in China

386 CE: Start of Northern Dynasty Period in China

387 CE: Partition of Armenia between the Roman and Sassanian Empires

391 CE: Christianity becomes official religion of Roman Empire and paganism is actively suppressed

394 CE: Battle of River Frigidus between the army of Theodosius I and the army of pagan-sympathising Western Roman ruler Eugenius.

395 CE: Buddhist King of Sri Lanka despatches gift to Emperor Xiaowu in China (which arrives 405 CE)

395–398 CE: Huns invade Roman territories.

395 CE: Theodosius I dies, causing the Roman Empire to split permanently.

399 CE: Chinese Buddhist monk Faxian travels on foot to India to acquire Buddhist texts.

401 CE: Chinese Buddhist monk Kumarajiva enters court in Chang'an and begins translations of Buddhist texts.

410 CE: The Sack of Rome by Visigoths led by King Alaric.

415 CE: Founding of Nalanda University in India by Kumaragupta

INTRODUCTION

T he surviving hewn-stone piers of a once-proud but now broken
bridge stood staunchly against the rushing force of the Tiber.
Nearby, in striking contrast, a series of wooden boats, hastily tied
together and roofed with boarding to create a usable pontoon bridge,
heaved and tremored with the current. The fading stone structure, the
Milvian Bridge, had once carried the great Via Flaminia across the Tiber
and on towards its terminus in the beating heart of Rome. The ram-
shackle pontoon now served as the final means of escape for men fleeing
death at the hands of fellow Roman citizens.

Piercing the air were the tumultuous sounds of the sharp clash of
swords, the heavy clatter of solid armour hitting the ground and the
bewildered shouts of soldiers in retreat. The rough-hewn boarding lain
on top of the boats was slippery with a mix of river water and blood,
the wood broken in many places. Disorderly columns of men, reeking
of fear and confusion, snaked their way towards this unstable, bucking
bridge, hoping to cross it and head for the safety of Rome's walls.

Many never made it. Panic, exhaustion and a cut-throat desire to
survive fed a stampede. The already-weakened bridge splintered under
the weight. Thousands slipped, were shoved or just collapsed under the
duress of their armour and injuries, so falling into the roaring waters
and drowning. Among them was a man called Maxentius – one of four
joint rulers of the Roman Empire – who was 'pressed by the mass of
those fleeing and hurled into the Tiber', devoured by the currents as he

tried in vain to escape.[1] He died on the sixth anniversary of his accession to power. The date was 28 October 312 CE – henceforward a key turning point in history.

*

Huge events, great powers and individuals had continued to reshape the ancient world over the four and a half centuries since a connection was forged between the growing empire of Rome in the west and that of the Han dynasty in the east. By the time of the birth of Jesus, these two empires had expanded to such an extent that half of the entire human species were under their control.

The Han, first under Emperor Wu and then his successors, had constructed more than 22,000 miles of highway criss-crossing their empire, to improve trade and communication; and they had adopted Confucianism as their guiding governing principle. Their capital city at Chang'an had grown, as the eastern terminus of the Silk Roads, into a bustling commercial hub that was home to well over a quarter of a million people. They had also expanded Chinese control west, in part to protect the developing network of trade routes known collectively as the Silk Roads, and in part to gain control over the most-prized possession that the East thought the West had to offer: the fast horses of the central and western Asian plains, acclaimed in Chinese sources for their capacity to sweat blood.

In 9 CE the golden age of the Han dynasty was interrupted briefly, by a usurper who proved incompetent to rule and was duly overrun by a peasant rebellion that destroyed the capital at Chang'an just over a decade later. The Han were reinstated and built themselves a new capital further east at Luoyang (former seat of the illustrious Zhou dynasty from the era of Confucius). Over the following centuries the Han learnt more and more about their far-flung trading partners: from the third century CE there survives a Chinese record entitled 'The Peoples of the West', offering brief descriptive insights into what each group of people was like and what they preferred to buy and sell. (The Roman world, it recorded, was a source of fine linens and excellent gold and silver coins, and it seemingly could not get enough of Chinese silk.)[2]

At this same time the Yuezhi tribes who had taken over the kingdom of Bactria – buoyed by their prime spot at the 'roundabout' of the Silk Roads – developed a sedentary dominion of their own in central Asia, known as the Kushan Empire.[3] This was a cosmopolitan world. At Tillya Tepe, some 60 miles west of Bactra (the old capital of Bactria), a burial site of one wealthy – perhaps royal – Kushan male and five aristocratic women has been found from the first century CE. Their bodies were buried in lavish clothes rich in gold thread. They had perfume flasks from the Mediterranean, mirrors from China, gold coins from central Asia placed in the hands (echoing a Greek burial tradition) as well as jewellery from central Asia and northern India depicting Greek and nomadic themes, deities and creatures.[4] Equally, at Kapisa near Begram in modern-day Afghanistan, two sealed storerooms thought to belong to Kushan kings have been discovered, piled high with goods dating from the first to early second centuries CE, coming from – and depicting ideas and myths originating from – Rome, Egypt, India and China.[5]

To the west, the beleaguered remains of the Seleucid Empire were slowly subsumed by Bactria's rebellious neighbour Parthia, so begetting a Parthian empire that also fed off Silk Roads trade, leading to the expansion and elaboration of major trading settlements like Dura Europos (in modern-day Syria).[6] And on the eastern Mediterranean coast, a new power emerged in the first century BCE, led by Mithridates of Pontus, son of a Seleucid princess, who in time would be recognised by Rome as an enemy with shades of Hannibal about him.

Meanwhile, in Rome, the political system of the republic continued to perform well under stress. Rome's mastery over the Mediterranean became ever deeper engrained: having destroyed Carthage and Corinth in 146 BCE, it extended its control over Numidia in North Africa at the end of the second century; then pushed into central Europe and dealt with internal rebellion in Italy in the first century BCE, while also facing up to Mithridates in the pursuit of further influence into Asia.[7] In the course of all these doings Roman engineers created more than 48,000 miles of road linking the empire like the veins and arteries of the human body.

Eventually, though, as Scipio Africanus possibly foresaw, the republican system was ripped apart at the end of the first century BCE, in civil war between men competing for power. The instigator of the upheaval is usually identified as Lucius Cornelius Sulla Felix, known simply as 'Sulla'. During the 80s BCE he had halted the advance of Mithridates, besieged a newly belligerent Athens into submission and destroyed its last vestiges of independent rule and, eventually, marched his army on Rome, where he was appointed dictator – the first time this emergency office had been used since the time of Hannibal. Though Sulla eventually gave up his power, a troubling precedent had been set. Akin to the narratives put forward by Confucius that explain the decline of a dynasty in light of its losing the mandate of Heaven to rule, the Roman Republic became riddled with the disease of self-serving contenders for despotic power, aware and emboldened as to how they could snatch it. Eventually some remedy emerged in the shape of a new ruler who was able to enforce unity once more and promised a return to the core values of Roman society: the first emperor, Augustus.

In the following centuries the Roman Empire, now (just like the Han Empire in the east) under the control of one man, continued to expand west (into Britain) and east (against Parthia, which itself fell victim to a new dynastic Asian family, the Sassanids, in the early third century CE). At the same time its control of Egypt now opened up its eyes – and its merchant fleet – to even more trade with the East via India.[8] The second-century CE Roman orator Aelius Aristides eulogised Rome's growth:

What was said by Homer 'The earth was common to all' you [Rome] have made a reality, by surveying the whole *oikoumene* ['inhabited world'], by bridging the rivers in various ways, by cutting carriage roads through the mountains, by filing desert places with post stations, and by civilizing everything with your way of life and good order . . . and now indeed there is no need to write a description of the world, nor to enumerate the laws of each people, but you have become the universal geographers for all by opening up the gates of the *oikoumene* and by organizing the whole *oikoumene* like a single household.[9]

In that transformation to 'world empire', something strange happened to the term 'democracy'. Once reserved for the radical direct representation in Athens and other such city-states of the Aegean, it begins to be used in the first century CE to describe the now-lost Roman Republic.[10] In his time Aelius Aristides went even further, claiming in the eulogy to Rome quoted above that 'there has been established throughout the world alike a democracy – under one man, namely the best ruler and leader of this universal empire'.[11] By a remarkable contortion, in other words, democracy was being hymned as the outcome of one individual's universal rule.

Yet as Rome expanded and continued its boundary conflicts in the east against the Parthians and later the Sassanids, its new 'democratic' emperor felt the same strains that the Qin, Han and Seleucid rulers had suffered in keeping their enormous worlds together and defending their boundaries. By the mid-third century the Roman Empire had been divided up into three competing segments and, despite a brief period of unification, as of 293 CE it was ruled by four men, collectively known as the Tetrarchy – a quartet of two senior emperors (*Augusti*) and two juniors (*Caesares*) – who each held responsibility for their own part of the Roman world, in an attempt to ensure stability. This system, though, was doomed to an early demise by the vying ambitions of its office-holders. Maxentius, who met his end at the Milvian Bridge in 312 CE, was a tetrarch and so, too, was his triumphant opponent on that day.

·*

On 29 October 312 CE Maxentius's adversary advanced and ordered his troops into formation to march over the hastily repaired pontoon – with relative ease, compared to the blind terror in which Maxentius's men had tried to take flight (he would later also see to the restoration of the broken stone Milvian Bridge as part of his memorial to his victory). Among the decaying bodies washed up on the river's banks and tangled in the tyings of the pontoon itself, the troops discovered Maxentius's drowned corpse. His head was unceremoniously severed, fixed atop a pike and carried aloft, as proof of the victory won by the men now arriving into Rome under their general – the erstwhile tetrarch, Constantine.

Constantine's father, Constantius, had been one of the first junior tetrarchs (*Caesares*) appointed on 1 March 293 CE. Come 1 May 305, Constantius and his fellow junior ruler Galerius had succeeded to *Augusti*, promoted to the positions of senior rulers upon the orderly retirement of their predecessors, Diocletian and Maximian. The smooth course of this handover of power had not, however, lasted long. Constantius died at York on 25 July 306, whereupon his army took it upon themselves to proclaim Constantine – who had no previous formal position in the ruling quartet – as one of the new *Augusti* alongside Galerius, the other surviving senior ruler. Galerius immediately objected, as did the junior ruler who believed the position was rightfully his. In October that year, things were complicated still further when the troops of Maxentius (son of the retired Maximian), along with the Senate of Rome, proclaimed Maxentius as a new *Augustus*, despite his also having never served as *Caesar*. The senior management of Rome was suddenly looking very crowded, especially when Maximian supported his son's claim.

Over the next five years the ruling quartet of the Roman Empire challenged one another for their right to wield authority. In battle Constantine defeated Maximian, who then killed himself. His son Maxentius never forgave Constantine, and from his base of operations in Rome he ordered all statues of his fellow ruler torn down and declared a war of vengeance on the 'murderer'. In turn, it is said, Constantine was not only incensed by tales of Maxentius's mistreatment of the people of Rome, but also took umbrage at his rival's 'most despicable small size', and decided to liberate the city from its diminutive tormentor.[12] The stage was set for the battle that culminated by the old Milvian Bridge, and which ended with Constantine entering Rome in triumph, his troops bearing Maxentius's head on a spear.

Maxentius had led his troops out to battle confidently that day, because a consultation of the oracular Sibylline Books – reputedly purchased from a Greek priestess by Rome's last king, Tarquinius Superbus, and consulted by Romans at moments of great peril – had revealed to him that this was the day on which an enemy of Rome would perish.[13] In Maxentius's mind, no doubt, he was Rome's defender and Constantine the malefactor, since Constantine was the one attacking the city. But it is possible Maxentius knew inwardly that his chances of carrying the day were slim. Before leaving the safety of Rome he hid his most precious symbols of power – three lances, four javelins, a base for the imperial standard, three glass and chalcedony spheres and a sceptre, all wrapped in linen and silk and placed inside a wooden box – under an altar on the imperial Palatine Hill so that they would not fall into Constantine's hands if he took Rome. (In this, if nothing else, Maxentius seems to have been successful, hiding these treasures so well that they were only uncovered by excavations in 2006.[14])

In advance of the Battle of Milvian Bridge both sides had laid on it weighty historical resonance. Maxentius was keen to style himself as a new Horatius Cocles 'the Cyclops' – that hero of the early Roman Republic, who held off the invading Etruscans almost single-handedly and whose example was a model of valour. In contrast, Constantine portrayed Maxentius, and his defeated father Maximian, as new Tarquins – the harsh, arrogant, hated Kings of Rome against whom the people had rebelled to form the republic. At stake was not only who held political and military power, but also the right to decide where Rome stood in its history: on the cusp of being saved once more from marauding outsiders, or of being liberated from subjugation to despotism. In victory, Constantine made it very clear how this day should be remembered: thereafter 28 October was celebrated as 'Expulsion of the Tyrant Day'.[15]

Constantine stayed in Rome for two months after his victory. With Maximian and Maxentius dead, he was declared *Augustus*, undisputed master in the west of the Roman Empire. Statues of Constantine were re-erected at his behest and golden statues of Nike (Victory) and of Roma (personification of the spirit of Rome) were also set up across the sprawling metropolis. Constantine renovated parts of the city, built new bath complexes and presided over gladiatorial games. A triumphal arch to celebrate his victory at Milvian Bridge was completed in 315 CE and still stands by the Colosseum today, the different reliefs on its arches portraying Constantine hunting; making sacrifices to Apollo, Diana and Heracles; and fighting for the freedom of the Roman Empire – all surrounded by images of Roman soldiers and captured barbarians, of Sol the divine sun, Luna the divine moon, and winged Victories. The inscription offers understandably fulsome praise of

Constantine: 'Inspired by the divine, and by the greatness of his mind, he, with his army, avenged the State upon the tyrant and his whole factions at the same instant with just arms.'

That potent phrase 'inspired by the divine' has attracted much scholarly attention, not least because of the dominant literary narratives surrounding the Battle of Milvian Bridge, both those written at the time and in the decades to come. As the triumphal arch was being constructed, another version of the conflict was being composed by one Lactantius, a native of North Africa who grew to be a professor of rhetoric at Nicomedia in the eastern Roman Empire under Diocletian, and eventually served as tutor to Crispus, Constantine's son. (Constantine had probably met Lactantius in Nicomedia around 293 CE while being held hostage by Diocletian, as a form of insurance that his father Constantius would abide by the agreed division of rule in the early days of the Tetrarchy.)

Lactantius was also a Christian. It has been estimated that, as of 312 CE, between 5 and 10 per cent of the population of the Roman Empire were Christians. They had suffered a number of official persecutions over the previous century, the most severe of which were inflicted in 303–11 CE. In 314 Lactantius published a text called *On the Death of the Persecutors*. In it, he recounts the final days of a number of rulers who had mistreated and oppressed Christians, some of whom are said to have died in particularly gruesome pain as punishment for their cruelty. But he also suggests a striking set of motivations behind Constantine's actions at Milvian Bridge, which give a precise shape to the phrase 'inspired by the divine':

> Constantine was advised in a dream to mark the heavenly sign of God on the shields of his soldiers and then engage in battle. He did as he was commanded and by means of a slanted X with the top of its head bent round, he marked Christ on their shields.[16]

Twenty-three years later, the Christian Bishop Eusebius from Caesarea (in modern-day Israel on the eastern Mediterranean coast) published a *Life of Constantine* shortly after the emperor's death. Eusebius was a close confidant of Constantine in the last decade of his life and reports that 'a long while after' the Battle of Milvian Bridge, Constantine had personally imparted to him what really occurred:

> About the time of the midday sun, when day was just turning, he said he saw with his own eyes, up in the sky and resting over the sun, a cross-shaped trophy formed from light, and a text attached to it which said 'By this sign conquer.' Amazement at the spectacle seized both him and the whole company of soldiers which was then accompanying him on a campaign he was conducting somewhere, and witnessed the miracle.[17]

These accounts of what Constantine saw and did in advance of the battle serve to frame one of the most famous historiographical dilemmas from antiquity, made all the more significant by Constantine's renown as the first baptised Christian emperor who began the formal process of converting the entire Roman Empire to Christianity. Both of these later accounts – published after Constantine had made official public steps towards ending the persecution of Christians and, in the case of Eusebius, towards supporting Christian teaching – contradict contemporary Roman ('pagan') sources. There, as we have seen, Milvian Bridge was a relatively clear-cut clash, arising from the violent dispute over political and military supremacy at the top of Rome's command structure, albeit polished up with the veneer of a historical remake of the birth of the republic.[18] For Lactantius and Eusebius, though, Constantine's triumph was to be cast as a pivotal moment in which the soon-to-be-ruler of the entire Roman world discovered and embraced Christianity as the true faith, and used it as his guiding light to secure victory. It was the moment at which, in Eusebius's words, a new 'Moses' conquered the 'Egyptian Pharaoh', who was washed away in the flood.

Many scholars have disputed this matter and tried to determine what truly was meant by the ambiguous 'inspired by the divine' on the arch of Constantine in Rome. Consequently Constantine has been characterised as everything from 'a cruel and dissolute monarch', to a 'fortunate opportunist who cared little about god and humanity', to 'a heavenly authority' on earth.[19] And yet to rest on a single interpretation is to miss the complexity of the realities faced by Constantine in his wider task as a ruler. Just like the Qin, Han and Seleucid rulers whose exploits we observed in Part II, and just like his imperial Roman predecessors – not to speak of the rulers of the other empires of Asia, such as the Parthians, Sassanids and Kushans – Constantine's very survival depended on his ability to lead, solidify, defend and maintain the world under his rule. In the Roman Empire, that job had come to seem an impossible task for one man: thus the Tetrarchy. But the attempted rule of four had devoured itself. Now Constantine would move to once again unite the Roman Empire under his single rule, and his greater challenge would be to make such rule endure.

His attempt was made at a time in which the religious landscape of the Roman world was in flux. Polybius, writing back in the second century BCE, had argued that, alongside the strength of the republican system and the insistence on individual valour, *deisidaimonia* – superstition, religious belief – was a prime ingredient in 'maintaining the cohesion of the Roman state'.[20] Man's relationship with the divine was part and parcel of the relationships between individuals and between communities. If Constantine wanted to be the sole ruler of the Roman world, he would have to become involved with, tackle the problems of and harness the cohesive power of its faiths, believers and religious communities, among them the relative newcomer, Christianity.

The fourth century CE became, as a result, *the* critical period in the story of Rome's relationship with Christianity – part of the wider narrative of the empire's gradual adaptation to the ancient world around it. That story will take us from the Milvian Bridge to the developing crises of Christian theology and practice in North Africa in the now-rebuilt Roman city of Carthage; to imperial attempts to link Christian beliefs and the stability of the Roman Empire in the eastern Mediterranean. We will encounter the balancing of Christian and pagan traditions by Constantine in his attempt to be sole ruler to all in this diverse and changing world; the birth of a new pagan-Christian imperial city at the meeting point of Europe and Asia; and, eventually, the emergence of Christianity as the official religion of the Roman world, and a new relationship between spiritual and secular authority at the heart of its empire.

Yet this era is crucial not merely to the annals of Christianity and the Mediterranean. Arguably the first realm to officially embrace the Christian religion was the kingdom of Armenia, between the Black and Caspian Seas, whose ruler Tiridates the Great was said to have forcibly imposed the faith on his subjects in the early 300s, albeit with varying degrees of success. At stake was not only Tiridates' personal redemption, but the power of the monarch within the decentralised Armenian state, and the safety and security of his kingdom and rule – sandwiched as Armenia was between the Roman world to the west and the Parthian and later Sassanid Empires to the east. Once again, man's relationship with the divine was fundamentally bound up with the relationships between individuals and between communities. The outcome of Tiridates' efforts would be a Christianity very different from that of Rome, and a much more bloody and fraught relationship between sacred and secular authority.

Christianity, moreover, was by no means the only religion of the fourth century CE to flourish and develop by interaction with a worldly ruler. Indeed, two more of the four biggest religions in our world today were also in a crucial period of development and expansion at the time: Hinduism and Buddhism.[21] In India, the Gupta dynasty rose to power on the back of religious change motivated by the interaction of Hinduism and Buddhism; an unstable dynastic landscape still feeling the effects of nomadic influx since the second century BCE; and a society being transformed by wealth from the newly created east–west trade routes. In turn, the Guptas gradually developed a very particular combination of new and old elements of Hindu worship to create a religion, a vision of the divine and a society that supported their rule, thus integrating secular and spiritual authority. Their rule was to be a golden age in India's history, one of religious diversity and cultural growth.[22]

In China, the Silk Roads leading straight to the new Han capital at Luoyang had meant a flow not merely of commodities but of compelling ideas into China, among them Buddhism, which began life in the India of the 'Axial Age'. Over the first centuries CE varying forms and ideas about Buddhism had slowly made their way into Chinese thought via central Asia and India. But the fourth century CE would prove a critical turning point in the story of Buddhism's introduction, translation, configuration and acceptance by China's people and its ruling elite as an official religion, at a time when the Han dynasty had itself ceased to exist and China was broken politically and militarily into numerous kingdoms and dynasties.

With all of these stories we are graced on the one hand with a collection of contemporaneous sources – from practitioners developing their viewpoints and arguments and setting out their stands, as well as religious texts outlining the evolution of theological beliefs and their versions of what happened during this tumultuous century – and, on the other, with a number of later historical commentators, fighting to make sense of their societies and to commemorate events to suit their particular purposes. At the same time, thanks to the now-connected nature of the ancient world, we are afforded insights into a particular culture both from those operating within it and from those outside – especially in the east, as Chinese Buddhists began to make regular pilgrimages back to India. *In toto* these accounts offer us a picture of a crucial period in world history, when three great religions were engaged in a dialogue of adaptation, development and survival with the society and rulership of different communities and empires spread across a connected globe. Man's relationship to man, the relationships between communities, as well as that between humans and the divine were inextricably bound together on a journey of dramatic change.

CHAPTER 7

Religious Innovation from Inside and Out

One of her hands is placed provocatively on her slender waist, the other caught in a tentative caress of her thigh. Her ample bosom, emphasised by her clinging, flimsy clothes, is turned towards her companion. Her head, also looking his way, is framed by large gold earrings. His muscular arms are open and turned upwards in welcome, his pelvis arched towards hers, his left foot off the ground as if he were dancing with joy in her presence. His body is adorned by a gilet of the type favoured by Kushan (formerly Yuezhi) rulers of central Asia, its curves and pointed ends emphasising the length of his torso. Behind him is a staff mounted by a circle, denoting his authority. In one of his upturned hands, as he gestures towards the woman, is a ring. The two appear deep in conversation, their close heads surrounded by a halo.

This is, we think, the moment of proposal of marriage between a man called Chandragupta and a woman called Kumaradevi, as depicted on a coin produced by their future son. We have met a man of that name already in these pages. It was Chandragupta Maurya who was credited with unifying India at the time of Alexander the Great's invasion from Greece. Chandragupta was also the man in whose court Megasthenes sat as ambassador to the first Seleucid king, Seleucus I. It was he who commanded the great palace of Pataliputra, a city founded by Heracles. (Whenever he washed his hair, Megasthenes told us, his people celebrated a festival.) And he was the founder of the Mauryan dynasty who established the largest land empire in India's history – one that, as we saw earlier, is said to have disintegrated only in the hands of his grandson, Ashoka, who converted to Buddhism and decided to give everything away as part of a ruling ethos tied to the Buddha's teachings, rather than, as with his predecessors, based on conquest.

The central and northern half of India had been fragmented into warring communities ever since, beset by incursions from an expanding Bactria; by the establishment of, and wars between, different Indo-Greek kingdoms; and subsequently by the migration into India of Greeks and central Asian Saca nomads fleeing the arrival of the Yuezhi, who had established themselves just to the north of India as the Kushan Empire of central Asia and then, over the following centuries, expanded to rule much of northern India, with their southern capital in Mathura.

It is the Kushan-style outfit worn by the Chandragupta shown on this coin that dates the marriage proposal not to the fourth century BCE, but nearly 650 years later. The coin depicts the betrothing of a man who came to power in February 320 CE and called himself Chandragupta I of the Gupta dynasty. We don't know whether or not that was his real name. But his choice was very evidently steeped in reverence for the long-lost era of Chandragupta Maurya, its deployment here an unmistakable marker of this ruler's goal to create a new 'golden age' in Indian history.

As we shall see, both Chandragupta in India and Constantine in the Mediterranean would be required to reckon with religious innovation emanating from within their own realms. In both cases the development of faiths, while somewhat destabilising to society, also offered an opportunity to harness that religious belief towards the security and expansion of imperial power. In China, meanwhile, there were efforts to accommodate the arrival of Buddhism to the religious landscape. Buddhist beliefs had entered China over previous centuries, thanks to the newly connected nature of the ancient world whereby Buddhist missionaries could trek along the trade routes running east. Buddhism's advocates now faced a difficult challenge: how to gain favour and support while China itself was ripped apart politically and socially.

Similarly, in Armenia, a country perpetually in strife owing to its position as the buffer zone between the might of the Roman and Parthian/Sassanid Empires, the new religion of Christianity made a spectacular impact because of its patronage by King Tiridates the Great, who would instigate a dramatic change in religious orientation for his entire country – one that had consequences not only for the Armenian people and their religious observance, but also for the organisation of Armenia's political hierarchy and its position in the wider geopolitics of the ancient world.

Religious Innovation from Within

If we trust later accounts given by Chinese travellers in India, then Chandragupta was not the first Gupta ruler.[1] Rather, that was Sri Gupta, who came to power around 275 CE (close to the birth of Constantine) and whose son Ghatotkacha succeeded him in 300 BCE (while Constantius, Constantine's father, was enjoying his share of ruling the Roman world as a junior *Caesar*). Ghatotkacha's son was Chandragupta. We know next to nothing about the personalities of these first three Gupta rulers. But we do know that Chandragupta saw his rule as an advance upon that of his predecessors: whereas his father had called himself simply *Maharaja* ('Great King'), Chandragupta took the title of *Maharajadhiraja*, 'King of Kings'.[2]

This was clearly a man concerned with fashioning for himself a position of high stature; and so the public emphasis on marriage – on union – upon his sons coinage might at first appear curious. Indeed, the image could be taken to suggest that Chandragupta's wife held him in a sort of seductive thrall, rather than being subservient to him.

Kumaradevi came from the Licchavi family, an established tribal confederation ruling between the Ganges plain and the Terai region of Nepal. The Guptas ruled slightly further to the south, in the area known as Magadha, from which the Mauryan rulers had come centuries before. The marriage of Kumaradevi and Chandragupta thus seems to have conjoined two important families to create a large single area of influence. Yet we have a hint that there was more to it than that. Chandragupta's son chose to refer to the marriage on his own coins, and his official inscriptions also noted his descent from the Licchavi family. What the Licchavi alliance seems to have given the Guptas as a ruling family was, above all, respectability.[3]

To understand why the Guptas desired such an enhancement of their standing, we need to appreciate the nature of society and religion in India at this time. In the *Rig Veda* – the earliest known ancient Hindu text, composed between 1500 and 1200 BCE – different groups within human society are represented as if they were different parts of the body of the cosmic figure Purusha: his mouth, arms, thighs and feet.[4] Over the centuries that followed, these different elements of society (known as *varnas*) came to form the caste system, which imposed a strict social order in which each *varna* had a specific role to perform in society, and each enjoyed specific rights. The *Kshatriya* was the *varna* of kings (and were Purusha's arms); the *Brahman* was the *varna* of individuals who took care of sacrificial ritual (and were Purusha's mouth); the *Vaishya* incorporated men and women engaged in agriculture and trade (who were Purusha's thighs); and the *Shudras* was made up of labourers and those who performed other servile tasks (who, fittingly, were Purusha's feet). And while in reality there seem to have been several examples of those who managed to escape the rigidity of the system (earlier dynasties like the Nanda, for instance, were said in later sources to have been from the non-ruling *varna*), by the first century CE the rhetoric of these distinctions was rigid enough to make movement between *varnas* very difficult – even intermarriage between *varnas* was outlawed.

This social and religious division was supported by a wide range of religious writings dating from different times. First were the *Vedas* – four sets of sacred texts composed roughly between 1500 and 1200 BCE, of which the *Rig Veda* was acknowledged as the oldest, and which offer a gradually strengthening link between certain social groups and their particular (and protected) roles in society.[5] Access to them too was a protected privilege: only the top three *varnas* had the right to read the *Vedas*. Next were the Sanskrit epics such as the *Ramayana* (the story of the good king Rama, claimed by some modern scholars to be an Indian version of the Greek *Iliad*) and the

Mahabharata (the longest epic poem in existence, telling the story of the dynastic struggle for the throne of Hastinapura), both originally composed around the fifth century BCE, although they continued to evolve over the following centuries.[6] Lastly there were the *Puranas*, created perhaps around the time of the *Vedas*, but not written down until the first centuries CE and continually modified right through to the modern era, especially during the years of the Gupta dynasty. The *Puranas* were genealogical records of great families and gods. Of particular importance within all of these texts was the concept of *dharma*: that evolving and multiplicitor sense of order and balance, which in turn made the universe possible. Part of pursuing *dharma* (and the prescription inevitably varied for each *varna*) was not to challenge the segmentation of society. To do so was to risk cosmic imbalance.

As of the late third/early fourth centuries CE the Guptas, it has been argued, were *Vaishya*, and so had apparently managed to bypass the precedent of rulers having to belong to the *Kshatriya*.[7] This was thanks in no small part to developments in the ritual landscape in India, which had increasingly helped to muddy the distinctions within the caste system.

One of these developments was Buddhism. By Chandragupta's time Buddhism was around 800 years old and could boast many noteworthy adherents, not least the Mauryan king Ashoka, who was said to have proselytised for the faith and whose embrace of its selfless teachings may have brought about the collapse of his Mauryan dynasty.

The high profile of Buddhism within Indian society had posed a challenge to the Hindu *varna* system. In particular Buddhism, which in its early phases had little interest in officials of any sort, had served to query the system's stipulation of only one group – the *Brahmans* – having the right to undertake religious rituals for the community. This tradition compelled the society to place huge reliance on the specialist knowledge, training and activities of the *Brahman* as insurers of their salvation, indeed as veritable gods on earth. The *Brahmans* were people of tremendous power, instantly recognisable on the streets: half-naked, brandishing a stick with which to ward off evil spirits, hair gathered up in a topknot. (A *Brahman* would have his hair tied in this manner at the age of three as part of an initiation ritual, and the topknot was a treasured mark of distinction. *Brahmans* could not be sentenced to death, but they could be sentenced to have their hair knot cut off – a fate considered equally severe.[8]) In contrast, Buddhists advocated that each individual could work towards their own personal salvation – they didn't need a *Brahman* to do it for them (although Buddhists were at the same time keen for lay support to help sustain *them* as ritual specialists within their Buddhist monasteries).

At the same time, from the second century BCE, the apparent impermeability of the different *varnas* was further weakened as a number of *Brahmans* took on roles other than that of priest – becoming military and political leaders, and even spies, as well as taking up a range of more mundane jobs that kept society functioning, such as gaming-house owners, land overseers, actors and even butchers. At the same time the boundaries between the other *varnas* were likewise weakened by the increasing wealth and importance of members of the *Vaishya* class, who were benefiting from the abundantly profitable trade routes (including the new Silk Roads) and, in consequence, effectively becoming a new middle class.[9]

Finally, *varna* distinctions across India were further weakened by immigration. From the late second century BCE waves of Saca nomads – traditional inhabitants of central Asia on the borders of Bactria – streamed down south into the area of the Punjab in India. (The newly created Parthian Empire served to bar their way from heading west.) These Sacas had originally been displaced from their homeland by the Yuezhi, who fled the Han-dynasty expansion of the third century BCE and who, within a century, would dominate Bactria and develop into the Kushan Empire. During the first century CE the Kushans themselves began to push into India, driving the Sacas yet further south. These historically nomadic tribes brought with them a variety of religious beliefs and traditions, particularly focused around respect for the heroic warrior ruler, who did not have to come from a particular social background, but instead was judged by valour in battle and competence in rule; as well as the notion of elite warrior brotherhood that could expect lavish support from its community. Such ideas inevitably came to influence and challenge traditional religious beliefs in India, including the fixed-from-birth social and religious position of any one individual as delineated by the different *varnas*.

A notable difference remains, though, between becoming a king and becoming the 'King of Kings', as Chandragupta styled himself. As we have seen, Chandragupta from the start set his sights high on leading a ruling dynasty that would bring about a novel 'golden age'. In this climate of newly improved social possibility, his family's respectability and right to rule were bolstered by this new marriage bond of equality with a more traditional ruling clan who claimed real power and influence.[10]

The marriage, it should be noted, was also a shrewd tactical move to bulwark both families against a fresh era of turbulence in central Asia. The Kushan Empire to the north was now in serious trouble. Its new enemy was the emergent empire of western Asia: the Sassanids, who had overthrown the Parthians and were now expanding east into Kushan territory. During the third century CE the Kushans had crumbled, leaving the area of Asia centred around today's Afghanistan once again in uproar. At the same time the community of the Satavahanas in southern India, beleaguered by the weight of migrating Sacas, also came apart, leaving a political vacuum. In an area of southern central India known as the Deccan, this vacuum was soon filled by a new ruling clan, the Vakatakas, who subsequently allied with other neighbouring groups close to the Guptas.[11] The Gupta–Licchavi alliance may, therefore, have offered both parties a certain safety in numbers and protection from annihilation in a fast-changing and fraught political environment to their north and south.

And so, whatever he chose to call himself, whomever he allied himself to in marriage, Chandragupta still had much to do if he was to make real his aspirations. The changing religious landscape of India proved to be his greatest ally. The first crucial shift in religious outlook – the increased muddying of divisions between the *varnas* – made it more feasible for the Guptas to rule in the first place. And in response, Chandragupta and his successors seem to have tried to favour all sides: encouraging the concept of every individual's right and responsibility for ensuring their own (and their community's) salvation, while also supporting the ongoing social and religious importance of the Brahmans in return for their support of royal (and particularly Gupta) power. Around this time, for instance, the *Purana* texts – which many scholars believe to have been regularly written down only from the Gupta era onwards – came to be increasingly important relative to the more traditional *Vedas*. The *Puranas* offered a collection of genealogical stories of gods and families that emphasised both the importance of the Brahmans and rulers, as well as the importance of individual acts and personal piety to particular gods as a route to salvation.

The second major shift in Hindu worship at this time that proved helpful to Chandragupta and his successors was the rise to prominence of two gods above all others: Vishnu and Shiva. Vishnu was the four-armed saviour of mankind, a sort of epic and infallible king; Shiva the three-eyed god of both destruction and benefaction. Many other gods – also human heroes, such as King Rama, celebrated in the epic *Ramayana*, and even founders of other religions such as the Buddha – were increasingly portrayed as avatars (alternate forms) of Vishnu and Shiva. As a result, a more streamlined divine world came into conception alongside its more multiplicitous counterpart. A wide range of gods was still evoked and worshipped (and conflict between the different conceptions of the divine could, and did, break out), but ultimately there was also the potential for them to be related back to these two supreme deities, making possible the linkage of groups with different priorities of worship – even from different religions – into one greater community devoted to two ultimate figureheads.

India had evolved into a pluralistic society teeming with different peoples, ethnic identities and religious, social and political traditions. Its religious landscape now had the potential to support the creation of large cohesive political and religious communities without having to do harm to that pluralism. Much would depend, though, on the right kind of king and imperial family, if a new era of empire fit to compare with the Mauryans was to be forged. It was now in the hands of the Guptas as to whether they could be such rulers.

*

Constantine, too, had ambitions to harness the changing religious landscape of the Roman world in order to solidify and expand his power. After defeating Maxentius in 312 he was undisputed ruler of the western Roman Empire. In February 313 he held a meeting in Milan with Licinius, who was shortly to hold comparable authority over the east. It is said by the Christian writer Lactantius (who in 314 published his account of Constantine's Christian awakening at Milvian Bridge) that Licinius had also been aided in his victories by an angel of God who taught him a prayer for his troops to recite.

The two men probably made a contrasting pair. Statues of Constantine always show him as beardless, youthful, serene, his calm features emanating power. Licinius is always bearded, older and seeming somehow more worldly-wise. Between them, they presented distinct, if disparate, visual echoes of Roman power past. Constantine seems to recall Augustus, who was a boyish nineteen-year-old when he assumed the role of Julius Caesar's adopted heir and went on to fashion the Roman Empire out of the imploded republic. Licinius, meanwhile, might remind us of Diocletian, the low-born Dalmatian, forty when he became emperor, who stabilised the empire after a period of terrible trauma.

The friendship between Licinius and Constantine was sealed in Milan when Constantine's daughter was given to Licinius in marriage, though she was half his age. What they furthermore agreed on was a need for caution. The communiqué issued after their discussions did not demand that Romans convert to Christianity, or decree the destruction of pagan sites; rather, it called for the toleration of all religious beliefs, respect for diversity, and the restitution of property confiscated from persecuted sects. It offered 'to Christians and everyone else the free power to follow whatever religion each person prefers'.[12] While this, of course, particularly benefited Christians, it prioritised no one. Specific religious choice was, it seems, for Licinius and Constantine no longer the issue. Rather, they wanted religious calm.

This move – to actively embrace toleration rather than persecution – has been hailed as a defining moment in Western thought. In many ways it was also an intensification of the traditional Roman religious outlook. Just like those of Greece and India, the Roman religious world was inherently polytheistic: there was a smorgasbord of gods, and people had always had their personal and/or local favourites. New gods, and new variants of already established deities, continually entered Roman religion and were being worshipped with gusto. (For instance, in the early centuries CE the cult of Mithras seemed to enter the Roman bloodstream in the army, and among members of the imperial court in particular, and sites were founded for his worship across the empire). What did unite Roman religious worship was, first, the centrality of blood sacrifice to (often public) ritual action; and, second, the recognition that the figure of the emperor – generally worshipped and held as akin to the divine – commanded the ultimate loyalty and reverence of every Roman.

Christians, however, were different. They tended to meet in private, were not disposed to offer blood sacrifice and professed ultimate loyalty not to the emperor but to their God. As such, they had served to put an increasingly irritant thorn into the Roman psyche. The problem was not doctrinal so much as political and social: given their peculiar habits, were Christians to be considered good contributing members of Roman society or were they traitors in the midst? From the mid-third century CE onwards, the official mindset of the emperors had veered towards the latter view, so leading to periods of Christian persecution, the most serious under Diocletian between 303 and 311. But in 313 Constantine and Licinius – needing to secure and solidify their own rules over communities that were politicaly, socially and religiously divided – called for an intensified sense of religious toleration and respect, thereby permitting Christian as well as all the forms of polytheistic worship (later lumped together by Christian writers under the term 'pagan') to be practised alongside one another.

Over the next three years Constantine affirmed his commitment to this policy of toleration, in a tireless attempt to balance Christian and pagan traditions. He was the pagan emperor (he had not converted or been baptised) of an as-yet overwhelmingly pagan empire – despite Lactantius, in contemporary publications, claiming him for Christianity. He had refused pagan sacrifice as part of the celebrations to mark his ten years in power, but allowed the traditional pagan circus games. He had built new baths, but also new churches (including the first St Peter's) on imperial property or outside the city walls, so as not to threaten the traditional pagan temples at the heart of Rome. In their architecture these new churches used a well-known social and secular architectural form – the basilica – to minimise any discontent about their construction amongst the pagan majority. On his coinage Constantine continued to use the pagan image of the Unconquered Sun (*Sol Invictus*), which he claimed as his 'companion', and banned business on a Sunday so that the day could be dedicated to sun-worship (not in deference to Christian scripture that declared the seventh day as that of God's rest). Yet medallions bearing Christian symbols were also produced. Furthermore, Constantine appointed Lactantius as tutor to his son Crispus, extended the judicial authority of Christian bishops and gave permission for manumission of slaves to take place in churches.

Within the wider Christian community, however, Constantine's desire for even-handedness was by no means unanimously shared. On 15 April 313 his representative was met by an angry crowd in the streets of Carthage. (This great city – once the centre of opposition to Roman expansion in the Mediterranean – was now a rebuilt and flourishing Roman port and, most importantly, the centre of the Christian religious hierarchy in North Africa.) From the incensed mob Constantine's man received two packages. The first was sealed and contained a set of charges against the Christian Primate – Chief Bishop – of Carthage, a man called Caecilian. The second was an open letter of petition to Constantine, asking him to allow the Christian bishops of Gaul to hear their case.[13]

Constantine agreed and deferred the organisation of the hearing to the Chief Bishop of Rome, Miltiades, who made it into a much larger affair, stacking the jury with other bishops from Italy. On 2 October 313, after just three days of discussion, they delivered their verdict: far from agreeing with the grievances against Caecilian, they instead accused the group of Christians in Africa (led by a man called Donatus) of forming a schism in the Christian Church. Not to be dissuaded, Donatus and his fellow activists appealed directly to the emperor to overturn the decision.

The grievance at stake arose from the manner in which religious authority emanated from choices made during the era of persecution that Constantine and Licinius had recently outlawed. During that time

Christian bishops had been required to hand over copies of the scriptures. Those who did, and who complied in other ways with the Roman authorities – therefore compromising their Christian beliefs – were known as *traditores* (from the Latin *trado*, 'to surrender'). As persecution waned, the issue for Christians was whether or not to accept back into the fold those who had been *traditores*, and to what extent any of their performance of functions – particularly Christian rites such as baptism and ordination – carried sacred weight. The rigorists – those who felt that such men had lost all authority and that to associate with them would be to deny the joys of Heaven – had their stronghold of support in a town called Cirta, in the Numidian hinterland of North Africa back from the Mediterranean coast and Carthage, an area that had been hard hit by Christian persecution. They were led by the Primate of Numidia. The moderates – those who felt that the *traditores* should be forgiven – were led by the Primate of Carthage on the western North African coast.

In 311 the Primate of Carthage had died, and his archdeacon, Caecilian, had quickly prevailed upon three local bishops to elect him as successor before the Numidian contingent could travel to Carthage for the election. In 312 – as Constantine was taking Rome after the defeat of Maxentius – the Primate of Numidia, Secundus, at last held a council in Carthage, comprising seventy bishops from North Africa, which challenged the veracity of Caecilian's election. Not only did Secundus declare Caecilian a *traditor* (he was guilty of preventing food being given to Christians who were being starved to death by the Roman authorities), but also those who had ordained him: thus he believed that the election was null and void. Not that Secundus and a number of the bishops who supported him were free of such accusations themselves – many of them had confessed to being *traditores* at one point or another and had agreed to overlook one another's actions.

Secundus is said to have been aided in stirring up antagonism towards Caecilian by a Spanish lady of extreme wealth living in Carthage named Lucilla, who had never forgiven Caecilian for censoring her ostentatious style of Christian worship. Together she and Secundus elected an alternative rigorist candidate as their Primate of Carthage: Lucilla's personal chaplain, a man called Marjorinus. It was Secundus and Marjorinus who had written to Constantine in 313 asking him to resolve the issue, though Marjorinus had died shortly afterwards, being replaced as rigorist candidate for Primate of Carthage by Donatus, who was the face of their cause by the time Bishop Miltiades' ecclesiastical court in Rome made its ruling.

This battle in North Africa, however, was not simply an issue of theological doctrine – it was a geographical and class struggle, too. Carthage was a big, busy metropolitan city, firmly part of the Roman Empire since its humbling and destruction by Rome in the wars of the third and second centuries BCE. The population of the now-rebuilt harbour town was wealthy, with a burgeoning successful middle class whose sprawling villas surrounded the city, copying the vogues of design and decoration current in Rome. Its well-watered and fertile estates produced the corn that Rome – a city of more than a million people – depended on for its sustenance. Carthage had much to gain from its continuing good relationship with Rome, and Rome had significant interest in keeping Carthage close.

Conversely, Numidia – stretching across what is now Algeria and parts of Tunisia – was a territory made up of tiny villages. The heavy and sustained persecution against its Christian inhabitants in the early fourth century had decimated what towns there had once been. Numidia's high plains lacked natural rainfall and only the olive tree thrived in its soils. Amidst their groves, small rural communities descended from Berber nomads huddled around their olive presses and, increasingly, their Christian churches. These poorer, more rural, more isolated and more traditional communities were the bedrock of the Donatist movement – Donatus himself came from Casae Nigrae on the southern edge of the high plains of Numidia, looking out over the Saharan desert to the south.

The Donatist struggle was thus between the territory of Numidia and the city of Carthage, the lower classes and the more affluent ones; between Romanised Africans and those still attached to their traditional Berber ancestry; between a bustling urban community and isolated, struggling rural ones; between rigorists and moderates in Christian doctrine and action; between the rival bishops Donatus and Caecilian, and increasingly between the Donatists and the Roman Christian Church, not to mention Constantine himself.

For Constantine – seeking to secure his position as sole ruler of the western Roman Empire and reinforce its solidarity after a period of inter-ruler conflict – the Christian hierarchy in North Africa (like those elsewhere within his command) had no doubt seemed a useful tool for him to empower, as a way of reinforcing community cohesion under his rule. He had already given bishops increased juridical authority and had increased the number of social roles for churches within the community. In Carthage, Constantine had in the same way shown solid support for Caecilian, showering him with money and releasing from municipal taxes all clergy who worked with him. In tandem he is also said to have tried to scare those who threatened the peace and prosperity of his rule by sending Maxentius's severed head – or what remained of it by this stage, previously paraded around Rome atop a pike – to North Africa to show what happened to those who opposed him.

At the same time, Constantine was willing to hear Donatus's case against Caecilian, most likely because solving religious disputes was another way of achieving his greater goal of religious toleration and community cohesion. In addition, he may even have welcomed Donatus's demand for the emperor himself to hear the case and overturn the original bishops' ruling – because such an exercise of arbitration would position Constantine as the ultimate adjudicator on religious issues: it enjoined the Christian hierarchy with the imperial one, just as pagan religious hierarchies had traditionally placed the emperor at their top. (Constantine never relinquished his official pagan title of *Pontifex Maximus*.)

On 1 August 314 CE Constantine pursued this intertwining of imperial and Christian hierarchy by personally convening a council of Christian bishops at Arles – the first time a non-Christian authority (Constantine was still officially a pagan emperor) had claimed the right to call such a gathering. Their task, over several weeks of discussion, was to adjudicate on a number of outstanding issues of dispute within the Christian Church, from the 'Donatist' issue in Africa to the official date of Easter. In addition Constantine asked them to examine how Christians could be better integrated into the imperial order and, particularly, into its army – this being a furthering of the aspiration to see Christian and pagan hierarchies (and wider communities) better amalgamated.

In relation to North Africa this council, too, supported Caecilian, but once again the Donatists refused to accept their verdict. Constantine finally agreed to hear the case himself: the emperor of the western Roman Empire was to adjudicate on a matter of Christian doctrine in North Africa. And yet still the Donatists refused to accept his decision, which was one that gave continued support for Caecilian. The Donatists increasingly gave the appearance of being unyielding, puritanical obstructionists who were challenging the authority of Constantine as emperor. In 315 CE Constantine threatened to bring his army to Africa to deal personally with the situation and destroy those who acted against him. (Possibly the decayed remnants of Maxentius's head were brought back for public inspection once again.) But the army never arrived, because Constantine's attention was demanded on his northern and eastern fronts.

Throughout 314 and 315 CE Constantine had been otherwise engaged in fortifying his western Roman Empire against increasingly rebellious Germanic tribes in the north. He had also been dealing with the ruler of the east, Licinius, who had delivered Constantine a grandchild via his much younger wife. In 316, however, the relationship seems to have rapidly deteriorated. The coinage produced in Constantine's western half of the empire, which had proudly proclaimed the faces of both *Augusti*, henceforth depicted only Constantine. On 8 October 316 the two men met on the battlefield in Pannonia in the area of today's northern Balkans. In January 317 their troops clashed again, this time in Thrace, but there was no clear victor.

Over the next seven years an uneasy truce was maintained in which Licinius kept his official title but with much reduced authority. Yet by 324 both *Augusti* had amassed armies in excess of 100,000 men. Constantine defeated Licinius twice, on 3 July and 18 September. At both encounters Constantine's men had gone into battle under Christian standards, echoing those Constantine had apparently used at Milvian Bridge. It was later said that Constantine ordered the Christian standard to be moved around the battlefield to wherever his men were wearying. Its sight had reportedly not only given them fresh strength, but had struck dismay into the troops of Licinius. As the later historian and Christian bishop Eusebius recounted, this conflict had become a battle of Christianity versus paganism.

According to the later Christian sources, the reason for this resort to hostilities between co-rulers formerly devoted to religious toleration was that Licinius had over the past seven years diverged from the agreed policy and, increasingly, persecuted Christians in the east. He had devoted himself to the god Jupiter, dismissed Christians from imperial service, ordered them not to worship in church but in the open outside the city gates, and forbade bishops to visit one another's cities.

And so, when Licinius finally surrendered to Constantine at Nicomedia in 324, Constantine not only became undisputed master of the entire Roman Empire, but did so buoyed by a narrative of his own successful religious toleration *and* by strong Christian support. He now had to find a way to hold his empire together and to determine what role Christians and Christianity would play within his extended domains.

Religious Innovation from Without

By the time Ghatotkacha Gupta, the father of Chandragupta I, came to power in India around 300 CE, there were almost 4,000 Buddhist monks in China, the majority concentrated in the 180 or so Buddhist establishments constructed in the old Han capital (now rebuilt) at Chang'an and the new Han capital at Luoyang. This was a small number, vastly outweighed by those devoted to the predominant strains of worship and belief in China, focused mostly around lunar and solar festivals, ancestor worship and folk traditions based on belief in a multitude of divine beings.[14] And alongside these sat the still-developing philosophies of Daoism and Confucianism, both products of the 'Axial Age' in China.[15]

Throughout the era of the Han dynasty, Daoism – which advocated the setting of individual action in harmony with the greater rhythm of the universe – had continued to develop in myriad forms across different parts of China.[16] And during the same era, the Han emperors had also begun to embrace Confucianism, particularly as their philosophy of government. In 136 BCE the government established five areas of learning in which its civil servants were expected to be expert: five – now canonical – texts, including the *Spring and Autumn Annals*, supposedly written by Confucius. In 124 BCE an imperial academy was set up, through which it was necessary to pass to enter the administration, at the same time as 'inherited' imperial court positions (passed down through aristocratic families) were finally abolished. The result was the appointment as the emperor's chancellor of a man called Gongsun Hong, who had begun life as a swineherd, then became a Confucian scholar, prior to this remarkable elevation, which made real that which Confucius had dreamt of for himself: the acceptance of his philosophy of rule in China. It is no accident that around this same time the first biography of Confucius appeared, written by Sima Qian.

But despite Confucianism's new stature, its beliefs and principles were not necessarily fixed – not least because Confucianist disciples were constantly being required to adapt the master's thinking in response to problems of a kind that Confucius had never directly had to address (for instance, the concept of foreign policy in a new connected world, China having sent its first ambassadors to Rome in 130 BCE, Roman ambassadors making their way to the imperial court in 166 CE).[17] Similarly, the manner in which Confucius himself was remembered was to change dramatically. In 57 CE the imperial college began the practice of sacrifice to Confucius as more than a mere man. In 195 CE official veneration at his tomb began.

As such, the religious landscape of China was complex: older forms of ancestral worship and folk traditions, mixed in amongst developing forms of Daoist belief that stretched across the boundaries of philosophy and religion, itself cheek-by-jowl with the philosophy of Confucianism, whose late founder was now an object of ritual worship – and, in the midst of it all, Buddhism.

It was later reported that Buddhism had first been brought to Chinese soil by the Indian king and Buddhist convert Ashoka during the third century BCE.[18] Ashoka is said to have sent missionaries to western Asia to preach Buddhist doctrine, and to have sent his son to Sri Lanka to introduce Buddhism there. But he is also said to have built

84,000 *stupas* (mound-like structures encasing Buddhist relics that were used as a focus for meditation) across a wide area of India and central Asia. Some of these *stupas* were even reputed to have been built inside the territory of what would become the Han Empire, after Emperor Wu and his successors expanded west to protect the emerging Silk Road in the second and first centuries BCE.

Whether or not Ashoka did build here, the *stupa* without a doubt became a regular sight within Chinese territory in later centuries, and has a hugely important place in the history of Chinese architecture: it is the architectural ancestor of the now-ubiquitous Chinese pagoda. The Big Wild Goose Pagoda in the former Han capital city of Chang'an (in modern-day Xi'an) is still standing, created in the seventh century CE, and not only echoes Buddhist architecture, but was built to house Buddhist relics and *sutras* (manuals for Buddhist religious practice) brought back to China from India.

Buddhism – to a greater degree than its Indian counterpart Hinduism – was at its heart a missionary doctrine that urged its believers to spread its teachings.[19] As a result, from Ashoka's time onwards groups of Buddhist monks appeared in a number of Indo-Greek, central Asian and eastern communities. In the mid-second century BCE Buddhist monks won over the Indo-Greek king Menander (who ruled in north-west India in the last decades before Bactria and the surrounding area was overrun by the Yuezhi, having migrated into central Asia). Menander's conversion is celebrated in the later Buddhist text *Milindpanho – The Questions of Milinda (Menander)* – which in turn became part of a package of Buddhist texts to be exported even further afield: we know about *Milindpanho* thanks to its survival in Burmese and Chinese Buddhist literature. Equally, it was in Sri Lanka that some of the first Buddhist texts were written down (on palm leaves) around 43 BCE (Ashoka's son clearly met with some success in his mission there).[20] And by the first century CE Buddhism had spread to the north of India, supported officially by at least some of the rulers of the Kushan Empire.

In texts from the fifth and sixth centuries CE we also read of how the first Buddhist missionaries supposedly came to China. A Buddhist delegation is said to have arrived at the court of the First Emperor, Qin

Shi Huangdi, in the late third century BCE – whereupon the emperor, very much of the Legalist outlook, promptly threw the Buddhists in jail. But legend has it they were broken out of their prison by an enormous golden man who cowed the emperor into allowing them to continue with their worship.[21]

In the time of the Han dynasty, in contrast, Buddhists were said to have been actively sought out by the emperor, on the advice of his own learned men, in order to help with explanations for unnatural phenomena. During the construction of an artificial lake for the emperor, a dark black sludge deep in the ground was discovered. This baffled the Han experts, but was identified, it is said, by Buddhist authorities as the ashes left over from the conflagration of all that remained at the end of a *kalpa* – the Indian concept of a cosmic time period equating to 4,320,000 human years.[22]

In this same period the envoys of Han emperors also encountered Buddhism in India and central Asia: Emperor Wu's ambassador to the Yuezhi in the early second century BCE (he whose endless travels made his name one of high repute on the Silk Roads) spoke of Buddhism in his reports back to the emperor.

Then, in the second half of the first century CE, Emperor Ming was said – albeit in later reports not unlike those of Eusebius relating to Constantine and his purported visions at Milvian Bridge – to have dreamt of a golden deity and been told by one of his most trusted advisers that this figure was none other than the Buddha from India. Ming immediately despatched a delegation to search for Indian disciples of the Buddha and bring them back to his court. Upon their return, around 65 CE, they were accompanied by two Indian Buddhist monks, who rode on a white horse and clutched a number of relics as well as a text.[23] This was the first Buddhist writing to be translated into Chinese: the *Sutra* of forty-two sections. This, however, was no traditional Buddhist text of Indian provenance – but, rather, a compilation of different ideas about Buddhist worship purposely created for the export of Buddhism abroad.

In honour of the monks' arrival, the emperor built the first Buddhist monastery in China on the outskirts of the Han capital at Luoyang and, in recognition of the mode of their arrival, named it the White Horse Monastery. Ming did not stop there: his half-brother, Liu Ying, had also welcomed a Buddhist group and had even begun to worship the Buddha. The emperor now lent his public support for his half-brother's worship, in an edict sent to all his client kings: 'He [Ming's half-brother] respectfully performs the gentle sacrifices to the Buddha ... What dislike or suspicion could there be?'[24] Soon afterwards, however, Liu Ying suffered a fall from grace on account of his perceived attempts to rise above his station. Usurping the prerogatives of the emperor still mandated punishment, whatever religion one practised. After being found guilty and exiled from his kingdom he committed suicide in 71 CE.

From this point onwards Buddhist monks continued to flow steadily into China, driven by the desire to spread their beliefs. By around 100 CE Buddhist monks were sufficiently known – for their unflinching devotion to their worship, at least – to be used by the commentator Zhang Heng as the ultimate example of the seductive charms of the women in the city of Chang'an: 'with their lovely open eyes they cast bewitching glances upon the company. One look at them would make one surrender a city. Even the virtuous *Sramanas* [Buddhist monks] could be captivated by them!'[25]

Most of these monks travelled into Chinese territory along the northern Silk Road of central Asia, which, since the late second century BCE, had connected the Mediterranean, central Asia and China, passing through Chang'an and ending up at Luoyang. These missionaries slowly snaked their way on foot, by horse or in caravans, alongside traders, exiles and mercenaries, across the vast wide-open plains, steep mountain passes, deserts and grand roads of the Han Empire. It was often not an easy journey. In the late fourth century CE a Chinese traveller called Faxian, himself a Buddhist monk, travelled to India on pilgrimage and later described the agonising process of one section of the route that crossed the Gobi desert:

[T]here are a great many evil spirits and also hot winds; those who encounter them perish to a man. There are neither birds above nor beasts below. Gazing on all sides as far as the eye can reach in order to mark the track, no guidance is to be obtained, save from the rotting bones of dead men which point the way.[26]

Since the inception of the first Silk Road several other routes from the Mediterranean to China had developed. One of these alternatives, also used by Buddhist monks – especially those coming direct from India – is known as the 'southern' Silk Road, starting at the former capital of the Mauryans, Pataliputra, continuing through Burma and up over the mountains and across the river valleys to Kunming (Yunnanfu), the chief city of the southern province of China.

Increasing numbers also travelled by sea on the developing trade routes that ploughed the waters along the Persian Gulf around India, eventually ending their journeys at the port known to the Romans as Kattigara, in modern-day Vietnam. Buddhist teachings in these centuries travelled alongside precious goods such as silk, jade, cotton, ivory, musk, amber and oil, but also exotic animals, including elephants, monkeys and parrots; as well as more mundane goods, such as soya beans. And Buddhist ideas mingled with the enormously wide range of knowledge surging along these umbilical cords joining East and West, covering everything from astronomy, calendrical science and an understanding of the constellations to medicine and a working knowledge of crop rotation. Much of this specific expertise was carried by the same people: Buddhist monks also knew astronomy and medicine, for instance.

What it is crucial to understand is that Buddhism did not enter China at one time or from one place. For example, in the second and third centuries CE eighteen foreign missionaries (whom we know by name) were actively teaching Buddhist ideas in China: four were Indian, four Indo-Scythian, three Parthian, four Sogdians and three Khotanese.

Equally, and even more crucially, Buddhism did not enter China in one form: it was never a static creed, in much the same way that Hindu worship evolved in India and Confucianism in China (and as Christianity would change shape within the Roman world). After the death of the Buddha in the fifth/fourth century BCE various councils had been held to formulate and refine Buddhist ideas and practices in locations from India to the Kushan Empire in central Asia. This had led almost immediately to the division of Buddhism into two main strands: *Mahayana* ('Great Vehicle') and *Theravada* ('Lesser Vehicle', also known as *Hinayana*), differentiated in principle by their attitudes to *Bodhisattvas* (those who try to attain *bodhi*, or 'enlightenment', in imitation of the Buddha). At the same time, as Buddhism expanded into central Asia, it was also influenced by Greco-Roman traditions coming from the west, especially in the realm of artistic representation. One of the first surviving images of the Buddha appears on a coin struck by King Kanishka of the Kushan Empire, representing the Buddha in a Greco-Roman tunic and with wavy hair.

Buddhism was thus an ever-expanding and changing religious phenomenon, influenced by the major currents of ideas flowing across the connected ancient world, and expressed in a growing number of religious texts created for each of its major divisions in each of the regions in which it was worshipped (and to which it was exported). These texts covered how the Buddhist monastery (the *sangha*) and its monks should behave; the sermons and stories of the Buddha, known as *sutras* (including those of his 550 earlier lives), alongside stories of his disciples and songs of devotion; numerous commentaries on the teachings of Buddhism; reports of particular conversions (such as that of the Indo-Greek king Menander); sayings of the Buddha; and, particularly for followers of *Mahayana* Buddhism, additional texts said to have been revealed by the Buddha to certain of his disciples that backed up particular *Mahayana* beliefs. As a result, the sheer volume and diversity of Buddhist literature was overwhelming, all of it simultaneously feeding into China from different locations.

And by the later third century CE Chinese intellectuals had begun to travel back towards India specifically to seek out even more of it. From 260 CE we have the first record of a Chinese person leaving Chinese territory in order to bring back Buddhist texts. Zhu Shixing set out 'to secure certain canonical texts needed for the better understanding and practice of religion at home'.[27] He did not have to travel far, however. In Khotan on the southern edge of the Tarim basin, less than 3,000 kilometres from Luoyang, he found 25,000 new verses and duly returned home with his treasure.

As Buddhist ideas found their way into China across the first to fourth centuries CE and were received by a collection of intellectuals, emperors and travellers, few distinctions were made between this multitude of texts and the versions of Buddhism they proclaimed. In the mid-second century CE the Parthian An Shigao arrived in Luoyang. He was a royal prince who had renounced his privileged position and future throne (much like the Buddha himself) in order to become a Buddhist missionary. No fewer than 179 translations of Buddhist texts into Chinese were later ascribed to him, mostly focusing on *Theravada* Buddhism. At exactly the same time, also in Luoyang, another Buddhist missionary – a Kushan called Lokaksema – was translating principally *Mahayana* texts. In fact Lokaksema's Chinese translation of a text known as the 'Perfection of Wisdom' is the earliest surviving *Mahayana* text in existence anywhere.

The translating work of these two Buddhist monks was of fundamental importance. Despite the flood of Buddhist texts into China, few of them could be read by native Chinese without mediation. *Theravada* Buddhist texts were mostly written in Pali; *Mahayana* texts in Sanskrit. Very few Chinese understood either language and, equally, few foreigners spoke good Chinese. As a result, until the late third century CE, translation was a complicated process. It began with a Buddhist master who may have worked from texts or may have recited Buddhist teachings orally, but who did not himself speak Chinese. A team of translators, often much more skilled in one language than the other, listened to the master and/or read his texts and rendered the ideas into Chinese as best they could. These translations were then polished up into more erudite Chinese by educated Chinese scholars (who were often not Buddhists themselves) to create a Chinese-language Buddhist text, albeit one that could not be assessed for its fidelity by its author. In that the material under review offered complex ideas and new philosophies about life and the soul – many of which did not have direct translations from Pali or Sanskrit into Chinese – it is not hard to see how further confusion and variation might have crept in.

This unsatisfactory situation persisted until 286 CE, when the phenomenally talented Dharmaraksa, who had travelled through thirty-six countries having become a Buddhist monk at the age of eight, performed the first-recorded simultaneous translation in history. He had grown up in Dunhuang, a Chinese city located on the Silk Road that was alive with Buddhist ideas, and as a result he had learnt Chinese in his childhood. In the space of three weeks, between 15 September and 16 October 286 CE, Dharmaraksa read and translated out loud from Sanskrit into Chinese the *Saddharmapundarika*, the 'Scripture of the Lotus of the True Doctrine'.

While this scholarship gathered pace in China, however, the political framework, unity and continuation of the Han dynasty, which had lasted for nearly 400 years, collapsed. On 11 December 220 CE the last Han emperor, Xian, formally abdicated and ceded power to a man called Cao Pi. All power in northern China passed to Cao, who styled himself as the First Emperor of Wei. In the south, two kingdoms had already come into existence – the kingdoms of Shu and Wu. The question for Buddhism, given its monks' reliance on Chinese rulers and their accompanying intellectuals to support the work of translation and dissemination of Buddhist teachings, was whether or not the new rulers would be as supportive as the Han.

In the middle of the third century CE – around the time that the Kushan Empire was collapsing to the north of India, and the Satavahanas in the south of India – the Emperor of Wu, Sun Quan, interrogated a Buddhist monk called Kang Senghui, who had actually converted to Buddhism in the southern Chinese border town of Jiaozhou. Sun Quan challenged Kang to prove the veracity of his faith, which the monk managed to do by magically producing a Buddha relic.[28] Sun Quan's grandson, Sun Hao, was even more sceptical of Buddhist beliefs and is said to have used a Buddha statue, dug up by his staff in the park of an imperial harem, as a urinal. His regular 'ritual washings of the Buddha', as he called them, caused much hilarity among his courtiers, though in turn he was reported to have been afflicted by a nasty disease that lasted until he repented.

In 265 CE a rebellious general's son by the name of Sima Yan had dethroned the rulers of Wei and, over the next twenty years, added the Shu and Wu Empires to his kingdom, creating the Western Jin dynasty. During this period immigration from central Asia into China also rose: 250,000 people are thought to have resettled within the Jin Empire in the twenty years after 265 CE. Then, in 304 CE, Liu Yuan, 'supreme commander of the five Xiongnu hordes' – the same nomads who had caused havoc for the Han dynasty back in the third century BCE and had driven the Yuezhi west towards Bactria – attacked northern China.[29] The outcome was staggering in its magnitude: ten million people emigrated from the northern steppes into northern China, with an equal (if not greater) number of northern Chinese fleeing into southern China, which until then had only been home to around one-tenth of China's total population.

In 310 Liu Yuan died, to be replaced by his yet more fearsome son Liu Cong – the Attila of Chinese history. In 311 Luoyang – a city of 600,000 people, the fertile hub of Buddhist teaching and translation – fell. As many as 30,000 gentry were reportedly murdered and the Jin family tombs were desecrated. We hear of the destruction from a contemporary source who embodies the extraordinary cosmopolitan atmosphere created by the Silk Road. A Sogdian trading merchant, resident in Luoyang, wrote to his office back at home in Samarqand in central Asia, to describe the scene:

> And, sirs, the last emperor, so they say, fled from Luoyang because of the famine, and fire was set to his palace and to the city, and the palace was burnt and the city [destroyed]. Luoyang (is) no more, Ye (is) no more! . . . Ye, these (same) Huns [who] yesterday were the emperor's (subjects)![30]

The razing of Luoyang was followed, five years later, by the destruction of the comparably great city of Chang'an. Taken by force, it was left almost deserted, with no more than a hundred families remaining to scrape out a living within its battered walls. The beginning of the fourth century CE thus bore witness to the biggest upset in China's political, social and military framework for more than 400 years: the country divided, dealing with mass inward and outward immigration, and with destruction. At the same time Buddhism was a diverse and complex minority religion whose proponents, translating texts as fast as they could, were supported via a small circle of Chinese intellectuals and rulers within a much wider landscape focused on the varying principles of Daoism (which, some claimed, contradicted Buddhist teachings), ancestral worship, folk traditions and good Confucian governance. Buddhist ideas had made their way to China with relative ease: the uphill struggle now was for Buddhism and its supporters to find a way in which a much larger section of the population could engage with it, such that they might see a need for its counsels in the rapidly changing political and military atmosphere of a crumbling empire.

*

In the same year that Luoyang was destroyed, a group of thirty-three nuns are said to have fled the persecution of Christians within the Roman Empire and sought refuge in Armenia. Such a destination may seem a strange choice. Armenia is a large region between the Black and Caspian Seas, north of modern-day Iraq. It has few lowlands, being renowned instead for its lofty mountains, one of which, Ararat, was reputedly the pinnacle on which Noah's ark came to rest. In amongst the decaying remains of the Seleucid Empire, the new Parthian Empire and the kingdom of Mithridates of Pontus, a strong independent kingdom had been established in first-century BCE Armenia, under the rule of Tigranes II, who expanded his lands to touch the Mediterranean Sea close to Antioch in former Seleucid territory.

Around 69 BCE, however, Tigranes found himself under constant Roman assault – this the price of having taken in Rome's mortal enemy Mithridates of Pontus, whose own empire had also expanded to the Mediterranean coast, from where Mithridates had repeatedly attacked the Romans. Betrayed by his son, Tigranes finally surrendered to Rome and was allowed by the Romans to rule his original kingdom until his death.

But as Rome strengthened its grip on the coast of Asia Minor during the first century CE and came into direct conflict with the Parthian Empire, Armenia's fate was to be a focus of interest from both sides who wished to exert influence over its ruler. As part of a mid-century peace accord between Rome and Parthia, Rome agreed to the Parthian request that one of their king's brothers, Tiridates, be the ruler of Armenia and pass the throne to his descendants, but only on the condition that the Roman emperor – Nero – officially bequeathed the kingship to him. The Armenian king would thus have Parthian sympathies, but would owe his crown to Rome.

Tiridates I, now king, was also a priest of Zoroastrianism, a religion born in the Achaemenid Empire in Asia during the Axial Age of the sixth century BCE (at around the same time, in other words, as Buddhism). The faith's founding prophet, Zoroaster, had identified a single deity who controlled the world, Ahura Mazda ('Illuminating Wisdom'), yet who was split into opposing positive and negative forces. Zoroastrians believed that one honoured this single deity and the forces he embodied in part through ritual worship (Zoroastrianism was known for its focus on water and fire in rituals as the agents of purity), but also through the continual practice of good deeds, which helped to keep chaos at bay. Zoroastrianism had become the primary religion of eastern Asia in the period before Alexander the Great's invasion, and was taken up again by the Parthian Empire when it came to power during the second and first centuries BCE.

When Tiridates I travelled to Rome in 66 CE to be crowned king by Nero, he did so surrounded by 3,000 Parthian cavalry and his Zoroastrian priests. This large retinue travelled only by land, respecting the Zoroastrian principle of the purity of water, which would be sullied if they sailed upon it. The coronation was adorned by Roman ceremonies, celebrations and games. Observing a display of Roman wrestling, Tiridates saw a contestant fall to the ground and continue to be punched by his opponent; the new king is said to have remarked upon the unfairness of it all, so indicating his fidelity to Zoroastrian principles on the importance of good deeds.[31]

In all, though, Armenia may not at first glance have seemed the obvious destination for fleeing Christian nuns – given the inhospitality of its landscape, the distance necessary to reach it, its underlying obligations to Rome and its native, powerful Zoroastrian ancestry. By the early fourth century, however, much had changed since the crowning of Tiridates I. In 224 CE the Parthian Empire to Armenia's east, ancestral home of its ruling family, had fallen in battle to the Sassanids, whose original power-base was in northern central Asia. As a result Armenia had aligned itself even more closely to Rome against their newly shared enemy. In 257 CE a Sassanid plot to assassinate the Armenian royal family had left only two surviving infants: one the son of the murdered king (the future Tiridates the Great), the other the son of the regicide himself (a boy named Gregory). The former was taken to Rome, the latter to Caesarea on the eastern Mediterranean coast, where he was given over to a Christian family to be raised and educated. The royal orphan, the future Tiridates the Great, found protection and education under Licinius, soon to be ruler of the eastern Roman Empire, and so grew up with an intimate, first-hand knowledge of the difficulties facing the Roman world.

Our understanding of what happened next has in large part been dominated by three surviving ancient texts by Armenian writers, all entitled *History of the Armenians*. The first – written, we think, in the fifth century CE, was by Phaustus: he may have been Greek, and may have been a Christian bishop in Armenia, but nothing about his identity is certain. His surviving work, however, offers a rich account of events.

The second is by Agathangelos, who claims within his text to be a learned Roman scribe and eyewitness to some of Tiridates the Great's actions in the fourth century CE. In fact his *History* dates from the following century at the earliest, and indeed many scholars – noting how the manuscript has survived in a number of conflicting editions – believe it to be the work of several authors over many generations (rather as 'Homer' is held by some to be shorthand for generations of oral performers who perfected the *Iliad* and the *Odyssey*). In any event, the *History* we credit to 'Agathangelos' covers the period from the assassination of Tiridates' father, through to a meeting of Constantine and Tiridates on the eastern Mediterranean coast in the 320s CE, culminating in the death of Gregory, Armenia's first Christian *Catholicos* (head of the Armenian Catholic Church). In a manner followed by later biographies of saints, its aim is not to provide a straightforward history but, rather, to describe the miraculous power of Christian faith in the life of its subject so as to inspire readers to yet greater faith.

The third *History of the Armenians* was by a man called Moses Khorenatsi, a Christian bishop and grammarian, who wrote perhaps in the eighth century CE. We know he travelled widely across the Mediterranean before becoming a bishop in service to an Armenian prince, who duly commissioned him to write his history.[32] Moses Khorenatsi was the first to write a history of Armenia from its mythical origins up to his own time. (He is sometimes called the 'father of Armenian history', 'the Armenian Herodotus'.) What makes his text feel more like history as we know it is his familiarity with the historical narratives of the period created both by Armenian authors and by authors across the Greco-Roman and Asian worlds.[33] Nonetheless we cannot overlook his Christian sympathies and the circumstances of his commission, writing for an Armenian prince whose family and ancestors he wastes no opportunity to praise.[34]

From these sources we take it that at some point in the final decades of the third century CE Tiridates the Great was restored to power as king of a united Armenia. The precise date is disputed both because of difficulties within the surviving texts and because of what we know about the wider geopolitical environment in this period. Agathangelos says Tiridates was placed on the throne by a Roman emperor whose life he had saved in battle. Moses Khorenatsi tells us the emperor was Diocletian, the year the third of his reign, 287–8 CE.[35] But historically that date jars with what we know about Armenia at this time, particular the fact that it was still divided between Roman and Sassanid control. For many, the return to power of Tiridates could not, and did not, happen until 298 CE.[36] What is clear is that Tiridates – Parthian by birth, Roman-educated – took charge of an Armenia struggling to align its social, civic and religious traditions (both Parthian and Zoroastrian) with a political-military allegiance to Rome.

Agathangelos delights in telling us of the confused mishmash of religious practices in Armenia at this time, the plethora of diverse worships and sanctuaries for Zoroastrian and Semitic gods, for Persian, Greek and Roman gods.[37] To which must be added the Christian God. Christian worship had spread east in the first century CE, up from the area around Jerusalem via the city of Edessa (on the border of modern-day Turkey and Syria). There Armenians living in Edessa became Christian converts and were responsible, along with Assyrian Christian priests like Bardatsan of Edessa, for spreading Christianity into southern Armenia (Christianity also spread from Edessa into the Parthian Empire in this period).[38] Both Phaustus and Moses Khorenatsi briefly allude to how the Apostle Thaddeus was supposedly sent from Edessa to bring Christianity to southern Armenia, while the Apostle

Bartholomew was tasked with the north.[39] In the second century CE the North African Christian bishop Tertullian stated that there was a Christian community in Armenia.[40] In 248 CE (at the moment the emperor of the Wu state in southern China, Sun Ch'uan, was ordering the Buddhist Kang Senghui to prove the legitimacy of his faith) the Bishop of Alexandria in Egypt sent a letter to a Christian bishop in Armenia called Meruzanes. The letter proves not only that there was a Christian community in Armenia, but an organised one; and one that, scholars have argued, was oriented towards caring for the spiritual needs of the mass of the people, espousing democratic principles and communal philosophies.[41] It was also a community subsequently persecuted by the country's ruler, Tiridates' father, Khosrov, in tandem with the persecutions of Christians ordered by various Roman emperors during the second half of the third century CE.

During Tiridates' reign, however, Christianity also dramatically entered Armenia from the Roman west, led by Gregory, the son of the former regicide who had been taken to Caesarea and was raised as an educated Christian. It is the narrative of Gregory's introduction of Christianity to Armenia on which Agathangelos, Moses and Phaustus principally focus; and, as we shall see, they made it a gripping (if fantastical) story, to which the thirty-three nuns escaping from Rome were absolutely essential as the touchpaper for Armenia's conversion, led by its king Tiridates. Yet once again we are uncertain of the date, again because of both textual uncertainties and our knowledge of the geopolitical environment. Depending on when you think Tiridates was placed in power, Armenia's conversion took place (according to Agathangelos) either thirteen or fifteen years after that date: that is, in either 301/303 BCE or 311–12/313–14 BCE.[42]

The main problem with 301–3 as a date is that it would have put Tiridates in a difficult position politically vis-à-vis the Roman Empire and Tiridates' Roman imperial sponsor, Diocletian. For as Tiridates, with Gregory's help, was supposedly converting Armenia to Christianity in the first years of the fourth century CE, Diocletian in 303 BCE issued his first edict of Christian persecution, demanding that all Christian scriptures be handed over to the authorities across the entire Roman Empire, followed by further edicts in that autumn, winter and in spring of 304, which ordered the arrest of Christian bishops, the imprisonment of Christians and their execution if they refused to submit to the emperor. Thus began a new wave of persecution, which would continue in an uneven manner across the whole empire – though it was especially harsh in the east – until 311 CE. Whereas the alternative chronology for 311–12/313–14 not only allows for the Armenian conversion to have taken place when persecution in the Roman Empire had died away, but also chimes with the fact that Gregory was officially ordained by a Roman council of bishops in his position as head of the Christian Church in Armenia (in the position of *Catholicos*) in 314 CE.[43]

The thirty-three nuns who escaped persecution in the Roman Empire were thus either running from Diocletian's persecutions (if we follow the traditional Armenian histories) or, more likely, escaping from persecution in the eastern Roman Empire in 311, conducted under the auspices of one of the joint Roman emperors, Maximian, before Constantine and Licinius became *Augusti* in 312 and 313 and jointly declared their edict of toleration.

Agathangelos's *History of the Armenians* presents an appalling tale of how those fugitive nuns were treated when they arrived in Armenia, as part of his mythologisation of the miraculous introduction of Christianity to Armenia. According to Agathangelos, having found their way to the capital Vagharshapat, they there eked out a living by selling handmade glass pearls and otherwise keeping themselves to themselves.[44] Then a letter allegedly from Diocletian reached Tiridates, requesting that he find the nuns and kill them, but send back to him – or keep for himself, if he wished – a nun of surpassing beauty named Rhipsime. Tiridates did as he was told: the nuns were captured and crowds gathered to glimpse the rumoured beauty of Rhipsime, the air thick with the base desires of the jostling men.

The next day, Agathangelos tells us, Tiridates sent for Rhipsime, planning to make her his wife, but she refused to come. In response, he ordered her brought before him by force. Once they were alone together Tiridates attempted to rape her, but she fought him off 'like a man', or even 'a beast', for seven hours.[45] Tiridates then threatened to execute one of Rhipsime's fellow nuns unless she surrendered to him, but this nun advised Rhipsime to stand firm, so Tiridates' men knocked all her teeth out and broke her jaw. Rhipsime and Tiridates continued to struggle all night until *she* had stripped *him* naked, knocked off his crown and left him exhausted on the floor while she escaped through the city. But soon enough the king's executioners caught up with her. They tore out her tongue, stripped her of her clothes, tied her to four stakes and roasted her alive, cutting out her intestines and plucking out one of her eyes, finally dismembering her.[46] Of the remaining nuns, some were killed immediately, others were tortured by flaying. The corpses were left as food for the dogs in the streets and the birds in the sky.

And yet, as any good story of religious miracle requires, horrendous deeds brought down horrendous punishment. In the days after the atrocity the king decided to go hunting, during which he was, according to Agathangelos, struck by 'an impure demon'.[47] He began to rave and eat his own flesh, believed himself to be a boar (his name Tiridates means 'Gift of the Wild Boar God') and insisted on living among fellow beasts, feeding on grass and wallowing naked. His facial muscles retracted to make his face seem boar-like. He had sported a short beard, but now thick black hair sprouted all over his body. His hands and nails became like claws, his teeth grew to boar tusks and his speech became incoherent. In this state he was trapped until his sister, Khosrovidukht, received word in a vision that Gregory might be able to help him.

And here comes the miraculous redemption, thanks to an even more miraculous survival. The problem – as the people who heard Khosrovidukht's idea pointed out – was that Gregory had been cast down into a deep pit almost fifteen years previously by King Tiridates himself (this is the thirteen- to fifteen-year gap calculated in the dating of events in this period). The reason for his incarceration was twofold. Gregory was the son of the man who had murdered Tiridates' father. The two infant boys – Tiridates and Gregory – had been smuggled out of Armenia: Tiridates to Rome and Gregory to Caesarea. In turn Gregory had been brought up as a Christian and had returned to Armenia in order to pay his debt to his fatherland. But when Tiridates, now also returned to Armenia as its ruler, asked him to worship the Parthian goddess Anahit, Gregory refused. For the past actions of his father and his now-Christian beliefs, Tiridates ordered that Gregory be tortured.

On an altar curtain made in 1789, now in the Museum of the Catholicate in Armenia, are depicted twelve images of Gregory's ordeal: he had sacks of cinders tied to his head, funnels placed in his anus and water poured into his intestines; his sides were torn with iron scrapers; his knees broken; melted lead was poured over him; and he was hung upside down and flogged. Later he was cast into a deep pit, which formed the dungeon of the fortress of Artaxata, and from which there was no escape (and which today can be visited as the thriving monastery of Khor Virap). Everyone presumed he was dead.

But against all the odds, implausible as it sounds: according to Agathangelos, when Tiridates' sister sent guards to see if Gregory was still alive, he was – sustained by a loaf of bread thrown down into the pit every day by a kindly local widow. Long ropes were lowered into the pit and Gregory was dragged out. When he came into view, his body was blackened like coal, but he was otherwise intact. Brought before Tiridates, he miraculously cured the king of his afflictions and restored his mental health, commanding that the bodies of the murdered nuns be given special burial and shrines as recompense. In response to Gregory's miraculous work, the king converted to Christianity. In the aftermath, Gregory is said to have held a meeting for sixty-six days in the royal vineyards just outside the capital, undertaking mass conversions of huge numbers of Tiridates' subordinate nobles to Christianity. Then Tiridates gave Gregory the authority to destroy the very memory of the previous gods that Armenians had worshipped and to remove them from their midst.

Some scholars have attempted to link elements of Agathangelos's story with at least some kind of more plausible reality, including the identification of Tiridates' boar-like transformation with ergot-poisoning from eating bread made with contaminated rye flour. [48] Yet we don't have to go so far to see the grittier political reality underpinning this later fantastical story of nuns, miraculous survival of cruel punishments, severe disfiguration and redemption.

Tiridates, as ruler, faced two major and linked problems. The first was Armenia's perilous geopolitical position between the Roman and Sassanian Empires, whose politics and desires had already intruded significantly into Armenia's history and politics. Tiridates' foreign-policy objective was the settled dynastic rule of his family, safe (and independent) from Sassanian intervention, backed up by the support of Rome. From this perspective, particularly after 312, the acceptance of Christianity – not that Christianity seeping into Armenia from the south and from Edessa, but that explicitly nurtured and brought from, and confirmed by, the Roman world – was very attractive.[49]

But Christianity could also help to solve Tiridates' second major dilemma as ruler. Since taking power, he had struggled to centralise the hierarchies of power within Armenia by reorganising the territorial jurisdictions of local governors and undertaking massive land surveys to enable more efficient taxation. Now Christianity – as it would do for Constantine in time – offered itself as a monotheistic form of worship, which could further support, philosophically, religiously and ideologically, the centralisation of power around the monarchy and the king in the service of God.[50] And in adopting Christianity, Tiridates could not have hoped for a better accomplice than Gregory, the descendant of a powerful and noble Armenian family, now a committed Christian who was educated within, and endorsed by, the Roman world.[51] However incredible the accounts of its provenance there, Christianity certainly found an official home in Armenia in the early fourth century CE, and the future biographers of St Gregory were to be blessed by yet more vivid material with which to work.

*

By 324 CE, from one end of the Silk Road to the other, rulers of empires of differing shapes and sizes had engaged with the different religious landscapes, problems and opportunities of their worlds and had set the tone for how religion and rule would interact across the century.

In India, the newly emergent Guptas were riding the wave of the changing nature of native ancient Hindu worship, which had made possible their rise to power, but now also offered potential support for an extension of their empire. In China, as political and military disaster fragmented what had been a unified world, a tolerated but confused and multiplicitous new introduction – Buddhism – was on offer to those who sought to rule afresh in China and those who sought to re-establish their dominance. In Armenia, thanks to apparent divine intervention, the king was poised to embark on a deliberate extermination of embedded religious life in favour of the newly embraced Christianity. And in the Roman world, Constantine was now sole ruler of a reunified Roman Empire: a still officially pagan emperor of an overwhelmingly pagan world, with a track record of religious toleration and Christian sympathies.

Within the next two decades many of these leaders would be dead; but their actions in the interim would not only define the future paths of religious practice within their own countries, but the nature of these religions themselves.

CHAPTER 8

Enforcing, Mixing and Moulding Religion

In the aftermath of the decisive defeat of Licinius and his surrender at Nicomedia in 324 CE, King Tiridates the Great of Armenia travelled to meet the newly victorious and all-powerful Constantine.[1] The outcome of the meeting, we know, was a new Armeno-Roman treaty of friendship, no doubt based in part on mutual distrust of the Sassanid Empire to the east. However, later Armenian histories and more fanciful retellings depict the meeting as one of high spiritual significance between Christian rulers and their key church leaders, one that deepened not only their mutual respect, but their respective commitments to Christianity.[2]

Tiridates the Great is said to have travelled with 70,000 Armenians over land and sea (with none of the Zoroastrian sensitivities that had forced Tiridates I to keep to terra firma on his journey to be crowned by Nero). Their meeting was celebrated by the cancelling of taxes and the freeing of prisoners. Agathangelos, in the closing sections of his *History of the Armenians*, recounts how Tiridates hailed the resilience of the nuns who had fled to Armenia, and of the divinely inspired defiance of the fair Rhipsime on whom he had tried to force himself.[3]

The fictional *Letter of Love and Concord*, composed in late twelfth-century Armenia, but purporting to be a communiqué exchanged between Tiridates and Constantine, as well as their top religious representatives (Gregory for Armenia and Pope Silvester for Rome) after this meeting, would have us imagine that Tiridates and Constantine 'mixed Christ's blood in the ink' of their accord, and solemnly took an oath to stay faithful to each other 'until the end of the world'.[4] It purports that Constantine issued an edict assigning Tiridates the eastern provinces of Rome to rule in Constantine's name, and charging him to lead the Roman effort against the Sassanids.[5] He is said to have showered Tiridates with gifts and territorial donations of cities like Bethlehem. In return Tiridates is said to have left Constantine 300 hardened Armenian soldiers as bodyguards.[6]

Constantine is said to have revealed that he suffered from leprosy until he was healed by Silvester, mirroring Tiridates' affliction until his cure by Gregory.[7] But then – to all their surprises – a miracle of light appeared over Gregory's head and Constantine himself fell to the ground asking for the benediction of the world, before showering Gregory and the Armenians with even more lands and gifts.[8] On their triumphal return to Armenia, Gregory and Tiridates travelled in golden carriages and, on arrival back home, dedicated all Constantine's gifts to the chapels of the martyred nuns established by Gregory or to embellish their new Christian churches, which had been set up by this time throughout the land.[9]

Whatever amity and mutual respect actually attended the meeting of Constantine and Tiridates, we may be sure the two men were at very different stages in their relationship with Christianity. Tiridates, with Gregory, was in the process of attempting to impose Christianity upon his people, in order to support his administrative centralisation of power and at the same time shore up Armenia's difficult geopolitical position. Constantine was neither baptised nor converted to Christianity, and ruled a recently unified empire containing many more pagans than Christians, for which his priorities were twofold: first, a return to toleration for, and mixing of, all religions (as long as they did not refute his power to rule or threaten the stability and unity of his empire); and second, the strengthening of his rule by implicating himself in Christian religious hierarchies, just as the position of emperor was already implicit in pagan observances.

In India and China the moulding of religious practice by rulers was done by different means. The Guptas of India sought to mould old and new Hindu practices together to reinforce their own credibility as rulers as well as the stability and unity of their empire. In China, contrastingly, given the collapse of Chinese political unity and renewed military conflict, Buddhist missionaries sought to repackage and reshape the faith, the better to align and overlap itself with traditional Chinese religious thought and social conventions, as well as the needs of its new and multiple rulers.

The result across the ancient world would be massive changes, both in the place of each of these religions within their respective societies and in their theological doctrines and beliefs.

Enforcing New on Old

In 325 CE, with his life's work seemingly done, Gregory died. The Armenian Church would commemorate him with the honorific of 'The Illuminator'. Together with Tiridates, he had harrowed Armenia's formerly rich landscape of Greco-Roman, Zoroastrian, Semitic and Persian religious activity – itself the outcome of Armenia's position within the land mass of Asia, subject to the constant toing and froing of empires and ideas over the previous centuries. Following his purported mass conversions in the vineyards of Tiridates' palace (probably around 314 CE), Gregory had been charged not simply with adding another religion to this mix, but with wiping out all in favour of one. This was easier said than done. And none of what *was* done seems to have been part of the discussion (real or imagined) in the meeting of 324 with Constantine – perhaps because of the blood that was shed in achieving it.

Armenian society – not unlike the *varna* system in India or the traditional divisions in Chinese society from the time of Confucius onwards – was divided into three great estates: the magnates (*nahapets*), who controlled the land and guarded Armenia's borders; the junior nobility (*azats*), who held land tenure and acted as the cavalry; and the mass of the population (*anazats*, or 'not nobles'), who were peasants and traders. In addition Armenian tradition placed a huge importance on hereditary positions of power, from the king downwards. This was not unusual: most dynastic families from China to the Mediterranean aimed to keep power within the family. But in Armenia it was not just the kingship that passed from father to son, but every noble and religious position in the land.

What made Armenia even more unusual was that these hereditary nobles and priests did not by right have to agree with the king or do his bidding – unlike in the more centralised Sassanid and Roman Empires to its east and west. This decentralisation was at the root of Tiridates' dilemma when it came to strengthening his hold over Armenia. And it was not simply a question of obeying Tiridates' domestic policies. These nobles also held wider religious and political allegiances – many of which made them more sympathetic to the Sassanians to the east (because of their Zoroastrian religious beliefs, or family and political connections with the nobles of the Sassanid Empire) than to the Romans, with whom Tiridates had allied Armenia, to the west. As such, these nobles – funded and backed up by significant power-blocks within Armenia; recalcitrant, obstinate, sometimes downright disloyal and potentially treacherous – were a huge threat to Tiridates, to Armenia's internal stability and to its position on the global stage. Tiridates, we think, had turned to Christianity because its monotheistic religious hierarchy could be a bolster to his own policies of centralisation. But it also gave him an excellent excuse to attack the rich and wealthy holdings of many of these difficult and disloyal nobles: the pagan sanctuaries of Armenia.

These sanctuaries were rich: shrines in Armenia were gifted vast estates from which to produce income, they were exempt from taxes and even received up to a one-fifth share of any spoils of war won by nobles and the king. The Roman geographer Strabo, for example, describes the incredible lengths to which the Armenians went in worship of Anahit, their version of the goddess of love and fertility. Female slaves were dedicated in the temple as prostitutes to be used as part of Anahit's worship, after which they were released and freed and were highly sought-after as marriage material by Armenians.[10] And these sanctuaries were run by chief priests (themselves nobles) whose own positions were also hereditary, creating personal religious fiefdoms, often staffed by large numbers of slaves. Moreover, unlike in the

Roman and Greek worlds where sanctuaries relied for protection on the city, state or ruler to whom they belonged, the shrines of Armenia were not defenceless enclosures manned by unarmed priests. Often they could comfortably afford their own fortifications and even private armies. To turn Armenia Christian meant having to shut down these wealthy independent enclaves and potentially having to defeat them in armed conflict. But the prize was also the destabilisation of the traditional power-bases of Armenian nobles and the resultant opportunity to centralise control (and wealth) in the king's hands.

Tiridates, and his religious emissary Gregory, in adopting Christianity, also faced the task of convincing the mass of the people to give up their long-held and deep-seated beliefs, customs and traditions. This was not even as simple as getting them to exchange the name of one god for another, to be worshipped in much the same way. Zoroastrianism taught that divergence from its beliefs would be punished by hellfire – a concept unknown in Greco-Roman religious beliefs that stipulated no specific theological penalty for worshipping other gods. (Problems only arose in relation to Christianity if people did not observe the law and worship the emperor as well.) Zoroastrianism also permitted marriage between blood relatives – indeed, encouraged it as an act of particular virtue, because it was seen as helping keep the all-important hereditary bloodlines pure for the key noble and priestly positions, to which end the offspring of these marriages were often considered with particular respect. Conversion to the Christian faith, however, would require the abandonment of such practice. The acceptance of Christianity therefore posed a direct and serious threat to the existing balance of social relations, not to speak of Armenians' conceptions of their prospects in the afterlife. But demanding such a change in allegiance and belief would also provide Tiridates with an ideal opportunity to identify and isolate those who were of pro-Sassanian beliefs (those who refused the Christian message), neutralise them (such people lost all privileges within Tiridates' new Christian Armenia), and in turn build a new hierarchy of loyalties based on a new ideology and set of institutions that would not only strengthen him in his role as king, but also establish more resoundingly Armenia's geopolitical position as an ally of Rome.[11]

The fight to impose Christianity on Armenia was thus a fundamental struggle not simply to introduce a new religion, but, more
importantly, to break down the traditional way of life and administration of the Armenian state, rebuild it in a much more centralised and
hierarchical way and give it a new, more unified, religious and political
stance in ancient world affairs.

How this was supposedly achieved is recounted for us in the
texts written by Agathangelos and Moses Khorenatsi and characteristi-
cally laced with miracles. It is written, for instance, that merely by
making the sign of the cross Gregory was able to direct divine forces
to bring the temple of Anahit crashing down into oblivion: wood,
stone, gold, silver, priests and all. At the site of the Vahevahean temple
at Ashtishat – which contained altars to the god Vahagn and the god-
desses Anahit and Astghik – the soldiers first sent by Gregory were
said to have been led astray by demons and unable to find the entrance;
then their iron tools were unable to blunt the sanctuary walls. But
Gregory ascended to a nearby hill and simply raised his cross, emanating from which came a wind that reduced the temple to ash.[12]

At the temple of Erez, where female slaves were dedicated as prostitutes, Gregory is said by Agathangelos to have directed an attack by
troops against armed 'demons' (more likely hired mercenaries).[13] Moving like an elemental force across the Armenian landscape, backed by
Tiridates' troops, Gregory destroyed a litany of formerly sacred sites,
including the temples of Tyr at Erazamuyn, Barsamina at Tortan,
Aramazd at Fort Ani, Nana at Til and Mithras at Pacarij. Other temples he is said to have forcibly converted into Christian churches, and
to have installed Christian relics and prevailed upon the previous pagan
priests to act as Christian clerics.[14]

Politely put, it is impossible for us today to verify the details of
Agathangelos's account.[15] But Gregory and Tiridates were not said
simply to destroy; they also built, funding the construction of new
Christian churches throughout Armenia, the results of which we can
see today. (The Etchmiadzin Cathedral in Vagharshapat is on the site
of an original built by Gregory, said to be where a pagan temple had
previously stood, its siting suggested to Gregory, Agathangelos says, by
a vision of Christ striking the ground with a gold hammer.[16]) In the

manner of their pagan predecessors, these new Christian foundations were granted their own estates to live off, ripped from the hands of the previous pagan nobles. Meanwhile any of the nobles who stood in the way of Gregory were slowly and carefully disenfranchised, wherever possible. Tiridates ensured that the lands of recalcitrant nobles – once their bloodlines were exhausted, most often by unnatural deaths – were transferred to support a new Christian Church.[17]

Gregory even established schools for the creation of new priestly families and Christian soldiers. Such education Gregory is recorded by Agathangelos as valuing highly, so that 'in the twinkling of an eye these savage and idle and oafish peasants suddenly became acquainted with the prophets and familiar with the apostles and heirs to the gospel and were fully informed about all the traditions of God'.[18] Gregory was given the money to carry out this expensive campaign of education, recruitment, destruction and construction by Tiridates, who is said to have increased Gregory's family wealth and power by gifting him vast territories within Armenia.[19]

In 314 CE – while Constantine was dealing with the Donatists in North Africa and calling the council at Arles to help integrate imperial and Christian hierarchies – Tiridates is said to have called a grand review of his armies and officials. Before the gathered crowd he proposed the election of Gregory to the position of *Catholicos*: the official ordained Christian overseer of the Armenian people. But according to Agathangelos, Gregory, humble in the extreme, declined the invitation. 'I am unable to undertake this because of its immeasurable height,' Gregory is said to have replied. 'But let them seek and find one who is worthy.'[20] Despite repeated protestations from Tiridates and the assembled masses, it is said that only a divine vision eventually persuaded Gregory to accept this high honour.

He was sent off in the king's golden chariot drawn by white mules, surrounded by sixteen provincial governors and endless troops, gifts and ornaments, to journey to Caesarea on the eastern Mediterranean coast, there to be ordained by Bishop Leontius at a meeting of Roman Christian bishops. There he was received with great pomp and ceremony and his ordination happily confirmed, in a move that linked the emergent Armenian and Roman Christian communities together, which would again be reinforced by the meeting of Constantine and Tiridates, Gregory and Silvester in 324 CE.

On his return journey, while crossing Armenia, inspired by his now-official position, Gregory is said to have continued his destruction of non-Christian sanctuaries, razing temples to the ground and redistributing their gold and silver, as well as building new Christian churches. He conducted mass conversions – converting, it was said, more than 190,000 people over twenty days. When he arrived back in the capital, he soon set off again on a number of journeys criss-crossing the country, converting people and establishing churches and priesthoods. The king came to meet him by the Euphrates River, where they held a thirty-day fast and session of prayer, whereupon the king and his wife, more than 150,000 soldiers and four million men, women and children were said to have been baptised in a single week. According to Agathangelos, the Christian God naturally registered his pleasure at this extraordinary event by stilling the waters and then restarting them, accompanied by a shining pillar of light.[21]

Gregory's position as *Catholicos* was, per Armenia's traditions, hereditary: for the next 100 years the head of the Armenian Church would be one of Gregory's descendants, ruling out of the place of worship (now Etchmiadzin Cathedral) that Gregory had built at Vagharshapat. One of his sons, Aristakes, had lived all his life as a hermit in the mountains. 'He had given himself entirely to spiritual affairs – to solitude, dwelling in the mountains, hunger and thirst and living off vegetables, being shut up without light, wearing a hair shirt, using the ground as a bed, often spending the sweet repose of night – the need of sleep – in the wakeful vigils on his feet. This he did for no little time,' Agathangelos claimed.[22] But before Gregory's death, Aristakes was persuaded by Tiridates to leave his isolation and help the king while his father continued to journey around the country performing his missionary work. Aristakes, imitating his father's reluctance to take up the position of *Catholicos*, was initially said to have refused to leave and rejoin the outside world. He was eventually persuaded not by a divine vision, but by his fellow Christian hermits. 'The task of God's labour is better for you than this solitary living in the desert,' they argued.[23] Aristakes returned to the king's court and was subsequently ordained as *Catholicos* after Gregory's death.

*

Agathangelos's narrative of Gregory's and Tiridates' swift, resolute and thorough conversion of Armenia to Christianity whitewashes over the sheer difficulty of what they were attempting: to use religious change as a way of breaking down the way the country worked, thought and believed, and rebuilding its hierarchy and administration centred around the king and the Christian God. Many nobles who had governed with such independence from Tiridates were not ready to accept Tiridates' and Gregory's new religion – particularly when it entailed a break with past traditions, such as the acceptance and importance of blood-marriage, and the cutting of long-standing loyalties to family and fellow nobles in the nearby Sassanian Empire. And at the same time Gregory's version of Christianity – one formed in the heart of the Roman Empire and intended to strengthen a centralised hierarchy with the king at its apex – meshed badly with the form of Christianity that *had* established itself in the south of Armenia coming up from Edessa, which was more focused on caring for the masses. As such, it is without doubt the case that Tiridates, Gregory and his successor, in trying to employ Christianity to increase Armenia's coherence and unity, ended up simply adding a religious dimension to the already dynamic administrative, economic and geopolitical problems that Armenia faced. And even the texts that focused on the miraculous work of Gregory and his successors cannot entirely ignore the problems they faced in their campaign.

Moses Khorenatsi claims, for instance, that 'by nature presumptuous and perverse, [the Armenian nobles] opposed the King's will concerning the Christian religion, following the will of their wives and concubines'.[24] The opposition was such that soon after 327 CE, according to Moses, Tiridates left his throne and headed for the mountains, where he 'cast off his earthly crown . . . and lived in mountain caves as a hermit'.[25] Having attempted to unite Armenia, Tiridates had in fact left it with even greater divides than before – whether north–south

(Roman Christianity versus Syrian) or east–west (Roman sympathies versus Sassanian). Some ancient historians even believed that Tiridates never got the chance to skulk off into the mountains – that he was instead assassinated by pro-Sassanian nobles.[26]

If so, he was not the only one so despatched. Moses records an instance of especially vehement opposition dating from 333 CE, when Aristakes, son of Gregory and now *Catholicos*, was murdered by an Armenian noble called Archilaeus, whom Aristakes had reprimanded for his non-Christian ways.[27] Archilaeus was said to have met Aristakes on the road and cut him to pieces with his sword. Aristakes' successor, Gregory's other son Vrtanes, was pursued in Taron by an angry mob of 2,000 pagans, emboldened by the queen (Tiridates' daughter-in-law) whom Vrtanes had rebuked for her adulterous and dissolute ways. The mob was said to have been held back only by 'an invisible hand' who bound them up individually in invisible chains, suggesting that what actually happened is that soldiers were still supporting the *Catholicos* in his work of imposing Christian worship on Armenia and acting as his bodyguard where necessary.[28] Vrtanes' son Grigoris, a local bishop, was later trampled to death under the stampeding horses of a group of local nobles.[29] Vrtanes' other son, who became *Catholicos*, would also be killed by the Armenian nobility.

The enforced acceptance of Christianity in Armenia, while seemingly effortless in the saintly biographies, was by no means complete or certain and had left Armenia perilously unstable within a changing geopolitical world.

Mixing New and Old

Newly ruling Rome's empire alone, as of 324 CE, Constantine took measures in respect of religion that were very different from those taken by Tiridates. He first sought to rectify the imbalance in religious toleration created especially in the east, where Licinius's return to pagan ways in his last years had left its mark. He ordered the release of all Christians who had been condemned to forced labour, enabled the return of Christian exiles and the restoration of their property, and encouraged Christian bishops to repair damaged churches and build new ones. Constantine also seems to have been keen to continue his policy of intertwining the ecclesiastical and imperial bureaucracy, especially in the eyes of the people in the east: when famine beset Antioch in 324 CE, it was through the Christian churches that the city authorities distributed the grain to help its people – both Christian and pagan – survive.

In 325 Constantine made more strident anti-pagan moves, technically outlawing gladiator shows and crucifixions (although they continued for another century in the western empire, where pagan traditions remained popular and strong, particularly in Rome itself). In his Good Friday address of 325, preserved for us by the Christian historian Bishop Eusebius and thought to have been delivered from Antioch, Constantine reiterated his belief in the huge potential for the entwining of Christian and imperial hierarchies. Whereas pagan worship supported the idea of multiple rulers like multiple gods, Christianity, he argued, with its single God, could provide strong support for his vision of a single unified community under a single ruler: a union of Church and State, Empire and Christianity, the Emperor and God.

Yet it would be a mistake to see these moves as Constantine completely eschewing his duties to the overwhelmingly pagan majority of the empire. He retained in his service a pagan *augur* (diviner) named Sopater, along with other pagan priests, and never gave up his pagan religious title of *Pontifex Maximus*, which ensured the traditional and long-standing overlap between pagan and imperial hierarchies. Moreover, while he issued proclamations banning certain pagan practices, he was never keen (unlike Tiridates) on enforcing their imposition.

In the same year that he beat Licinius and met Tiridates, Constantine began perhaps his greatest endeavour to mix the Christian and pagan elements of his realm – on a strip of land at the meeting point of Europe and Asia where, since the sixth century BCE, had stood the Greek colonial settlement of Byzantium. On 8 November 324 Constantine inaugurated a new city over the old. He did so with both traditional pagan ritual and Christian rites. The boundaries of this new city had been drawn out on the ground with a spear by Constantine himself some weeks before, backed up by another pagan ceremony in which a priest ploughed a furrow in the spear's wake to ensure the city's good fortune. As ever, balancing his pagan and Christian credentials, Constantine is also said to have later told people that the Christian God ordered him to name the city after himself: Constantinople.

It is said that Constantine's initial idea was to build his new city over the ruins of the ancestral origins of the Romans at Troy, further down the eastern Mediterranean coast. A divine vision, however, directed him north to Byzantium/Constantinople. Edward Gibbon, author of *The History of the Decline and Fall of the Roman Empire*, later described Byzantium as having been 'formed by nature for the centre and capital of a great monarchy'. Overlooking the narrow sea lane between Europe and Asia while controlling the access route through to the Black Sea, Byzantium was at the hub of civilisations, trade and the movement of people. More importantly, it was laid out on the pinnacle of a stout finger of land now known as 'the Golden Horn'. Protected on two sides by narrow defensible sea channels, its community could be made almost impregnable to land attack by the construction of a single city wall across its northern front.

For Constantine, his Constantinople reflected the new era upon which the Roman world had embarked. Once more united under a single ruler, the Roman Empire – stretching from Britain to Syria – had a new city that bridged continents and would soon come to surpass Rome as its capital. Indeed, while Rome was burdened by centuries of history and overwhelmed with the markers of traditional pagan religious worship (not to mention the old-fashioned and traditionally pagan Roman Senate), Constantinople could be crafted to reflect Constantine's preoccupations and tastes as leader of both pagans and Christians. On 25 July 326, as tradition demanded of him, Constantine entered Rome to celebrate the twentieth anniversary of his accession to power. But after declining the customary pagan sacrifice on which the Senate insisted, he left Rome and never came back. His eyes were firmly on his new city and his new world.

On 11 May 330 Constantine's new capital was formally dedicated. His pagan *augur* had picked the date, which was to be a public holiday thereafter. Over the first two days of celebration there was a noisy procession through the streets to the new forum of Constantine, culminating in the placement of a new statue of the emperor atop a 36-metre-high Egyptian porphyry column. The next day the city's population gathered in the new sporting arena to witness chariot races. The emperor was amongst them, wearing a crown set with pearls and precious gems. In a gesture of largesse, a large wooden statue of Constantine was presented to the cheering crowds and it was decreed that such a statue would be presented every year. The celebrations continued for more than a month, culminating on the final day when a statue of the pagan goddess of luck and fate, Tyche, was carried through the streets and placed in the shrine of the pagan goddess Cybele – one of at least three major pagan sanctuaries still open and flourishing in the city. Important pagan sculptures from sanctuaries and cities across the empire were brought and erected in Constantinople, making this new city feel like a microcosm of the wider Roman Empire and a container of all the best that the Mediterranean had ever produced.

Coins minted for the festivities portrayed a personification of the city carrying a crossed sceptre on its shoulders. And as well as the importation of pagan statues, work soon began on the construction of new Christian churches, dedicated to personifications of virtues and desirable entities that both pagans and Christians could agree on: the church of Hagia Sophia (Holy Wisdom) and that of Hagia Eirene (Holy Peace). Amongst all this, at the entrance to Constantine's imperial palace in the city, a new tableau was created showing Constantine using his Christian military standards to pierce the flank of a great dragon, whose head plunged into an abyss below.

The new statue of Constantine that was dedicated on the first days of celebrations in his new forum summed up this mixing of religious traditions, and of Constantine's place within the religious and imperial hierarchies. On top of Constantine's head, a crown of seven rays was placed as if he were *Sol Invictus*, the Unconquered Sun. At the same time, in the statue's head, it was said, was a nail found by his mother Helena during her pilgrimage in the Holy Land, one that had been used to fix Jesus to his cross. And at the column's base was an altar containing a fragment of the True Cross found in Jerusalem. Constantine's statue reflected a blend of pagan and Christian beliefs and traditions, but also portrayed him as the embodiment and meeting point of all of them. It is said that during the rest of his rule he developed an increasingly sacred air around his person: there had, for example, to be a respectful silence in his presence. Similarly, art historians reflect on the way that, after 324, Constantine's portraits always look upwards. He did not portray himself as a god, but as the apex of the earthly sacred and secular, pagan and Christian hierarchies, looking upwards in turn towards the divine.

And yet Constantine was beset by two major divisions within the Christian community itself, which threatened the unity, cohesion and balance that he had so painstakingly sought to achieve under his rule. The first was the ongoing dispute in North Africa. Back in 315 CE, exasperated by the Donatists who had refused to accept his adjudication over who was and was not *traditor* and official Primate of Carthage, Constantine had confiscated their property, exiling their leaders and even supporting attempts to expose some of them as *traditores* themselves. But by 321 CE he seems to have reconsidered his strategy, possibly reflecting on how little the persecution of Christians had achieved within the Roman world over the previous half-century. Now he spoke of toleration. In a letter to African bishops he asked: 'for what is it in this age to conquer in the name of God if not to bear with unmoved breast the lawless attacks of those who harry the people of the law of peace?'[30]

This policy of toleration became one of feigned ignorance after his final victory over Licinius and his move to become sole ruler of the Roman Empire: 'what each has seen and understood, he must use, if possible, to help the other, but if that is impossible, the matter should be dropped'.[31] And in 329 CE, the year after he inaugurated his new city of Constantinople, he wrote to the bishops in North Africa again, arguing that the matter should be left to the Almighty: 'God indeed promises to be the avenger of all; and when vengeance is left to God a harsher penalty is exacted from one's enemies.'[32]

Constantine's policy seems to have become pragmatic: turning a blind eye, leaving the determining and deliverance of punishment to the higher authority. One can see the attraction, especially given that Donatus had begun to ask the question 'What has the church to do with the emperor?'[33] The very people who had first vaunted the role of

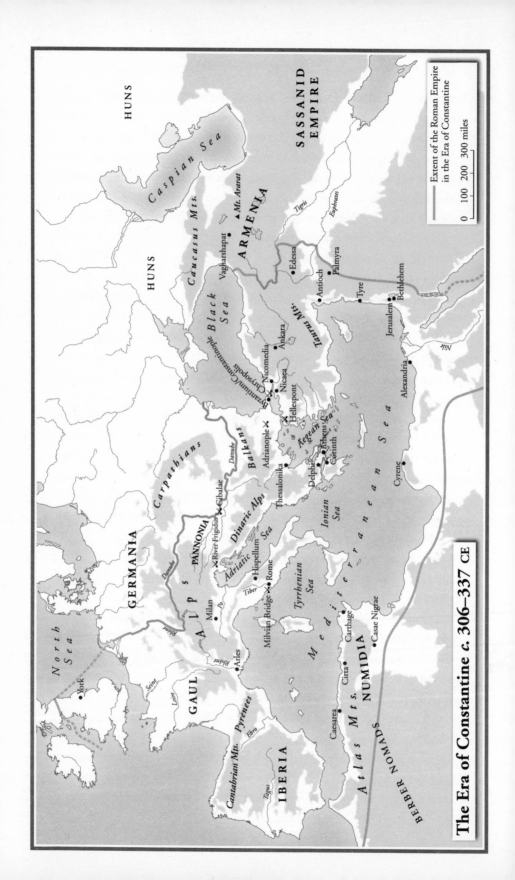

The Era of Constantine *c.* 306–337 CE

HUNS

HUNS

SASSANID EMPIRE

ARMENIA

▲ Mt. Ararat

Caspian Sea

Caucasus Mts.

Tigris

Euphrates

Vagharshapat •

Black Sea

• Edessa

Antioch •   Palmyra •

Tyre •   Bethlehem •

Jerusalem •

Nile

Ankara •

Taurus Mts.

Nicomedia •
Byzantium/Constantinople
Chrysopolis
Nicaea •

Hellespont ✕

Alexandria •

GERMANIA

Carpathians

Balkans

Danube

Adrianople ✕

Aegean Sea

Athens ✕
Corinth

Delphi

Cyrene •

Thessalonika •

Dinaric Alps

PANNONIA
✕ River Frigidus   ✕ Cibalae

Ionian Sea

Rhine

A l p s

Milan •

Po

Hispellum ✕
✕ Rome

Tiber

Adriatic Sea

M e d i t e r r a n e a n   S e a

Tyrrhenian Sea

North Sea

GAUL

Seine

Loire

Rhône

Arles •

Pyrenees

Cantabrian Mts.

IBERIA

Tagus

Ebro

Atlas Mts.

NUMIDIA

Caesarea •   Cirta •   Carthage •

• Casae Nigrae

BERBER NOMADS

York •

Milvian Bridge ✕

emperor as final arbiter of Christian theology (by sending their grievances to him) now questioned that connection between imperial and
Church authority. Despite applying a tourniquet of isolation and non-
engagement to the Donatist poison, Constantine's actions did not
succeed in killing off the cause. They did, however, prevent the Donatist
issue from breaking his carefully constructed alliance between the
emperor and the Church more widely across the Roman Empire.

The second major dilemma to face Constantine from within the
Christian community could not, however, be so well contained on
the shores of North Africa. Back in 312 CE, just as Constantine was
victorious at Milvian Bridge, a bishop called Arius had argued that the
figure of Jesus Christ was subordinate to God, instead of equal to
God – part of a wider discussion about the relationship of the individual elements of the Holy Trinity. By 318 CE his arguments had led to
his excommunication from the Christian Church, but there were many
who supported Arius's position.

In the momentous year of 324 Constantine also despatched a trusted
bishop named Ossius to Alexandria, there to resolve this growing
schism in the Church. Constantine is later said to have called the dispute 'a silly question', and to have argued (just as with the Donatists)
for toleration, or else feigned ignorance of the discord: 'even if you
cannot bring yourself to a single point of view, [these views] ought to
remain in the mind, guarded in the hidden recesses of thought'.[34]

The bishops, however, refused to reserve their opinions to themselves. Indeed, Ossius's intervention served only to bring about the
excommunication of yet more notable bishops. As Ossius himself is
later recorded to have said, 'Confusion everywhere prevailed . . . to so
disgraceful an extent . . . that Christianity became a subject of popular
ridicule, even in the very theatres.'[35] Wishing to treat this open wound
and restore unity, Constantine acted in his self-created role as non-
ecclesiastical leader of the Christian community by summoning the
First Ecumenical Council of the Christian Church. As a later Church
historian, Socrates, recounts: 'When the emperor thus beheld the
Church agitated . . . he convoked a general council, summoning all the
bishops by letter to meet him at Nicaea in Bithynia.'[36]

In fact the original intention was that the bishops should gather in

Ankara, modern-day capital of Turkey. But the Arian controversy got in the way: the Bishop of Ankara was so vehemently against Arius and his ideas that any council held there could not hope to achieve compromise. Nicaea (now Iznik in Turkey) was suggested as a relatively neutral location, although the official story was that it was more accessible and the air was better. In late May 325 CE Constantine welcomed bishops from all over the Christian world, including the new *Catholicos* of Armenia, Aristakes, to his summer palace on the lake at Nicaea. Every lodging room in the city had been hastily but lavishly refurbished to receive such a large number of important guests.

The occasion must have worn a strange cast. Some bishops still bore the physical and mental scars of persecution inflicted upon them by the Roman authorities at the beginning of the century. Some, probably, had not met previously. Many had not seen Constantine in the flesh before. Most were from the East: Spain and Britain did not send bishops, Africa only one, and even the bishop in Rome claimed illness and sent deputies. There were representatives from outside the Roman Empire: not just from Armenia, but also a bishop representing Christians from within the Sassanid Empire. There, too, was Constantine's daughter, Constantia, who – that very spring – had seen her father renege on his solemn promise not to kill her husband, the captured Licinius.

As they all took their places in the Great Hall of the palace at Nicaea, in the middle of them sat Constantine, undisputed and ruthless ruler of the Roman Empire, seemingly tireless seeker of toleration within the Roman world, now self-styled guardian of unity in the Christian Church, resplendent in his imperial robes. The hubbub of noise and cacophony of accents fell quiet as Constantine – speaking in Latin, with simultaneous Greek translation – set out his goals: harmony, unity and the eradication of dissension. He then burnt every petition and accusation the bishops had sent him, before their eyes, saying, 'Christ enjoins him who is anxious to obtain forgiveness to forgive his brother.' After this opening salvo, the bishops set to work debating their beliefs, often overseen by Constantine, who himself interjected regularly into the discussion. Some may have resented (even privately denied) his authority to intervene, but there was no way that Constantine's comments could be ignored.

Following several days of testy and strained debate, the council's deliberations focused around the basic creed – the statement of core Christian beliefs – suggested by Eusebius of Caesarea, a supporter of Arius and the same Eusebius who would later write the *Life of Constantine* and the Church history of this period. In response to the Arian debate over the nature of the relationship between the elements of the Holy Trinity, Constantine had personally intervened to suggest a made-up Greek word to describe Christ and God as being 'of the same substance', which would fudge the issue and offer something everyone could get behind.

On 19 June 325 CE the council agreed an official version of the text: the First Nicene Creed, a statement of what all Christians believed, and which, it was hoped, would put an end to internal Christian dissent. It was paraded around the hall for the bishops to sign. For the next month the council continued to debate a range of other issues that were seen to hamper the unity of the Church: from the date of Easter; to how to resolve other more minor theological schisms in particular areas of the Roman Empire, such as Egypt; and how to make decisions on the systems of Church hierarchy.

On 25 July 325 CE – the anniversary of Constantine's accession to power – he invited all the bishops to a grand banquet at his palace at Nicomedia, spoke to them once again about the need for concord, and instructed them to write to their respective churches announcing the agreements that had been reached. (Constantine would follow with letters of his own, announcing the new-found unity of faith.) With that, he bade farewell to the gathering.

Despite his efforts, though, the First Nicene Creed failed to gain universal agreement. The disputatious Arius refused Constantine's Greek compromise, and two other bishops refused to sign up to the council's condemnation of Arius, both of them embarrassingly local – Theognis of Nicaea and Eusebius of Nicomedia (as distinct from Eusebius of Caesarea, who had proposed the basic creed in the first place). Arius, Eusebius and Theognis were officially exiled from the Christian Church.

Constantine had failed in his effort to unite the Church with him at its head. But that did not stop him continuing to press his case. Arius, harried for a further two years, finally relented, agreeing to keep his beliefs to himself and offering a bland statement of support for the emperor. This was adequate for Constantine, who demanded that Arius, and his supporters Eusebius and Theognis, should be reinstated. But the Bishop of Alexandria, with whom the decision rested, refused. In 327 CE Constantine reconvened the bishops at a second Council of Nicaea – at which the Armenian *Catholicos* Aristakes was also present – with the purpose of returning Arius, Eusebius and Theognis to the fold. While Eusebius and Theognis seem to have been reaccepted, the Bishop of Alexandria continued to resist the notion of Arius. This stalemate endured for another seven years. In 335 CE Constantine convened one further council at Tyre, ancestral homeland of the Carthaginians and the starting point of the Silk Road east towards China.

The bishops, once assembled at Tyre, travelled north to Jerusalem to see the dedication of the new Church of the Holy Sepulchre on 13 September. This church was a symbol of Constantine's desire to rectify the wrongs of his predecessors through his quest for religious toleration. The magnificent new Christian edifice was built on top of a pagan sanctuary of Venus now demolished by Constantine, originally constructed by Hadrian so as to conceal the site of Jesus' burial. Evidently overcome by the symbolic force of what Constantine had engineered, the bishops voted finally to reinstate Arius. (They later found the dissenting Bishop of Alexandria guilty of sufficiently serious charges to have him deposed from office.)

Constantine's biographer, Bishop Eusebius of Caesarea, later summed up Constantine's approach to the testy negotiations over the last decade: 'such as he saw able to be prevailed upon by argument, and adopting a calm and conciliatory attitude, he commended most warmly, showing how he favoured general unanimity, but the obstinate he rejected'.[37] Constantine had – in theory – his unified Church, and Christianity had a set of core beliefs on which the faithful could, more or less, agree. With the matter at last officially settled, Arius himself was to drop dead within a year, while visiting a public latrine in Constantinople.

Constantine is a hard man for history to get to grips with. He was a brilliant military leader, endowed with the necessary ruthlessness to conquer his way to sole rule of the Roman Empire, and to maintain his authority and dynasty. Not only did he kill his daughter's husband

Licinius, but also their child – his own grandson – to ensure neither would pose a threat to his other offspring in the future. And yet he was also, it seems, easily manipulated, especially by the women around him. In 326 CE he killed his son Crispus (to whom the Christian writer Lactantius had been tutor), supposedly at the instigation of his new wife Fausta, who feared for the claim of the children they had reared together.[38] He is later said to have boiled Fausta alive in her bath, having been reprimanded by his mother Helena for having listened to his wife.[39] It was this family rampage that sent Helena off on pilgrimage to the Holy Land, where she would find the pieces of Jesus' cross.

For all that Constantine was turbulent and unpredictable in his personal affairs, he seems to have relentlessly pursued a policy of toleration and balance between Christianity and pagan traditions, alongside tireless efforts to resolve disputes within Christian belief, in his new role at the apex of religious and imperial rule. By such a policy he no doubt sought to strengthen and unify the community under his command, a community that was to be centred around his new city, which in turn was a microcosm of that world and reflected his preferred mix of civic, political and religious life.

Moulding New with Old

In 335 CE – as the Council of Tyre put a seal of unity upon the Christian hierarchy, and the Church of the Holy Sepulchre was dedicated in Jerusalem – India was witnessing a scuffle over the Gupta throne.

Chandragupta, as we have seen, had risen to power on the back of social and religious change, most especially the weakening of the boundaries between the *varnas*. He faced an extremely unstable India, as new migrations of Sacas and Kushans came down from the north and new kingdoms were founded to the south. But he was also presented with an opportunity to engage with religion for the promotion of the stability and expansion of his realm. For one, the gathering sense that it was the duty of everyone in society – not simply that of *Brahman* priests – to keep the gods content and the cosmic circle turning made a strong argument for a cohesive community. For another, the distillation of the former multitude of Hindu gods into two chief deities had created figureheads and focus points for just such a unified and yet still-diverse community.

In the last years of his life Chandragupta seems to have made good use of both of these strands of religious change. But upon his death the Gupta dynasty was confronted by a succession dilemma, thanks to a number of potential – and keen – new rulers. Samudragupta, who would emerge the victor, was quick to point out in his official inscriptions that he was his father's choice as heir. This claim, along with many others about Samudragupta's rule, is preserved for us today on what is known as the Allahabad Pillar, named for the city where it is found in the state of Uttar Pradesh in northern India (bordering modern Nepal). A shaft of polished sandstone, it stands just over 10 metres high and was originally constructed in the third century BCE as a monument to the greatness of King Ashoka of the Mauryans, who inscribed upon it some of his ruling edicts. Five centuries later Samudragupta followed Ashoka's example, evidently seeking to place Gupta authority on a comparable plane with that of the Mauryans. The point about his undisputed accession is made painfully clear:

'Come, oh worthy (one)' [said Samudragupta's father] and embracing (him) with hair standing on end and indicating (his) feeling, (his) father, perceiving (him) with the eye, overcome with affection, (and) laden with tears (of joy), (but) discerning the true state (of things) said to him 'so protect (thou) the whole earth', while he was being looked at with sad faces by others of equal birth, (but) while the courtiers were breathing cheerfully.[40]

The preferred candidate of the courtiers, accepted more grudgingly by his fellow royals, Samudragupta – at least according to his own account – was crowned successor. In another surviving pillar inscription of his, the Eran inscription, the point is underlined: Samudragupta's father was pleased by his son's devotion, correct judgement and valour, which were, it said, 'irresistible'.[41] Yet around 335 BC coins were minted to celebrate the name of another Gupta ruler from this time: Prince Kacha. What happened to him we do not know; perhaps we may infer

姓嬴名政始目始皇乙卯即王位庚辰併天下稱皇帝
在位三十七年居王位二十五年即帝位十二年壽五十

9. Zhao Zheng was twenty when he fully assumed the reins of the state of Qin in 240 BCE. By 221 BCE he had taken it from being one among many 'warring states' to the sole and victorious survivor, uniting much of what is now central China for the first time in its history and establishing himself as Qin Shi Huangdi, First Emperor of the country of Qin. Soon he would order the construction of a great wall to run more than 500 miles along the limits of the new Qin Empire.

10. On his death in 210 BCE Qin Shi Huangdi was laid to rest in a vast burial-tomb complex which had required the labour of hundreds of thousands. Posted as guards of this necropolis were 8,000 'soldiers' – life-size sculptures in terracotta, each individually designed. The First Emperor's 'terracotta warriors' still keep their vigil today.

11. When Publius Cornelius Scipio first went to war, Rome was only one of several powers in the Mediterranean. By his death – thanks in no small part to his efforts – the Mediterranean was Rome's world. He was twenty-five when elected to a military command in 210 BCE in Rome's protracted fight against Hannibal. Following a great victory at Zama, Rome hailed their winning general as 'Scipio Africanus'. Yet it is said he retired from public life embittered by political squabbles, denying Rome the honour of burying him. He died in 182 BCE, the same year as his great antagonist Hannibal.

12. Eucratides I was a usurper who seized the throne of Bactria for himself and his lineage, displacing the Euthydemid dynasty of Greco-Bactrian kings. Thereafter he faced up to internal rebellion and invasion by Parthia, pursued an expansion of influence into India and was, according to one interpretation of sources, killed by his own son. His importance is evidenced by his creation of an illustrious coinage that included the largest and most valuable gold coin in the Hellenistic world.

13. *The Battle of the Milvian Bridge*, a fresco in the Vatican painted to a posthumous design of Raphael's by Giulio Romano *c.* 1520–4. It depicts the battle of 312 CE between Constantine I and Maxentius – ostensibly a violent dispute for supremacy in Rome. But in 314 CE the Christian writer Lactantius suggested that Constantine had been divinely inspired to his victory. So began the recasting of this triumph as the moment when the soon-to-be-ruler of the Roman world embraced Christianity as the true faith. In the painting, Constantine's soldiers bear crosses into battle and sword-bearing angels fly above the fray.

14. The attraction seems clear, judging by the body language and closeness of their haloed heads: this is, we think, the moment when Gupta emperor Chandragupta I proposed marriage to the Licchhavi princess Kumaradevi, as depicted on a coin produced by their future son. The image might suggest that the emperor's future bride held him in a sort of seductive thrall; the truth could be that the Guptas were boasting of a union well made.

15. This copper engraving of the 1700s depicts the baptism of Armenian king Tiridates the Great by Gregory the Illuminator, an act that enshrined the nation's conversion to Christendom *c.* 324 CE. The two were not always so amicable: Gregory was the son of the man who murdered Tiridates' father. Holding both that and his Christian beliefs against Gregory, Tiridates ordered him to be tortured in numerous ways (shown around the borders of the image) then cast into a pit, where he languished for years – until Tiridates suffered a seeming demonic possession brought on by his malign behaviour; and Gregory's piety supposedly engineered both Tiridates' physical recovery and his spiritual repentance.

16. The marble head of a colossal statue of Constantine that once stood 12 metres high in the west apse of the Basilica of Maxentius on the northern boundary of the Roman Forum. The statue had originally been intended to represent the emperor Maxentius, but it was Constantine who had this work completed after defeating his rival at the Milvian Bridge in 312, and the likeness was duly re-sculpted to represent the victor. Pieces of the Colossus of Constantine now reside in the Courtyard of the Palazzo dei Conservatori of the Musei Capitolini on the Capitoline Hill.

17. Coinage of Gupta ruler Samudragupta commemorates his resurrection of the early Vedic practice of the *ashvamedha* or horse-sacrifice, formerly banned by his predecessor Ashoka after Ashoka's conversion to Buddhism. The coin depicts the chosen horse before an altar billowing smoke, as it waits to be smothered to death and dismembered. This popular ritual occasion served to confirm Samudragupta as *chakravartin* – a benevolent universal ruler, and guardian of the spiritual wellbeing of his people.

18. The Allahabad Pillar in the state of Uttar Pradesh in northern India. A shaft of polished sandstone, it stands over 10 metres high and was originally constructed in the third century BCE as a monument to the greatness of King Ashoka of the Mauryans, who inscribed upon it some of his ruling edicts. Five centuries later Samudragupta followed Ashoka's example, seeking to place Gupta authority on a plane comparable to that of the Mauryans.

19. A deepening overlap between the god Vishnu and the ruling Guptas of India brought forth, from the end of the fourth century CE, a new form of Hindu religious architecture: the stone temple, grand and free-standing. The porches of these temples were often decorated with glorious reliefs: for example, at Deogarh in Janesi, known also as the Dashavatara Temple because it represents the stories of the ten avatars (*Dash-avatara*) of Vishnu.

that some were not quite as willing to ruefully accept Samudragupta's accession, and instead tried to set about ruling themselves. The complete subsequent absence of Kacha from the historical record tells us all we need to know about what the outcome was.

The Allahabad inscription is a poetic eulogy written by Samudragupta's own court poet, Harishena (who was also Minister for Peace and War). In it, Chandragupta is said to pose his successor a challenge: 'to protect the whole earth'. To do so would require Samudragupta to become not just a good and fair king, but also a brave warrior. And, most importantly, it would require that he act correctly with regard to the gods, continuing his father's work to use religion to stabilise and unify the realm.

In respect of his valour in combat, Samudragupta's own pillar publications leave no room for doubt (the Edwardian British historian Vincent Smith would dub him 'the Indian Napoleon'). By his own estimation he was:

> skilful in engaging in hundreds of battles of various kinds, whose only ally was valour [*parākrama*] through the might of his own arm, and who (has thus) the epithet *Parākrama*, whose body was most charming, being covered over with the plenteous beauty of the marks of hundreds of promiscuous scars, caused by battle-axes, arrows, spikes, spears, barbed darts, swords, iron clubs, javelins for throwing, barbed arrows, span-long arrows and many other weapons.[42]

Samudragupta had more than mere scars to show for his endeavours – he also had the crowns of captured kings. Under his rule the Gupta Empire expanded massively across the northern half of India: the Allahabad inscriptions list the many regions that succumbed to him – nine kings of north India and eleven in the south, with a further five compelled to pay tribute. Many have argued that in reality his direct rule extended probably only to the Ganges plain, accompanied by a wavering control over north-western India. Moreover, he did not conquer the Sacas in western India, and the kings of the south and the Deccan paid him homage, but no more. Still, it was an impressive achievement.

Arguably of greater significance is the degree to which Samudra-gupta's inscriptions extol his religious zeal. According to the Eran inscription, he gave away gold to support religious activity amongst his people, as well as hundreds of thousands of cows, and he worried con-stantly about the relief of the lowly, poor, destitute and afflicted. The Allahabad inscription claims that religion was Samudragupta's daily companion, and he was its 'refuge' – he was the person who guarded and watched over the empire's spiritual well-being.

To this end, Samudragupta reinstated a religious practice long since discontinued, directly associated with the kind of early Vedic worship from which the Guptas had otherwise departed: the *ashvamedha*, or horse-sacrifice. His successor Chandragupta II, in a pillar inscription of his own at Mathura, would recall Samudragupta as 'the very axe of the god Kritana, the giver of many millions of lawfully acquired cows and who was the restorer of the *ashvamedha* sacrifice that had long been in abeyance'.[43] Samudragupta's own coinage underlines his decision to resurrect this ritual: on one side a horse is represented, standing on a pedestal, looking towards an altar already billowing thick smoke into the sky. On the other side we see Samudragupta's queen, clothed in a sari and short corset, her neck, wrists and ankles bearing precious bands, her ears heavy with large circular earrings. She holds a fly-whisk in one hand and looks towards a ceremonial lance stuck into the ground.

It may seem a peculiar pairing: a horse and the ruler's wife, in cele-bration of Samudragupta's attainment of the *ashvamedha*. But, in fact, both parties were necessary for the ceremony's completion, its point being to confer universal sovereignty on the ruler. It was a costly and onerous sacrifice, with preparations beginning up to two years in advance. For a year the horse chosen for sacrifice was allowed to roam free across the land, escorted by members of the *Kshatriya varna* – the nobles of Gupta society – who prevented its coupling with any mares. Any land over which the horse moved was said to be the king's, and the royal escort was on hand to deal with anyone who refuted the claim. Upon the horse's return home, a huge crowd of people from all parts of Gupta society gathered on a specially prepared area of ground in the royal city. Sacrificial stakes were set up and for three days and nights a

fire was kept alight with continual animal sacrifices: at one such ceremony 609 victims had their throats slit to keep the flames burning.

On the second day, to the sound of drums, the chosen horse was
harnessed to a gold-encrusted royal war chariot in which stood the
king and the chief *Brahman* priest. The horse pulled the chariot with its
occupants to the sacrificial area. Amidst the blood of the ongoing sacrifices to feed the fire, the noise of the drums and the tumult of the
gathered masses, the horse was fettered and decorated by the queen,
before being smothered to death on the edge of the arena. All of the
king's wives would then encircle the lifeless beast, murmuring loving
phrases over its body and fanning it with their skirts. The queen herself
lay down by its side as if to copulate with the animal, while the king and
his other wives stood by making obscene ritual remarks. The idea
behind the ceremony seems to have been that the 'union' between the
queen and the sacrifice mimicked a union between the ruling couple
and the gods. In this, it was not unlike a traditional annual ceremony in
ancient Athens during the period of its democracy, in which the wife of
the chief magistrate was 'married' to the god Dionysus in order to
bring good fortune to the city during her husband's tenure.

After the feigned coitus between queen and horse, the horse's
corpse was dismembered with a golden knife and its blood offered to
the fire. Through the night, lit by torches, the celebration continued,
with the smell of roasting flesh and spilled blood mingling in the air
with the crackle of flames, the ritual whispering of the priests, the
music and dancing. On the third and final day, as all the attendees prepared to bathe and purify themselves, twenty-one sterile cows were
sacrificed and the king gave plentiful gifts to his *Brahman* priests and to
his wives.

The *ashvamedha* sacrifice had been banned by King Ashoka upon his
conversion to Buddhism, along with all other animal sacrifice, because
of the Buddhist belief in the reincarnation of spirits in both the human
and animal worlds. And yet, despite the fact that in every other respect
the Guptas wished to be seen as the new Mauryans, this ceremony was
worth bringing back, in so far as it served to emphasise the successful
job Samudragupta was doing as king. The horse's free wanderings were
seen as representing territory that the king was said to have 'conquered'.

The ceremony's crucial focus on the king and queen as the carriers of the ritual reinforced the sense of their particular role within Gupta society as the guarantors of peace, stability and divine goodwill (with the mutual support and respect of the *Brahmans*). And the communal aspects of it, in which all parts of society had a role to play – even if only as spectators – simultaneously reinforced the roles they all had in ensuring the fertility and prosperity of their world, and thus strengthened the stability and unity of the Gupta community as a whole.[44]

It appeared, then, that Samudragupta had made a consummate job of kingship: no mere military conqueror, but an ethical and benevolent ruler, who was also the 'refuge' of religion and the religious protector of the people. As such, he could claim to have performed the role of the *chakravartin* – the ideal universal ruler who rules benevolently and watchfully over his people, keeping the cosmic forces of the universe turning, just as Chandragupta Maurya had been hailed for doing centuries before. The performance of the horse-sacrifice proved his right to claim universal sovereignty, making him a ruler not unlike those in China who, from the Qin and Han dynasties onwards, claimed to govern with the mandate of Heaven.

If these were his virtues, Samudragupta did not hide them under the proverbial bushel. In his official inscriptions he was claimed as equal to the gods 'Dhanada, Varuna, Indra and Antaka . . . the very axe of the god Krtanta'. And, crucially, Samudragupta was equated with one of the supreme gods into which all others linked: he was given the same epithet as Vishnu, *apratitatha* ('matchless warrior'). He was decisively hailed as 'a mortal only in celebrating the rites of the observances of mankind but otherwise a god, dwelling on earth'.[45]

In asserting his own quasi-divine status, Samudragupta made religious and imperial rule in Gupta India effectively one and the same thing. From this point we start to see the use of the Garuda – a large bird-like creature akin to a phoenix, said to serve as the mount of the god Vishnu – as the symbol of the Guptas under Samudragupta. In addition, on the same coins that display the horse-sacrifice, Samudragupta chose to inscribe a description of himself: 'the overlord of kings, who has performed the *ashvamedha*, having protected the earth, conquers the heavens'.[46] He had, at least according to his own coins, met his father's challenge to protect the earth and asserted himself as a universal ruler of a stature to make Constantine in the West or the Chinese rulers in the East seem almost retiring figures by comparison.

With the ruler so claiming quasi-divinity the Guptas naturally sought to restructure their relationship with the religious hierarchy below them. The *Brahmans* were still, despite the relaxing of tradition around the roles of each *varna*, an important group within society, symbolised by the fact that they still had particular roles to perform within the *ashvamedha* sacrifice. Their stature was reflected also in the tradition of gift-giving from rulers to *Brahmans*, a mark of respect, respectfully received, so reinforcing a virtuous circle of reciprocal reward. But this circle the Guptas now sought to reconfigure as a vertical hierarchy of patronage.

The most sought-after gift was land, on which one could mine for gold and keep cattle. During the fourth century CE there were vast increases in land grants to *Brahmans* from both the Guptas and other noble families in imitation. These grants were recorded on copper plates bound together with a ring that carried the seal of the donor – making the direction and hierarchy of the patronage clear to see. And it was, ultimately, a gift that could be revoked, especially by the king, if the situation called for it (though many of the grants offer a rhetorical diatribe against such an action). As such, while continuing the tradition of honouring the *Brahmans* and thus reinforcing their own right to rule, the Guptas were able to reconfigure the system so as to emphasise the origins of patronage as descending from themselves, ensuring that the bonds that held their community tight were all, ultimately, linked to them.

Ultimate Gupta authority was not the only positive outcome of this practice of land gift-giving to *Brahmans*. The land they were given was often chosen very specifically. *Brahmans* might find themselves masters of un-irrigated rural lands into which they had to make significant investments of time and effort. But *they* increasingly became effective land-managers (a manual was even developed to help them, called the *Krishiparashara*), and they brought important benefits to rural areas – from irrigation to regular cultivation, even helping to create new villages and towns. In turn, the other *varnas* in Gupta society benefited, especially the *shreni* (the merchants and traders), who had new outlets for their work.

The Guptas were not the only ruling family in India at the time to develop such techniques. The Vakatakas to the south were even greater land-donators to *Brahmans* than the Guptas (in one case they handed over thirty-five villages). So, too, were the Satavahanas even further to the south. But it was amongst the Guptas that the concept seems to have reached its most sophisticated formulation: as presiders and donators over an increasingly structured hierarchical society, which mutually reinforced and legitimated political and religious positions and authority, at the same time as helping to develop their economy and integrate their society. The Guptas – armed by their self-identification with the supreme Vishnu, validated by the resumption of older Vedic rituals like the horse-sacrifice, and presiding over a self-legitimating system of patronage and societal development – had managed to cast themselves as living embodiments of the epic kings of Indian imagination. The possibilities seemed limitless.

Midway through Samudragupta's reign he received a request from the King of Sri Lanka to erect a monastery and rest house near the Bodhi Tree (in modern-day Bihar). The rest-house would be for Buddhist monks and visitors making a pilgrimage from Sri Lanka to this sacred location, where the Buddha had once meditated and obtained enlightenment. Sri Lanka had been one of the places to which Ashoka had sent Buddhist missionaries, and indeed is where the earliest surviving Buddhist texts come from. It was, by the time of Samudragupta, a community in which Buddhism thrived and from which Buddhists were now themselves expanding, both back to the key places of pilgrimage from the Buddha's own life and, along the increasingly complex trade routes, east towards China.

Samudragupta was no stranger to Buddhism. He had even appointed a Buddhist to oversee his son's education because of their reputation for extraordinary learning. What he was perhaps unaware of was the seismic leap that Buddhist worship had taken in China, in and around the years that he himself had come to power.

*

China had faced massive disruption in the years after 304 CE. An invasion by a number of Xiongnu and other nomadic hordes into northern China had brought about not only the destruction of great cities like Chang'an and Luoyang, but mass immigration into the north, and an immense migration of northern Chinese into southern China. In the north the many invading tribes set up a multitude of mini-kingdoms (historians speak of 'The Sixteen Kingdoms Period') that fought for power amongst themselves over the next hundred years. Eventually one tribe, the Xianbei – themselves descendants of the Donghu tribe defeated by the Xiongnu in the third century BCE – emerged triumphant to form the Northern Dynasty.

In contrast, the remnants of the Western Jin dynasty – the ruling house that had managed to conquer and unite the kingdoms of Wei, Shu and Wu – fled south-east in the early fourth century following the influx of Xiongnu tribes, to re-establish themselves around a new capital, Jianking, in the area of today's Nanjing, and began life as the (now) Eastern Jin dynasty, which would survive for another century.

The political and military history of China in the fourth, fifth and sixth centuries CE is one of intensive upheaval and fragmentation, sandwiched as it is in the annals between the unifying empires of the Western and Eastern Han on the one hand, and the emergence of the Sui and Tang dynasties from the late sixth century CE on the other. Within this challenging and disparate world, what hope did Buddhism have to become embedded in Chinese society? After all, it was, at best, a religion tolerated by Chinese intellectuals and rulers, but one still overwhelmingly practised by foreigners, reliant on the importation and (often imperfect) translation of texts, which were themselves confusing and sometimes contradictory, reflecting a religious practice that was itself divergent, multiple and constantly evolving.

In fact Buddhism not only survived, but prospered in this splintered environment, and for a number of reasons. Most profound, perhaps, was the uncertain and unsettling nature of the world in which many – both elite and ordinary laypeople – found themselves. Life was an ongoing struggle against natural disasters, plagues and famines, punctuated with periodic ravages by external invaders and internal turf wars.[47] Buddhism's focus on the futility of worldly ambition (given the ceaseless nature of the cycle of reincarnation) may well have chimed with the pessimism of the age. At the same time, thanks to its emphasis on the cycle of good deeds and intentions creating good effects as the only route to an exit from the cycle of rebirth (*karma*), Buddhism also offered something hopeful and attainable to individuals at every level of society. As the Buddha was quoted as saying – a credo in sharp contrast to the religious hierarchies entrenched in the Roman world, Armenia and India – 'my doctrine makes no distinction between high and low, rich and poor; it is like the sky, it has room for all; like water it washes all alike'.[48]

This was also a time when China's main philosophical traditions, Confucianism and Daoism, were both suffering declines in popularity. Confucianism – the mainstay of the Western and Eastern Han dynasties, which had led to the ritual worship of Confucius himself – had failed to arrest its fall. Likewise Daoism, in all its various forms, had failed to give succour to the people amid the disruption caused by the northern invasion of the Xiongnu and the southern flight of the Jin. Moreover, neither Confucianism nor Daoism had much to say about two issues that were, given the instability of the period, on everyone's minds: the nature of death and the hereafter, two topics absolutely central to Buddhist thought. Far from being an impediment to Buddhism's development, then, it turns out that the fragmented and fraught atmosphere of fourth-century CE China was well suited to its spread amongst a much wider range of the population, when their traditional religious and political ideas failed to provide sufficient guidance.

We must distinguish, however, between the ways in which Buddhism came to prominence in the north and the south during this period. In the north Buddhism came swiftly to the attention – and gained the approval – of the newly arrived rulers. Just before the destruction of Luoyang by the invading Xiongnu in 311 CE, a Buddhist monk named Fotudeng from the former Kushan Empire in central Asia had found his way to the city, no doubt along the trade networks that connected the Mediterranean to China. He had come in order to establish a new religious centre, only to find his mission overtaken by events with some alacrity. As Luoyang was looted around him – its buildings plundered, its women raped, those who could not escape murdered – Fotudeng, it was later claimed, made recourse to his extraordinary ability to produce striking supernatural effects.

One of the new Xiongnu rulers – who would become the Emperor Shi Le of the Later Zhao dynasty, one of the warring Sixteen Kingdoms – challenged Fotudeng to demonstrate the power of his religion. On burning incense and uttering a spell over a bowl of water, he produced blue lotus flowers (one of the symbols of the Buddha) said to be so bright that they dazzled the eyes. With spirits as his messengers, Fotudeng was also able to draw water from dried-up wells. Legend has it that by such impressive feats he not only managed to convert Shi Le to Buddhism, but became his respected adviser, built a number of Buddhist temples, and led a community of Buddhist monks in their continued work of translating and communicating Buddhist thought.

What attracted not just Shi Le but a number of Xiongnu tribal leaders (now heads of nascent Chinese kingdoms) to adopt Buddhist practices was the very fact that Buddhism was a foreign religion. Northern China was, of course, awash with foreigners and foreign interaction: even before the Xiongnu invasion, it is estimated that half of the population of Chang'an were foreigners. The interaction (both diplomatic and economic) with the kingdoms of central Asia – many themselves centres of Buddhist practice – was constant. And despite the inevitable slowing of such interaction that the destruction of Chang'an and Luoyang (not to mention ongoing regional disturbances) brought with it, new arrivals were still pouring into north China. In engaging with Buddhist practice, therefore, Shi Le and other Xiongnu tribal leaders were pointedly eschewing old Jin-dynasty practice and responding to the very international nature of the communities they ruled. Whereas Tiridates in Armenia attempted to force a new religion upon an established and embedded population, in northern China the new could be preached to the new.

At the same time, the shamanistic figure of a Buddhist monk such as Fotudeng struck a chord with traditional Xiongnu ideas of what religious practice should look and feel like, given their love for associating divine signs with major events. Consequently what developed in the north across the fourth century CE was a Buddhism free of entanglement with other Chinese schools of philosophical and religious thought, reflecting the international nature of its population and rulers. This Buddhism was mixed with elements of older ancestor worship, divine signs and miracle-working, and focused on the issue of salvation through devotion for the ordinary people, while providing reinforcement of the right to rule for those in charge.

It was also a form of Buddhism particularly attached to images: a tradition that had begun in central Asia in the era of the Kushan Empire, and in turn reflected Greco-Roman influence in the region dating back to the era of Alexander the Great. It is symbolic of this connected global world that one of the first Buddha images surviving in northern China from the beginning of the Sixteen Kingdoms period was owned by a Yuezhi patron living in Chang'an, whose distant ancestors had fled west, eventually creating the Kushan Empire. It is a small statuette in gilt bronze, measuring just 13.5 centimetres in height, representing the Buddha seated in meditation in central Asian-style robes, seated on a rug with central Asian motifs.[49] In one object we see influences, ideas, historical events and peoples from several centuries that span the ancient globe from the Mediterranean to China.

In southern China, however, the story of the development of Buddhism follows a different trajectory. Alongside the gentry who streamed south in flight from the Xiongnu invasion were a number of Buddhist monks who had been working and translating in the great cities of Chang'an and Luoyang. As they re-established their homes and communities in the south – sometimes even setting up new villages and towns and naming them after the places where they had lived in the north – many of these refugees experienced the common feeling of despondency in regard to the pressures of the time, and the apparently inadequate response to the same provided by Confucianism and the varying forms of Daoism. For some time so-called 'Dark Learning' – a quest for a permanent substrate underlying this world of change – had mixed in with Confucianist and Daoist beliefs amongst the Chinese scholar gentry. This quest had been a principal element of intellectual discussions that took place during orchestrated tea parties known as Qingtan – 'pure conversation' sessions. These exclusive events were the dynamic and selective hub into which Buddhism would have to break in the south, if it was to become more than a tolerated foreign cult.

The process by which Buddhist teachings and teachers did so had begun much earlier, however. In the late second century CE the great Buddhist teacher Mouzi had been asked why he constantly explained and supported his arguments for Buddhist ideas by quoting Chinese texts. His reply was simple and practical-minded: 'It is because you know the contents of the Classics that I quote them. If I should speak about the words of the Buddhist sutras and explain the essential meaning of Nirvana it would be like speaking about the five colours to the blind, or playing the five tones to the deaf.'[50]

Mouzi was not underestimating the difficulty of enabling the Chinese to understand the concepts of Buddhism. It was not merely a translation problem. Rather, there was an issue in that many of the concepts of Buddhism did not even exist in Chinese thought. Nirvana – the quenching of the cycle of rebirth in the attainment of a place of perfect enlightenment – had no equivalent in Chinese.

It was a very different kind of problem from that experienced in other parts of the ancient world. Within the dominion of Rome, Christianity's doctrinal beliefs were not so far removed from those surrounding several pagan deities – rather, the real difficulty that the faith faced in being accepted had always derived from the way in which Christianity put its followers at social and political odds with the rest of Roman society. In India, a religious evolution emerged from the naturally multifaceted nature of Hindu worship. In Armenia, what occurred was not a growing correspondence but, rather, the blanket replacement of one religion with another. In China, however, Buddhist missionaries had the arguably unique challenge of how to explain to and convert people who could not comprehend the beliefs to which they were being asked to devote themselves.

Moreover, it had to be faced that many of these new central Buddhist ideas ran directly contrary to the traditions of Chinese society. Confucianism (in a way not dissimilar to the traditional Hindu *varnas*) advocated a community-focused sense of one's place in the world: in his *Analects*, as we have seen, Confucius had made plain that the epitome of kingcraft came about 'when a king is king and the minister is minister, when the father is father and the son is son': in other words, when no one usurps their place in society.[51] Buddhism – with its emphasis on individual karma and individual paths to salvation – advocated the absence of hierarchy replaced by a central focus around the institution of the *sangha* (the Buddhist monastery), in a manner that had contributed to the weakening of the *varna* system in India.

The crucial Buddhist institution of the *sangha,* which welcomed anyone from any background to become a monk and sat, as an institution, both outside traditional social and political hierarchies while, at the same time, claiming to be a crucial part of the society's hope for salvation and enlightenment, also posed a problem for Chinese society. While such inclusiveness chimed with Confucius's desire to establish educational establishments for all, the *sangha*'s claim to be outside Chinese society made an ill fit with the highly structured and aggressively hierarchical nature of the Chinese community.

Since the second century CE Buddhist teachers had sought to counteract the perceived misalignment of Buddhist and Chinese traditions not simply by using Chinese texts in support of Buddhist arguments, but also by attempting explicitly to integrate Buddhist and Daoist ideas, stories and concepts, so as to make the Buddhist teachings appear less threatening, less foreign. The principal idea of '*dao*' in Daoism – the 'Way', 'path' or 'principle' by which one should live life – was used as a translation for *dharma,* for example; and explanations of *karma,* as well as defences of the *sangha,* were made right through into the fourth century CE with quotations from, and allusions to, Daoist and other Chinese classics.[52]

The endeavour was evidently successful. Back in the second century CE Emperor Huan of the Han dynasty was said to have performed a joint sacrifice to Laozi (the fictional 'founder' of Daoism) and the Buddha; and the idea was formulated that Laozi had disappeared from China and become the Buddha in India. In this way Daoism and Buddhism came to be seen no longer as opposites, but linked across time and space.[53] And from the third century CE onwards we see works of Chinese art that freely match Daoist and Buddhist ideas, as well as the first reports that Confucius may also have become the Buddha (a stunning reversal of earlier Daoist claims that Confucius learnt at the feet of Laozi).[54] Such suggestive overlaps paved the way for the more difficult reconciliation of Confucianism and Buddhism within Chinese thought.

If in India the Guptas had sought to mould old and new Hindu traditions together, what Buddhists in southern China were attempting was to merge different religions – a reflection of the manner in which so many disparate people, traditions and cultures had been mixed in China, as well as across eastern and central Asia, by migrations, imperial expansions and the development of trade routes since the third and second centuries BCE. And to merge these religions was to merge also the histories of different worlds. Just as Megasthenes, Greek ambassador to the Indian court, had connected the early histories of these worlds by noting the arrival of the god Dionysus in India and the birth of Heracles there, now, too, the early histories of India and China were melded by stories of the joined-up lives of the respective founders of great religions.

Buddhist thinking in China had also evolved on its own terms to align more with the key questions and issues being discussed by the Chinese elites, particularly in relation to 'Dark Learning'. A school of what would be called 'Prajna' Buddhism emerged, probing specifically into the nature of the ultimate reality underlying the variant nature of human experience that so plagued Chinese intellectuals.

In all, by the time Chinese elites had reconstituted themselves in southern China in the fourth century CE, Buddhism was well positioned to become part of their conversation. This was made all the more possible by a new generation of naturalised foreign monks, but also by equivalent numbers of Chinese Buddhist monks, who could be part of these elite discussions because they were themselves naturally part of the higher echelons of Chinese society. They had the breeding, the eloquence and educational background to be heard and understood within the Qingtan, and most importantly, they had the authority to be listened to.

Among these new Buddhist elites were men such as Gaozuo, formerly a Kushan prince who had given up the throne to become a monk. First resident in the north, he had drifted south following the Xiongnu invasions, before being discovered by a leading member of the elite Wang family in the new capital of the Eastern Jin. It was the Wang family who invited Gaozuo into their Qingtan, not least probably because two members of their own family were Buddhist monks.

Gaozuo gained huge respect from the local gentry – even though all his interventions in the Qingtan were via interpreter – because he was said to display a kind of 'silent understanding' that was felt to greatly enrich the conversation.

Buddhism, then, increasingly entered the lifeblood of Chinese elite circles in the south in the fourth century CE as Buddhists became not just part of the Qingtan, but also preachers, chaplains, advisers and friends to the Chinese aristocracy. In turn, the gentry became great sponsors of Buddhist churches, monasteries and ongoing translation efforts. During the period of the Eastern Jin it is estimated that 17,068 Buddhist temples were built in China, alongside the translation of 263 volumes of Buddhist texts.

Despite these successes, however, Buddhism would continue to attract ardent critics who still felt threatened by the socio-political implications of Buddhism for Chinese society, particularly in the shape and function of the *sangha*. If Buddhism was to be more than an intellectual fad in the south, or a fabled conjuror of lotus flowers from thin air in the north – if it was to make a comfortable long-term fit for Chinese society and its rulers, within China's religious and political landscape – then it would need to find a way to appease critics of its most prominent institution.

*

At the outset of the latter half of the fourth century a wealth of diverse forms of worship were in varying states of accommodation with the great rulers of far-reaching realms.

The recorded narrative of Tiridates' and Gregory's swift, divinely aided conversion of Armenia masks a more difficult and uneven reality that eventually sent Tiridates running from power to live as a hermit, or perhaps had him assassinated, leaving Armenia even more divided and unstable. Across the Mediterranean, Constantine had created a new capital to embody his fine balance and commingling of pagan and Christian traditions, and had tried to ensure that doctrinal Christian disputes did not sow perpetual disorder amid the unity of his realm. He had above all attempted the fusion of Church, pagan and imperial authority in his person, placing himself at the apex of the system.

In India, the Guptas had surpassed their wildest dreams in not only moulding old and new religious traditions together, to reinforce their rule and the stability of their community, but in the process generating a stronger social hierarchy that was ultimately dependent on them as quasi-divine rulers. And in China, Buddhists had managed to make their religion appealing to the new rulers of the north, and moulded it in the south so that it could be accepted into elite circles of conversation and thinking, in so doing linking the histories and religions of India and China together.

In each case, though, the position of these religions and of their proponents remained precarious. For Christianity within the Roman Empire, despite Constantine's interest and involvement, was still a minority religion and the Roman emperor was by no means a Christian. For Christianity within Armenia, despite the miraculous work of Gregory, it was unclear to what extent the religion had been embedded with the population (let alone with the Christianity of southern Armenia, with its different, more people-focused ethos) and there were gathering tensions in the relationship between the king and the *Catholicos*. For Buddhism in China, the fate of this new religion was yet to be decided in both the north and the south, within a still rapidly changing political and military climate. In each case it remained to be seen whether the faith had a future as an accepted national religion, not least because, unlike in Gupta India, the relationship between religion and rule had yet to be fully negotiated.

CHAPTER 9

Religion and Rule

In early April of 337 CE Constantine felt the onset of illness. For the good of his health he decided to leave Constantinople and travel east to Nicomedia. There he summoned his bishops; and, according to Eusebius of Caesarea, it was only now that Constantine was finally baptised into the Christian faith. St Jerome (writing forty years after Eusebius) tells us that the baptism was conducted by the *other* Eusebius, Bishop Eusebius of Nicomedia – he who had refused to sign the First Nicene Creed in 325 CE and been sent into exile, only to be accepted back by Constantine in 327. It would appear that Constantine held firm on his commitment to toleration and inclusiveness. Following his baptism, freshly forgiven of his sins, he is said to have refused to dress in colourful imperial robes, instead donning the plain white garb of a Christian convert.

It was at Nicomedia, on 22 May 337 CE, that Constantine – unifier of the Roman Empire, creator of its new capital at Constantinople and architect of its policy of religious toleration – died. He was surrounded by his Christian bishops and his pagan prefect, Evagrius, a suitably mixed group in an appropriate setting replete with memories of his rule. Nicomedia, after all, had been the scene of the surrender of Licinius, when Constantine became sole ruler of the entire Roman Empire. It had seen the meeting with King Tiridates the Great of Armenia, as well as the grand dinner for the attendees of the First Council of Nicaea.

Constantine's body was transferred back to Constantinople, and it was here that the ultimate expression of his place at the apex of Christian and imperial hierarchy was articulated. In accordance with his wishes, his body was placed under the central dome of the Church of the Holy Apostles. Surrounded by the cenotaphs and memorial gravestones of the Twelve Apostles, Constantine's sarcophagus was positioned symbolically in the centre of them, as a thirteenth Apostle. By the fifth century CE it had become fashionable (especially in the east) to call Constantine *isoapostolos* – 'equal to the apostles'. In later Byzantine histories of Constantine he would be hailed in even more glowing terms, akin to the descriptions of the Gupta rulers in India by their court poets as published on pillar inscriptions:

> The saintly Constantine was indeed a man distinguished in every way for the courage of his spirit, the keenness of his intelligence, the erudition of his discourse, the uprightness of his sense of justice, the readiness of his benevolence, the propriety of his appearance and the bravery and fortitude he showed in war; he was of great reputation among barbarians and unequalled among those of his own race, firm and unshaken in honesty. Furthermore in looks and in elegance of beauty he was both the most seemly and the most handsome ... [A]gainst all his enemies, it was by prayer that he brought victory within his grasp.[1]

And yet at the time of his death, Constantine's empire was still not officially Christian. Indeed, less than 50 per cent of the empire's seventy million-plus population professed the faith. It was only over the next sixty years that Christianity would develop into the true religion of the Roman Empire – amidst huge political and military upheaval across the Mediterranean – and, in the process, be honed into a single acceptable faith against which any and all deviations were held to be heresy. In that final journey towards one official Christianity, the relationship between religion and ruler as forged by Constantine – with the emperor as an apostle figure linking Christian and imperial hierarchy – would be first strengthened and then finally frustrated, to be replaced by a new battle between the spiritual authority of Christian bishops and the earthly authority of the emperor.

That same conflict between spiritual and earthly authority would develop in even more bloody form in Armenia, fuelled by the ruler's desire for more centralised authority, the struggle to adapt Christianity to the native religious and social landscapes, and the impact of political, military and religious decisions made by the Roman and Sassanid Empires that surrounded it. In Gupta India, however, the crafting of religion and rule that had taken place under previous rulers was only strengthened in the second half of the fourth century CE. With it came political, economic and military stability, which led – unlike the adoption of very particular kinds of Christianity in Rome and Armenia, and the official outlawing of all others – to a flourishing of religious diversity, respect and toleration.

In China, Buddhist practitioners continued their efforts to counteract negative impressions of their practices within Chinese society, with the result that Buddhism gained its first official ruling converts and ongoing royal support, part of a developing relationship between ruler and religion that – in some instances, at least – blossomed into mutual respect for each other's authority.

One Religion, Two Rulers

On his deathbed Constantine was attended by both Christian and pagan officials. The architecture of his new city, Constantinople, still reflected this mix of traditions, whereas older cities such as Rome remained overwhelmingly pagan in their feel and outlook, steeped as they were in centuries of pagan history and construction dating back to the foundation of the republic and to the era of Rome's kings before that.

In the years immediately before his death, Constantine was still granting people the right to worship as they wanted. That even included the right to worship him, as previous Roman emperors had been worshipped. The Italian community of Hispellum asked permission to build a temple in honour of Constantine and his family. He agreed, as long as 'no temple dedicated in our name shall be defiled by the deceptions of any contagious and unreasonable religious belief'.[2] Typically ambiguous, this communiqué left unstated exactly what 'unreasonable' religious belief might look like.

Constantine's authority over the developing Christian Church and its community within the Roman Empire was never absolute. In North Africa the schism between the Roman-approved Christian Church and the Donatists had continued to grow. In 330 Constantine, keeping to his policy of ignoring religious misdemeanour on the African continent, stood by and watched as the Donatists seized a church that he had himself paid for (on the proviso that it be used by those who followed the 'official' church hierarchy), and simply gave money for another to be built. Their leader Donatus, up to his own death in 335, was said to have 'claimed for himself sovereign authority at Carthage, who exalted his heart and seems to himself to be superior to other mortals'.[3] The Donatists even attempted to expand their influence beyond Africa by putting forward a Donatist candidate for the prestigious position of Bishop of Rome. And even after Donatus was gone, the movement continued to be extremely popular: in 336, 270 Donatist bishops gathered for an assembly in North Africa.[4]

Constantine had also been unsuccessful (despite his pragmatic approaches at Nicaea and Tyre) in resolving the other great schism of the Christian Church, over the issue of the relationship between Jesus Christ and God. His final attempted solution had been little more than a fudged compromise held together by his personal authority. As such, its endurance depended entirely on whether Constantine's successors chose to uphold it. They did not, as things transpired, have a great deal of time in which to prioritise religious matters.

Constantine was survived by three children by the same woman, Fausta, whom he had murdered in her bath after she had persuaded him to kill his child from a previous marriage. On his death the Roman Empire, united so painstakingly under his rule, once again split between those three surviving children: Constantius II commanded the east, Constantine II the west and Constans the centre and North Africa. Constantius II in the east was wholly occupied with fending off renewed attacks by the Sassanid Empire. In contrast (if akin, perhaps, to Constantine's tussles with Maxentius), Constantine II and Constans quickly came to be locked in conflict with one another, for sole control of the western and central empire. By 340 Constantine II had been killed and Constans took charge of two-thirds of the Roman world. He lacked, however, his father's ability to command loyalty, for just a decade later, in 350, he was murdered following a rebellion led by Magnentius, commander of an imperial guard unit, who subsequently took charge of what had been Constans's share of the empire.

Constantius II, having pushed back the Sassanids in the east, now returned west to deal with the usurper. From 351 to 353 the two faced up against one another in several battles, eventually leading to Magnentius's death. But still Constantius won himself no breathing space. Encouraged by the ongoing struggle for control of the empire, tribes on its northern borders had begun to invade and Constantius II now devoted his energies to defeating them. Having pushed them back, he was met with bad news from the east: the cousin he had left in charge there had wholeheartedly failed to balance the demands of his command and had upset pretty much every constituent part of Roman society within his realm. There were tales of brutally put-down rebellions, mob riots, the strong-arming of the legislature, the murder of Roman officials, as well as the fake trial and execution of wealthy citizens to commandeer their wealth. Constantius recalled his cousin from command and eventually had him executed. But no sooner had he done that than he was faced with another rebellion in Gaul, led by another Roman deserter. Realising he could not hold the empire together himself, Constantius II elevated his sole remaining male relative, Julian, to be his junior emperor and tasked him with taking on the rebellion in Gaul. In turn, Constantius eventually returned east to face the Sassanids, who were once again massing on the Roman border.

It is amazing to think that during this fraught period Constantius – as he moved across the entirety of the Roman Empire, fighting off external enemies and putting down internal ones – had any time whatsoever to consider the religious equilibrium of his realm. In most areas he seems to have maintained the balancing act of toleration practised by Constantine – except in relation to the particular question of the relationship between the elements of the Holy Trinity, on which his view was adamant. On 22 May 359 CE Constantius II, on the twenty-second anniversary of his father's death, and just as he was about to head east once more to fight the Sassanids, renounced the First Nicene Creed, refuting his father's personal formulation of the relationship of Christ and God as 'of the same substance'. Instead he described Jesus as 'like his father', creating a new Nicene Creed text to reflect this formulation.

We will never know what Constantius II planned next. The following year Julian, having taken care of the Gaulish rebellion, was proclaimed senior emperor by his troops. Constantius – still fighting off the Sassanids in the east – chose to return west to deal with this new threat, but died en route in early November 361 CE.

The events leading up to this moment are related to us by Julian himself. He wrote letters to the key cities in Italy and Greece defending his actions: only the letter to the city of Athens survives, in which Julian praises Athens' historic role in defending Greece against the Persian invasions of 490/480 BCE, and praises the city's reputation for justice above all else from the period of its great democracy. It was on the basis of this renowned admiration for justice that Julian wrote to Athens to lay open his own conduct for their judgement:

> then if this was your conduct of old, and from that day to this there is kept alive some small spark as it were of the virtue of your ances-tors, it is natural that you should pay attention not to the magnitude merely of any performance, nor whether a man has travelled over the earth with incredible speed and unwearied energy as though he had flown through the air; but that you should rather consider whether one has accomplished this feat by just means.[5]

We don't know for sure if Athens' response supported Julian's version of events; but, to some extent, it no longer mattered: Julian was now sole emperor of the Roman world.

His reign took shape around two key policies, the first forced on him, the second his personal choice. The first was to counter the on-going threat of the Sassanid Empire in order to secure the empire's eastern border and, even more importantly, to bolster his authority as a ruler of military prowess equal to – even surpassing – his predecessors.[6] The second, however, must have come to the Roman world as a complete surprise. Julian had been born and brought up as a Christian, but the ongoing arguments over Christian doctrine – particularly the relationship between the elements of the Holy Trinity – had disillusioned him. Thus he had returned to worship of the pagan gods.

In one of his later hymns to the pagan sun god Helios, Julian claims that 'from my childhood an extraordinary longing for the rays of the god penetrated deep into my soul'.[7] Believing that Christianity would destroy itself in time by dint of its own internal discord, Julian advocated a return to former pagan practices, which had in contrast stood for time immemorial. (He was said, by the later fifth-century Church scholar Socrates of Constantinople, to believe himself to be Alexander the Great in another body, on account of the transmigration of souls, as advocated by the philosophers Pythagoras and Plato.[8])

On assuming imperial command in 361 CE Julian did not, however, seek to eradicate Christianity – not least because he knew all too well that the persecutions by Valerian, Diocletian and Galerius had manifestly failed in that regard. Instead he sought to deprive the faith of its influence by expelling it from positions of authority and encouraging Christianity's own internal dissension, the better to accelerate its decline. He withdrew the rights of Christians to teach outside their churches; purged the imperial staff of Christian worshippers; withdrew imperial stipends from Christian bishops; and recalled exiled bishops whose views were at odds with the official creed of the Church, in order to ferment that hoped-for dissent. He further decreed the reopening of pagan sanctuaries and the return of their confiscated property.

Julian is, in fact, the last known consultant of the famous pagan oracle at Delphi. And yet the response relayed to him offered little hope for a return to pagan worship:

> *Go tell the king the wondrous hall is fallen to the ground.*
> *Now Phoebus [Apollo] has a hut no more, no laurel that fortells,*
> *No talking spring; the water that once spoke is heard no more.*[9]

Julian was killed, just two years into his reign, fighting the Sassanids on the eastern borders of his empire, and his dreams of returning the Roman world to paganism died with him. In truth, his attempts to disenfranchise Christianity probably served only to stimulate its development within the Roman world over subsequent decades. His plan to introduce dissenting Christian voices and antagonistic debates within the faith rather backfired, in that these debates spilled out from rarefied circles to become a hot topic of conversation across all levels of society: in Constantinople, it was said that even the bath attendants were keenly discussing Christian theology.

Moreover, by seeking to disenfranchise rather than persecute Christianity, Julian had allowed Christians enough leeway to entrench and define their history, key stories and figures, around which they could develop an even stronger religious and social identity. In Rome, for instance, the Christian bishop was busy in this period identifying the burial sites of Christian martyrs and embellishing their tombs so that they could become objects of worship and pilgrimage.

A third and possibly fatal flaw in Julian's plans was that the message of Christianity – like that of Buddhism in China in this same period – seemed to resonate amid the unstable military-political mood of the times. For the two decades after Julian's death the Roman world was splintered by multiple simultaneous rulers governing different areas for often short-lived reigns, this turmoil accompanied by ongoing threats to Rome's borders, particularly in the north and east. Christianity preached kindness and the importance of helping one another: its message gained many adherents in this tumultuous time. The result was a significant increase in the number of Christians across the empire: by the 380s well over half the population of the Roman world were Christian.

That said, Christian belief remained riven by internal disagreements. Over the same period a deepening geographical split had become apparent, particularly over the issue of the Holy Trinity, between the Western Roman world (which followed the First Nicene Creed created by Constantine) and the East (which preferred Constantius II's version). What seemed to be needed was a clear statement once and for all on what official Christian theology and practice actually were. But for such an authoritative declaration, the Roman world needed the voice of an undisputed ruler.

Theodosius, Roman emperor from 379 to 395, was the first of his kind in well over a decade to rule the whole empire single-handedly for any length of time. (Indeed, he would be the last.) In January 380, at Thessalonika in northern Greece, Theodosius issued an imperial edict on the question of the relationship of Christ and God. The edict proclaimed a familiar belief in a single deity 'of the Father, son and the Holy Ghost under a concept of equal majesty and of the Holy Trinity'. But this time the Roman emperor went further. He declared that any other version of the divine relationship was no longer merely in contravention of the official imperial and ecclesiastical lines; rather, it was demented and insane, and would incur the wrath of both God and the emperor.

This was a crucial moment not only in the development of Christian belief and the concept of heresy, but in the relationship of Christianity, the Church and the emperor. Constantine had posited himself at the apex of the imperial and church hierarchy, a 'Thirteenth Apostle' overseeing the publication of statements of belief by ecclesiastical councils and punishing dissenters who threatened unity. But he had not declared that such dissent would incur the wrath of God, or made it known that the emperor would be the hand through which that wrath was delivered. Theodosius, in contrast, had taken such steps. In November 380 he entered Constantinople and demanded that its bishop, Demophilus, accept the imperial edict. The bishop refused and was immediately deposed, replaced by Gregory of Nazianzus, a Greek-born bishop who was no friend of Arianism with its concept of the relationship of the holy trinity. But Gregory proved so unpopular with the population of the city that he required a bodyguard of imperial troops. Theodosius, it seemed, was promoting and protecting a particular version of Christianity as the will of God, against the will of a noteworthy proportion of the Roman people.

In January 381 Theodosius went yet further. He declared that only those with 'the faith of Nicaea' could be appointed bishops: those who refused were stripped of their privileges and expelled from cities. He followed this up with a new council in Constantinople, which – after much wrangling and the resignation of Gregory from the bishopric of Constantinople – led in July to another version of the Nicene Creed, which Theodosius ordered his civil servants and soldiers to impose widely. Every other version of Christian belief was, from 383 CE, declared 'heresy' – officially, legally and theologically wrong.

The motivation behind Theodosius's hardline stance was simple: the need to unify and stabilise a huge empire in a time of significant external threat. Theodosius had grown up in Spain as a soldier. He had proven himself in the rigours of battle time and again. What he had learnt was that the success of the empire depended above all upon authority and unity in a crisis, just as the great military leaders of the third and second centuries BCE had sought to achieve. The empire had been splintered politically and militarily for the last decades, and was also still at war with the Sassanid Empire to the east. In such a difficult political and military environment, religious unity and loyalty were crucial.

Theodosius was now confronted, though, by the problem that his edict on the Holy Trinity had sided with Western sympathies in contrast to those in the Roman East. Given that the East was the critical front against the Sassanid onslaught, Theodosius was particularly concerned that it should accept his decision – hence his marching to Constantinople to confront Demophilus. Thereafter he also tinkered with the Christian Church hierarchy to ensure the subjugation of the East to the West: the Bishop of Constantinople was made secondary to the Bishop of Rome. Politics, war and religion, in the context of a connected ancient world, had been fused together in this new settlement for the Roman Empire.

Theodosius's strictures in respect of Christianity had obvious repercussions, too, for pagan worship in the empire, since it was technically within the 'demented and insane' spectrum of beliefs now outlawed. During the 380s attacks by Christians on pagan sites of worship intensified. The pagan orator Libanius complained of 'the black-robed tribe who hasten to attack the temples with sticks and stones and bars of iron . . . utter desolation follows, with the stripping of roofs, demolition of walls and the tearing down of statues'.[10] And yet the pagan Olympic Games were still celebrated in 381 CE, and Theodosius himself visited the still strongly pagan Senate in Rome in 389 and was received with traditional pagan sacrifices. It was not until 391 and 392 that Theodosius officially moved to outlaw key pagan practices such as sacrifice, and the use of its major symbols and images. The Church historian St Jerome commented on the results: 'The gilded capital falls into disrepair, dust and cobwebs cover all Rome's temples . . . the city shakes on its foundations and a stream of people hurry, past fallen shrines, to the tombs of the Martyrs.'[11]

It was not just in Rome that the effects of the outlawing of paganism were felt. In Egypt, where looting of pagan sanctuaries in cities such as Alexandria had been particularly widespread (spurred on, even, by Alexandria's Christian bishop), the study of the ancient Egyptian script of hieroglyphics inscribed onto its ancient pyramids and temples was now abandoned as heresy. (The ability to read the script was lost from human memory for the next fourteen centuries, until redeciphering became possible once more in the nineteenth century, thanks to the discovery of the multilingual Rosetta Stone that now sits in the British Museum.)

Old habits, however, die hard. However moribund its temples had become, paganism still had strong and powerful supporters, especially in the Roman Senate. In the same year that Theodosius banned pagan symbols, an altar of the pagan goddess Nike ('Victory') was reinstalled in the Senate house in Rome. In Theodosius's new world, where religious choice was mandated by the emperor, religious dissension now constituted political rebellion, and that meant war. A man called Eugenius defended the Senate's right to choose their own religious observances, and challenged Theodosius for the throne.

In early September 394 CE, at the River Frigidus in modern-day Slovenia, Theodosius led a Roman and allied army under Christian standards, against Eugenius's forces of Franks and Gauls fighting in the name of the pagan gods Jupiter and Heracles. For two days the two sides were locked in bloody combat to determine both political leadership and religious freedom. Christian writers would later claim that a fierce tempest sent by God served to break the lines of Eugenius's troops. Theodosius was victorious. It was the last serious military challenge to the adoption of Christianity within the Roman Empire.

Theodosius died the following year. His eulogy was pronounced by Bishop Ambrose of Milan, who articulated yet another twist in the development of the relationship between religion and rule. Ambrose began by describing the idea of a Christian ruling dynasty, as initiated by Constantine (although Constantine had not officially converted until just before his death). However, Ambrose went on, this did not mean that the emperor was the ultimate authority over the Church, as Constantine and his successors had positioned themselves: in fact, it was the bishops who had religious authority over the emperor.[12]

This much Ambrose had made clear to Theodosius himself before his death. Ambrose had excommunicated Theodosius from the Church for his decision to massacre 7,000 people at Thessalonika in punishment for a revolt against Roman rule back in 390 CE. He had told Theodosius that the only way to be readmitted to the fold was to repent, and after months of penance Theodosius was indeed received once more. As Ambrose put it in his eulogy, with Theodosius's son among the listeners: 'he showed himself to be humble and asked for forgiveness, when sin stole upon him'.[13] The Roman world now had one religion, but two rulers: one earthly, one spiritual, the latter in the ascendant. Little wonder that, early in the fifth century CE, the Church writer St Augustine, who had been baptised into the Christian faith by Ambrose, claimed that 'the authority, which the Christian faith has, is diffused the world over'.[14]

*

This tussle between ecclesiastical and imperial authorities, as part of the continuing evolution of Christian thought and worship, was not unfolding in the Roman Empire alone. Indeed, a very different form of Christianity – and an even more bloody and divisive split between secular and sacred rule – was played out in Armenia over the same period.

Tiridates the Great (as king) and Gregory (as *Catholicos* and head of the Christian Church) had worked together to impose Christianity on Armenia, with varying degrees of success, depending on the sources you follow. After Gregory's death and the continuation of his work by his successors, beginning with Aristakes, what ensued were forms of Christian worship and architecture that were remarkably different from those that developed in the Roman world, resulting from a number of acculturations that were made to help Christianity embed itself both with the Armenian nobles and with the wider population.

In 335 CE – as Constantine settled the question of the Holy Trinity at Tyre and consecrated the Church of the Holy Sepulchre in Jerusalem – the Bishop of Jerusalem, Macarius, wrote to the 'Christ loving and reverend chief bishop' Vrtanes, successor to Aristakes as *Catholicos* of Armenia.[15] Macarius's letter followed a visit by a delegation of Armenian clerics to Jerusalem, and it outlines their discussions over correct procedure in performing baptisms and the Eucharist. Macarius is not shy in blasting Vrtanes and the Armenian Church for their odd practices: they seemed to have an aversion to the use of fonts, instead employing any old vessel to perform baptism; any priest seems to have been allowed to consecrate the holy ointment; and some of them were supporters of Arius and his version of the relationship of the Holy Trinity, despite the First Nicene Creed having been brought back to Armenia by Aristakes, who had attended the Councils of Nicaea in 325 and 327 CE.

Macarius, though, did not know the half of it. The fairly elaborate architecture of early Armenian churches shows that they took over the pagan Armenian traditions of accumulating and displaying wealth. (Many were amply endowed in that regard, on account of all the land grants they were given.) More strikingly, the architectural outlines show that a space was left in church design for the ritual killing of animals at the end of Christian services. This is thought to have been part of the original compromise between Gregory the Illuminator and the existing pagan priesthood, many of whom agreed to become Christian priests. (The alternatives were to run to the hills or else face Gregory's army.) But if they chose Christianity, it was said, Gregory allowed them to continue with their traditional sacrifices, which afterwards could be eaten communally. Armenian Christians, including the priests, also had little truck with celibacy, especially since the important religious positions (not least *Catholicos*) were supposed to be hereditary. And crucial festivals such as the Midsummer Rose Festival dedicated to Anahit (goddess of fertility, healing and wisdom) were allowed to remain, albeit recast as celebrations of Jesus' transfiguration.

Out among the lay population of Armenia, the degree to which this acculturated mishmash of Christian and pagan practice made an impact was minimal. Phaustus, in his fifth-century CE history of fourth-century Armenia, characterises the response in the most functional terms:

> From the earliest times, when they took upon themselves the name of Christianity, it was merely a human religion, a necessary human superstition, and not as was becoming from a warm piety, in knowledge, hope and faith, for those only understood it by little or much who were somewhat familiar with either Greek or Syrian letters.[16]

The key problem was that until the early fifth century CE there was no Armenian script: the language could not be written down unless it was translated into another tongue. This was a different problem from that which beset efforts to introduce Buddhism to China during the first part of the fourth century. In China there had been two perfectly good languages that could be written and spoken, but there were just not enough people who understood both well enough to translate Buddhist Sanskrit texts faithfully into Chinese. Here, in contrast, the problem was that nothing could be written down in the Armenian native tongue at all, however good the translators were.

Armenian culture was overwhelmingly oral, built upon communal storytelling. But Christianity increasingly relied upon key texts, which, given the lack of Armenian script, remained in either Greek or Syriac. Unless people could read these languages, or personally attend events at which Christians expounded Christian teachings in Armenian, it was impossible for Christianity to take root and grow among the wider populace. On top of this obstacle was the ongoing tenacious desire of Armenians to hang on to much of the imagery of their pagan past. The use of serpents, as well as scenes of hunting, banqueting and feasting on gravestones as images of the afterlife, continued to be popular long after Armenia's purported conversion to Christianity. Indeed, some pagan practices, like sun worship and, especially, the highly prized practice of consanguineous marriage to protect hereditary positions, are said to have continued for centuries.

The textual problem would not be solved until around 405 CE, when an Armenian monk called Mashtots (born in 361, the year Rome's last pagan emperor Julian came to the throne) officially introduced a script for writing down the Armenian language, devised while he was living as a Christian hermit in the desert. Learning at Mashtots's feet was said to have been the later Armenian historian Moses Khorenatsi, from whom we have heard many of the stories of the difficulties of imposing Christianity on Armenia back in the time of Tiridates and Gregory. And it is said that the first phrase Mashtots wrote in the new Armenian script was a meaningful quotation from the opening line of the Book of Solomon: 'to know wisdom and instruction; to perceive the words of understanding'. The invention of the script would be a huge boon for the strength and popularity of the Christian Church in Armenia, because it enabled Christianity's message to be understood and spread much more easily and quickly and, as a result, a more concrete Armenian Christian identity to form.

But Armenian Christianity faced an even more difficult task in being accepted at the royal court, particularly against the background of the ongoing geopolitical tensions that beset Armenia, stuck between the Roman and Sassanian Empires. Aristakes, Gregory's son, had been murdered by Armenian noblemen for chastising them over their unchristian ways. His successor, Vrtanes, was pursued by an angry mob inspired by the queen, who resented his preaching. Vrtanes' son, a local bishop, was trampled to death. The next *Catholicos* was a man called Yusik, ably described for us by Phaustus in his fifth-century *History of the Armenians*:

> Though he was but a lad, he was robust and tall, was extremely hand-some and attractive, to the point that he had no equal throughout the country. With a soul clean and radiant he did not occupy himself at all with mundane things. Rather, he was like a brave warrior of Christ, like a champion hero who, from his boyhood onward scorned and threatened the invisible enemy with victory. He never showed partiality or bias toward anyone, but rather bore the message of the Holy Spirit like a sword fixed to his waist. The grace-giving Spirit filled him with knowledge with which, like a fountain, he irrigated the ears and souls of all listeners of the country.[17]

The irrigation does not, however, seem to have been received particularly well:

> With words of priestly authority [Yusik] threatened and reproached them for impiety, adultery, homosexuality, the shedding of blood, dispossession, ravishment, hatred of the poor and numerous other sins such as these.[18]

Phaustus tells that on one annual feast day in 347, when Yusik had lambasted the king and other nobles for coming to church and darkening its doors with their sins, he was set upon and done to death.[19] According to Moses Khorenatsi, Yusik was 'beaten for a long time with thongs of ox hide, until he gave up the ghost under the whipping'.[20] This murder may not have been solely thanks to his insistence on Christian ways of behaving, but also to wider geopolitical interested parties. The ruler of the Sassanian Empire, Shapur II, had been keenly in favour of pro-Sassanian nobles within Armenia – something that Rome had been actively supporting the Armenian king, Tiran, to suppress, even if that meant the elimination of a *Catholicos*.[21] Yusik's replacement resigned within a year, and no further *Catholicos* was appointed until 353 CE.

During that time, according to Phaustus, the people of Armenia strayed even further from their Christian teachings:

> [They] were given the soul of erring: eyes which do not see, ears which do not hear and hearts which do not understand and do not turn to atonement. Benighted, they reached the abyss of destruction, having cut their own road, they were ruined and fell, and there was no one to be shamed by their acts and sins of frenzy, since they remained without a leader . . . They resembled that flock of sheep which made its own protecting and guarding dogs depart, and by its own will was betrayed to the enemy wolves, becoming their food, just like the great city of Athens.[22]

We don't know exactly to which era of Athens' decline Phaustus was referring, but it is tempting to take his comments as an allusion to the negative effects of democratic 'mob' rule, when the people make their own decisions unguided by wise leaders. (Such was the view of Polybius back in the second century BCE, when he critiqued democracy as a system of government.) However, it was not only the mass of the Armenian people who strayed from the Christian path. In this period even Yusik's own sons were said to have failed to live up to their father's reputation: 'The two brothers went and entered the episcopate and drank wine with whores, harlots, bards, and jesters, and, scorning the blessed and sacred places, they trampled on them.' Later, so Phaustus says, both were struck by lightning and killed.[23]

In 353 CE, finally, a worthy successor was appointed to the position of *Catholicos*: a man called Nerses, Yusik's grandson. Phaustus describes him in a remarkable paean as:

> a tall man, of pleasing size and captivating beauty, so much so that his equal in good looks could not be found in the world. Everyone looking at him found him desirable, amazing and venerable, and he displayed enviable courage in military training. He had the fear of God in his heart and stringently upheld His commandments. He was humane, pure and modest, very intelligent, unbiased, just, humble, a lover of the poor, proper in married life, and perfect in the love of God.[24]

The different surviving histories of Armenia all credit Nerses with a crucial role in helping to solidify the establishment of Christianity within the country. He was said to have resembled 'the first trees and during the course of his teaching he brought forth the same and similar ripe fruits for all, offering them generously, nourishing them with the spiritual field'.[25] More prosaically, he is believed to have convened the first Armenian Christian council at Taron in 353 CE. This council, like the gatherings called in the Roman world by Constantine and his successors, established a series of canonical regulations and set about establishing countrywide Christian missions of different sorts, which would help to embed Christianity across all levels of Armenian society.

The council established Christian almshouses for lepers who were otherwise ignored, and hospitals for the sick, granting each establishment 'town and fields, fertile in fruits of the land, in milk from herds, and wool, that these through their taxes might cater for their needs from a distance'.[26] It also prescribed that lodges and inns be built for travellers, and hospices for orphans, the old and the poor, as well as monasteries and hermitages in the deserts. It furthermore substantially increased the number of Armenian bishops serving the *Catholicos*. At the same time it banned a number of ongoing pagan practices, in moves reminiscent of those pursued by Theodosius in the Roman world. Consanguineous marriage was outlawed for the first time (although it would continue to be practised for a long time to come), as well as the wailing and laceration of arms and faces that were traditionally enacted at Armenian funerals.

Crucially, the council at Taron had begun to give Christianity a key role to play in the social fabric of Armenian society, one that echoed the original version of Christianity which had found acceptance in the south of the country in the early centuries CE: providing help, respite and care to those who needed it, alongside a more complex and complete Christian hierarchy. But despite these steps forward, things became infinitely more complicated over the next two decades, thanks to the impact of religious and political change on the wider global stage.

In 359 CE, as we have seen, Constantius II attempted to renounce the First Nicene Creed and constitute a new one, distinctly different in its view of the relationship between God and Jesus Christ compared to the first. He expected his bishops to follow it, and his secular allies in power to ensure that their populations did likewise in their respective countries. Yet in Armenia, Nerses refused to renounce *his* Church's adherence to the First Nicene Creed, as brought back to Armenia by Aristakes, son of Gregory. However, King Arshak II had no choice but to follow the wishes of his Roman ally, not least because of the ongoing war of Rome and the Sassanids, between whom Armenia was stuck in the middle. Once again war, politics and religion were fused together across a connected world, this time driving a profound rift between king and *Catholicos*.

The rift deepened across 361–3 CE when Julian came to the throne and attempted to turn the Roman world back towards paganism. Once again Arshak was prevailed upon to follow the emperor, and Nerses was set even more firmly in opposition to him. Though this division receded quickly with the death of Julian and the return to a Christian agenda, it seems that during the 370s the *Catholicos* ordered that all his priests wear military dress: a decree that surely reflects not only the ongoing tension, but also the increasing military nature of the conflict, between secular and religious authority within Armenia.

One evening in 373 CE Nerses accepted an invitation to dine with King Pap, the Rome-approved ruler of Armenia since 370, at the king's mansion. There Nerses drank from a wine cup at the king's proffering and knew instantly that he had been poisoned. Returning to his home, he showed his companions a blue swelling above his heart the size of a small loaf.

> After this for about two hours, globules of blood started to ooze from his mouth. Then he arose to pray. He kneeled and asked forgiveness for his murderers. After this he recalled everyone in his prayers, those near and far, the dishonored and the honored and even those whom he had never known. Upon completion of the prayers he lifted his hands and eyes to Heaven, and said: 'Lord Jesus Christ, accept my soul.' Having said this, his soul was released.[27]

When in 387 CE the war between Rome and the Sassanids finally came to an end upon Theodosius I signing an agreement with the Sassanid king Shapur III, one of the outcomes was the forced division of the land between them. As such four-fifths of Armenia was given over to the Sassanids, the remainder staying as part of the Roman Empire, with its Christian populace absorbed into the Roman Christian world. Christians in the Sassanid area faced persecution, but would eventually (in the first half of the fifth century CE) win their independence again following a revolution.[28]

The ironies of the partition were heavy. Tiridates the Great had been established on the Armenian throne thanks to the Romans having the upper hand over the Sassanids. And while Tiridates' conversion to Christianity would be attributed by pious historians to his heavenly punishment and repentance for the attempted rape of the beautiful nun Rhipsime, more hard-headed observers read his new devoutness as a desire to improve his power and control over his realm, as well as distance Armenia from the Sassanids and from his father's murderers and their Zoroastrian religion.

Tiridates had achieved as much by aligning Armenia squarely with Christian Rome (at least officially), so putting clear religious waters between Armenia and the Sassanid world to the east. But the reality on the ground meant that he left Armenia more divided than ever before, now with an additional set of religious divisions to contend with, and with a burgeoning rift between the king and *Catholicos*. In addition, Armenia's geographical location – for ever caught between the two great empires – had confounded Tiridates' plan, and that of his successors, to achieve wider geopolitical stability. In the end it was Rome that delivered the death-blow by carving up Armenia in order to secure its own peace and security. Ultimately, war and global politics had put paid to the aspirations of centralised hierarchy and religious unity for Armenia.

Many Religions, One Ruler

In the Roman world religious authorities had claimed superiority over secular ones. In Armenia, the tussle between the two had erupted in bloodshed prior to the tearing of the realm in half. In India, contrastingly, there was a blossoming of a wide diversity of religious life within the stable and unified community created by the quasi-divine Gupta rulers.

Samudragupta I, reviver of horse-sacrifice, died in 375 CE, and what happened next was to inspire a famous drama composed several centuries later by the playwright Vishakhadatta. Entitled the *Devi-ChandraGupta,* it tells the story of Samudragupta's first successor, Rama, who attempted to expand the Gupta Empire by taking on the Sacas to the west and south. Humiliated in battle, Rama was forced to give up his wife, Dhruvadevi, to the Saca king as tribute. But the Gupta king's younger brother, Chandragupta – outraged by Rama's willingness to concede in this manner – took it upon himself to dress up in Dhruvadevi's clothes and travel in disguise to the Saca king's court. There,

Chandragupta managed to enter the king's presence, murder him, then escape back to the Gupta court. Encouraged by popular support for his actions, emboldened by his own courage and audacity, Chandragupta next murdered Rama, took his throne and married his widow Dhruvadevi, whose future he had saved by his earlier cross-dressing mission to the Sacas.

Chandragupta II – as he became known – ruled over the heyday of the Gupta Empire. Following thirty years of fighting, he finally managed to defeat the Sacas completely and expand the reach of the empire from the north-west coast of India all the way to the north-east, thus permitting direct access to the ports of the Arabian Sea and an undisturbed route for Western trade through to India and the East and back the other way. Chandragupta also managed to gain control over vast swathes of the rival Vakataka kingdom to the south, by marrying his daughter to the Vakataka king whose death, just five years into the union, conveniently left his widow in a position to administer the province.

In the gold coins minted during his reign, this impressive military record is placed front-and-centre. Chandragupta II is shown turned to the right, wearing a tunic tied tight around his waist with a cord, its two ends fluttering behind him as if caught in a strong breeze. Covered in bracelets and jewellery, Chandragupta holds in his hands a bow, fully tensioned and ready to shoot. His prey, at the extreme right, is a lion rearing on its hind legs and baring its teeth. The inscription on the coins reads: 'The King Chandragupta, a renowned warrior, achieves victory with the bravery of a lion.' On the reverse, a goddess is shown riding a lion, representing what the inscription calls 'possessing Lion courage'. In this leonine martial valour, Chandragupta is evoked, like his ancestors, as being on the level of the divine. In a further series of coins, Chandragupta continues the emphasis on his – and his ruling family's – quasi-divine nature by showing himself receiving holy favours from the supreme god, Vishnu. And this special relationship was also reinforced in the text of one of his own pillar inscriptions, which describes how Chandragupta had 'a beauty of countenance resembling the full moon, and has fixed his mind with devotion on Vishnu'.[29]

At the same time as the ruler was brought closer to the god, the god was increasingly made to resemble the ruler. Vishnu in the art of this period was often depicted in the guise of a head of state, carrying emblems relating to warfare and protection of the realm, not unlike the fourth-century CE Roman iconography of God and Jesus Christ, increasingly shown in the guise of imperial rulers sitting on thrones. Similarly, at the rock-cut caves at Udayagiri in central northern India, Chandragupta invested huge amounts (what inscriptions call a 'meritorious gift') to the god in the carving of a complex set of iconographic scenes depicting Vishnu.[30] In intense deep-cut relief, a giant Vishnu – in the form of Varaha, the Boar – rescues the earth from cosmic chaos. Many scholars have seen the choice of imagery as intended to reflect not only the Guptas' special relationship with Vishnu, but also the similarity between them: just as Vishnu saves the earth, so, too, had the Guptas (specifically Chandragupta II) saved the Gupta Empire from the precarious chaos around it.

And from this deepening overlap between the god Vishnu and the Guptas as rulers came, from the end of the fourth century CE, nothing less than a new form of Hindu religious architecture: the temple. Previous preference had been for the adaptation of rock-cut caves, like those at Udayagiri. But increasingly grand free-standing stone temples, raised high on resplendent platforms, were developed for the worship of the supreme gods.[31] The Gupta term for a temple was *prasada* – originally a palace or royal mansion – and the term used to describe offerings to Vishnu within a temple was *bali* (the old Vedic term for royal revenue). These temples were the palaces of the ruler gods. They often had porches that were highly decorated with beautiful relief sculpture: for example, at Deogarh in Janesi, known also as the Dash-avatara Temple because it represents in superb relief on the temple walls the stories of the ten avatars (*Dash-avatara*) of the god Vishnu.

What is most notable about the reigns of Chandragupta II and his successors, though – in contrast to the situation in both Armenia and the Roman world – is the way in which, at the same time as there was such a strong bond between a particular religious and ruling hierarchy, multiple religious faiths were also embraced, encouraged and protected within the empire. At Mathura a pillar inscription dating from the fifth

year of Chandragupta II's reign, 380 CE – the same year that Theodosius was eliminating alternative versions of belief in the Roman
Empire – testifies to the flourishing of a religious group who were an
offshoot of those who worshipped Shiva. This group had a teacher
who had set up statues to his own teachers in Mathura, and professed
no problems with publicly proclaiming their religious choice. Indeed,
the pillar was intended as a public focus for cult worship by his sect,
and came with a threat that anyone who destroyed it would end up
languishing for ever in great sin.[32]

That toleration extended to Buddhism, too, despite the fact that it
specifically rejected many of the hierarchical tenets of Gupta religious
practice. Indeed, the Guptas seem to have appointed an official charged
with looking after Buddhist affairs and the thousands of Buddhist
monks in the city of Mathura, as well as the hundreds in the Gupta
capital at Pataliputra. The Sanchi Stone inscription, from towards the
end of Chandragupta II's reign, records how the ruler granted the
profits of a village to a community of Buddhist monks to help sustain
their monastery. What is fascinating about this inscription is not simply
that the king is providing for Buddhist worship, but that he did so in
touchingly diplomatic terms. Gupta inscriptions have long been noted
for their very earthy language and grammar: they were, it is argued,
meant to be read and understood by everyone. But in the Sanchi inscription Chandragupta has given careful consideration to the sensitivities of
the group he was addressing. Traditionally in royal inscriptions the king
was described with the epithet 'top devotee of Vishnu', but the term is
eschewed here, the inscription claiming only that 'perfection has been
obtained'.[33]

In the reign of Kumaragupta – successor to Chandragupta II from
415 CE – we note the ultimate example of what diversity can bring. It
was in his reign that the Buddhist monastery and university at Nalanda
was created, and it went on to become one of the great seats of learning
in Asia. By the seventh century CE it boasted 500 students, thirteen
monasteries, seven halls, 300 teaching rooms (interspersed with deep
pools filled with blue lotus flowers); and all of this sustained by a land
grant of more than 200 villages, which enabled its upkeep. Crucially,
students did not study Buddhist texts alone, but also the *Vedas*, Hindu

philosophy, logic, grammar and medicine. And thanks to the integrated and connected nature of India to central Asia and China, students came from far and wide. A later Chinese visitor described what awaited them:

> From morning till night the monks engage in discussion; the old and the young mutually help one another. Learned men from different cities, who desire to acquire renown . . . come here, and then their wisdom spreads far and wide. For this reason they style themselves Nalanda students, and are honoured as a consequence.[34]

Seats of learning, meditation and debate such as these, open to students professing a range of religions and philosophies and hailing from many different places, helped to make this period one of the most remarkable in Indian history, in terms of its philosophical, scientific and literary outpourings.[35] This was the era of Kalidasa, the 'Shakespeare of India'; the era of the final formulation of grand epic poems such as the *Mahabharata*, perhaps the longest poem in human history, which told the story of epic dynastic struggle in past ages, and which had long been a stable part of the core Hindu set of sacred texts; and it was the era of men such as Aryabhata (later dubbed the 'Newton of India'), who discovered, inter alia, that the moon rotates on its own axis.

The tolerance shown by the Guptas towards Buddhism extended also to Jainism, a sect that had emerged at around the same time as Buddhism in the Axial Age of the sixth and fifth centuries BCE. This is surprising, however, in that Jain beliefs stood even more ardently in opposition to the hierarchical nature of Gupta religion and society than those of Buddhism. Jainists believed that austerity and monasticism were the sole routes to salvation. They eschewed the trappings of wealth to such an extent that some groups only wore white robes, while others went entirely naked. They sought to be entirely outside society, rather than wrapped up in an increasingly hierarchical religious system with Vishnu, Shiva and the Guptas at the top.[36]

Gupta tolerance for the Jainists looks especially open-minded when compared to the treatment of such groups in other Indian kingdoms at

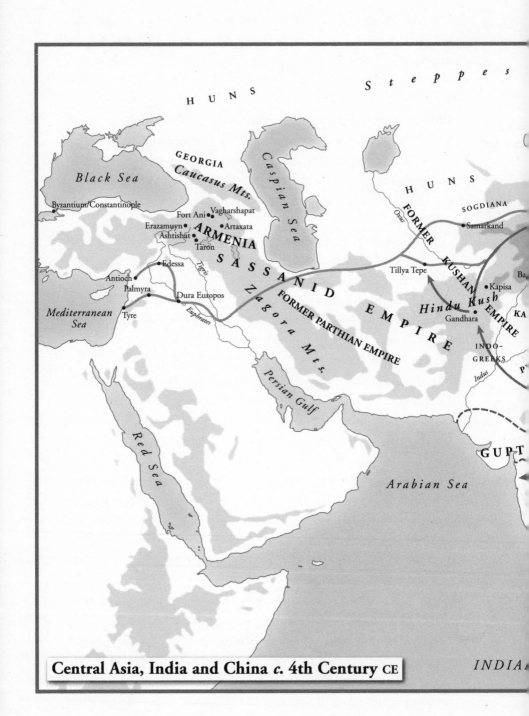

H U N S

S t e p p e s

GEORGIA

Caucasus Mts.

Black Sea

Byzantium/Constantinople

Fort Ani
Vagharshapat
Erazamuyn
Ashtishat
ARMENIA
Artaxata
Taron

Caspian Sea

H U N S

SOGDIANA

Samarkand

FORMER

Oxus

S A S S A N I D

E M P I R E

KUSHAN

Antioch
Edessa
Palmyra
Tigris
Dura Europos
FORMER PARTHIAN EMPIRE

Mediterranean Sea

Tyre
Euphrates

Zagora Mts.

Tillya Tepe

Hindu Kush

Gandhara

Kapisa

EMPIRE

KA

Ba

Red Sea

Persian Gulf

INDO-
GREEKS

Indus

P

Arabian Sea

GUPT

Central Asia, India and China *c.* 4th Century CE

INDIA

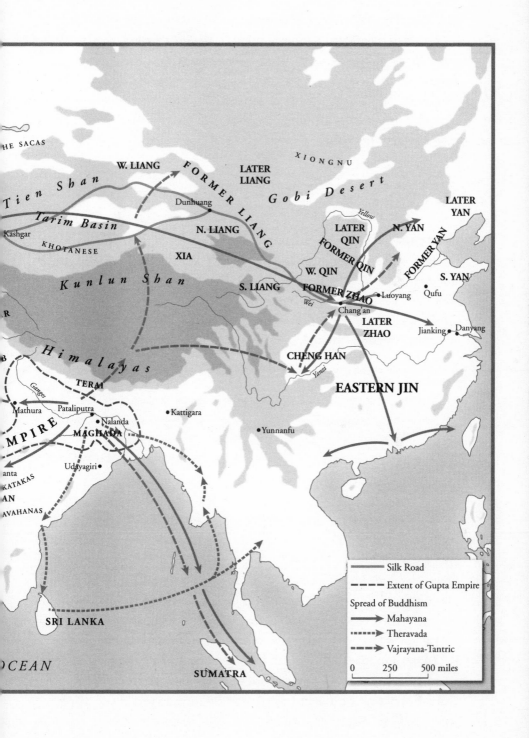

THE SACAS

Tien Shan

W. LIANG

LATER LIANG

XIONGNU

Gobi Desert

LATER YAN

FORMER LIANG

Dunhuang

Yellow

Tarim Basin

LATER QIN

N. YAN

Kashgar

KHOTANESE

N. LIANG

XIA

FORMER QIN

FORMER YAN

S. YAN

Kunlun Shan

S. LIANG

W. QIN

FORMER ZHAO

Luoyang

Qufu

Wei

Chang'an

LATER ZHAO

Jianking

Danyang

Himalayas

TERM

CHENG HAN

Yanzi

EASTERN JIN

Ganges

Mathura

Pataliputra

Nalanda

Kattigara

MPIRE

MAGHADA

Yunnanfu

Udayagiri

anta

KATAKAS

AN

AVAHANAS

SRI LANKA

OCEAN

SUMATRA

	Silk Road
	Extent of Gupta Empire
	Spread of Buddhism
→	Mahayana
⇢	Theravada
⇢	Vajrayana-Tantric

0   250   500 miles

this time. The Vakatakas to the south, under the influence of the Gup-tas via Chandragupta II's sister, supported Buddhism and helped make possible the great Buddhist carvings and paintings at the caves of Ajanta and Bagh. But in the southern kingdoms of the Pallavas and the Pandyans, Jains were routinely persecuted and even murderously repressed; this despite the fact that Jains believed in non-violence and even forswore the killing of insects.

Many Religions, Many Rulers

During the reign of Chandragupta II a Chinese Buddhist monk named Faxian came to India on a pilgrimage to the key sites in the life of the Buddha. Faxian's account, which exudes positive feelings about the condition and popularity of Buddhist worship in India, also comments on the lavish conditions at the court of Chandragupta II at Pataliputra, and more broadly upon life in India at this time (the early fifth century):

> The people are numerous and happy: they have not to register their households, or attend any magistrates . . . the kings govern without decapitation or other corporal punishment. The criminals are sim-ply fined. Even in the case of repeated attempts at wicked rebellion, they only have their right hands cut off.[37]

We might recall the observations on Indian crime and punishment made by Megasthenes in his fourth-century BCE account of the soci-ety of Chandragupta Maurya. The lopping-off of hands may seem a draconian punishment by today's standards, but it was lenient in com-parison to what we have seen of Roman, Armenian and Chinese histories, where 'wicked rebellion' was, without doubt, a capital offence.

Faxian was roughly sixty-five years of age when he began (in 399 BCE) the journey from China to India over land, along the great trade routes of the Silk Road. His account of the difficulties of crossing the Gobi desert we have already noted. The pilgrimage would last fifteen years in all, its objective to collect Buddhist scriptures from India to bring back to China. Faxian made this journey at a momentous point in the history of Chinese Buddhism, when this foreign religion received official public sanction from the rulers of China and articulated its relationship with the multiplicity of powers within the fractured realm.

The socio-political upheavals of the fourth century had, ironically, helped Buddhism to become part of elite life in both Xiongnu northern China and the Qingtan conversation circles of the south. But it could not have attained or held on to such status without some degree of compromise and argumentation. As we have seen, many Buddhist monks actively sought to discuss Buddhist ideas through the language and terminology of Daoism, even linking the narratives of these religions to make Laozi – the fictional founder and guide to immortality – and the Buddha the same figure, and pursuing a similar policy in relation to Confucius. This was not only to improve the Chinese grasp of Buddhist concepts, but also to counter any suggestion that Buddhism was a mere foreign barbarian creed unsuited to the civilised Chinese.

Whereas in Armenia pagan practices were enfolded into Christian churches and rituals in a more or less unalloyed form, Buddhist missionaries chose to edit out of their teaching ideas that might be distasteful – if not anathema – to the Chinese mindset. That included any use of the language of kissing and embracing as part of the Buddhist practice of worshipping *Bodhisattvas*: this was felt to be inappropriate for a society so respectful of complex and fixed ritual for the management of relationships between people, as advocated centuries before by Confucius and others. (The nakedly sexual elements of the later-arriving Tantric Buddhism would also be suppressed in China.)

The Chinese were similarly resistant to two central aspects of the lives of Buddhist monks. The first was their celibacy, a commitment that, for the Chinese, threatened the very continuity of the family – one of the cornerstones of society. (It was as alien a concept to them as to Armenians, who favoured hereditary succession to official positions, this mandating the production of offspring.) The second was the idea that Buddhist monks, so conspicuous in their yellow robes, ought regularly to beg in the streets for their food and other necessities. Within India this process was part of the way in which society helped to ensure everyone's cosmic salvation – by providing for the physical needs of the monks who would, in turn (it was hoped), look after the cosmic-salvation part. But in China begging was a practice that signified a negative dependence on others: consequently Buddhists desisted from practising it in China.

The institution of the *sangha* (or Buddhist monastery) proved yet more problematic for Chinese society, in terms of its purported transcendence of social hierarchies. The Buddha had once described the *sangha* as like the ocean in which the waters from the five great rivers (echoing the *varnas* of Indian society) lose their identity. Over the centuries since Buddhism's introduction to China, thanks to royal and elite patronage, *sanghas* had multiplied in many of the major cities in the north and south. They had attracted many individuals of the lower classes, who saw in the *sangha* not simply a refuge from the rigid boundaries of society, but also an opportunity for self-improvement: many monasteries were also places of education (as at Nalanda in India). The famed monk Dao'an, a notable translator of Buddhist texts and a fierce proponent of the system of equating Daoism and Buddhism, had entered a *sangha* aged eleven and received most of his education within the monastery. The *sangha*, then, was not merely a place in which to shun society, but a potential vehicle through which to uplift one's place in that society.

There were more dimensions to the *sangha* even than that. As we have seen, many foreign Buddhist monks working in China came from elite (even royal) backgrounds in their home countries. From the beginning of the fourth century CE, as the Xiongnu streamed into the north and millions of Chinese flooded into the south, the *sangha*, with its sense of detachment from worldly affairs, became a desirable refuge particularly for elite intellectuals and other literati, not to mention those avoiding military service. (Christian monasteries, and the very idea of Christian monasticism, grew similarly in the Mediterranean amid the difficult and unstable political-military circumstances of the third and fourth centuries CE.) Within decades the *sangha* had taken the shape of a curious mix of the elite and the low-born, now intermixed as an independent priestly class, yet unbound by the hierarchies of Chinese society, claiming to be not answerable to the authorities while also asserting that the salvation of society depended upon them.

Many of them were also sponsored by wealthy families, enabling those families to avoid paying tax to the authorities, and this also contributed to the tension surrounding the *sangha*'s place in Chinese society.

So as much as Buddhism enjoyed intellectual entrée within the Qingtan in southern China, and transformed itself so as to accommodate itself to the miracle-loving Xiongnu rulers in the north, the *sangha* nonetheless came in for intense criticism. In the mid-fourth century CE the northern Xiongnu ruler, Shi Hu (nephew to the former ruler, Shi Le), issued a proclamation that the selection of monks entering into the *sangha* should be overseen and enforced:

> Nowadays the monks are very numerous: among them are scoundrels and evaders of labour-service, and many of them are unfit to perform their religious duties. Let this be considered and investigated, and let the veracity and falsehood of the individual monks be discussed in all details.[38]

The accusations only got worse. In 389 CE the northern general Xu Yong described the Buddhist clergy as 'vile, rude, servile and addicted to wine and women', and complained that the monks 'oppress and pillage the people, considering the collection of riches as wisdom'.[39] In 400 CE, in the south, Jin dynasty ruler Huan Xuan undertook to 'purify' the *sangha* through a thorough investigation of all monks. Only three types were allowed to continue: those who were found to have profound knowledge of Buddhist scriptures; those who strictly observed the rules of the *sangha*; and those who dwelt in the mountains, cherishing Buddhist ideals and not engaging in vulgar activities.

Perhaps the most serious interrogation of the usefulness of monastic life and Buddhist philosophy was on the issue of whether it delivered any concrete results in this world. A critique on these lines was advanced in a Buddhist apologetic from the mid-fourth century, *Zhengwu lun*, which set up contemporary criticisms of Buddhism, the better to respond to them. The *contra* argument was framed as follows:

> There are many monks in Luoyang, but I have never heard that they are able to prolong the life of the ruler. They are unable to

harmonise yin and yang, to make the year abundant and the people rich, to prevent natural disasters, eliminate epidemic diseases and soothe trouble and disorder.[40]

Buddhist rebuttals to such criticisms across the second to fourth centuries CE show us how sensitive they were to the fundamentals of the Chinese mindset: the need to demonstrate utility in this world, and the ability to transform individuals by instruction; the need to support (and not undermine) hierarchical authority; the need to appear innately 'of' the country rather than from outside it; and the need to uphold the sacred canons of social behaviour rather than deny them.

The Buddhist defence was ingenious – arguing that the monk was, in truth, an official emissary of human society to what lay beyond. Just as the emperor's court would supply an official envoy to a foreign court with everything they needed to represent the emperor in a good light, so too should the state support the *sangha* and its monks. But as an additional safeguard, to ensure that the *sangha* was not felt to be ripping family life asunder or threatening regal/imperial authority, it was agreed that no one should be able to join the *sangha* without parental permission, or if they were in the service of the king or emperor.

Moreover (as the apologists put it) the Buddhist community as a whole was a force to ensure lasting peace and prosperity in this world, which – given the current political and military situation – was tremendously useful. Above all, it was not foreign: Buddhism had been on Chinese soil since the time of Ashoka, great builder of *stupas*, in the third century BCE, through the rise of the Qin and Han dynasties, and was – at least now – explicitly entwined with the development of Daoism and Confucianism. Together they were all mutually complementary, like head and tail, and their basic purpose was one and the same.[41]

These arguments did not silence all criticism. And at the same time, as in the Roman Empire and in Armenia, there arose the thorny issue of the relationship between increasingly respected (Chinese) Buddhist monks and the many rulers among whom command of China was fragmented. In 379 CE a northern ruler called Fu Jian ordered the famed monk Dao'an to come from his home to the city of Chang'an.

It was a time of intense activity for Buddhism in northern China, now benefiting from a new influx of missionaries and more large-scale translation projects. But Fu Jian's order also raised the question of who could order whom. Monks who had withdrawn into the *sangha* had chosen to renounce the temporal world. Could a ruler really demand that they leave the *sangha* and attend court? Dao'an, for one, chose to comply and upped sticks to Chang'an.

The same dilemma confronted Buddhist monks in the south. Emperor Ai, who ruled the Eastern Jin for a short time in the 360s CE was another of those zealous Chinese seekers after the secret of immortality (he died after ingesting some purportedly magical pills that did the opposite of what they promised). Ai routinely commanded famous Buddhist monks to come to his capital to preach and, if he had found their sermons pleasing, on their journey home they received imperial military protection, along with plentiful gifts of money, silks, summer and winter garments, as well as a spectacular carriage to ride in. But not all monks were willing to leave the *sangha* and engage with court life. When the Buddhist Zhu Daoyi was summoned in 387 CE by the prefect of Danyang on order of the royal court, he wrote a letter protesting that a monk should always have freedom of movement and be left in peace. His objection struck home: the order to attend the court was cancelled. Ultimately the emperor did not want to compel the monk against his will.

This developing relationship between imperial power and Buddhist practice was to be officially formulated in the 370s and 380s CE. The Eastern Jin emperor, Jianwen, became the first of his kind to officially employ a Buddhist priest on behalf of the court (for the express purpose of averting a perceived evil omen). His successor, Emperor Xiaowu, came to the throne in 372–3 CE at the tender age of ten, then, at thirteen, married a Buddhist follower who became Empress Wang (and who died barely five years later in 380 CE). In 381 Emperor Xiaowu, not yet twenty, became the first emperor to formally accept the Buddhist doctrine as his religion. That spring in the capital at Jianking a *vihara* (individual Buddhist monastery) was established within the palace, monks were invited to dwell in it and some Buddhist texts were officially placed in the royal library. Buddhism would have an official position at the imperial court for the next four centuries.

Xiaowu was also a firm supporter of Buddhist nunneries, and one nun in particular, called Miao-yin, was a great favourite of his. She presided over a nunnery of a hundred devotees built in the capital, and her literary Qingtan conversations became renowned. This was a mark of how far Buddhism had travelled: from seeking entrée to these elite tea parties, to a Buddhist nun running the most influential of them all. Miao-yin came to be so powerful that innumerable clerical and non-clerical people were dependent on her to obtain advancement, and from whom she received endless gifts. Each day more than a hundred horse-drawn carriages pulled up outside the gates of her monastery and stood there as their occupants waited patiently to gain a few moments of Miao-yin's attention.

Thus by the end of the fourth century CE Buddhism was strongly ensconced in the south at the Eastern Jin capital, and in the north at the capitals of many of the Sixteen Kingdoms, and particularly of the expanding Northern Wei, who would come to rule most of the north before the middle of the next century. Its development and spread was further fuelled by a new generation of translators of Buddhist texts. A man called Zhu Fonian became the first Chinese monk to master Sanskrit and so be capable of performing his own translations direct from Buddhist texts. But many of these new translators came from northern India and Kashmir, an area brimming with cultural and religious life, thanks to the light-touch rule of the Gupta Empire, then enjoying its heyday.

In 401 CE (just before the Christian monk Mashtots invented the Armenian alphabet), perhaps the greatest translator of all arrived at Chang'an from Kashmir: the monk Kumarajiva. Born around 344 CE to a Buddhist Kuchean princess and a *Brahman* Indian father, at the age of seven Kumarajiva followed his mother when she went to join the Buddhist order, and together they travelled to Kashmir to study the sacred texts. From Kashmir they went to Kashgar, where he studied the Buddhist *sutras* and the Hindu *Vedas* as well as books on astronomy, maths and science. Finally he found *Mahayana* Buddhism, a discovery that, it was later said, he described as akin to realising that he had been looking at gold and seeing only stone.

At the age of twenty Kumarajiva became a Buddhist monk and began to translate important texts. By 379 CE his fame in this regard had reached northern China on the lips of numerous Indian and central Asian monks who had travelled to the region. The then-emperor of the Later Qin – one of the Sixteen Kingdoms struggling for domination in northern China alongside the Northern Wei – sent a general with an army to conquer the area where Kumarajiva resided, in no small part in order that the monk might then be carried back to his court. But the general turned rogue, captured Kumarajiva and kept him hostage on the edge of Chinese territory for well over a decade. A new ruler of the Later Qin – Yao Xing – had to despatch another army to kill the renegade general, release Kumarajiva and finally bring him to the court in 401 CE. There, along with the 3,000 other monks for whom Yao Xing made personal provision, Kumarajiva remained until his death at the age of seventy in 413 CE, just as the Buddhist monk Faxian was returning to China from his pilgrimage to India.

It now appeared to be the habit of Chinese rulers to go to war to free noteworthy religious thinkers – not only because the authority of their rule had been questioned, but because the presence of such spiritual luminaries at their courts seems to have become an important part of their apparatus of rule.

Working feverishly both during his impromptu and extended captivity on the Chinese borders as well as during his years at court, Kumarajiva not only mastered Chinese, but translated (it was later said) ninety-eight Buddhist texts alongside improving many of the previous translations, thanks to his now-perfect knowledge of the necessary languages. He not only translated the *Brahmajala-sutras* (crucial for followers of *Mahayana* Buddhism, and subsequently among the most popular *sutras* in China), but also clarified great numbers of doctrinal questions that had been long obscured in the hazy ambiguity of imperfect translation. He led a team of perhaps a thousand individuals, including editors, sub-editors and doctrinal discussants (in effect an early publishing house), working out of the manicured gardens at the capital that had been laid at their disposal by Yao Xing. Kumarajiva was honoured with the title of *guo shi* or 'National Teacher';

and so desperate was Yao Xing for his genius to continue that he installed ten beautiful women to live with the monk – each in their own separate quarters – so that as many sons and heirs as possible might be conceived to carry on his work. To this end Kumarajiva appears to have been enticed from the traditional Buddhist celibacy, siring many sons, though none who would live up to his intellectual calibre.

While Kumarajiva's bloodlines and brilliance were cultivated in Chang'an at the capital of the Northern Later Qin, news of Xiaowu's 'conversion' at the Eastern Jin capital in today's Nanjing (and of Buddhism's integration into southern Chinese life) spread far and wide along the trade routes of the connected ancient world. So impressed was the King of Sri Lanka by Xiaowu's zeal for Buddhism that in 395 CE – similar to the way in which Constantine and Tiridates were said to have bonded over their religious enthusiasm – he despatched a Buddhist monk to the Chinese court, bearing with him a valuable Buddha statue four feet and two inches high and made entirely of jade, to be presented to the emperor as a token of their cordial feelings as Buddhist rulers. The journey – for unknown reasons – took ten years and so the precious statue was eventually presented to Xiaowu's successor, Emperor An, in the early fifth century CE.

What the Sri Lankan monk found was, if anything, a yet more keenly Buddhist court than the one he had left. The new emperor had a dominant and ardent Buddhist uncle, Sima Daozi, who served as regent, and who seems to have gone overboard in his support of Buddhism. He was not only a fervent admirer of the nun Miao-yin, but also, according to the later histories of the Jin dynasty, 'revered and believed in the teachings of the Buddha, such his excessive waste in spending money for religious purposes made life intolerable for the common people'.[42] Chinese rulers were now giving preference to the *sangha* and to Buddhism over their own people. The irony is that it was also under Emperor An that Faxian returned to China after his long voyage to the East and his stay in India, bringing back his considered view of how good and tolerant were the (non-Buddhist) Gupta rulers of northern India, and how their people flourished under them.

In 402 CE another of the powerful nobles at An's court summed up Buddhism's journey over the course of the previous century:

> Formerly, there were among the people of Jin hardly any Buddhists. The monks were mostly Barbarians, and, moreover the [Chinese] rulers did not have any contacts with them. It was only therefore that the government could tolerate their local customs, and did not restrain them [in the practice of their creed]. But nowadays the rulers and highest dignitaries venerate the Buddha and personally take part in religious affairs: the situation has become different from former times.[43]

There had been a similar meteoric rise for Christianity, and for the new formulation of ancient Hindu worship promoted by the Guptas: these religions had either not existed in their particular formulations or had been the religions of minorities and foreigners – even the subject of persecutions – just a century before. In the second half of the fourth century CE each faith had been subject to an internal process of theological discussion and debate amongst followers, as well as to an outward process of adaptation to take account of local traditions and beliefs, not to mention political and social hierarchies and military realities. Man's relationship with the divine had been recast in tandem with relationships between communities and between individuals. In Rome and Armenia, this had led to the definition of a single kind of Christianity being accepted at the expense of others. In contrast, in India and China there was a diversity of religious practice, mandated by the different religions inherent to the country, but also in China by the diffuse way in which Buddhism had arrived in so many different forms (not to speak of China's ongoing political fragmentation).

Across the ancient world, broadly seen, religion, war and politics had been fused together. In the Roman world emperors fought battles to enforce their version of official religion as the hand of the will of God, and subsequently came to blows with the Church in what would become a near-perpetual conflict between spiritual and earthly authority. In Armenia, the king and the *Catholicos* were often at deadly odds with one another, sometimes because they struck different religious positions and at other times (just as in Rome) because spiritual authority was pitted against earthly powers. In Gupta India, in contrast, the entwining of religion and rule chimed with the establishment of political, economic and military stability, creating a golden age in Indian history of religious diversity and intellectual creativity. And in China, as Buddhism saw off its critics and came to be an official religion of courts, rulers had in some cases commanded Buddhist monks into their presence; in others, had respected their spiritual independence; and in others still, had gone to war to secure their release.

The fourth century, as a result, deserves its renown as a decisive moment in history, not simply because it saw dynamic change in the religious and political make-up of vast swathes of a truly connected ancient world, but also because those changes still impact today upon the way our world works and many of the ideas by which we live.

Coda

Our story in this Part has been concerned with three of the four most popular religions in our world today, and how the fourth century CE was such a critical period in their theological development, growth, acceptance and integration within human societies. These dynamic processes were made possible by the newly connected nature of the world at that time: connections developed over the preceding centuries. Each of the faiths, it should be said, underwent a degree of modification in the course of transmission.

This was particularly the case for ancient Hindu and Buddhist worship. The waves of migrations from the east to central Asia during the third and second centuries BCE caused the mass movements of the Sacas and subsequently of the Yuezhi down into India, not only destabilising India politically and militarily, but infusing its religious lifeblood. These communities honoured the idea of the warrior king, which, in turn, assisted the intertwining of religion and rule within the figure of the quasi-divine lion-like Gupta ruler.

Conversely, the development of trading links along the Silk Roads and by sea between India, central Asia and China created the potential for the spread of Buddhism first into central Asia and subsequently east into China, as generations of Buddhist monks crossed paths along the new arteries of travel. Some have argued that the development (most especially in central Asia) of *Mahayana* Buddhism, with its emphasis on the figure of the *Bodhisattva* (he who has the essence of Buddhahood, but remains in this world to help others), should be linked also to the contemporaneous spread of the stories of Jesus Christ as a saviour who gave his life for the forgiveness of human sin.[1] These stories, too, were carried east by Christian missionaries along the trade routes from the Mediterranean.

Meanwhile Greco-Roman aesthetics, long present in central Asia since the era of Alexander the Great's invasions, exerted a conspicuous influence on artistic representations of the Buddha, especially for those in central Asia during the first to fourth centuries CE.[2]

Over and above such comminglings, what also made the fourth century so critical in the history of these religions and of the ancient world was the way in which the problems concerning how to rule – and the opportunities provided by fragmented rule – chimed with the arrival and evolution of new religious ideas. In the Roman world, in Armenia and in Gupta India, new and developing religious beliefs became another way in which leaders could address the challenge of unifying, stabilising and strengthening their realms. In turn, this led in each place to a different relationship emerging between religion and rule: from the joining of spiritual and earthly authority in some places, to adamant antagonism in others. The irony was that this mingling of religion and rule brought together religions whose core message was based on peace, toleration and love with rulers whose reality, and actions, were ones of war and violence – a contradiction that has plagued the whole of human history.

The difficulty in such an approach for Roman and Armenian rulers – indeed, for Christianity as a religion – was that by identifying the ruler with a particular faith (or version of same), hostility towards every other kind of religious belief thus became officially sanctioned, as demonstrated by the vicious Christian attacks on pagan sanctuaries in the Roman world at the end of the fourth century. Furthermore, it opened up the possibility of political dissent against the ruler, in the event that the one faith decreed by the powers-that-be did not chime with the beliefs of the people.

In contrast, the message of Buddhism – increasingly carefully artic- ulated and translated by Buddhist missionaries – was able to strike resonant chords with the needs and interests of both the wider populace and their multiple ruling dynasts within a heavily fragmented and unstable era of China's history. Thus Buddhism became an accepted mainstream part of Chinese society, enjoying an equally varied relationship between religion and rule. Crucially, however, in China Buddhism remained but one of the sanctioned religions, alongside the philosophical doctrines of Daoism and Confucianism, with the beliefs of both in turn affected through their contact with Buddhism.

At the same time in Gupta India it was thanks to the polytheistic and flexible nature of Hindu worship – able to accommodate not only different variations of Hindu beliefs, but entirely different religions, like Buddhism, within its loose hierarchy – that diversity of religious worship could be achieved within a stable political community under a single ruler.

In the Roman and Armenian worlds especially this development of the relationship between religion and rule also led to a new level of overlap between religious and political identity. In the Mediterranean world, Eusebius of Caesarea (biographer of Constantine and the first great Church historian) arguably put a nail in the coffin of democracy as a political system by linking the Christian God with sole monarchical earthly rule. Aelius Aristides, back in the second century CE, had twisted democracy's meaning into a term applicable to the universal world rule of one man. In the writings of Eusebius, however, the good and enviable situation of one ruler (and one God), *monarchia*, is contrasted with *polyarchia* – the rule of many (the people) based on *isotimia*, 'equality of privileged' – which is inherently bad, inevitably leading to 'anarchy and civil strife'.[3] Eusebius proceeds to point out that there is only one God because, just as in earthly politics, any more would create chaos.[4] No wonder that by the sixth century CE, if people spoke of democracy, it was to denounce the negative effects of mob violence and riot. Democracy was not to recover from this defamation, and to reclaim a better name for itself, until the European revolutions of the eighteenth century.[5]

And yet while Christian theology concerning a single God was intertwined and made synonymous with sole monarchical rule, Eusebius was also keen to equate this kind of rule and religion with the entity of the Roman Empire. He is not interested in articulating the stories of Christians outside the Roman Empire: co-believers in Persia, for instance, receive short shrift from him, despite a Persian Christian bishop's presence at Nicaea in 325. Instead Eusebius seems to have been keen to advocate the overlap and mutual reinforcement of one empire, one ruler, one unified religious community and one God. A particular politics and a particular set of religious beliefs were now key parts of a Roman national and imperial identity, and had been shown, through victory on the battlefield, to be crucial to Rome's success.

Along similar lines, scholars have noted how the fifth-century CE Armenian historians often overlooked the earlier evidence for Christianity's slow absorption into Armenia over the first to third centuries CE via the Levant and western Asia. These historians preferred to focus on the dramatic interactions of Tiridates and Gregory the Illuminator as fateful stand-alone moments in Armenian history that tied in with its emergence as a unified nation, the better to conflate political and religious identity.[6] That effort was a success: Armenia's unswerving adherence to Christianity has continued to be one of the defining features of its history and identity up to today, and is in part why Armenia is so proud of its place as the first nation to officially convert to Christianity.

A similar pattern of relations between religious and political identity would emerge in China over subsequent centuries. In the mid-ninth century CE, when China was again unified politically under a single ruler by the era of the Tang dynasty, the foreign nature of Buddhism came to be perceived once again as a major problem. The emperor Wu-Zong led a crackdown on Buddhism, its practices and its monasteries – alongside a number of other 'foreign' religions – across the Chinese Empire, in order to reinforce the Tang dynasty's 'natural' religious and political identity as centred around Daoism and Confucianism (as well as, just as importantly, clamp down on the tax-avoidance vehicle, and the haven for avoiding military service, that the *sangha* had become).

The Roman world, Armenia, India and China were, of course, not the only communities for whom religion was in the process of change in the run-up to and during the fourth century CE; nor were they the only places where missionary religions such as Christianity and Buddhism were developing. Just as Armenia's ruling family was being converted to Christianity, so, too, was the ruling family of the state of Georgia to its north. There, in a conversion narrative just as dramatic as that of Tiridates in Armenia, Queen Nana of Georgia, grievously ill, was said to have summoned a slave woman called Nino who seemed to be able to heal the sick. Nino healed the queen, and sufficiently impressed the king for him to subsequently call on the Christian God to come to his aid when he got lost while out hunting. Finding his way home, he too converted and devoted himself to the conversion of his nation. Like Tiridates, he connected himself to the emperor Constantine, asking for help in Georgia's conversion, and indeed was baptised in the same year as Constantine: 337 CE.

More widely in this period, Christianity spread from the eastern Mediterranean along the trading routes (most often as the religion of traders) and south into Africa, particularly Nubia and Ethiopia. The Christian Frumentius – building on a small Christian community formed by refugees from Roman Imperial persecution – converted Ethiopia to become a Christian country in the 330s and 340s CE. Similarly during the fourth century Christianity also spread further east, as we have seen, into the Sassanid Empire and then to India and even into China, no doubt by the same routes down which Buddhism had ventured to and fro.[7]

And on that side of Asia, thanks to the connected nature of the ancient world and its pulsating trade routes, at the same time as Buddhism was being carried from India and central Asia into China, it was also reaching other parts of east Asia. In the area of modern-day Tibet, around 233 CE, the legend is that Buddhist texts fell out of the sky onto the roof of the palace of the ruler, the twenty-third monarch of the Yarlung dynasty, called Totori Nyentsen. The Chinese Buddhist monk Faxian saw Buddhism established in Sumatra in Indonesia. And the seventh-century Chinese traveller I Tsing spent ten years in a Buddhist monastery on the island and commented on the strong Buddhist communities now in Sumatra, Java and Bali. Buddhism moved on from these places, too: from Tibet it travelled into what is now Mongolia, and from China it spread to Korea and Japan.

As fast as some faiths spread, we should recall that at other times in other places the mills ground more slowly: for example, Theodosius's

Nicene Creed was not officially adopted in the west at Rome until 1014, more than 600 years after Theodosius had first attempted its enforcement.

Within their home world of India, Hindu and Buddhist worship – so welcomingly supported by the Guptas – was integrated even further during the fifth and sixth centuries CE. From the fourth century onwards this was accompanied (and aided) by the development of Tantrism, in which divine energy is said to be unleashed through sexual union. Tantrism deeply influenced Hindu and Buddhist worship, creating new sects in both religions, and new possibilities for their merger. As a result, over the following centuries leading up to the thirteenth century CE and the Muslim invasions of India, the worship of Buddhism as a distinct religion actually declined in the land of its origin. Today, it is the religion of a scant proportion (something between 0.1 and 1.9 per cent) of India's population.

Nonetheless, Buddhist worship continued to develop in different directions within each of the countries to which it had spread. In Tibet, for example, the high Buddhist priest came to exercise sovereignty over the laypeople as well as the Buddhist monk community: religion and rule were embodied in one and the same person. The new varieties of Tantric Buddhism that developed in India also spread out along the connecting networks of the ancient world, to enter and influence the types of Buddhism already established across the east, and to be influenced in turn by the respective religious and cultural landscapes of those communities (though, as we have seen, Tantric Buddhism's counsels with regard to sexual intercourse had to be moderated within Chinese hearing).

The fourth century CE did not, of course, see the end of the impact that the connected nature of the ancient world would have upon its constituent parts. The Roman military officer and historian Ammianus Marcellinus tells us that in 356–7 CE the Sassanid ruler, Shapur II, was forced to go to war against new nomadic invaders on the eastern borders of his empire. By the 370s CE reports were coming back to Rome of successful defeats of native tribes around the Black Sea by nomadic invaders, too; followed by mass immigration of tribes on Rome's borders to within the supposed safety of the Roman Empire. In 395

CE – just after Theodosius had marched to take on the pagan Eugenius in the Battle of the Frigidus River – these nomads seized on the opportunity of an unprotected northern frontier to raid within the Roman Empire itself. In 410 the city of Rome itself was sacked by tribes inspired, and pushed on, by these same nomadic arrivals.

Around the same time, far to the east in northern India, the peaceful reign of the Guptas was interrupted during the rule of Kumaragupta by nomadic invasions. These continued into his son's rule, spilled over the Khyber Pass and eventually brought about the end of the Gupta golden age. Ammianus Marcellinus, in the penultimate major history to survive from the ancient Mediterranean, described these nomads:

> They are quite abnormally savage ... They have squat bodies, strong limbs, and are so prodigiously ugly and bent that they might be two-legged animals ... They have no buildings to shelter them, but avoid anything of the kind as carefully as we avoid living in the neighbourhood of tombs ... They are ill-fitted to fight on foot, and remain glued to their horses, hardy but ugly beasts ...[8]

These were the Huns, whose different tribes and groups made swift war across central and western Asia and into Europe and the Mediterranean during the fifth century CE. Their most famous leader, Attila, came to terrorise the fragmented Roman Empire, threatening Constantinople and forcing the Roman emperor to abandon North Africa. While we cannot know for sure, it is entirely possible that the Huns were originally descended from the Xiongnu nomadic tribes that had troubled China since the fourth century BCE.[9] And while in China the fragmented kingdoms of the fourth and fifth centuries would eventually be reunited into a single dynasty once more, the Roman world was fated never again to be one empire.[10] These two realms, home to more than half of the world's human population, and for so long mirror-images of each other, now contemplated very different futures, as would the lands of Asia between them.

Conclusion

We have seen how, across ancient worlds, both great myths and histories (upon which so much of our understanding of ancient civilisations is based) were rearticulated and re-presented over time – and how such narratives, from very different societies, often have common themes and narratives. (Think of the Indian *Mahabharata* and its powerful affinities with Homer's *Iliad*.) The myths of our modern globalised age are most famously made by the movies – a global business long dominated by the Hollywood-based industry of the USA. But the march of globalisation has meant that Hollywood has steadily become as dependent on overseas markets as on its own large body of domestic customers. China is now the second-biggest importer of Hollywood films, and Hollywood has, naturally, adapted by trying to tailor its output towards the tastes of Chinese viewers (as have, for example, many of the world's luxury-goods makers). But we shouldn't be surprised that China now hankers to generate global blockbuster movies of its own; or that it should look to the histories of ancient worlds to find potential cinematic stories with a 'global' appeal.

It was by this strange route that on 19 February 2015 – Chinese New Year – Chinese movie-goers were treated to the release of *Dragon Blade*: the first motion picture financed with monies from the Beijing Cultural Assets Chinese Film and TV Fund; and a story within which the era of the Eastern Han dynasty meets martial-arts superstar Jackie Chan.

The film's main character is Huo An (played by Chan), leader of a Han-dynasty military squadron charged with protecting the Silk Roads and promoting the idea of peace along the trading network. Huo An encounters, fights against, but subsequently comes to bond with, the leader of a Roman legion in Asia (John Cusack). The two then join forces against an evil Roman overlord (Adrien Brody) who wants to claim the Silk Roads for himself. Into this conflict are poured troops from all corners (and eras) of the ancient globe: Huns, Uighurs, Turkics and Indians, all battling to preserve the safety and peace of the Silk Roads. The film ends with Huo An's mission accomplished, and the surviving Roman legion establishing a new city under his command, by the official sanction of the Han emperor. Subsequently lost in the sands of time, the city is uncovered in the present day by a team of Asian–American archaeologists, who marvel at this evidence of the interconnectedness of the ancient past, as exemplified by the dual Chinese/Latin inscriptions they find.

Dragon Blade was a huge hit in Chinese cinemas, grossing $120 million during its first month of release. In the West it was received less keenly, praised for its fusion of Hollywood and East Asian styles of cinema, but also lambasted as 'Chinese propaganda' and criticised for its plot and historical unfaithfulness. To my mind, whatever the movie's pros and cons as a piece of cinema, it undeniably makes a fantastic symbol for many of the historical themes and ideas we have met in this book.

The legendarily haughty Gore Vidal might not have welcomed the comparison; and yet *Dragon Blade,* in a manner analogous to Vidal's novel *Creation,* plays with time and the historical record, to create a world in which key characters from opposite ends of the ancient globe interact to a degree that simply was not possible in reality. And in this respect the film sits in a long tradition that stretches all the way back to the ancient world itself. Livy, in his great historical treatise on the development of Roman power down to the first century BCE (*Ab Urbe Condita*), was aware that Rome's military power grew just as Alexander the Great was conquering his way through Asia (and fashioning the world to be inhabited by Megasthenes, with whose adventures in India we began this book). Thus Livy wonders, at some length, what would have been the outcome, had Rome come to fight against Alexander. (No surprises that he believes, with reason, that Rome's military machine would have been able to outlast Alexander's charismatic generalship).[1] At any rate, what the imagined confrontations and connections of Livy, *Creation* and *Dragon Blade* have in common are their roots in the reality of a connected ancient world, the developing story of which we have explored within these pages, at three crucial moments.

In Part I, surveying the 'Axial Age' of the sixth century BCE, we observed how the ways in which humans interacted with one another within social groups were subject to dynamic changes in different societies across the ancient globe – in Athens, Rome and the Lu state of Zhou-dynasty China. In each, the effects of war, tyranny, administrative inefficiency and socio-economic inequality had driven a need for change. And in each, war – in different forms, at different moments and arising from different quarters – had a galvanising effect on the political systems that subsequently developed, all of which remained fragile and flexible for decades to come, as these systems slowly matured within their respective populaces.

In Rome and China the systems that emerged saw each section of society as having a different and self-contained role in the function of the whole, akin to the different parts of a human body. But in Athens such an analogy was inapplicable to a system in which each individual was meant to fulfil several roles. Whatever these distinctions, power in Athens, Rome and China would within centuries swing back into the hands of individuals, who ruled, to varying degrees, with a presumption of moral judgement and honour that political theorists from the Mediterranean to China had thought highly desirable.

Today, in a world of much larger populations and – in many parts of the world, at least – much greater representation of different social groups, we still face the same spectrum of choice for our social and political organisation as the ancients did. Like them, we have to interact both with those whose choices we agree with, and with those whose we don't. And in that ongoing process of engagement and interaction, the ideas born in this crucial era of our ancient past remain in flux. Perhaps the most dynamic of all of these has been the legacy of Confucius.

From the sixteenth to nineteenth centuries in China, Confucius was extolled as the sage and teacher par excellence, and his system – with its stresses on moral integrity and filial piety – was adopted at all levels of government. But by the end of the nineteenth century China's failure to keep pace with the West had bred disillusionment. In 1905 the Confucian-based exam system was abolished, and in 1911 the Republic of China was established after the overthrow of the imperial family. Confucius was blamed for China's apparent backwardness ('Down with Confucius and sons!' was the protest chant) and from the 1920s the Chinese Communist Party officially endorsed this sentiment, preferring Legalist philosophies.[2] When Mao Zedong's 'Cultural Revolution' was instigated from 1966 to 1976, Confucius was a prime target: his temples were destroyed, his books obliterated – the Red Guards even dug up his grave to make sure he was definitely dead.[3] In a similar spirit, opponents of the Communist Party and of Mao, such as military leader and minister Lin Biao, were likened to Confucius (for instance, in the 'Criticise Lin, Criticise Confucius' campaign of the 1970s).

And yet in countries such as Korea, Japan and Vietnam, Confucius became increasingly popular through to the twentieth century. Indeed, it was in part thanks to the economic success of these countries in the 1950s to 1970s – success gained while still embracing Confucianist ideas – that Confucianism became more acceptable once again back in China and is now regarded as carrying a promise of economic growth, as well as an antidote to Western materialism. Today, Confucianism in China is promoted on two levels: first, as religion – a spiritual counter to Western pollution; and second, as political force – a potential form of democracy suited to the East.[4]

In Part II of this book we surveyed a gallery of ancient rulers who were responsible for renegotiating relationships between communities, and who consequently forged closer global connections in the third to second centuries BCE. It was in this era that *symploke* ('interconnectedness') became indispensable to military and political strategy in the Mediterranean; when ruthless, respected and energetic rulers fought for the survival of their realms in western, central and eastern Asia, creating (and fragmenting) empires in the process, with knock-on effects for one another. The creation of these behemoths in turn kick-started processes of global migration that came to connect up the horizons of historians of East and West, and encouraged the growth of trade routes across the ancient world that made for a newly enmeshed organic whole. That trade network – the 'Silk Roads' – remained the paramount engine of world trade through to the sixteenth century, only being overtaken by the discovery of America and global trade via the western oceans. And yet, as I noted in the Introduction, we stand today on the brink of the creation of a new set of Silk Roads, and a new era of connectivity across these long-trodden paths.

Across that increasingly interconnected and entangled world stage, as we saw in Part III, ideas – especially about the relationship between human and divine worlds – spread and mutated with ease. In the course of a single century three of the world's major religions were actively disseminated across vast regions of the globe and/or were fundamentally altered in their theological and ritual make-up within their home worlds. This came about partly because of the missionary nature of certain faiths (especially Christianity, which travelled across the Mediterranean into central Asia; and of Buddhism, borne along the Silk Roads across China). But the process was further assisted by the opportunities created by political and military events, and by the careful curation of relations between the divine and worldly rulers – often carried out by the rulers themselves, or else by their missionary supporters.

This interaction between religion and ruler – which created superficially bizarre pairings of ruthless rulers and religions with peace and goodwill at the core of their message – was intended most often to support the ruler's efforts in controlling and maintaining their dominions: a means of accounting for their successes and of undermining their rivals.[5] Man's relationship to man, the relationship between communities, and the relationship between humans and the divine became ever more intrinsically interlinked, just as the ancient world itself became an increasingly complex network of interaction. But quite often the outcome of this linkage of rulers and religions was that the faiths championed by earthly powers proved to be inflexible in relating to other sets of religious beliefs, in turn straining relationships between communities for centuries to come and curtailing the ability of those religions to continue to spread. The embracing of Christianity by Roman emperors across the fourth century CE, for example, effectively ruled out the possibility of Christianity's spread and adoption further east among Rome's political and military rivals, and indeed contributed to a hardening of religious fervour in opposition.[6]

*

This book, then, has sought to explore the gathering connectivity of the ancient world through the lens of three crucial moments and three particular themes. We have seen how political, military and religious innovation, re-articulation and engagement shaped individual communities from the Mediterranean to China and thereby affected the nature and development of the ancient world as a whole. We have explored how the developments of these crucial eras were made possible by what had come before, as well as thanks to the societal forces and powerful individuals of the time; and we have examined how many of the outcomes of these critical moments laid the foundations for the way our world still works – and for debates that we continue to have – in this day and age.

The curious case of *Dragon Blade* echoes another key idea in this book: the use (and abuse) of history itself. *Dragon Blade* not only imagines a fanciful interaction between Rome and China, but also conjures up a very particular view of ancient world priorities: namely, the safety, peace and communality of the Silk Roads as a shared goal of disparate peoples. And yet, are the creative liberties taken by the film's writer-director Daniel Lee really so different from the ways in which we have seen key historians, powerful individuals and whole communities represent their pasts in the ancient world to suit present ends or reflect particular realities?

Consider the Greek historians who put forward very different rationales for the actions of key figures in the development of democracy in Athens; or the rich soup of myth and endlessly varying stories about the origins of Rome and its republic that swirled around the city; or the ways in which key rulers sought to cloak their actions in the costume of particular historical moments and individuals, or to characterise themselves as definitively breaking with the way things had been done previously. Think, too, of the calls to action based on purported comparisons between past and present; or of the endless reconfiguration of the meaning of ideas, which saw the concept of democracy, for example, interpreted as everything from 'power of the people' to 'mob-rule' and 'individual monarchical rule'. All of these examples point to crucial ways in which the ancients imagined and reimagined their pasts, and made that past part of their ongoing dialogue and debate about themselves, their present and their future.

The past then, we should understand, is always a work in progress, a malleable tool that contributes to self-understanding and identity.[7] And under that broad umbrella, the ways in which each ancient community envisaged and articulated its own particular relationship to the past were influenced (or were considered to have been influenced) by many of the key political and religious ideas – as well as powerful rulers and individuals – that we have met in these pages. In China, for example, the understanding of rulership from its earliest dynasties, echoed by Confucius, was based on the offering of the mandate of Heaven, which would be withdrawn and given to a new dynasty whenever the current rulers lapsed into a pattern of unethical behaviour. This cyclical notion of history meant that the job of the historian became the discovery of the patterns of good and bad behaviour, so making them the creators of a de facto guide to good rule. No wonder later observers would credit Confucius – renowned sage and advocate of the wise and just ruler, and of the importance of looking to the past – with the creation of the *Spring and Autumn Annals,* that key historical record of the patterns of the past.[8]

Such patterns were disrupted in ancient Chinese history at the end of the third century BCE by the arrival of China's first empire, the Qin, under Qin Shi Huangdi, who broke with notions of the cyclical and presented his rule as the beginning of a new order that was no longer reliant on the mandate of Heaven. (It was no accident that Legalist, rather than Confucianist, ideas motivated the Qin.)[9] But with the fall of the Qin and rise of the Han, another great debate arose over how to view the past, and which was the correct philosophy of political governance to embrace (Confucianism and Legalism vying amongst others); and eventually a dynastic cyclical purview returned to the forefront.

By contrast, in the Western world, Greek and Roman religious traditions pre-Christianity ran to a linear rather than cyclical conception of time: of the world as a past creation ruled over by gods for eternity. The adoption of Christianity from the fourth century CE only reinforced that linear sense of a divine plan: from creation, to the coming of Christ, to an anticipated Day of Judgement.[10] Perhaps it is small wonder that the West, broadly speaking, has been much more willing to embrace the (false) idea of the past as bygone, worthy of understanding in a strictly retrospective manner, but not as a source of useful instruction for our own times.

The ways in which different societies chose to conceive of the past, and relate themselves to it, have also influenced (and indeed been influenced by) the position that history and historians occupied in that society's social hierarchy.[11] It is not hard to see why in China, where history was thought to be cyclical and to contain the key warnings and teachings for present-day rulers, the study of history – and the place of historians in society – was tightly controlled. For instance, Sima Qian, responsible for the first wide-ranging Chinese history, *Shiji,* was the court astrologer to the Emperor Wu and offered the emperor counsel on state affairs.[12] Similarly, in the eleventh century the great historian Sima Guang, as high chancellor to the emperor, was officially requested – and given official resources – to write his history of the period 403 BCE–959 CE under the title *Zizhi Tongjian* ('Comprehensive Mirror for Aid of Government').[13]

This picture of the official place of history in China – and the monopolisation of the right to authorise its composition by Chinese rulers – is often compared to the example of the Roman world. It is no accident that one of the earliest authors of Roman history, Quintus Fabius Pictor, was also a senator, military general and trusted statesman. Indeed, the way in which the republic conceived of time – dating periods according to the individuals who held the position of consul – fundamentally linked history to the state and its most influential individuals. Equally, Roman historians of the imperial period came from the aristocratic class, had careers in high government service as well as in writing history, and were dependent on the continued goodwill of the emperor both for their own survival and for the survival of their work.[14] In contrast, it has been argued that Greek historians – while often belonging to elites, and sometimes active participants in government – were also regularly political exiles or outsiders, motivated by particular strands of enquiry and often writing for a wide-ranging pan-Hellenic audience within a self-standing philosophical, oratorical and historical tradition, rather than at the behest of rulers: a condition that encouraged their tendency, amongst others, to write wider universal histories (for example, Herodotus, Strabo and Diodorus Siculus).[15]

It has often been lamented that the communities of ancient India seem to have had no sense of history and no place for the historian; or, at least, that they produced no counterpart of Herodotus or Thucydides, Livy, Tacitus or Sima Qian.[16] Indeed, an absence of such kinds of history-writing was later used as part of the justification for the colonial occupation of India by the West.[17] But what such accounts miss are the different – and conflicting – ways in which ancient Indian communities did think about their past as a result of their complex mix of religious and socio-political traditions. On the one hand, ancient Hindu texts such as the *Rig Veda* provided a strong sense of the development of key elements and codes of Indian society, while the *Puranas* (meaning, literally, 'That which is ancient') offered genealogical stories linking the past and the present, created in particular under the imperial Guptas in the fourth century CE as part of the articulation of their rule.

This linear form of mytho-history was complemented both by the pillar and rock inscriptions used by successive Indian rulers to legitimise themselves in relation to successful predecessors (such as the Guptas – and later Mughal rulers – writing their own achievements on the pillar edicts of Ashoka Maurya); and by the development of date-specific biographies, particularly of the Buddha (of which there were conflicting versions amongst the different religious communities, just as there are still ongoing disagreements today amongst scholars over the date of the Buddha's birth and death).[18]

But these multiple linear narratives also sat alongside a cyclical notion of the past that was much bigger than that which governed Chinese approaches to history, in which time was made up of a 'great age' divided into sections (*yugas*), with a cataclysmic collapse of the universe or the arrival of a saviour figure occurring at the end of each great age, inaugurating a new great age and the beginning of another cycle.[19] Such immensely long time-cycles – the inevitability of them, and thus the ultimate insignificance of all that occurred within them – sat in tension with the multiple linear understandings of the past, even within individual religious traditions, especially that of Buddhism.[20] Indeed, far from India having no sense of history, it had in many ways too many senses of history for any one to dominate, in the way that occurred in other societies.

All of this should make us reflect on the place of history and historians, and how we relate to the past, within our own modern worlds. No longer advisers to rulers, historians today go about their work as a professional body seemingly remote from (and thus impartial to?) centres of power. But that does not mean that history itself is no longer just as usable, abusable and malleable as it once was.

Dragon Blade's vision of East and West factions united by a desire to protect the freedom and safety of the Silk Roads possibly reflects how the modern world might want to engage with the – soon to be created – 'new Silk Road' trading routes in our own times. It is a vision uncovered and endorsed by the movie's modern-day Asian–American archaeologists: an exemplar of ancient globalisation, reinforcing the synergy between the ancient and modern worlds and giving legitimacy to them both.

This is a role the ancient world is used to playing. The oracular sanctuary of Delphi in Greece, for example, has been employed as a symbol of ancient (Mediterranean) unity to support modern calls for European nations to work together. The now-idealised example of ancient Athenian democracy has been used to lambast the perceived laxity and unconnectedness of modern democratic societies (particularly in the USA).[21]

I would like to think that the examples described in this book offer readers a way to see the ancient world playing such a role even more effectively – in particular reminding us not simply of far-removed cultures (or elements of them) as magnificent stand-alones but, rather, as part of a much wider interactive web of human connection. Likewise, I hope that the vision of our ancient past offered here will encourage people to see places such as modern-day Afghanistan – such a fixture of our news cycle, yet so seemingly remote – in the context of a geographical region that once played host to Greek cities, Greco-Bactrian riches, great empires and the meeting of East and West, both on the battlefield and in historical record; one that, moreover, acted for centuries as a cultural roundabout for objects, ideas and beliefs for societies from the Mediterranean to China. Similarly we would be better to perceive a site such as the caravan trading centre of Palmyra in Syria as an ancient cosmopolitan melting pot, a space in which people from numerous religious and cultural backgrounds could engage freely with one another – an image that assumes intense sadness and poignancy in light of the recent destruction of Palmyra (among other sites) by Daesh, a group intent on allowing only one version of religious, political and cultural life.

Furthermore, I hope that the vision of a global connected ancient world set out here gets us thinking more about where we stand in our current global outlook in relation to the past, present and future. In the Introduction we saw how an interest in global history had developed in the ancient world following on from the era of Megasthenes, leading to the universal histories and viewpoints of writers such as Diodorus and Strabo. Come the seventeenth century, Walter Raleigh among others felt the necessity for a global history in light of the needs and discoveries of the age.[22] Now, after the world wars of the twentieth century and the increasing globalisation of trade and politics, we once again contemplate the global approach to history.

In past examples a resurgence of closer political horizons caused a decline in the nascent global historical perspective. The universal histories and approaches of Diodorus and his successors were overshadowed by the growth of Rome, which became the centrifugal force for historical thought in the West, until the break-up and decline of the Roman world in the fifth century CE; a point in time that also marked the 'first great divergence' between societal development in East and West, as China – in steep contrast to the disintegrating Roman world – began its journey back to unity, political and economic supremacy.

The Raleigh-era efforts for a global approach were quashed over time by the Industrial Revolution and the rise of the nation state in the West during the eighteenth and nineteenth centuries, which marked the beginning of the second great divergence between East and West, as the West, for the first time since the fifth to sixth centuries CE, became more advanced than China.[23]

Today's twenty-first-century global historical focus has been spurred by world wars, the loss of Western authority on the world stage and the Eastern resurgence to economic global power. And our contemporary appreciation of globalisation and its effects has a seeming permanence to it. There are so many weighty issues for the world's attention that seem to require a global perspective and global action – whether climate change, migration, disease or trade. But surveying the fate of previous global 'turns' could easily lead us to wonder: could our horizons yet roll back again? What might be the occurrence or upheaval that next turns us away from a global perspective? Can we imagine the major shift in the balance of world power that would accompany it?

History shows us that a vision of a larger connected world – one that contains lessons greater than those encountered in one's own back-yard portion of the globe – must be nurtured and championed and fought for. I hope this vision endures, and that our appreciation of the global perspective continues to encompass not just our times, but those of ancient worlds, too.

Notes

INTRODUCTION

1 A paraphrase of Megasthenes, *Indica*, Fragment 39 (Strabo, 15.1.44); Fragment 40.B (Dio Chrysostom, *Discourses*, 35)
2 Cf. N. Kalota, *India as described by Megasthenes*, 1978; R. Majumdar, *The Classical Accounts of India*, 1960
3 Some scholars have argued that these large ants were in reality marmots: J. Boardman, *The Greeks in Asia*, 2015, 130
4 Megasthenes, *Indica*, Fragment 12 (Strabo, 15.1.37)
5 Megasthenes, *Indica*, Fragment 29 (Strabo, 15.1.57), 30 (Pliny, *Natural History*, 7.2.14–22)
6 Cf. A. Bosworth, 'The Historical Setting of Megasthenes' *Indica*', in *Classical Philosophy*, 1996 (91), 113–27
7 Cf. S. R. Goyal, *The Indika of Megasthenes: its content and reliability*, 2000; S. R. Goyal, *India as known to Kautilya and Megasthenes*, 2001
8 Megasthenes, *Indica*, Fragment 25 (Strabo, 15.1.35–6), Fragment 26 (Arrian, *Indica*, 10)
9 Cf. P. Kosmin, 'Apologetic Ethnography: Megasthenes' Indica and the Seleucid Elephant', in E. Almagor and J. Skinner (eds), *Ancient Ethnography – New Approaches*, 2013, 97–116
10 Megasthenes, *Indica*, Fragment 27 (Strabo, 15.1.53–6)
11 Cf. Euripides, *Bacchae*, in which Dionysus talks of how he has come to Greece from the wealthy East. See also Strabo, *Geographica*, 3.5.6, and Apollodorus, 3.5.2, who recount the finding of pillars in India inscribed with deeds of Dionysus and Heracles; J. Boardman, *The Greeks in Asia*, 2015, 130
12 Megasthenes, *Indica*, Fragment 1 (Diodorus Siculus, 2.38–39)
13 Cf. B. de Give, *Les rapports de l'Inde et de l'Occident: des origines au règne d'Asoka*, 2005, 261, 303. We know that Megasthenes knew personally the ruler Seleucus Nicator, and was also associated with Sibytrius, the *satrap* (ruler) of Arachosia. He may also have met with the Indian King Porus, who fought

Alexander the Great. He may have been the negotiator in the agreed settlement of borders between the Seleucid and Mauryan Empires: P. Kosmin,
'Apologetic Ethnography: Megasthenes' Indica and the Seleucid Elephant',
in E. Almagor and J. Skinner (eds), *Ancient Ethnography – New Approaches*,
2013, 97–116

14 Cf. D. Vassiliades, *The Greeks in India*, 2000, 22

15 Cf. S. R. Goyal, *India as known to Kautilya and Megasthenes*, 2001. The Greeks had
been making voyages to examine the borders of the known world more widely
since at least the sixth century BCE; e.g. Hecateus of Miletus. Herodotus
reports that a Phoenician, Hanno, had sailed around the whole continent of
Africa with the sponsorship of an Egyptian pharaoh, to see if it was surrounded by water (no one else ventured around Africa until 1498 CE).
Phoenicians were also said to have ventured into the south Atlantic towards
the Canaries and Azores: P. Stearns, *Globalisation in World History*, 2010, 16

16 Cf. M. Sommer, 'Oikoumene: longue durée perspectives on ancient Mediter-
ranean "globality"', in M. Pitts and M. Versluys (eds), *Globalisation and the
Roman World: world history, connectivity and material culture*, 2015, 175–97. See also
Herodotus, 3.98, 4.40

17 Not to mention the city's architecture reflecting its cosmopolitan visitors:
stone capitals have been found there that mimic the Greek style, and have
Greek decoration: J. Boardman, *The Greeks in Asia*, 2015, 134

18 Megasthenes, *Indica*, Fragment 1 (Diodorus Siculus, 2.42)

19 Seleucus, his boss, also gave his daughter Helen in marriage to Chandragupta;
alongside Greek mercenaries who will have fought for Indian kings and
Greek artisans, doctors, astrologers and traders: S. R. Goyal, *The Indica of
Megasthenes: its contents and reliability*, 2000, 55

20 Patrocles, *Die Fragmente der griechischen Historiker*, 712; Demodamas, *Die Fragmente der griechischen Historiker*, 428. Cf. P. Kosmin, 'Apologetic Ethnography:
Megasthenes' Indica and the Seleucid Elephant', in E. Almagor and J. Skinner (eds), *Ancient Ethnography – New Approaches*, 2013, 97–116

21 Cf. P. Robb, *A History of India*, 2002, 40

22 *The Milindpanho 'Questions of King Milinda [Menander]'*. Cf. D. Vassiliades, *The
Greeks in India*, 2000, 59

23 Jeremy Tanner points to a number of reasons that the study of Greece and
Rome has remained so blinkered: the deluge of archaeological discovery, which
encourages specialisation; the place of Greece and Rome as the cornerstones of
European identity and as the 'ideological cement' of the ruling classes in the
nineteenth and twentieth centuries, as well as the prevalence of postmodernist
and post-structuralist notions of the uniqueness of entities: J. Tanner, 'Ancient
Greece Early China: Sino-Hellenistic studies and comparative approaches to
the Classical world', in *Journal of Hellenic Studies*, 2009 (129), 89–109

24 E.g. J. Anderson, *Hunting in the Ancient World*, 1985; J. Landels, *Engineering
in the Ancient World*, 1978; C. Gill and T. Wiseman (eds), *Lies and Fiction in
the Ancient World*, 1993; E. Cantarella, *Bisexuality in the Ancient World*,
1992, T. Whitmarsh, *Atheism in the Ancient World*, 2015. The list goes on,
including – mea culpa – one of my own titles: M. Scott, *Delphi: centre of the
ancient world*, 2014.

25 E.g. A.J. Toynbee, *A Study of History*, 1934-54

26 F.Braudel, *La Méditerranée et le Monde Méditerranéen à l'époque de Philippe II*, 1949

27 Work on the Mediterranean and the Roman Empire as a unit: P. Horden and N. Purcell, *The Corrupting Sea: a study of mediterranean history*, 2000; D. Abulafia, *The Great Sea: A human history of the mediterranean*, 2011; K. Hopkins, *Conquerors and Slaves*, 1981; B. Cunliffe, *Greeks, Romans and Barbarians*, 1988. Works that have met with stiff resistance: e.g. M. Bernal, *Black Athena: the afroasiatic roots of classical civilisation*, 1987–2006. More recently on a networked approach to ancient history: M. Castells, 'Nothing new under the sun?', in O. LaBianca and S. Scham (eds), *Connectivity in Antiquity: Globalisation as a long-term process*, 2006, 158–67, and, on connecting the development of the Mediterranean into wider perspectives: C. Broodbank, *The Making of the Middle Sea*, 2013

28 P. Stearns, *Globalisation in World History*, 2010; N. Sitwell, *Outside the Empire: the world the romans knew*, 1984; L. Casson, *Travel in the Ancient World*, 1994; P. Curtin, *Cross-cultural Trade in World History*, 1998; P. DeSouza, *Seafaring and Civilisation: Maritime perspectives on world trade*, 2002; J. Boardman, *The Greeks Overseas*, 1980; *The Greeks in Asia*, 2015; J. Hill, *Through the Jade Gate to Rome: a study of the Silk Routes during the later Han dynasty*, 2011; F. Wood, *The Silk Road: 2000 years in the heart of Asia*, 2004; P. Frankopan, *The Silk Roads: a new history of the world*, 2015

29 C. Gizewski, 'Römische und alte chinesische Geschichte im Vergleich: Zur Möglichkeit eines gemeinsamen Altertumsbegriffs', in *Klio*, 1994 (76): 271–302; F. Mutschler and A. Mittag (eds), *Conceiving the Empire: Rome and China compared*, 2008; I. Morris and W. Scheidel, *The Dynamics of Ancient Empires: state power from Assyria to Byzantium*, 2009; W. Scheidel (ed.), *Rome and China: Comparative perspectives on ancient world empires*, 2009; J. Burbank and F. Cooper, *Empires in World History: geographies of power, politics of difference*, 2010; W. Scheidel (ed.), *State Power in Ancient China and Rome*, 2015; I. Morris and W. Scheidel (eds), *State Formation in Europe and China*, forthcoming. See also the Stanford Ancient Chinese and Mediterranean Empires Comparative History Project.

30 K. Raaflaub (ed.), *War and Peace in the Ancient World*, 2007; P. de Souza, *The Ancient World at War: a global history*, 2008; K. Raaflaub and N. Rosenstein (eds), *War and Society in the Ancient and Medieval Worlds: Asia, the Mediterranean, Europe and Mesoamerica*, 1999

31 For a summation of the scholarship so far in all these fields: J. Tanner, 'Ancient Greece Early China: Sino-Hellenistic studies and comparative approaches to the Classical world', in *Journal of Hellenic Studies*, 2009 (129), 89–109. In particular, for discussion: S. Shankman and S. Durrant (eds), *The Siren and the Sage: knowledge and wisdom in ancient Greece and China*, 2000; *Early China/Ancient Greece: thinking through comparisons*, 2002. In addition, more recently, see: H. Kim, *Ethnicity and Foreigners in Ancient Greece and China*, 2009. For the advantages of the comparative approach, see G. Lloyd and N. Sivin, *The Way and the Word: science and medicine in early China and Greece*, 2002, 8. Cf. M. Finley, *Use and Abuse of History*, 1986, 119, calling for a third discipline of comparative study. Also W. Scheidel, 'Comparing ancient worlds: comparative history as comparative advantage', in *2012 Proceedings of the International Symposium of Ancient World History in China*, forthcoming

32 Cf. B. Gills and W. Thompson, *Globalization and Global History*, 2008.1. The same is true of other periods; e.g. medieval history so often reduces to the

story of European knights, at the expense of what else was going on around the world at this time.

33 Indeed some scholars even deny the ancient world was globalised. For debate see: I. Wallerstein, *The Modern World System*, 1974; R. Robertson and D. Inglis, 'The Global Animus: in the tracks of world consciousness', in B. Gills and W. Thompson (eds), *Globalisation and Global History*, 2008, 32–47; C. Cioffi-Revilla, 'The Big Collapse', in B. Gills and W. Thompson (eds), *Globalisation and Global History*, 2008, 79–95; C. Chase Dunn and T. Hall, *Rise and Demise: comparing world systems*, 1997; A. Frank and B. Gills (eds), *The World System: Five hundred years or five thousand?*, 1994; J. Jennings, *Globalisations and the Ancient World*, 2011; I. Morris, *Why the West Rules for Now*, 2010

34 Cf. B. Gills and W. Thompson (eds), *Globalisation and Global History*, 2008, 5; B. Mazlish and R. Buultjens (ed.), *Conceptualising Global History*, 1993, 1

35 This is despite the recent popularity of more global approaches to history in the public sphere e.g. the British Museum's hugely popular exhibition, book and radio series *A History of the World in 100 Objects*; I. Morris, *Why the West Rules – for now*, 2010; Y. Harari, *Sapiens: A brief history of humankind*, 2014; B. Cunliffe, *By Steppe, Ocean and Desert: the birth of eurasia*, 2015; P. Frankopan, *The Silk Roads*, 2015

36 Cf. P. Frankopan, *The Silk Roads*, 2015; R. McLaughlin, *Rome and the Distant East: trade routes to the ancient lands of Arabia, India and China*, 2010

37 Cf. Diodorus Siculus, *Bibliotheca Historica*; Strabo, *Geographica*; Pliny, *Natural History*; Claudius Ptolemy, *Geographica*

38 I. Morris, *Why the West Rules – for now*, 2010; *Foragers, Farmers and Fossil Fuels*, 2014; *The Measure of Civilisation*, 2015. W. Scheidel, 'Introduction', in W. Scheidel (ed.), *Rome and China: Comparative perspectives on ancient world empires*, 2009, 3–10: 'the study of ancient civilization . . . has much to gain and nothing to lose from broader perspectives'; W. Scheidel, 'Comparing comparisons: ancient East and West', in G. Lloyd, Q. Dong and J. Zhao (eds), *Ancient Greece and China Compared*, forthcoming

39 In the spirit of Winston Churchill's famous dictum: 'the farther back you can look, the father forward you are likely to see'.

PART I: POLITICS IN AN AXIAL AGE

INTRODUCTION

1 K. Jasper, *Vom Ursprung und Ziel der Geschichte*, 1949, 19–42. Cf. S. Eisenstadt (ed.), *The Origins and Diversity of Axial Age Civilisations*, 1986; R. Bellah, 'What's axial about the Axial Age', in *Archives Européennes de Sociologie*, 2005 (46): 69–87

2 Cf., however, recent attempts to deny the attribution of the development of democracy to Greece and its existence as an originally Western idea: A. Sen, 'Democracy as a Universal Value', in *Journal of Democracy*, 1999 (10.3), 3–17; B. Isakhan and S. Stockwell (eds), *The Secret History of Democracy*, 2011. The most recent rebuttal of this position is P. Cartledge, *Democracy: a life*, 2016

3 'Until the 20th century, China was so inseparable from the idea of Confucius that her scheme of government and society, her concept of the self and human relationships, and her construct of culture and history all seemed to

have originated from his mind alone': A. Jin, *Confucius: a life of thought and politics*, 2007, 2. 'The rich civilization of China . . . owes more to the impress of Confucius' personality and teaching than to any other single factor. Chinese civilization may truly be called a Confucian civilization': D. Howard Smith, *Confucius*, 1973, 9

4 The title of 'Senate' for a modern political assembly is found in a number of countries, from the USA to Rwanda; cf. M. Beard, *SPQR: A history of ancient Rome*, 2015, 26

5 Cf. J. Roberts, *A History of China*, 1999, 75

6 W. Faulkner, *Requiem for a Nun*, 1951, Act 1, Scene 3

CHAPTER 1: ATHENIAN DEMOCRACY AND
THE DESIRE FOR PEOPLE-POWER

1 Herodotus, 5.72.2

2 J. Ober, *The Rise and Fall of Classical Greece*, 2015, 160

3 Cf. Herodotus, 5.72.1–2

4 This was also the same Persian king, Darius, who sent Gore Vidal's character Cyrus in *Creation* off to be the Persian ambassador to India.

5 The term 'tyrant' – while an ancient Greek word – did not necessarily have negative connotations in the ancient world. It could mean a good strong ruler or an oppressive ruler, as it does today.

6 Herodotus, 5.66, 5.69.2

7 Herodotus, 5.66.2

8 'Cleisthenes introduced the tribes and the democracy to the Athenians': Herodotus, 6.131

9 Pseudo-Aristotle, *Constitution of the Athenians*, 20–1

10 Herodotus, 5.67–9

11 Herodotus, 5.71

12 Cf. J. Ober, *The Rise and Fall of Classical Greece*, 2015, 76–85

13 Ironically, the text of Draco's legislation that actually survives to us details the circumstances in which a man can be let off involuntary homicide.

14 Solon, Fragment 5.1; cf. Pseudo-Aristotle, *Constitution of the Athenians*, 9.1

15 Solon, Fragment 35; cf. Pseudo-Aristotle, *Constitution of the Athenians*, 12.4

16 Cf. Pseudo-Aristotle, *Constitution of the Athenians*, 12

17 Herodotus, 1.59; cf. Pseudo-Aristotle, *Constitution of the Athenians*, 13.4, who recasts these geographical parties as those with actual political agendas. The people of 'the shore' wanted a 'moderate constitution', the people of 'the plain' wanted an oligarchy and the people of 'the hill' were the discontented populace.

18 Herodotus, 1.59

19 Pseudo-Aristotle, *Constitution of the Athenians*, 14.4

20 Herodotus, 1.61

21 Pseudo-Aristotle, *Constitution of the Athenians*, 13–17; Aristotle, *Politics*, 5.1313b

22 Aristotle, *Politics*, 5.11

23 Cf. Athenaeus, *Dinner Table Philosophers (Deipnosophistae)*, 695A–B; *Inscriptiones Graecae* I³ 131; Thucydides, 65.4–6

24 Thucydides, 6.54–6

25 Herodotus, 5.61

26 Herodotus, 5.73

27 Herodotus, 5.78

28 There is an ongoing debate in scholarship over the extent to which the emergence of democracy in Athens pre-dates the emergence of democracies elsewhere in the Greek world. Some scholars argue for the existence in the seventh and sixth centuries of a much wider regional manifestation of the 'middling' ideology, in which the very rich and the very poor were scorned in favour of the middle: I. Morris, 'The strong principle of equality and the archaic origins of Greek democracy', in J. Ober and C. Hedrick (eds), *Demokratia: a conversation on democracies, ancient and modern*, 1996, 19–48. Others point out that, despite this, Athens developed a recognisable democracy faster and earlier than anywhere else: democracy 'seems to me to be found no where else in the world before the late 6th century BCE in Athens': P. Cartledge, *Ancient Greek Political Thought in Practice*, 2009, 56

29 R. Osborne, *Greek History*, 2004, 1

30 For a collection of the surviving fragments, see T. Cornell (ed.), *Fragments of the Roman Historians*, 2013

31 Cf. B. Gibson and T. Harrison (eds), *Polybius and his World*, 2013

32 Polybius, 6.43.3, 44.4

33 Cf. K. Bringmann, *A History of the Roman Republic*, 2007, 1–2

34 Other key Greek historical events were used as markers for dating the advent of the Roman Republic: the Greek historian Dionysius of Halicarnassus dated the creation of the Roman Republic as occurring in the year of the sixty-eighth Greek Olympic Games (508 BCE), to chime with the expulsion of Isagoras and the adoption of Cleisthenes' reforms; Polybius in the second century BCE also dated it as occurring twenty-eight years before the invasion of the Persian King Xerxes into Greece (508–7 BCE).

35 Polybius, 6.43.4; 44.3; 48

36 Demaratus, father of Tarquin the Elder, came to Etruria from Corinth: Pliny, *Natural History* 35.152–4; Numa was said to have been tutored by Pythagoras; cf. M. Beard, *SPQR: A history of ancient Rome*, 2015, 100, 104

37 Strabo, 5.3.3. Heraclides, a fourth-century BCE Greek, referred to Rome as a Greek city: Heraclides Ponticus, Fragment 102 (in Plutarch, *Life of Camillus*, 22.2). For discussion, cf. M. Beard, *SPQR: A history of ancient Rome*, 2015, 74

38 M. Erasmo, *Roman Tragedy: theatre to theatricality*, 2004, 93–4

39 In his work Diodorus offers a complaint that echoes the Introduction to this book, on the lack of global approaches to ancient history even in his own day: 'although the profit which history affords its readers lies in its embracing a vast number and variety of circumstances, yet most writers have recorded no more than isolated wars waged by a single nation of a single state'. Diodorus Siculus, 1.3.2

40 Dionysius of Halicarnassus, 1.11

41 Cf. A. J. Ammerman, 'Looking at Early Rome through fresh eyes: transforming the landscape', in J. DeRose-Evans (ed.), *Companion to the Archaeology of the Roman Republic*, 2013, 169–80; R. Scott, 'The Contribution of Archaeology to Early Roman History', in K. Raaflaub (ed.), *Social Struggles in Archaic Rome: New perspectives on the conflict of the orders*, 2005, 98–106. The first-century BCE Roman landscape had key markers from its origins also still visible:

'Romulus' hut' on the Palatine, the fig tree in the Forum under which Romulus and Remus had been placed as babies, the Temple of Jupiter Stator, built by Romulus; cf. M. Beard, *SPQR: A history of ancient Rome*, 2015, 70

CHAPTER 2: ROME, THE REPUBLIC AND
THE PERFECTION OF GOVERNMENT

1 Livy, 1.58.5
2 Livy, 1.59.1
3 Although scholars have commented on the Athenian 'flavour' to the story of the rape of Lucretia, in linking the fall of tyranny with sexual crimes, e.g. the Tyrannicides (at least according to Thucydides) in 514 BCE; cf. M. Beard, *SPQR: A history of ancient Rome*, 2015, 121
4 Tacitus, *Annals of Imperial Rome*, 1.1
5 Livy, 1.49
6 Livy, 1.46–8
7 So too was Servius Tullius's predecessor, Numa Pompilius, who is accredited in the later sources with the foundation of Rome's religious infrastructure; cf. M. Beard, *SPQR: A history of ancient Rome*, 2015, 101
8 Livy, 1.43.10
9 Only, however, in the imperial period did the term *res publica* come to denote a specific form of governance with a specific political flavour – what we now call the Roman Republic and a 'republican' constitution. During the republic's early history, *res publica* denoted simply an organised political community in which power could be distributed in many different ways.
10 Although at the time the position was known formally as *praetor* – a term meaning 'to go before'. The term 'consul' came into use in the fourth century BCE in order to distinguish it from another set of *praetors*: T. Cornell, *The Beginnings of Rome*, 1995, 226; G. Forsythe, *A Critical History of Early Rome*, 2005, 151; F. Pina Polo, *The Consul in Rome*, 2011
11 The inspiration to have two consuls may have come from the concept of collegiality in the colleges of priests or public magistrates: G. Forsythe, *A Critical History of Early Rome*, 2005, 153. It has been argued that this 'twin' position was also the inspiration for the story, which emerged only from the fourth century BCE, of the twins at the heart of the foundation of Rome itself, Romulus and Remus: T. P. Wiseman, *Remus: a Roman myth*, 1995
12 Livy, 2.19
13 The last three kings of Rome had Etruscan connections, which some scholars have interpreted as an Etruscan takeover of Rome (seeing Servius Tullius as an Etruscan armed adventurer taking the city by force); cf. M. Beard, *SPQR: A history of ancient Rome*, 2015,111–15
14 Livy, 2.6.8
15 Livy, 2.7
16 Tacitus, *Annals of Imperial Rome*, 3.72; Pliny, *Natural History*, 34.139. Credence to the story of real destruction in Rome around this time is given by the layer of fire debris found in the archaeological levels of the city, dating to around 500 BCE; cf. M. Beard, *SPQR: A history of ancient Rome*, 2015, 132
17 Polybius, 6.55

18 Livy, 2.10; Dionysius of Halicarnassus, 5.24. A tale even Livy described 'as more famous than credible in posterity': Livy, 2.10.11

19 Livy, 2.12.9–11

20 Livy, 2.12.14

21 Sallust, *History of Rome*, Fragment 11

22 Livy, 2.32

23 Cf. Sallust, *History of Rome*, Fragment 11, which argues that it was only the external threat that compelled Rome's leaders to deal fairly with the Roman masses.

24 The city of Cincinnati in the USA was named in memory of Cincinnatus's example in being willing to give up supreme power.

25 Cf. K. Raaflaub, 'Between Myth and History: Rome's rise from village to empire', in R. Morstein-Marx and N. Rosenstein (eds), *Wiley-Blackwell Companion to the Roman Republic*, 2006, 125–46; K. Raaflaub, 'The Conflict of the Orders in Archaic Rome: a comprehensive and comparative approach', in K. Raaflaub (ed.), *Social Struggles in Archaic Rome: new perspectives on the conflict of the orders*, 2005, 1–46. This hierarchical structure was also reinforced in social as well as political aspects of society: the power of the *paterfamilias* as head of the household, and of the extensive patronage and client-systems cascading downwards through Roman society from rich individuals, for example.

26 F. Millar, 'The political character of the classical Roman Republic', in *Journal of Roman Studies*, 1984 (74), 1–19; *The Roman Republic in Political Thought*, 2002

27 Cicero, *On the Commonwealth (De Re Publica)*, 2.67–9

28 Polybius, 6.11

29 In particular, Polybius argued, the people should have the right to confer honour and inflict punishment – as the 'only bonds by which kingdoms and states . . . are held together': Polybius, 6.14.4

30 Polybius, 6.10.14

31 Although it seems that some Plebeians had been consuls at least in the first part of the fifth century, including Lucius Junius Brutus himself; cf. M. Beard, *SPQR: A history of ancient Rome*, 2015, 150–1

32 E.g. S. Oakley, 'The Early Republic', in H. Flower (ed.), *The Cambridge Companion to the Roman Republic*, 2004, 15–30; M. Beard, *SPQR: A history of ancient Rome*, 2015, 153–8

CHAPTER 3: CHINA, CONFUCIUS AND
THE QUEST FOR THE JUST RULER

1 According to the later Chinese historian Sima Qian, writing the first broad history of China, entitled *Shiji 'Records of the Grand Historian'*, c.110 BCE. For a translation of the biography of Confucius, see *Library of Chinese Classics: Selections from the Records of the Historian, Vol. 1*, 2008 (and for his account of the eighty women: 2008, 231–2). Other sources mention Confucius's discontent at not being given a portion of the public sacrifice as leading to his decision to leave Duke Ding and go into exile: A. Jin, *Confucius: A life of thought and politics*, 2007, 27

2 This book uses the Hanyu Pinyin for the transcription of Chinese names (although popular alternatives are sometimes given in brackets).

3 Sima Qian, *Records of the Grand Historian (Shiji): Library of Chinese Classics: Selections from the Records of the Historian, Vol. 1*, 2008, 233

4 D. Howard-Smith, *Confucius*, 1973, 54

5 B. Kelen, *Confucius: in life and legend*, 1974, 58

6 F. Fénelon (1712), however, wrote, in his *Dialogues des morts,* an imaginary dialogue between Socrates and Confucius. (Gore Vidal's character Cyrus in his novel *Creation,* in contrast, only met Socrates and Confucius individually.) Cf. B. Kelen, *Confucius in life and legend*, 1974, 12

7 Cf. S. Shankman and S. Durrant (eds), *Early China–Ancient Greece: Thinking through comparisons*, 2002

8 E.g. L. Raphals, *Knowing Words: wisdom and cunning in the classical traditions of China and Greece*, 1992; G. Lloyd, *Ancient Worlds, Modern Reflections: philosophical perspectives on Greek and Chinese science and culture*, 2004; G. Lloyd and N. Sivin, *The Way and the Word: science and medicine in early China and Greece*, 2002

9 E.g. W. Scheidel (ed.), *Rome and China: comparative perspectives on ancient world empires*, 2009; F. H. Mutschler, *Historiographical Traditions of Imperial Rome, and Han China*, 2007; C. Gizewski, 'Römische und alte chinesische Geschichte im Vergleich: Zur Möglichkeit eines gemeinsamen Altertumsbegriffs', in *Klio*, 1994 (76): 271–302

10 L. Shihlien Hsü, *The Political Philosophy of Confucianism*, 1975, 24

11 Cf. Sima Qian, *Records of the Grand Historian (Shiji)*.

12 For discussion of Confucius's life and literary goals: B. Watson, *Sima Qian Grand Historian of China*, 1958. A full translation of Sima Qian's text is still not available in English. Major sections have been translated: B. Watson, *Records of the Grand Historian: Qin Dynasty*, 1993; B. Watson, *Records of the Grand Historian: Han dynasty, Vols 1 and 2*, 1961. Most recently, see the selected translations of Sima Qian published in three volumes as *Selections from the Records of the Historian*, in the *Library of Chinese Classics* series (2008).

13 Although later scholars thought the *Spring and Autumn Annals* were written by Confucius, this entry, along with a number of others, makes modern scholarship very doubtful of this attribution: J. Roberts, *A History of China*, 1999, 36

14 Cf. L. von Falkenhausen, *Chinese Society in the Age of Confucius 1000–250 BC: the archaeological evidence*, 2006

15 *Analects*, 13.12

16 *Analects*, 16.2

17 *Analects*, 2.4

18 The mandate to rule as the gift of the gods is something one sees in Homer's epics in the Greek world; cf. J. Haubold, *Homer's People: epic poetry and social Formation*, 2000

19 Cf. I. Morris, *Why the West Rules – For Now*, 2010, 131

20 The origins of the name 'China' are uncertain, appearing in English from the mid-sixteenth century. It was originally argued to have been derived from the name of the Qin dynasty in the late third century BCE. But more probably it may have come from the Persian word for 'porcelain', describing one of China's best exports. However, it may also have originated in Indic texts to describe a particular tribe in Chinese territory. The word *'thin'* to describe Chinese territory is also found in a first-century CE Greek text, *'Periplus of the Red Sea'*.

21 In terms of bureaucratic procedure, it was virtually impossible 'with the resources and techniques available to them to organize and maintain a centralized administration adequate to control the broad territories to which

[the king] made claim': H. G. Creel, *The Origins of Statecraft in China, Vol. 1: the western Zhou*, 1970, 417; M. Lewis, *Sanctioned Violence in Early China*, 1990; Chang Chun-shu, *The Rise of the Chinese Empire, Vol. 1: Nation, state and imperialism in early China 1600 BCE–CE 8*, 2007

22 N. Rosenstein, 'State Formation and the Evolution of Military Institutions in Ancient China and Rome', in W. Scheidel (ed.), *Rome and China: comparative perspectives on ancient world empires*, 2009, 24–51. This was also the period that military specialists appeared in China: like Sun Tzu, who wrote *P'ing Fa* ('The Art of War') during the fifth century BCE.

23 Estimates vary as to exactly how many were still 'surviving' at any one time; e.g. some argue that as many as forty states were still operational in the 470s BCE: L. Dian Rainey, *Confucius and Confucianism: the essentials*, 2010, 7

24 H. Jin Kim, *Ethnicity and Foreigners in Ancient Greece and China*, 2009, 2

25 J. Roberts, *A History of China*, 1999, 13

26 Many scholars argue over the degree to which the era of the Shang dynasty and that of the Western Zhou can be described as slave or feudal systems, and the degree to which Marx's analysis of the Asiatic Mode of Production, which characterises Chinese society as fundamentally different from that in the West, is a fair reflection of the economic realities of this period in China: J. Roberts, *A History of China*, 1999, xii; Li Jun, *Chinese Civilisation in the Making 1766–221 BCE*, 1996, 4

27 L. Jun, *Chinese Civilisation in the Making 1766–221 BCE*, 1996, 105

28 J. Roberts, *A History of China*, 1999, 39

29 Cf. N. Rosenstein, 'War, State formation and the evolution of military institutions in Ancient China and Rome', in W. Scheidel (ed.), *Rome and China: Comparative perspectives on ancient world empires*, 2009, 24–51

30 L. Dian Rainey, *Confucius and Confucianism: the essentials*, 2010, 11

31 *Analects*, 4.15

32 *Analects*, 2.15

33 *Analects*, 11.16

34 *Analects*, 4.14

35 *Analects*, 12.11

36 *Analects*, 17.8

37 *Analects*, 12.7

38 Polybius, 6.14.4

39 For the importance of *Ren*, see *Analects*, 4.15.

40 *Analects*, 15.23

41 *Analects*, 12.19

42 Examples of such moral force would in turn encourage the people to exhibit *Te* as well: *Analects*, 2.3

43 *Analects*, 17.23

44 Greeks and the new: P. Cartledge, 'Democracy, origins of: contributions to a debate', in K. Raaflaub, J. Ober and R. Wallace, *Origins of Democracy in Ancient Greece*, 2007, 155–69

45 Cf. L. Shihlien Hsü, *The Political Philosophy of Confucianism*, 1975, 175–97

46 Cf. L. Dian Rainey, *Confucius and Confucianism: the essentials*, 2010, 184–93

47 For comparisons between Greek and Confucian philosophies of rule: L. Shihlien Hsü, *The Political Philosophy of Confucianism*, 1975; W. Teh-Yao, *Confucius*

and Plato's Ideas on a Republic, 1978; M. Sim, *Remastering Morals with Aristotle and Confucius*, 2007

48 He seems to have continued to annoy people in power during this time – some sources speak of an assassination attempt on his life during this time: J. Roberts, *A History of China*, 1999, 52

49 *Analects*, 17.7

50 *Analects*, 7.7. Cf. *Analects*, 15.38

51 *Analects*, 14.41

52 Containing as one of its most famous phrases 'the journey of 1,000 miles starts with the first step'; cf. J. Miller, *Daoism: a short introduction*, 2003, 4

53 Cf. J. Roberts, *A History of China*, 1999, 15; J. Miller, *Daoism: a short introduction*, 2003, 4; L. Kohn, *Daoism and Chinese Culture*, 2001, 11, 16

54 Cf. R. Dawson, *Confucius*, 1981, 4–5

55 L. Dian Rainey, *Confucius and Confucianism: the essentials*, 2010, 73–5

56 The advantage of this period of intense competition was that it actually encouraged each of these different schools to articulate more clearly their beliefs and principles, spurring on their own individual development; cf. L. Kohn, *Daoism and Chinese Culture*, 2001, 11–16

57 Mencius, 2a.2. For a translation: D. Lau, *Mencius*, 1970

58 Mencius, 7b.14; cf. Mencius, 1b.7. Following Mencius was a man called Xunzi, living in the third century BCE, who similarly altered and adapted Confucian teachings at the same time as building Confucius's reputation as a legendary sage. Xunzi underlined the Confucian demand for strenuous learning in order to perfect one's character, because morality was not set by Heaven, but was created by rulers and society. His catchphrase was 'the nature of man is evil; goodness is acquired'. It was under Xunzi's influence that a list of 'set texts' for those following Confucius's ideas was established, including the *Spring and Autumn Annals*. Cf. B. Watson, *Hsün Tzu (Xunzi): Basic Writings*, 1963. It was Xunzi's brand of Confucianism that would be most popular in China until the twelfth century CE, when Mencius's version would prevail (with which the West came into contact in the sixteenth and seventeenth centuries, which is why we use the Latinised 'Mencius', but there is no equivalent for Xunzi's name).

59 Han Fei, in the mid-third century BCE, began as a follower of Confucius, but eventually turned against Confucianism and became a follower – and eventual an articulator – of Shang Yang's Legalist ideas, also advising the rulers of the state of Qin: J. Roberts, *A History of China*, 1999, 21

CODA

1 I. Morris, *Why the West Rules – For Now*, 2010, 261

2 I. Morris, *Why the West Rules – For Now*, 2010, 245

3 Herodotus, 3.80–2.

4 J. Ober, *The Rise and Fall of Classical Greece*, 2015, 101–5

PART II: WAR AND A WORLD IN CHANGE

INTRODUCTION

1 Diodorus Siculus, 4.19.3
2 Appian, *Roman History Book 7: The Hannibalic War*, 1.4
3 Polybius, 3.39.12
4 Livy, 21.30
5 Although later literary sources quote a monument erected by Hannibal him-self in southern Italy in which he lists his achievements (including the number of troops he brought with him safely through the Alps); cf. Livy, 28.46.16
6 Polybius, 3.20.5
7 Polybius, 3.48.12
8 Polybius, 1.1.5
9 'the chief cause of success or the reverse in all matters is the form of a state's constitution: for springing from this, as from a fountain head, all designs and plans of actions not only originate, but reach their consummation': Polybius, 6.2.9–10. For Rome's constitution at its best under stress: Polybius, 6.18.2. For Rome's ability to command plentiful supplies, Polybius, 6.50.6. Seager has recently argued that Polybius deliberately omits discussion of elements of the Roman constitution in order to make his point about balance stronger: R. Seager, 'Polybius' Distortions of the Roman Constitution: a simpl(istic) explanation', in B. Gibson and T. Harrison, *Polybius and His Worlds: Essays in honour of F. Walbank*, 2013, 247–56. The idea of the balanced constitution is made even more strongly by Strabo, writing in the first century BCE, who claimed it was Rome's geographical location in the middle of the Mediterra-nean and its command over natural resources (and allied troops) that enabled its mastery of the Mediterranean: Strabo, 6.4.1
10 Polybius, 6.11.2
11 Polybius, 9.24.6–7
12 Livy says that Hannibal's engineers cut down trees and, setting light to them, used them to super-heat rocks pre-soaked in vinegar, which made them eas-ier to smash apart: Livy, 21.37.2–3. But this story is doubtful, not least because of the scarcity of wood to fell at the summit of the Alps.
13 In the eighteenth century a complete skeleton of an elephant was found in one of the summit mountain passes of the Alps; but it is impossible to know if it was one of Hannibal's elephants that succumbed to the cold on those pitiful days of waiting: C. Torr, *Hannibal Crosses the Alps*, 1925, 28
14 Polybius, 3.60.6
15 Polybius, 3.56.4

CHAPTER 4: A NEW GENERATION ARISES

1 Cornelius Nepos, *Hannibal*, 13. (Nepos wrote a series of biographies of the lives of eminent military commanders from Mediterranean history.)
2 Diodorus Siculus, 25.10.4
3 Cornelius Nepos, *Hannibal*, 1.2–6; Polybius, 3.11; Livy, 21.14
4 Valerius Maximus, *Nine Books of Memorable Deeds and Sayings*, 9.3 ext. 2

5 Virgil, *Aeneid*, 1.621, 729; Silius Italicus, *Punica* 1.71–7

6 Indeed Erskine has recently argued that analyses of Polybius have tended to underplay the importance Polybius attributes to the make-up of Rome's army in its success: A. Erskine, 'How to Rule the World: Polybius Book 6 reconsidered', in B. Gibson and T. Harrison, *Polybius and His World: Essays in honour of F. Walbank*, 2013, 232–47

7 Polybius, 6.52

8 Polybius, 6.51

9 Polybius, 6.56. Erskine has underlined the efficiency of the Roman system as being crucial to its success, and its willingness to subordinate the individual to the needs of the whole: A. Erskine, 'How to Rule the World: Polybius Book 6 reconsidered', in B. Gibson and T. Harrison, *Polybius and His World: Essays in honour of F. Walbank*, 2013, 232–47

10 Arrian, *Anabasis*, 1.17; P. Rhodes and R. Osborne, *Greek Historical Inscriptions*, 2003, No. 84; *Sylloge inscriptionum graecarum, 3rd ed* , 284

11 M. Austin, *The Hellenistic World from Alexander to the Roman Conquest*, 2006, No. 55

12 S. Burstein, *The Hellenistic Age from the Battle of Ipsos to the Death of Kleopatra VII*, 1985, No. 16.11.4; 22.8; S. Carlsson, *Hellenistic Democracies: freedom, independence and political procedure in some east Greek city-states*, 2010

13 Polybius, 2.38.7

14 For discussion: F. Walbank, *Philip V of Macedon*, 1967, 18

15 A copy of the letter was said to have been found in the first century CE by the Emperor Claudius in the Roman archives: Suetonius, *Life of Claudius*, 25.3. For discussion of date: J. D. Grainger, *The Roman Wars of Antiochus the Great*, 2002, 11

16 A. Toynbee, *Between Oxus and Jumna*, 1961, 2

17 Cf. B. Cunliffe, *By Steppe, Desert and Ocean: the birth of Eurasia*, 2015, 160–4 (Assyrians), 204–12 (Persians)

18 Cf. B. Cunliffe, *By Steppe, Desert and Ocean: the birth of Eurasia*, 2015, 218–20; L. Martinez-Sève, 'The Spatial Organisation of Ai Khanoum, a Greek City in Afghanistan', *American Journal of Archaeology*, 2014 (118), 267–83

19 Cf. text and translation p. 274 n.39 in L. Martinez-Sève 'The Spatial Organisation of Ai Khanoum, a Greek City in Afghanistan', *American Journal of Archaeology*, 2014 (118); 267-83

20 *Analects*, 2.4

21 Plutarch, *Life of Alexander*, 62.9

22 Arrian, *Anabasis*, 5.6

23 In particular see the Sri Lankan early chronicles, the *Dipavamsa* and *Mahavamsa*. For discussion: I. Habib and V. Jha, *Mauryan India*, 2004, 20; U. Singh, *A History of Ancient and Medieval India*, 2008, 331

24 N. Khilnani, *Panorama of Indian Diplomacy*, 1981, 8. Cf. Rock Edict 13 (*Shahbazgrahi text*). For a recent translation: V. Singh (ed.), *Indian Society: Ancient to Modern, Vol. 1*, 2006, 201–25

25 Rock Edict 7 (section 7); cf. V. Singh (ed.), *Indian Society: ancient to modern, Vol. 1*, 2006, 201–25

26 Cf. A. Sen, 'Democracy as a Universal Value', in *Journal of Democracy*, 1999 (10.3), 3–17

27 H. Raychaudhuri, *Political History of Ancient India*, 1923, 348. Although H. G. Wells, in his *Outline of History*, 1920, comments: 'Amidst the tens of thousands of names of monarchs that crowd the columns of history, their majesties and graciousnesses and serenities and royal highnesses and the like, the name of Ashoka shines, and shines, almost alone, a star.'

28 C. Gizewski, 'Römische und alte chinesische Geschichte im Vergleich: Zur Möglichkeit eines gemeinsamen Altertumsbegriffs', in *Klio*, 1994 (76), 271–302; W. Scheidel, 'From the "Great Convergence" to the "First Great Divergence": Roman and Qin-Han state formation and its aftermath', in W. Scheidel (ed.), *Rome and China: comparative perspectives on ancient world empires*, 2009, 11–23

29 Wu Qi, *Wuzi* (text on military strategy), Section 2, 'Evaluating the Enemy'

30 Polybius, 2.31.7

31 Florus, *Epitome of Roman History*, 1.22.9

CHAPTER 5: MAKING CONNECTIONS

1 Livy, 23.34.1–10

2 Polybius, 5.104.7–8

3 Polybius, 5.101.10–102.1

4 Polybius, 7.9.1–17

5 Silius Italicus, *Punica*, 1.60. Cf. Seneca the Younger, *On Anger*, 2.5.4

6 Cf. Livy, 28.12.3; Cassius Dio, Fragment 54

7 This was despite the fact that Hannibal took the town and, according to Livy, gave orders that no one should be left alive: Livy, 21.14.3. Although Plutarch argues that he allowed the people to leave with their clothes, but not their weapons: Plutarch, *Moralia*, 248F

8 Cf. R. Garland, *Hannibal*, 2010.57

9 Polybius, 3.33.1–4

10 And just as Alexander the Great was said to have been told at Ammon that he was the son of the god himself, so too was it later said that Hannibal, setting out on his expedition to take on Rome, saw the vision of a youth sent by the great Carthaginian god Ba'al, who promised to lead them to victory: Livy, 21.22.5–9. Not for nothing did Hannibal's name mean literally 'touched by Ba'al'. Cf. R. Garland, *Hannibal*, 2010, 18

11 Polybius, 3.62.6–63.14

12 Polybius, 3.78.1–4

13 Polybius, 3.71–2

14 Polybius, 6.52.11

15 Livy, 22.4.2

16 Polybius, 3.84.7

17 S. Hornblower and A. Spawforth (eds), *Oxford Classical Dictionary*, 2003, 286. Polybius puts the casualties at 48,200 Romans killed: Polybius, 3.117.2–4

18 Cf. R. Garland, *Hannibal*, 2010, 87

19 Livy, 22.49.10

20 Polybius, 6.18.2

21 Polybius, 6.55

22 Polybius, 6.58

23 Which enabled the Roman dictator appointed to deal with the threat of Hannibal time not only to prepare Rome for siege, but also to raise more legions. It was, for some, 'perhaps his most important decision in the war': D. Hoyos, *Hannibal*, 2008, 51

24 Livy, 23.45.2–4

25 Polybius, 10.26; Livy, 27.31; Plutarch, *Moralia* 760A

26 Sima Qian, *Records of the Grand Historian (Shiji)*, 6

27 Sima Qian, *Records of the Grand Historian (Shiji)*, 6

28 It has been argued that the realism of these warriors is owed to Chinese interaction with the realistic sculpture of the Greek world brought east by Alexander the Great, although so far examples of Greek work can only be traced as far east as the Taklamakan desert: J. Boardman, *The Greeks in Asia*, 2015, 120; B. Cunliffe, *By Steppe, Ocean and Desert: the birth of Eurasia*, 2015, 267

29 Cf. B. Cunliffe, *By Steppe, Ocean and Desert: the birth of Eurasia*, 2015, 269–70

30 The Raphia Stele: M. Austin, *The Hellenistic World from Alexander to the Roman Conquest*, 2006, No. 276

31 Polybius, 5.58.13

CHAPTER 6: EMPIRES IN EAST AND WEST

1 The quantities were huge: in 1 BCE the Xiongnu were sent 30,000 rolls of silk and a similar amount of raw materials, as well as 370 items of clothing: P. Frankopan, *The Silk Roads*, 2015, 10

2 'Song of the Great Wind'. For discussion: V. Mair (ed.), *The Columbia History of Chinese Literature*, 2013, 249

3 Sima Qian, *Records of the Grand Historian (Shiji)*, 110

4 Sima Qian, *Records of the Grand Historian (Shiji)*, 110

5 Plutarch, *Life of Fabius*, 23.1

6 Livy, 27.51

7 Polybius, 11.3.6

8 Diodorus Siculus, 27.9; Livy, 30.20.6

9 Livy, 30.20.3–4

10 Polybius, 15.8.14

11 Polybius, 15.14.7

12 The geographer Strabo (14.2.5), at the end of the first century BCE, would describe Rhodes' political system as: 'The Rhodians care for the common people, although they do not live under a democracy.'

13 Polybius, 1.3.3–14; 1.4.11; 4.28.3–4

14 Livy, 31.6.3–5

15 Livy, 31.7.8–9, 11–12

16 Livy, 31.44.2–9; Polybius, 16.25–6

17 Plutarch, *Life of Flaminius*, 10.1–6

18 Polybius, 16.22

19 Justin, *Epitome (abridgement of the Philippic Histories of Pompeius Trogus)*, 30.2.8–30.3.4

20 Polybius, 18.50

21 Polybius, 18.51

22 Livy, 33.46.8

23 Livy, 33.49.5
24 Livy, 34.60.3–6
25 Cornelius Nepos, *Hannibal*, 1.2–6
26 Livy, 34.52.9
27 Livy, 35.33.8
28 Polybius, 20.8.1–5
29 Aulus Gellius, *Attic Nights*, 5.5.5
30 Appian, *Roman History Book 11: The Syrian Wars*, 4.16–20
31 Livy, 37.44.1–2
32 Polybius, 21.438
33 The geographer Strabo (11.11.1) even indicates that the Bactrians extended their empire east in this period as 'far as the Seres and the Phryni'. The Seres were inhabitants of the area of Serica – literally, 'the land where silk comes from'.
34 Juvenal, *Satires*, 10.160–2
35 Livy, 39.51.9

CODA

1 Polybius, 6.43–4
2 Justin, *Epitome (abridgement of the Philippic Histories of Pompeius Trogus)*, 41.6
3 Cf. B. Cunliffe, *By Steppe, Desert and Ocean: the birth of Eurasia*, 2015, 233–6
4 Strabo, 11.5.11; Justin, *Epitome (abridgement of the Philippic Histories of Pompeius Trogus)*, 42.2.2. Cf. W. Tarn, *The Greeks in Bactria and India*, 1966, 284–6
5 Sima Qian, *Records of the Grand Historian (Shiji)*, 123
6 H. Sidky, *The Greek Kingdom of Bactria from Alexander to Eucratides the Great*, 2000, 218
7 Cf. Sima Qian, *Records of the Grand Historian (Shiji)*, 123; P. Frankopan, *The Silk Roads*, 2015, xv; B. Cunliffe, *By Steppe, Desert and Ocean: the birth of Eurasia*, 2015, 261
8 Chinese officials had argued that giving the Xiongnu so much silk would soften their behaviour and bring them to be dependent on China and easily conquerable: Sima Qian, *Records of the Grand Historian (Shiji)*, 110
9 Cf. P. Frankopan, *The Silk Roads*, 2015, xv–xvi; F. Wood, *The Silk Road: 2000 years in the heart of Asia*, 2004; P. Perdue, 'East Asia and Central Eurasia', in J. Bentley (ed.), *The Oxford Handbook of World History*, 2011, 399–417 (404)
10 Sima Qian, *Records of the Grand Historian (Shiji)*, 123

PART III: RELIGIOUS CHANGE IN A CONNECTED WORLD

INTRODUCTION

1 Lactantius, *On the Deaths of the Persecutors*, 44.9
2 Yu Huan, *Weilue*, 'The Peoples of the West', section 12, written in the third century CE (quoted in the fifth-century CE *Sanguo Zhi*, 'Record of the Three Kingdoms')
3 Cf. B. Cunliffe, *By Steppe, Desert and Ocean: the birth of Eurasia*, 2015, 277–80
4 J. Boardman, *The Greeks in Asia*, 2015, 110
5 B. Cunliffe, *By Steppe, Desert and Ocean: the birth of Eurasia*, 2015, 279
6 J. Boardman, *The Greeks in Asia*, 2015, 73

7 Macedon was officially turned into a full Roman province with a Roman governor and military garrison in 147 BCE.
8 Cf. P. Frankopan, *The Silk Roads*, 2015, 15
9 Aelius Aristides, *To Rome*, 26.101–2
10 Cf. Josephus, *The Jewish War*, 19.162, 187
11 Aelius Aristides, *To Rome*, 26.60
12 Latin Panegyric 12(9), 2.4; 16.3
13 Lactantius, *On the Death of the Persecutors*, 44.7–8
14 D. Potter, *Constantine the Emperor*, 2013, 142
15 In 321 CE a Roman panegyrist called Nazarius would claim that Constantine's victory at Milvian Bridge had, above all, strengthened the power and prestige of the Senate, not least through its re-enactment of the struggle to found the republic: Latin Panegyric 4 (10), 35.2
16 Lactantius, *On the Death of the Persecutors*, 44.4–6
17 Eusebius, *Life of Constantine*, 1.28–32
18 Although one anonymous panegyrist also attributed Constantine's victory to a divine vision, but of the god Apollo, when Constantine visited a shrine in Gaul in 310: 'For you saw, I believe, O Constantine, your Apollo, accompanied by Victory, offering you laurel wreaths, each one of which carries a portent of 30 years ... you saw, and recognized yourself in the likeness of him to whom divine songs of the bards that prophesied that rule over the whole word was due.' Latin Panegyric 6 (7), 21.4–5
19 Gibbon, *Decline and Fall of the Roman Empire*: cruel and dissolute. Voltaire, *Philosophical Dictionary*: fortunate opportunist. Eusebius, *Life of Constantine*: heavenly authority
20 Polybius, 6.56.6
21 The fourth religion is of course Islam, which, in the fourth century CE, had still to begin its journey as a world religion. It was not until the early seventh century CE that the prophet Muhammed, believed to be the last of the law-bearing prophets to appear on earth after Jesus, Moses, Abraham, Noah and Adam, created a single Muslim community centred around Medina and Mecca in the Middle East.
22 'Hinduism' is a relatively recent word, first used in 1816–17, while the word 'Hindu' originally meant a description of people who lived around the Indus River. Modern Hinduism has no founder, no fixed canon, no organised priesthood, and is marked by a great variety of beliefs, practices, sects and traditions, which do not always equate with ancient practices. The scholarly terminology to describe ancient Hindu worship varies according to period: Vedic Ritualism, *c.* eighth to sixth centuries BCE; early Brahmanism *c.* sixth to second centuries BCE; Brahmanism *c.* second century BCE to second century CE; classical Hinduism fourth to twelfth centuries CE. In this text I refer collectively to these forms of worship as 'ancient Hinduism'.

CHAPTER 7: RELIGIOUS INNOVATION FROM INSIDE AND OUT

1 Our only evidence for Sri Gupta comes from the seventh-century CE Chinese traveller I Tsing and his *Biography of Eminent Monks Who Went to the Western World in Search of the Law during the Great T'ang Dynasty* (*Gaosend Zhuan*). I Tsing

visited India, and claims in the preface to his work that Sri Gupta had sup-ported Buddhist worshippers with the building of a temple and the allocation of revenue for its maintenance. For an English translation of the text: L. Lahiri, *Chinese Monks in India*, 1995 (for the section on Sri Gupta, see p.49)

2   A title which itself copies that taken first, we think, by Persian kings in the sixth to fourth centuries BCE.

3   Chandragupta I marked his accession by founding a new date era. The sys-tem he chose was one also used by the Licchavi family: R. Mookerji, *The Gupta Empire*, 1947, 15

4   *Rig Veda*, 19.90

5   For discussion: P. Robb, *A History of India*, 2002, 29

6   On knowledge of Homer in India: Dio Chrysostom, *Orations*, 53.6–8; T. McEvilley, *The Shape of Ancient Thought: Comparative studies in Greek and Indian philosophies*, 2002, 387. For discussion of possible influence also from East to West (of Indian texts on Virgil's Aeneid): P. Frankopan, *The Silk Roads*, 2015, 7

7   For discussion: R. Thapar, *Early India from the origins to CE 1300*, 2002, 282; A. K. Narain, 'Religious Policy and Toleration in Ancient India with particular reference to the Gupta Age', in B. L. Smith (ed.), *Essays on Gupta Culture*, 1983, 17–52; M. Brannigan, *Striking a Balance: a primer in traditional Asian values*, 2010

8   The picture that emerges of the powerful and high distinct *Brahmans* comes in no small part from the *dharma* sastric literature in the first centuries CE, which may have been intended to distance the *Brahman* from Buddhist (and Jainist) conceptions of religion, religious order and personnel. In essence, the image of the *Brahman* became more severe and distinct from the threat posed by alternative conceptions of religious community.

9   The hoards of Roman coins found in ancient Indian ports attest to the brisk and lucrative volume of trade from which India benefited in this era: S. Wolpert, *A New History of India*, 2009, 78

10 Though it has also been argued that the Licchavis were Buddhist and so would not have subscribed to the importance of *varna* regardless: A. Narain, 'Religious Policy and Toleration in Ancient India with Particular Reference to the Gupta Age', in B. Smith (ed.), *Essays on Gupta Culture*, 1983, 17–52

11 For discussion: P. Robb, *A History of India*, 2002, 40

12 Eusebius, *History of the Church*, 10.5.1–14; Lactantius, *On the Death of the Persecu-tors*, 48.2–12

13 Augustine, *Letters*, 88.2; Optatus, *Against the Donatists*, 1.22

14 Cf. L. Kohn, *Daoism and Chinese Culture*, 2001, 62; J. Miller, *Daoism: a short introduction*, 2003, 22

15 Scholars often refer to 'proto-Daoism' in the period before the second cen-tury CE, as it was not until then that formal Daoist movements were crystallised (e.g. the Way of Great Peace, Way of Orthodox Unity), which themselves continued to evolve through contact with Buddhism and Confu-cianism, as well as through contact with traditional Chinese religious attitudes, until the fifth century CE, when Daoism ritual was classified into three forms (by Lu Xiujing), which created the basis for Daoist influence on Chinese religious life: J. Miller, *Daoism: a short introduction*, 2003, 7–10; L. Kohn, *Daoism and Chinese Culture*, 2001, 30, 43–4

16 Particularly in the publication of Laozi's *Daodejing*, with commentary in the third century CE (by Wang Bi), as well as commentaries on the crucial *Zhuangzi* (named after its author) and the *Neige* text, which form the three principal texts of proto-Daoism. This was complemented in the second century CE by the creation of formal religious Daoist movements (the Way of Great Peace, Way of Orthodox Unity), as well as by ongoing interaction and development with the newly emerging procedures of government under the Han: J. Miller, *Daoism: a short introduction*, 2003; L. Kohn, *Daoism and Chinese Culture*, 2001

17 The 'five' Confucian virtues – humaneness, dutifulness, observance of ritual, wisdom and good faith – for instance, are not recorded in the *Analects* anywhere as a group. They are a later categorisation by Chinese intellectuals, who wanted five virtues to parallel the five elements, five canonical texts, etc: R. Dawson, *Confucius*, 1981, 51

18 Cf. Y. Kumar, *A History of Sino-Indian relations 1st century CE–7th century CE*, 2005, 34

19 Ancient Hinduism was spreading in this period into South-East Asia, mainly as a consequence of *Brahman* migration.

20 Cf. M. Wangu, *Buddhism*, 2006, 70

21 For discussion: E. Zürcher, *The Buddhist Conquest of China: the spread and adaptation of Buddhism in early medieval China*, 1959, 19–20

22 For discussion: E. Zürcher, *The Buddhist Conquest of China: the spread and adaptation of Buddhism in early medieval China*, 1959, 20

23 Wei Shou, *Wei Shu*, 114.1a; cf. E. Zürcher, *The Buddhist Conquest of China: the spread and adaptation of Buddhism in early medieval China*, 1959, 22

24 *History of the Later Han (Hou Han Shou)*, 12.5a (a fifth-century CE document covering the history of the Han dynasty, 6–138 CE)

25 Zhang Heng, *Poetical description of the Western Capital (Xijing Fu)*; cf. E. Zürcher, *The Buddhist Conquest of China: the spread and adaptation of Buddhism in early medieval China*, 1959, 29

26 Faxian, *Record of the Buddhist Kingdoms (Fuguoji)*, section 1

27 Y. Kumar, *A History of Sino-Indian relations 1st century CE–7th century CE*, 2005, 79

28 E. Zürcher, *The Buddhist Conquest of China: the spread and adaptation of Buddhism in early medieval China*, 1959, 52

29 He did so claiming that he was himself part of the Han dynasty, given that the Han had regularly sent royal Han brides to the Xiongnu leader as part of their bribes to the Xiongnu not to invade, from the third century BCE onwards. At the same time he claimed himself to be desecended from Maodun, the heroic and bloodthirsty Xiongnu leader from the third to second centuries BCE: E. Zürcher, *The Buddhist Conquest of China: the spread and adaptation of Buddhism in early medieval China*, 1959, 58, 83

30 *Sogdian Ancient Letters*, No. 2

31 Cassius Dio, *Roman History Book*, 62, 63.7.1

32 Moses Khorenatsi, *History of the Armenians*, 3.60–2

33 His opening too is suitably grand, in the style of Herodotus: 'For even though we are small and very limited in numbers and have been conquered many times by foreign kingdoms, yet too, many acts of bravery have been performed in our land, worthy of being written and remembered, but of which no one has bothered to write down': Moses Khorenatsi, *History of the Armenians*, 1.4

34 For discussion: S. Payaslian, *The History of Armenia from the Origins to the Present*, 2007, 34; R. Thomson, *Agathangelos: History of the Armenians translation and commentary*, 1976; R. Thomson, *Moses Khorenatsi: History of the Armenians translation and commentary*, 2006

35 Agathangelos, *History of the Armenians*, 152; Moses Khorenatsi, *History of the Armenians*, 1.82

36 E.g. R. Thomson, *Studies in Armenian Literature and Christianity*, 1994, 31; R. Thomson, *Agathangelos: History of the Armenians translation and commentary*, 1976, xxxv–vi; B. Zekiyan, 'Christianity to Modernity', in E. Herzig and M. Kurkchiyan (eds), *The Armenians: Past and present in the making of national identity*, 2005, 41–64. Indeed Thomson argues, as do other historians, that this Tiridates replaced on the throne in 298 was actually Tiridates IV, not III. For discussion: C. Toumanoff, 'The Third Century Armenian Arsacids: a chronological and genealogical commentary', *REA*, 1969 (6), 233–81

37 Agathangelos, *History of the Armenians*, 777–90

38 S. Payaslian, *The History of Armenia*, 2007, 35

39 Thaddeus: Phaustus, *History of the Armenians*, 3.1; Moses Khorenatsi, *History of the Armenians*, 2.33–4

40 Tertullian, *Against the Jews*, 7

41 S. Payaslian, *The History of Armenia*, 2007, 35

42 Thirteen years (in section 122 of Agathangelos's *History*) or fifteen years (in section 211) after Tiridates' return to power (in 287/8 CE, according to Agathangelos and Moses). Thirteen years takes us to 300/1 CE, the official date celebrated in today's Armenian Church (in 2001 Armenia celebrated the 1,700th anniversary of the event as a defining moment in Armenian history), and fifteen years takes us to 302/3 CE. Cf. Sozomen, *Ecclesiastical History*, 2.8; V. Nersessian (ed.), *Treasures from the Ark: 1700 years of Armenian Christian art*, 2001; D. Lang, *Armenia: Cradle of civilisation*, 1970, 158; A. Casiday and F. Norris, *Cambridge History of Christianity, Vol. 2: Constantine to 600*, 2007, 136–9

43 For discussion: R. Cormack, 'Introduction', in V. Nersessian (ed.), *Treasures from the Ark: 1700 years of Armenian Christian art*, 2001, 11–25; N. Garsoian, 'The Arsakuni Dynasty: CE 12–[180?]–428', in R. G. Hovannisian (ed.), *The Armenian People from Ancient to Modern Times, Vol. 1: the Dynastic periods from antiquity to the 14th century*, 2004, 63–94; R. Thomson, *Studies in Armenian Literature and Christianity*, 1994, 31; R. Thomson, *Agathangelos: History of the Armenians translation and commentary*, 1976, xxxv–vi, lii; E. Gulbenkian, 'The Date of King Trdat's Conversion', in *Handes Amsorya: Zeitschrift für armenische philologie*, 1991, 75–87

44 Agathangelos, *History of the Armenians*, 150

45 Agathangelos, *History of the Armenians*, 181

46 Agathangelos, *History of the Armenians*, 198

47 Agathangelos, *History of the Armenians*, 212

48 Gulbenkian has suggested that this might have been the result of ergot-poisoning, from eating bread made with contaminated rye flour: E. Gulbenkian, 'The Date of King Trdat's Conversion', in *Handes Amsorya: Zeitschrift für armenische philologie*, 1991, 75–87

49 S. Payaslian, *The History of Armenia*, 2007, 35; R. Blockley, *East Roman Foreign Policy*, 1992, 10–11

50 S. Payaslian, *The History of Armenia*, 2007, 36
51 S. Payaslian, *The History of Armenia*, 2007, 35

CHAPTER 8: ENFORCING, MIXING AND MOULDING RELIGION

1   Agathangelos, in his fifth-century CE *History of the Armenians*, claims the meeting took place in Rome (874–5), although scholars have doubted the physical possibility of both men being in Rome in 324 CE.
2   In the twelfth century a fictional letter (the *Letter of Love and Concord*) between Constantine, Pope Silvester in Rome, King Tiridates and Gregory (or St Gregory the Illuminator, as he became known) was written, purporting to originate from this meeting: Z. Pogossian, *The Letter of Love and Concord: a revised diplomatic edition with historical and textual comments and English translation*, 2010
3   Agathangelos, *History of the Armenians*, 875
4   *Letter of Love and Concord*, sections 2–6; cf. Z. Pogossian, *The Letter of Love and Concord: a revised diplomatic edition with historical and textual comments and English translation*, 2010
5   *Letter of Love and Concord*, section 7
6   *Letter of Love and Concord*, section 8
7   *Letter of Love and Concord*, sections 12, 14–15, 16–17
8   *Letter of Love and Concord*, section 20
9   Agathangelos, *History of the Armenians*, 882
10 Strabo, 11.14.16
11 S. Payaslian, *The History of Armenia*, 2007, 36
12 Agathangelos, *History of the Armenians*, 779, 813
13 Agathangelos, *History of the Armenians*, 786, 778–9
14 Agathangelos, *History of the Armenians*, 809–15
15 Cf. A. Redgate, *The Armenians*, 1998, 107
16 Agathangelos, *History of the Armenians*, 814, 840
17 S. Payaslian, *The History of Armenia*, 2007, 36; G. Bournoutian, *A History of the Armenian People*, 1993, 63
18 Aganthangelos, *History of the Armenians*, 735
19 Agathangelos, *History of the Armenians*, 837
20 Agathangelos, *History of the Armenians*, 793
21 Agathangelos, *History of the Armenians*, 833, 834, 835
22 Agathangelos, *History of the Armenians*, 859
23 Agathangelos, *History of the Armenians*, 861
24 Moses Khorenatsi, *History of the Armenians*, 2.92
25 Moses Khorenatsi, *History of the Armenians*, 2.92
26 S. Payaslian, *The History of Armenia*, 2007, 38
27 Moses Khorenatsi, *History of the Armenians*, 2.91
28 Moses Khorenatsi, *History of the Armenians*, 3.2
29 Moses Khorenatsi, *History of the Armenians*, 3.3
30 Optatus, *Against the Donatists*, 9
31 Eusebius, *Life of Constantine*, 2.60.1
32 Optatus, *Against the Donatists*, 10
33 Optatus, *Against the Donastists*, 3.3
34 Eusebius, *Life of Constantine*, 2.71.7

35 Socrates, *Ecclesiastical History*, 1.6
36 Socrates, *Ecclesiastical History*, 1.8
37 Eusebius, *Life of Constantine*, 1.44.3
38 Aurelius Victor(?), *Epitome of the Caesars*, 41.11–12
39 Aurelius Victor(?), *Epitome of the Caesars*, 41.11–12
40 Allahabad Pillar inscription: J. Fleet, *Corpus Inscriptionum Indicarum, Vol. 3: Inscriptions of the early Guptas and their successors*, 1888, No. 1
41 Eran Stone Pillar, lines 14–16: M. Bannerjee, *A Study of Important Gupta Inscriptions*, 1976, 12; J. Fleet, *Corpus Inscriptionum Indicarum, Vol. 3: Inscriptions of the early Guptas and their successors*, 1888, No. 2
42 Allahabad Pillar inscription: J. Fleet, *Corpus Inscriptionum Indicarum, Vol. 3: Inscriptions of the early Guptas and their successors*, 1888, No. 1
43 Mathura inscription: J. Fleet, *Corpus Inscriptionum Indicarum, Vol. 3: Inscriptions of the early Guptas and their successors*, 1888, No. 4
44 The horse-sacrifice is also present in the fourteenth book of the great Indian epic, the *Mahabharata* (very much in vogue in this era). The scene presents the king and *Brahmans* working together (the king receives the earth from the *Brahman* in return for a sacrificial fee) within a Vishnu-centred world conducting the horse-sacrifice.
45 Allahabad Pillar inscription: J. Fleet, *Corpus Inscriptionum Indicarum, Vol. 3: Inscriptions of the early Guptas and their successors*, 1888, No. 1
46 Cf. R. Mookerji, *The Gupta Empire*, 1947, 30
47 China was also heavily hit by plague in the period 310–22 CE: I. Morris, *Why The West Rules – For Now*, 2010, 296
48 Cf. L. Stryk (ed.), *World of the Buddha: An introduction to buddhist literature*, 1968, xxxiv
49 J. Wyatt, *China: Dawn of a golden age 200–750 AD*, 2004, Cat. No. 44
50 Mouzi, *Treatise of Settling Doubts (Lihuolun)*, 26
51 *Analects*, 12.11
52 Interestingly in the surviving correspondence, however, between the fourth-century Buddhist monks Hui-Yuan and Kumarajiva on issues of doctrine no allusion to Chinese scripture or philosophy is used. It seems to have been a very purposeful 'outward-facing' technique for teaching to non-Buddhists: E. Zürcher, *The Buddhist Conquest of China: the spread and adaptation of Buddhism in early medieval China*, 1959, 12
53 This co-influence also led to the creation of Daoist monasteries in China following the Buddhist tradition: J. Miller, *Daoism: a short introduction*, 2003, 10
54 E.g. J. Wyatt, *China: Dawn of a golden age 200–750 AD*, 2004, Cat. No. 104

CHAPTER 9: RELIGION AND RULE

1 Anonymous, *Life of Constantine* (*Bibliotheca Hagiographica Graeca* 364)
2 *Inscriptiones Latinae Selectae*, 705
3 Optatus, *Against the Donatists*, 3.3
4 Donatists were officially declared heretical only in 405 CE. The last indisputable evidence for them comes in 596 CE, when the Bishop of Rome demanded sterner measures to deal with Donatists in Numidia.
5 Julian, *Letter to the Athenians*, 247–9

6 Such a war to expand Roman power into the east against the Sassanids was said to have been on Constantine's 'to-do' list as well, only being prevented by his illness and death in 337 CE.

7 Julian, *Hymn to King Helios*, (Oration 4) 130C

8 Socrates, *Ecclesiastical History*, 3.21

9 Philostorgius, *Church History*, 7.1c

10 Libanius, *Orations*, 30.8–9

11 St Jerome, *Letter to Laeta*, 107.1

12 Ambrose was not above insulting the imperial family, too: he called Helena, the mother of Constantine and discoverer of the True Cross in Jerusalem, a *stabularia* – a tavern maid: Ambrose, *On the Death of Theodosius*, 42

13 Ambrose *On the Death of Theodosius* 28

14 St Augustine, *Confessions*, 6.9.19

15 Macarius, *Canonical Letter to the Armenians*

16 Phaustus, *History of the Armenians*, 3.13

17 Phaustus, *History of the Armenians*, 3.12

18 Phaustus, *History of the Armenians*, 3.12

19 Phaustus, *History of the Armenians*, 3.12

20 Moses Khorenatsi, *History of the Armenians*, 3.14

21 S. Payaslian, *The History of Armenia*, 2007, 39; R. Blockley, *East Roman Foreign Policy*, 1992, 11–12

22 Phaustus, *History of the Armenians*, 3.13

23 Phaustus, *History of the Armenians*, 3.19

24 Phaustus, *History of the Armenians*, 4.3

25 Phaustus, *History of the Armenians*, 4.4

26 Moses Khorenatsi, *History of the Armenians*, 3.20

27 Phaustus, *History of the Armenians*, 5.24

28 S. Payaslian, *The History of Armenia*, 2007, 39–40; N. Garsoian, 'The Problem of Armenian Integration into the Byzantine Empire', in H. Ahrweiler and A. Laiou (eds), *Studies on the Internal Diaspora of the Byzantine Empire*, 1998, 54

29 Mehrauli Pillar inscription, New Delhi. Cf. M. C. Joshi, S. K. Gupta and S. Goyal (eds), *King Chandra and the Mehrauli Pillar*, 1989

30 J. Fleet, *Corpus Inscriptionum Indicarum, Vol. 3: Inscriptions of the early Gupta kings and their successors*, 1888, No. 3

31 Although most probably with some earlier antecedents, e.g. the Naga temples in Sonkh, cf. D. Chakrabarti, *India: an archaeological history*, 2009

32 Mathura Pillar inscription: J. Fleet, *Corpus Inscriptionum Indicarum, Vol. 3: Inscriptions of the early Gupta kings and their Successors*, 1888, No. 4

33 Sanchi Stone inscription: J. Fleet, *Corpus Inscriptionum Indicarum, Vol. 3: Inscriptions of the Early Gupta Kings and their Successors*, 1888, No. 5

34 T. Watters, *On Xuanzang's Travels in India, Vol. 2*, 1840–1901, 165

35 The Chinese Buddhist monk I Tsing spent many years studying at Nalanda in the seventh century CE. Alongside his *Biography of Eminent Monks,* he also wrote an account of his travels and of the university: *A Record of the Buddhist Religion: As practiced in India and the Malay archipelago*. For an English translation: J. Takakusu, 1966

36 It is this complete eshewal of hierarchy that has led some, including Amartya Sen, to argue for democratic tendencies in the beliefs of Buddhists and

Jainists in India from the era of their inception, the sixth century BCE, as a counterpoint to the European 'invention' of democracy in Greece: A. Sen, 'Democracy as a Universal Value', in *Journal of Democracy*, 1999 (10.3), 3–17

37 Faxian, *Record of the Buddhist Kingdoms (Fuguoji)*, section on the 'Middle Kingdom'; cf. H. Giles, *The Travels of Faxian (399–414 CE)*, 1956, 20–1

38 *Biography of Buddhist Monks (Gaoseng zhuan)*, 9.385.3.2 (compiled mid-sixth century CE by Huijiau, offering biographies of 257 major and 243 minor biographies of Buddhist monks in China from the first to early sixth centuries CE). See also the *Biqiuni zhuan (Biographies of Buddhist nuns)* compiled in the early sixth century CE.

39 *Book of Jin (Jinshu)*, 64.8b (historical account of the Jin from 265 to 420 CE)

40 *Collection of Apologetic Work (Hongming ji)*, 2.8.2.22 (created in the early sixth century by the Buddhist monk Sengyou, this was expanded in the seventh century by the monk Daoxuan in the *Guang Hongming Ji*)

41 *Collection of Apologetic Work (Hongming ji)*, 3.17.1.7

42 *Book of Jin (Jinshu)*, 64.8a

43 *Collection of Apologetic Work (Hongming ji)*, 12.81.2.7

CODA

1 Scholars have also argued for Buddhist influences on the West: the sect of the *therapeutai* in Alexandria in Egypt is very similar, in doctrinal belief, to Buddhists: P. Frankopan, *The Silk Roads*, 2015, 27

2 Cf. J. Boardman, *The Greeks in Asia*, 2015, 170, 186, 217

3 Eusebius, *Oratio de laudibus Constantini*, 3.6

4 Eusebius, *Oratio de laudibus Constantini*, 3.6

5 In the sixth century CE, cf. John Malalas, *Chronographia*, Book 18, for the equating of democracy and mob rule.

6 B. Zekiyan, 'Christianity to Modernity', in E. Herzig and M. Kurkchiyan (eds), *The Armenians: Past and present in the making of national identity*, 2005, 41–64; R. Thomson, *Studies in Armenian Literature and Christianity*, 1994, 24–30

7 A. Casiday and F. Norris (eds), *Cambridge History of Christianity*, Vol. 2, 2007, 139

8 Ammianus Marcellinus, *Affairs of State (Resgestae)*, 31.2

9 For discussion: B. Cunliffe, *By Steppe, Desert and Ocean: the birth of Eurasia*, 2015, 335–7

10 Cf. W. Scheidel, 'Comparing ancient worlds: comparative history as comparative advantage', in *2012 Proceedings of the International Symposium of Ancient World History in China*, forthcoming

CONCLUSION

1 Livy, 9.17–19

2 L. Dian Rainey, *Confucius and Confucianism: the essentials*, 2010, 178–9

3 A. Jin, *Confucius: a life of thought and politics*, 2007, 11

4 Cf. L. Dian Rainey, *Confucius and Confucianism: the essentials*, 2010, 184–93; L. Shihlien Hsü, *The Political Philosophy of Confucianism*, 1975, 175–97

5 Cf. M. Puett, 'Ghosts, Gods and the Coming Apocalypse', in W. Scheidel (ed.), *State Power in Ancient China and Rome*, 2015, 230–59; P. Frankopan, *The Silk Roads*, 2015, 28

6 Cf. P. Frankopan, *The Silk Roads*, 2015, 44
7 The idea that the past is something dead, and thus subject to 'laboratory historical analysis', did not appear until the eighteenth century; cf. Z. Schiffman, *The Birth of the Past*, 2011; M. De Certeau, *The Writing of History*, 1988
8 Cf. M. Puett, 'Classical Chinese Historical Thought', in P. Duara, V. Murthy and A. Sartori (eds), *A Companion to Global Historical Thought*, 2012, 34–46
9 Cf. M. Puett, 'Classical Chinese Historical Thought', in P. Duara, V. Murthy and A. Sartori (eds), *A Companion to Global Historical Thought*, 2012, 34–46
10 F. Cox Jensen, 'The Legacy of Greece and Rome', in P. Duara, V. Murthy and A. Sartori (eds), *A Companion to Global Historical Thought*, 2012, 139–52
11 D. Woolf, *A Global History of History*, 2011, 53
12 Cf. G. Lloyd, *The Ambitions of Curiosity: Understanding the world in ancient Greece and China*, 2002, 18–19
13 This sense of history as intended to give warnings and exemplars of good (and bad) behaviour to current rulers is present, of course, in the history of numerous societies, e.g. Livy's Preface to *Ab Urbe Condita*.
14 Cf J. Tanner, 'Ancient Greece, Early China: Sino-Hellenic studies and comparative approaches to the Classical world: a review article', in *Journal of Hellenic Studies*, 2009 (129), 89–109; F. Mutschler and A. Mittag (eds), *Conceiving the Empire: Rome and China compared*, 2008
15 Although they still needed to impress and persuade their audience, as well as be wary of whom they criticised: G. Lloyd, *The Ambitions of Curiosity: Understanding the world in ancient Greece and China*, 2002, 18–19
16 Cf. 'the empty shelf' of Indian history: R. Salomon, 'Ancient India: peace within and war without', in K. Raaflaub (ed.), *War and Peace in the Ancient World*, 2007, 53–65
17 Cf. R. Thapar, 'History as a way of remembering the past: Early India', in P. Duara, V. Murthy and A. Sartori (eds), *A Companion to Global Historical Thought*, 2012, 21–33. The absences of such traditions are ascribed to the absence of the same coherence of political community and hierarchical organisation as is found in, say, Rome or China alongside the plethora of ethnic groups and languages as well as religious traditions: D. Woolf, *A Global History of History*, 2011, 65
18 Cf. I. Harris, 'Buddhist Worlds', in P. Duara, V. Murthy and A. Sartori (eds), *A Companion to Global Historical Thought*, 2012, 63–77, and M. Puett, 'Classical Chinese Historical Thought', in P. Duara, V. Murthy and A. Sartori (eds), *A Companion to Global Historical Thought*, 2012, 34–46
19 Such longer cosmic (rather than dynastic) cycles of time came into vogue also in Chinese history in the era at the end of the Han dynasty – just as Buddhism started to become more well known within China: M. Puett, 'Classical Chinese Historical Thought', in P. Duara, V. Murthy and A. Sartori (eds), *A Companion to Global Historical Thought*, 2012, 34–46
20 I. Harris, 'Buddhist Worlds', in P. Duara, V. Murthy and A. Sartori (eds), *A Companion to Global Historical Thought*, 2012, 63–77
21 Using Athens as an example to castigate modern democracies: e.g. L. J. Salmons II, *What's Wrong with Democracy?: from Athenian practice to American worship*, 2004; E. Sagan, *The Honey and the Hemlock: Democracy and paranoia in ancient Athens and Modern America*, 1991. Cf. P. Cartledge, 'Democracy, origins of: contributions to a debate', in K. Raaflaub, J. Ober and R. Wallace, *Origins*

of Democracy in Ancient Greece, 2007, 155–69; M. Hansen, *The Tradition of Ancient Greek Democracy and Its Importance for Modern Democracy*, 2005; R. Dahl, *On Democracy*, 1998

22 Sir Walter Raleigh, *The History of the World, Vols. 1–2*, 1614

23 Divergence in the fifth to sixth centuries CE between East and West: the 'First' divergence: W. Scheidel, 'From the "Great Convergence" to the "First Great Divergence"': Roman and Qin-Han state formation and its aftermath', in W. Scheidel (ed.), *Rome and China: Comparative perspectives on ancient world empires*, 2009, 11–23. The 'Second' Great Divergence in the eighteenth century: K. Pomeranz, *The Great Divergence: China, Europe and the making of the modern world*, 2000; I. Morris, *The Measure of Civilisation: how social development decides the fate of nations*, 2013

Select Bibliography for Further Reading

PART I

Athens: J. Smith, *Athens Under the Tyrants*, 1989; J. Dunn, *Democracy: the unfinished journey 508 BC to AD 1993*, 1993; K. Vlassopoulos, *Politics: Antiquity and its legacy*, 2009; R. Osborne, *Greek History*, 2004; H. Sancisi-Weerdenburg (ed.), *Peisistratos and the Tyranny: a re-appraisal of the evidence*, 2000; John K. Davies, 'The historiography of archaic Greece', in K. Raaflaub and H. van Wees, *Companion to Archaic Greece*, 2009, pp.3–21; A. Snodgrass, *Archaic Greece: the age of experiment*, 1980; A. Queyrel, *Athènes: la cité archaique et classique*, 2003; M. Ostwald, *From Popular Sovereignty to the Sovereignty of Law: Law, society, politics in 5th century Athens*, 1986; R. Osborne, *Greece in the Making: 1200–479 BC*, 1996; R. Osborne, *Athens and its Democracy*, 2010; H. Beck (ed.), *Companion to Greek Government*, 2013; C. Carey, *Democracy in Classical Athens*, 2000; R. K. Sinclair, *Democracy and Participation in Athens*, 1988; M. I. Finley, *Democracy Ancient and Modern*, 1973; J. Ober, *The Athenian Revolution: Essays in ancient Greek democracy and political theory*, 1996; J. Ober and C. Hedrick (eds), *Demokratia: a conversation on democracies, ancient and modern*, 1996; C. Farrar, *The Origins of Democratic Thinking: the invention of politics in classical Athens*, 1988; K. Raaflaub, J. Ober and R. Wallace (eds), *Origins of Democracy in Ancient Greece*, 2007; P. Cartledge, *Ancient Greek Political Thought in Practice*, 2009; P. Cartledge, *Democracy: a life*, 2016

Rome: K. Bringmann, *A history of the Roman Republic*, 2007; G. Mason, *A concise history of Republican Rome*, 1973; P. Matyszak, *Chronicle of the Roman Republic*, 2003; H. Flower (ed.), *The Cambridge Companion to the Roman Republic*, 2004; T. Cornell, *The Beginnings of Rome: Italy and Rome from the Bronze Age to the Punic wars 1000–264 BC*, 1995; R. Bloch, *The Origins of Rome*, 1960; A. Everitt, *The Rise of Rome: the making of the world's greatest empire*, 2012; D. Potter (ed.), *Rome in the Ancient World: from Romulus to Justinian*, 2009; A. J. Ammerman, 'Looking at Early Rome with Fresh Eyes: transforming the landscape', in J. DeRose-Evans (ed.), *Companion to the Archaeology of the Roman Republic*, 2013, pp.169–80; D. Gwynn, *The Roman Republic: a very short introduction*, 2010; F. Millar, *The Roman Republic in Political*

Thought, 2002; R. Morstein-Marx and N. Rosenstein (eds), *Companion to the Roman Republic*, 2006; K. Raaflaub (ed.), *Social Struggles in Archaic Rome: new perspectives on the struggle of the orders*, 2005; D. Kagan, *Problems in Ancient History, Vol. 2: the Roman world*, 1975; G. Forsythe, *A Critical History of Early Rome: from prehistory to the first Punic war*, 2005; F. Pina Polo, *The Consul in Rome*, 2011

China: J. Roberts, *A History of China*, 1999; F. Michael, *China Through the Ages: history of a civilization*, 1986; L. Jun, *Chinese Civilisation in the Making: 1766–221 BC*, 1996; R. Dawson, *Confucius*, 1981; D. Keightley (ed.), *The Origins of Chinese Civilisation*, 1983; D. Howard-Smith, *Confucius*, 1973; D. C. Lau, *Mencius*, 1970; B. Watson, *Hsün-Tzu: Basic Writings*, 1963; D. Munro, *The Concept of Man in Early China*, 1969; J. Ching, *Confucianism and Christianity*, 1977; X. Yuanxiang, *Confucius: a philosopher for the ages*, 2006; F. Flanagan, *Confucius, the Analects and Western Education*, 2011; L. Dian Rainey, *Confucius and Confucianism: the essentials*, 2010; W. Teh-Yao, *Confucius and Plato's Ideals on a Republic*, 1978; M. Sim, *Remastering Morals with Aristotle and Confucius*, 2007; L. Stover, *Imperial China and the State Cult of Confucius*, 2005; P. Goldin, *After Confucius: Studies in Early Chinese Philosophy*, 2005; L. Shihlien Hsü, *The Political Philosophy of Confucianism*, 1975; L. von Falkenhausen, *Chinese Society in the Age of Confucius 1000–250 BC: the archaeological evidence*, 2006; A. Jin, *Confucius: a life of thought and politics*, 2007; W. Scheidel (ed.), *Rome and China: Comparative perspectives on ancient world empires*, 2009; H. Jin Kim, *Ethnicity and Foreigners in Ancient Greece and China*, 2009; L. Raphals, *Knowing Words: Wisdom and cunning in classical traditions of China and Greece*, 1992; S. Shankman and S. Durrant (eds), *Early China/Ancient Greece: Thinking through comparisons*, 2002

PART II

Hannibal and Rome: Sir Gavin de Beer, *Alps and Elephants: Hannibal's March*, 1955; Sir Gavin de Beer, *Hannibal: the struggle for power in the Mediterranean*, 1969; J. F. Lazenby, *Hannibal's War: A military history of the 2nd Punic war*, 1978; D. Hoyos, *Hannibal's Dynasty: Power and politics in the western mediterranean 247–183 BC*, 2003; T. Bath, *Hannibal's Campaigns*, 1981; G. Charles Picard and C. Picard Stevens, *Carthage*, 1987; R. Garland, *Hannibal*, 2010; S. Lancel, *Hannibal*, 1998; D. Hoyos, *Hannibal: Rome's greatest enemy*, 2008; A. Goldsworthy, *The Punic Wars*, 2000; D. Proctor, *Hannibal's March in History*, 1971; J. Prevas, *Hannibal crosses the Alps: the invasion of Italy and the 2nd Punic war*, 1998; S. Lancel, *Carthage: a history*, 1995; A. Toynbee, *Hannibal's Legacy: the Hannibalic war's effects on Roman life*, 1965; T. Cornell, B. Rankov and B. Sabin (eds), *The 2nd Punic War: A reappraisal*, 1996; N. Rosenstein, *Rome and the Mediterranean 29–146 BC*, 2012; D. Hoyos, *Unplanned Wars: the origins of the first and second Punic wars*, 1998; J.-P. Jospin and L. Dalaine, *Hannibal et les alpes: une traversée, un mythe*, 2011; C. Torr, *Hannibal Crosses the Alps*, 1925; D. Hoyos (ed.), *The Blackwell Companion to the Punic Wars*, 2011; N. Fields, *Hannibal: Leadership, strategy, conflict*, 2010; H. Scullard, *Scipio Africanus: soldier and politician*, 1970

Philip V of Macedon and Greece: G. Shipley, *The Greek World after Alexander the Great 323–30 BC*, 2000; P. Edwell, 'War Abroad: Spain, Sicily, Macedon, Africa', in D. Hoyos (ed.), *The Blackwell Companion to the Punic Wars*, 2011, pp.320–38; N. Rosenstein, *Rome and the Mediterranean 290–146 BC*, 2012; F. Walbank, *Philip V of*

Macedon, 1967; S. Dmitriev, *The Greek Slogan of Freedom and Early Roman Politics in Greece*, 2011; T. Harrison and B. Gibson (eds), *Polybius and his world: essays in memory of F. W. Walbank*, 2013

Antiochus III and the Seleucid Empire: D. Gera, *Judea and Mediterranean Politics: 219–161 BC*, 1998; L. Hannestad, 'The Economy of Koile-Syria after the Seleucid conquest', in Z. Archibald and J. K. Davies, *The Economies of Hellenistic Societies, 3rd–1st centuries BC*, 2011, pp.251–79; A. M. Eckstein, *Mediterranean Anarchy, Interstate War and the Rise of Rome*, 2006; A. M. Eckstein, *Rome Enters the Greek East: From anarchy to hierarchy in the hellenistic mediterranean 230–170 BC*, 2008; J. D. Grainger, *The Roman War of Antiochus the Great*, 2002; J. Ma, *Antiochus III and the Cities of Western Asia Minor*, 1999; M. Holleaux, *Rome, la Grèce et les monarchies Hellénistiques au IIIe siècle av. J. C.*, 1921; F. Walbank, *A Historical Commentary on Polybius* (3 vols), 1957–79; M. J. Taylor, *Antiochus the Great*, 2013; P. Green, *Alexander to Actium: the historical evolution of the Hellenistic age*, 1990; J. Lerner, *The Impact of Seleucid Decline on the Eastern Iranian Plateau*, 1999

Bactria, Central Asia and India: B. A. Litvinsky (ed.), *History of Civilizations of Central Asia (Vols 1–3)*, 1996; C. Beckwith, *Empires of the Silk Road: a history of central Eurasia from the bronze age to the present*, 2009; D. Anthony, *The Horse, the Wheel and Language: a history of central Eurasia from the bronze age to the present*, 2007; P. Leriche, 'The Greeks in the Orient: from Syria to Bactria', in V. Karageorghis (ed.), *The Greeks Beyond the Aegean: from Marseilles to Bactria*, 2002, pp.78–128; P. Leriche, 'Bactria: land of a thousand cities', in G. Hermann and J. Cribb (eds), *After Alexander: Central Asia before Islam*, 2007, pp.121–54; G. Lecuyot, 'Ai Khanoum Reconstructed', in G. Hermann and J. Cribb (eds), *After Alexander: Central Asia before Islam*, 2007, pp.155–62; F. Holt, *Alexander the Great and Bactria*, 1989; F. Holt, *Thundering Zeus: the making of Hellenistic Bactria*, 1999; F. Holt, *Lost World of the Golden King*, 2012; H. Sidky, *The Greek Kingdom of Bactria from Alexander to Eucratides the Great*, 2000; W. McGovern, *The Early Empires of Central Asia*, 1939; W. W. Tarn, *The Greeks in Bactria and India*, 1966; A. K. Narin, *The Indo-Greeks*, 1957; G. M. Cohen, *The Hellenistic Settlements in the East from Armenia and Mesopotamia to Bactria and India*, 2013; I. Habib and V. Jha, *Mauryan India*, 2004; U. Kiran Jha, *Some Aspects of Mauryan Society*, 2011; G. M. Bongard-Levin, *Mauryan India*, 1985; N. M. Khilnani, *Panorama of Indian Diplomacy*, 1981; I. Habib, *Post-Mauryan India 200 BC–AD 300*, 2012; E. Rosen Stone, 'Greece and India: the Ashokan Pillars revisited', in V. Karageorghis (ed.), *The Greeks Beyond the Aegean: from Marseilles to Bactria*, 2002, pp.167–88

China and the Nomadic Tribes: K. Czeglédy, *From East to West: the age of nomadic migrations in Eurasia*, 1983; J. R. Gardiner-Garden, *Apollodorus of Artemita and the Central Asian Skythians*, 1987; C. Rapin, 'Nomads and the shaping of central Asia: from the Early Iron Age to the Kushan period', in G. Hermann and J. Cribb (eds), *After Alexander: Central Asia before Islam*, 2007, pp.29–72; K. Abdullaev, 'Nomad Migration in Central Asia', in G. Hermann and J. Cribb (eds), *After Alexander: Central Asia before Islam*, 2007, pp.73–98; T. Barfield, 'The Hsiung-nu imperial confederacy: organization and foreign policy', in *Journal of Asian Studies*, 1981 (41), 45–61; P. Golden, *Central Asia in World History*, 2011; T. J. Barfield, *The Perilous Frontier: Nomadic empires and China 221 BC to AD 1757*, 1989; N. Di Cosmo, *Ancient China and its enemies: the rise of nomadic power in East Asian history*, 2002; R. Brentjes, *Arms of the Sakas*, 1996; H. M. Tanner, *China: A*

History, 2009; S. Whitefield, *Life along the Silk Road*, 1999; Chu-Shu Chang, *The Rise of the Chinese Empire, Vol. 2: Frontier, immigration and empire in Han China 130 BC–AD 157*, 2007; P. Nancarrow, *Early China and the Wall*, 1978; J. Man, *The Terracotta Army: China's first emperor and the birth of a nation*, 2008; M. Edward Lewis, *The Early Chinese Empires Qin and Han*, 2007; Li Feng, *Early China: a social and cultural history*, 2013; P. Ropp, *China in world history*, 2010; W. L. Idema and E. Zürcher (eds), *Thought and law in Qin and Han China: studies dedicated to Anthony Hulsewé on the occasion of his eightieth birthday*, 1990; M. Loewe, *Bing: from farmer's son to magistrate in Han China*, 2011; M. Loewe, *Everyday Life in Early Imperial China During the Han Period, 202 BC–AD 220*, 1973; L. Yang (ed.), *China's Terracotta Warriors: the first emperor's legacy*, 2012

PART III

Rome and the Mediterranean: T. Baynes, *Constantine and Eusebius*, 1981; N. Baynes, *Constantine the Great and the Christian Church*, 1977; A. Cameron, *The Later Roman Empire (AD 284–430)*, 1993; W. Frend, *The Early Church*, 1982; H. Pohlsander, *The Emperor Constantine*, 2004; R. Van Dam, *Remembering Constantine at the Milvian Bridge*, 2011; N. Lenski (ed.), *The Cambridge Companion to the Age of Constantine*, 2012; H. Drake, 'The Impact of Constantine on Christianity', in N. Lenski (ed.), *The Cambridge Companion to the Age of Constantine*, 2012, pp.111–36; R. MacMullen, *Constantine*, 1969; D. Potter, *Constantine the Emperor*, 2013; S. Lieu and D. Montserrat, *Constantine: History, Historiography and Legend*, 1998; S. Lieu and D. Montserrat (eds), *From Constantine to Julian: Pagan and Byzantine views: a source history*, 1996; P. Stephenson, *Constantine: Unconquered emperor, Christian victor*, 2009; M. Odahl, *Constantine the Christian Emperor*, 2004; T. Elliott, *The Christianity of Constantine the Great*, 1996; G. Dragon, *Constantinople and its Hinterland*, 1995; R. Van Dam, *The Roman Revolution of Constantine*, 2007; W. Frend, *The Donatist Church: a movement of protest in Roman North Africa*, 1971; B. Shaw, *Sacred Violence: African Christian and sectarian hatred in the age of Augustine*, 2011

Armenia: R. Wilken, *The First Thousand Years: A global history of Christianity*, 2012; V. Neressian (ed.), *Treasures from the Ark: 1700 years of Armenian Christian art*, 2001; F. Tournebize, *Histoire politique et religieuse de l'Arménie*, 1910; E. Dulaurier, *Recherches sur la chronologie arménienne*, 1859; N. Garsoian, *Armenia Between Byzantium and the Sassanians*, 1985; S. Neressian, *The Armenians*, 1969; A. Redgate, *The Armenians*, 1998; E. Gulbenkian, 'The Date of King Trdat's conversion', in *Handes Amsorya*, 1991, pp.75–87; T. Greenwood, 'Armenia', in S. Fitzgerald (ed.), *The Oxford Handbook to Late Antiquity*, 2012, pp.115–41; Z. Pogossian, *The Letter of Love and Concord: a revised diplomatic edition with historical and textual comments and English translation*, 2010; R. Hovannisian (ed.), *Armenian People From Ancient to Modern Times, Vol. I: the dynastic periods from antiquity to the 14th century*, 2004; D. MacCulloch, *A History of Christianity*, 2009; N. Sitwell, *Outside the Empire: the world the Romans knew*, 1986; S. Payaslian, *The History of Armenia from the Origins to the Present*, 2007; B. Zekiyan, 'Christianity to Modernity', in E. Herzig and M. Kurkchiyan (eds), *The Armenians: Past and present in the making of national identity*, 2005, pp.41–64; R. Thomson, *Studies in Armenian Literature and Christianity*, 1994

Gupta India and Central Asia: V. Smith, *Early India*, 1999; A. Agarwai, *The Rise and Fall of the Imperial Guptas*, 1989; U. Singh, *A History of Ancient and Medieval India from the Stone Age to the 12th century*, 2008; R. Majumda, *Ancient India*, 1977; H. Raychaudhuri, *Political History of Ancient India*, 1972; L. Sharma, *A History of Ancient India*, 1992; A. Bachan, *The Origin and Development of Hinduism*, 1991; B. Stein, *A History of India*, 1998; J. Auboyer, *Daily Life in Ancient India*, 1968; M. Willis, *Archaeology of Hindu Ritual, Temples and the Establishment of the Gods*, 2009; J. Williams, *The Art of Gupta India: Empire and province*, 1982; S. Wolpert, *A New History of India*, 2009; R. Thapar, *Early India – from the origins to AD 1300*, 2002; A. Bhattacharjee, *A History of Ancient India*, 1988; J. Harle, *Gupta Sculpture: Indian sculpture of the fourth to sixth centuries AD*, 1996; M. Banerjee, *A Study of Important Gupta Inscriptions*, 1976; A. Narain, 'Religious Policy and Toleration in Ancient India with particular reference to the Gupta age', in B. Smith (ed.), *Essays on Gupta Culture*, 1983, pp.17–52; B. Gokhlae, 'Buddhism in the Gupta age', in B. Smith (ed.), *Essays on Gupta Culture*, 1983, pp.129–56; J. Shaw, 'Archaeologies of Buddhist propagation in ancient India: "ritual" and "practical" modes of religious change', in J. Shaw (ed.), *Archaeology of Religious Change*, 2013, pp.83–108; J. Shaw, *Buddhist Landscapes in Central India: Sanchi hill and archaeologies of religious and social change c. 3rd century BCE to 5th century CE* 2007; S. Goyal, *A History of the Imperial Guptas*, 1967; S. Goyal, *The Imperial Guptas: a multidisciplinary political study*, 2005; S. Upadhyaya, *The Kama Sutra of Vatsyayana*, 1974; J. McKnight, *Kingship and Religion in the Gupta Age*, 1976 (PhD thesis); J. Fleet, *Corpus inscriptionum Indicarum, Vol. III: Inscriptions of the early Gupta kings and their successors*, 1888; J. Coulston, 'Central Asia from the Scythians to the Huns', in P. de Souza, *The Ancient World at War*, 2008, pp.217–27; C. Baumer, *The History of Central Asia (Vols I–II)*, 2014

China: T. Barfield, *The Perilous Front: Nomadic empires and China 221 BC to AD 1757*, 1982; N. Di Cosmo, *Ancient China and its Enemies: the rise of nomadic power in East Asian history*, 2002; X. Liu, *Ancient India and Ancient China: trade and religious exchanges*, 1994; J. Edkins, *Religions in China: a brief account of the three religions of the Chinese*, 1893; E. Zürcher, *The Buddhist Conquest of China: the spread and adaptation of Buddhism in early medieval China*, 1959; T. Weiming and D. Ikeda, *New Horizons in Eastern Humanism: Buddhism, Confucianism and the quest for global peace*, 2011; S. Sharot, *A Comparative Sociology of World Religions: Virtuosos, priests and popular religion*, 2001; B. Wang and T. Sen (eds), *India and China: interactions through Buddhism and Diplomacy*, 2011; P. Williams (ed.), *Buddhism: Critical concepts in religious studies (Vols I–VIII)*, 2005; F. Houang, *Le Bouddhisme de L'inde à la Chine*, 1963; V. Fic, *The Tantra: its origins, theories, art and diffusion from India to Nepal, Tibet, Mongolia, China, Japan and Indonesia*, 2003; J. Powers, *Introduction to Tibetan Buddhism*, 2007; J. Silk (ed.), *Buddhism in China: collected papers of E. Zürcher*, 2014; Y. Kumar, *A History of Sino-Indian Relations 1st century AD to 7th century AD*, 2005; Z. Tsukamoto, *A History of Early Chinese Buddhism from its introduction to the death of Hui-Yuan (Vols I–II)*, 1985; F. Sheng, *Chinese History*, 2012; M. Wangu, *Buddhism*, 2006; J. C. Watt (ed.), *China: Dawn of a golden age 200–750 AD*, 2004; W. Scheidel (ed.), *State power in Ancient China and Rome*, 2015; F. Mutschler and A. Mittag (eds), *Conceiving the empire: Rome and China compared*, 2008

Index